Courage, stubbornness, insight, intelligence, creativity and out-of-the-box thinking are all words that describe David Winstrom, the author of *I Choose Adam*. Beyond these words and far more important is the word *love*. David chose to love Adam and be his advocate. This book is the amazing and emotional journey of David, Jetta, his wife, and Adam their very special son who was born with both Autism and Down syndrome. I was blessed to have Adam at Zeeland Christian School and learned a great deal about life from him. You, too, will be blessed and will gain a new perspective of many life lessons by taking the time to read this book. Nothing would honor Adam's life more than making sure that every single child is given the opportunity to reach their full potential.

Bill Van Dyk
Principal, 1987-2016
Zeeland Christian School

The name Adam is embedded in the Hebrew word "adama" which literally means earth or earthy. As the Torah states, Adam was made from the dust of the earth. Upon his birth Jetta and David named their beloved son Adam. And rightfully so. Adam, for those who knew him was one of the most earthy, down to earth, caring persons any of us could ever hope to meet. Adam was about the meaningful mission of bringing all of us over-achievers down to earth. In and through Adam we discovered our own frailty, weakness of moral character and for those who were open to Him our own humanity. Accepting Adam brought some closer to accepting God and his beloved - persons of inestimable worth in a kingdom of grace and beauty.

David tells his son's story with honesty, compassion and a determination to help the reader know that all life matters to God and therefore should matter to us. The story of Adam to various degrees is a part of our own story as we journey to know more fully the ultimate meaning of life on this sod. David has chosen to be vulnerable in this storytelling in order to open the door to our own recognition as vulnerable beings.

Andy DeJong
Adam's Pastor

This book describes the role of love, tenacity, courage, advocacy and often unpredictability in David and Jetta Winstrom's life journey with their son, Adam. It also describes how they turned the challenges they faced together into extraordinary developmental opportunities for Adam.

In this sometimes uncomfortable, always instructive and touching reading about Adam, David offers his very frank perspective on how people, institutions and the social environment influenced and were influenced by Adam. This book is important reading for parents, educators, religious leaders, helping professionals and policy makers. David insightfully shares the impact of his advocacy on individual and societal expectations, policies and decisions. The reported process and outcomes of this advocacy on Adam's opportunities and life development and the changed perceptions of those around him engage each reader emotionally and intellectually. Implicit in the book is the question that each of us must ask: Are our perceptions, expectations and actions constricting and inhibiting or expanding and encouraging greater growth and opportunities for those around us?

James C. Piers
Professor of Social Work
Hope College

I Choose Adam: Nothing "Special" Please

By David Winstrom

All Scriptures are from New International Version (NIV) Holy Bible, New International Version®, NIV® Copyright ©1973, 1978, 1984, 2011. Used by permission. All rights reserved worldwide.

Books may be purchased in bulk by contacting the publisher or author at: Info@IChooseAdam.com

ISBN: 978-0-9985303-0-7 I Choose Adam by David Winstrom (Softcover)
ISBN: 978-0-9985303-1-4 I Choose Adam by David Winstrom (eBook)

Printed in the United States of America

Published by Lightning Tree Creative Media: LTCMedia.com.

Editing, book design and cover design by Keren Kilgore
of Lightning Tree Creative Media
Denver, Colorado

I am the kernel forced open by the son
I am the possibility of every parent
Compelled not intended, bent knee instructed
Given a precious gift and obligated by love
I became that I am, my intended self.
David Winstrom

Contents

Dedication

To Barb Newman. Thank you for dedicating your life to inclusion. For your support and understanding and efforts to teach others that living together in faith was better than living separated by fear–fear that we will not know how to live together or that life will get too messy or be too much of a burden if we are *all* included.

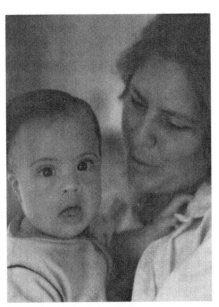

To all of Adam's community. Thank you for loving him as much as I did and for accepting his love for you.

To Jetta. My beloved wife of 40 years. Your goodness and mercy guided us well.

To Adam. Thank you for trusting me enough to do the difficult and sometimes painful work to live in community.

Adam and Jetta Winstrom

Foreword

This book will completely alter the way you look at intentions, methods and interactions with friends, school systems, even churches. Over the last 20 years, David has given me the gift of seeing things differently, and now he offers that gift to you in this book. David dedicated his life to finding ways to bring out the best in his son, himself and those around him to create a community where everyone is welcomed equally and without apology for their differences.

I first met David as the parent of a student we accepted into Zeeland Christian School (ZCS). While professionals in various school systems had some "fear and trembling" over the path that led him to our school, David, and his wife, Jetta, seemed like parents who had a deep desire for Adam, their only child, to be part of an educational setting where he would be valued for the gifts he brought and be supported in the areas his neurological anomaly (Down syndrome and Autism). Sometimes these anomalies caused us difficulties. Adam would be considered a student along with all the other children at ZCS and included as an honored member of the body of Christ as we lived out God's invitation to community in the halls and classrooms of our school—a community where each one is valued, respected and welcomed.

When I first met David, he was discouraged, having spent many years trying to find such a school. We were eager to partner with the Winstroms knowing that Adam would touch lives and that we would learn from one another at ZCS. I had no idea at that point in time that God would use Adam's life to offer me a profound picture and testimony to inclusive education and give my voice even greater confidence in the writing, speaking and teaching that I do for Christian Learning Center Network and Zeeland Christian School.

Soon after Adam started at ZCS, we discovered that he was not the only one who brought gifts to our community. David, as Adam's primary caregiver, came with degrees, experiences and a heart that we soon put to work in our community. He became our consultant when a student displayed behavioral or emotional concerns that begged for intervention beyond what we knew how to give. David once described his private practice as, "I only treat zebras,"—children with unique neurological and behavioral anomalies, and so we would call on Dr. Winstrom when some of our students started to display those stripes.

We watched David sit beside a child who refused to do nearly everything we asked as they gently threw grass at one another on the hillside. When the bell rang to come inside everyone except the two grass throwers came. When the child was ready to go, they came in together.

I asked what had happened and David said the child had thrown some grass at him to see what would happen. He said he could have said, "Stop" and probably more grass would have flown. Instead, he threw some grass back, gently. He said it was like playing catch and teaching her turn taking until they found their rhythm together. When the bell rang, the child stiffened and paused, again waiting for a control struggle. He just threw a little more grass. The child joined in again, but this time David had led, and the child followed. He told me he just started talking about what was going on inside the school. There would be lunch and then a classroom full of new friends. He told the child when she was ready he would like to go in with her. When the child said, "Okay," David responded, "Please wait for just one more minute. Let's make sure you are okay with going in. If you feel afraid or confused or uncomfortable when you are in school, just stop and wait. A teacher or I will come to you to make sure you are okay." David said that was how to assess and make a behavior plan with a contingency plan for situations that could become oppositional.

Jetta, David and Adam Winstrom

We navigated parent meetings or medical meetings where he gave such valuable direction that it was clear he saw things in a way no others seemed to see. My colleague and I were ready to put together a bracelet that said, "WWDD" (What Would David Do?) as we asked that question frequently when he was not in the building. Just imagining the solutions he would offer gave us new direction and ideas to try.

At some point, the Newman family and Winstrom family became friends. My sons enjoyed playing with Adam, and my husband and I enjoyed watching David and Jetta in action. As we prepared to join their family for New Year's Eve, David advised us that we would actually be celebrating the midnight hour at 10:00 p.m. This allowed Adam to get the sleep he needed and still understand the holiday. Changing clocks at that point in time was much easier to accomplish! It was a solution we all enjoyed.

We watched Adam's parents train him to work, relate and care deeply for others. Each interaction could have a life lesson, and it was profound to see how the Winstroms arranged people and opportunities around them to make this happen in multiple ways.

As Adam left ZCS and moved on to high school, I enjoyed hearing about Adam's life with his friends and on the football team. And I still would ask for David's wisdom with some of the students at our school. When one of my sons could drive, there were times he would take Adam to events. When my children were sick, Adam would call them on their cell phones and offer encouragement or support. He did that with me, too. I looked forward to that call, knowing that Adam was thinking about me at that time.

While I will offer a few other stories as part of this book, may I suggest that you are beginning a journey—one that will give you as parents or educators new tools and one that will give any individual a new perspective as you live in community with persons of varied abilities. It's possible that at the end of this book you, too, may wish to have a bracelet that says, "WWDD."

Barbara J. Newman

Introduction

Adam was a remarkable person. I don't know how to best tell you who Adam was. He was my son whom I loved from the first moment I looked into his eyes and heard him take his first breath until the moment he looked back into my eyes and released his last breath. And I love him still. When he was small, I used to hold him high and say, "This is my son in whom I am well pleased!" His connection to me was strong. His connection to God, his Father, was even stronger. His life was a gift to all who could embrace him. People often came at Adam to "help" him but quickly discovered that what they gave they received back tenfold because they became infected by the spirit of who Adam was.

The story I can tell is about how difficult it was to live in this world with my son, Adam. In 1984, children with unique neurological anomalies such as Autism and Down syndrome scared people and challenged traditional systems. Schools in Michigan were still segregated 20 years after President Johnson signed into law the Civil Rights Act. Segregation was not based on race; it was based on genetics and mental acuity. Doctors, nurses, teachers and friends as well as Jetta and I had to come to terms with our own interpretations and visions of what the world was intended to be. Was there room for divergent thinking children in our public schools? Would we welcome divergent people into our culture, our world, our neighborhood, our lives? Could our friends accept our having Adam and remain our friends?

Choosing Adam compelled his mother Jetta and I to make those choices. Once we chose to support him and his right to be included in all aspects of our world, the world as Jetta and I knew it changed. It was the beginning of our lifelong struggle with our world to be allowed to include our son in all aspects of our life.

Every day having Adam as our son created situations that invited others to reconsider their basic belief systems. Is the world ready to celebrate differences? Is segregation going to continue to be the only choice to educate unique children? Is the possibility of living peacefully together in heart-to-heart relationships possible? It appeared that inclusion never seemed possible to most of the people we were surrounded by when Adam was young. Because Adam was different, we were encouraged to take advantage of the special, alternative world. There were all the kind protections they call "special." And our family was told that we should be grateful for their efforts in "making protective programs so children like our son can have their own place" and "be with their own kind." Their thinly veiled message was clear: We were no longer their kind of people. Segregation did not seem special to us. Their gift of "special" would isolate us and remove us from their life. It was illegal. For 20 years, segregation had been illegal ruled by the Supreme Court to be destructive and hurtful. It was immoral. "The Lord sees not as man sees: man looks on the outward appearance, but the Lord looks on the heart" (1 Samuel 16:7). The professionals could not see Adam's heart. They never knew his spirit. And many decided he was an expendable person, unworthy of their effort. Adam was a challenge for Jetta and me, but the educational and initial medical systems were a bigger challenge because they were oppressive and occasionally hostile.

Barb Newman and others are hopeful that by reading Adam's story you may gain some new understanding of how to cope, how to adapt and even how to alter the personal behaviors and societal responses that systematically alienate and disable unique people. As you read on, I hope you will come to understand that behavioral changes are not one-sided; it is not just "them" who need changing. In telling Adam's story, I will share many of the skills I learned to create conditions for myself and others to live peacefully together. My hope is that you may discover Adam's way. He took all I knew and added his own touch. Adam's technique was to find God in each new person he met–to seek, find and nurture the best in each person until all they could do was become their best manifestation of God in the flesh. As an adult, every next person became his friend. There was no escaping Adam's love. His world view was that we are all capable of friendship, kindness and mutual support. He surpassed his father to be more like his Father. The Scripture, "Whatever you neglected to do unto the least of these, you neglected to do unto Me" (Matthew 25:45) spoke to my heart about what was at stake. I am going to tell you about my life with Adam. Then I will let his community tell you who he was to them.

Adam had Autism; Autism never had him. He had Down syndrome; Down syndrome never had him. He was himself and was unique. He fully lived life. When he was a youngster, the school system and community tried to tell me what kind of a person he was and would be because "he was autistic" and a "Down's child." Jetta and I never accepted their definition of our son. We never allowed external labels to eclipse Adam's unique abilities and talents and personhood. He once told me he wished he was smarter because someone told him that being autistic meant he was ret…. I told him that being smart was not such a grand thing—that he would see the world differently, feel and experience it more completely and understand other people's feelings as well as they did. And so, he would have to work harder to be around other people. And if they were smart, they would discover the treasure of who Adam was and they would learn together what friendship really meant. Adam's life was full and filled with many smart friends who learned from Adam.

To all of Adam's community, thank you for loving him as much as I did and for accepting his love for you.

David Winstrom

Chapter 1
Beginnings Start Before You Know It

All journeys have a beginning. My journey to becoming Adam's father started long before Adam was born. It started long before my wife, Jetta, after 12 years of marriage, announced that she had changed her mind and wanted to have a child. My becoming Adam's father began when I was a child.

I am now 68 in this year 2017. In retrospect, I see how I was made ready to be Adam's father and was transformed into my intended self. We all have some kernel within us, an oft dormant seed that once awakened compels us to become more than we imagined ourselves capable of being. Once our seed finds fertile ground, the thorns and brambles that choked our potential fall away. All the lessons of my past life and childhood gained reason and purpose as I grew into being Adam's father. Mark Twain wrote that there are two important days in a person's life—the day he is born, and the day he discovers the reason he was born.

Jetta Changed Her Mind

The foundation for becoming who we were intended to be runs deep in each of us and can take a lifetime to figure out. My discovery began the day Jetta announced her desire to have a baby. The cesspool of my childhood demons were once again freed from their encapsulation. The ghosts spoke to me from the core of my being: children are not safe in this world, and people will hurt your child just like they hurt you.

What I did not know and could not see was that all my reasons for not having children and not being a father were exactly why I was just right to be Adam's father. Jetta had her own issues as an adopted and only child and found a way through her past. And this was also why Jetta's early life was just right to prepare her to become Adam's mother.

I loved my wife. I was, I think, a good husband and a good man to her. I had given Jetta the key to my fortress; I had allowed her into my heart. We had created a wonderful life together. Then, after 12 years, she asked for what I thought I never wanted—children—and what I thought I never wanted to be—a father. I didn't want to take any chance that another child might have to endure my childhood experiences. When I proposed to Jetta, I made it clear that marriage to me would not include children. Ever.

I was shocked by her request and even more shocked when I heard my voice saying, "Yes, of course." I would do whatever I could for Jetta, the woman I forever loved. Our years together had already begun transforming me. I understood it was my fear rather than real reasons that had formed my decision not to have children. I could see in her eyes that being a mother was her dream blossoming and emerging. In my world, dreams always trump fears. Our 12 years of loving each other had softened my once-adamant position of not bringing children into this world. Jetta had found a way through her past. Now it was my turn to make my fears wither away.

Vanquishing Monsters

I knew it wouldn't be very long before Jetta was pregnant. I had at least nine months to find my monsters and release myself from their influence...nine months to rid myself of the old memories buried but not dead. As a child, I was tormented because I could not read or spell. I was branded "stupid" and made to feel ashamed and unacceptable. I had nine months to shed this too-tight coat that I continued to wear. Socially, I had learned to live with their idea of me and had accepted their idea as being who I was. I accepted others' judgments of me and even expected them to occur as they always did. Every day I wanted to be surprised, but it just didn't happen. The feigned deference I learned at an early age allowed them room to play with me in ways a harder presentation from me would not. I smiled, even managed laughter at their jokes. It was my childhood way to deflect wounding.

Now, thanks to my loving wife, I had nine months to face my fear of bringing my own child into this world, to become a father. Nine months was a long time and would come like tomorrow morning at 5 am. I knew instinctively I did not need to get ready to be a father, what I had to do was release my fears and stop the imprisonment of my old memories of being shamed as a child. Stop my replayed visions of being hurt. Stop thinking that what I had experienced would be my own child's experience. It was time to let myself out of jail so I would be present when my child needed me to be father David in 1984.

I did know something about being a good father. I had one. My first lessons about how to care for a child came to me when I was a child myself, from my mother and father and my community. I grew up in a town that looked out for all children and was surrounded by the love and attention of family and friends. I belonged to and grew up in a community where neighbors knew every family and every child in the neighborhood and where families watched over all the children. In my early experience, everybody cared for everyone. All children belonged and were accepted. I believed that this was how it would always be.

It was not until I left my home and my neighborhood and went to school that I began to learn about "them"—the children who did not fit in. When I went to school, there was no understanding or expectation that the school would make any accommodation for a child being different mentally or physically. The expectation was either fit into the regular classroom or be left behind and moved to the room at the end of the hall where "they" were sent. Or worse, sent to the *special* place no one knew where it was, but once there, they never returned. Initially, I was one of "us," but over time I became one of "them."

Last Seat in the Classroom

Like most of us, I grew up with "normal privilege"—the belief that others will recognize something of themselves in you and welcome you into the group without reservation. It is a ticket to full inclusion, instant belonging, a social shield against being shunned. It comes with a package of unearned assets that we do not acknowledge or even think about but accept as just the way things are. Because it is unearned, people who exercise normal privilege are most often completely unaware of their privileged behaviors. It would be wonderful if everyone shared the experience of being welcomed and greeted as a fellow human being wherever they went, but we do not. It is from normal privilege that bias, then prejudices and ultimately discrimination blossom. It is the basis for inclusion or exclusion. The seed of exclusion grows rapidly: from ignoring to teasing to bullying to physical intimidation to shunning and, finally, segregation. When my classmates no longer recognized themselves in me because I failed to learn to read or write, my belonging was revoked. I never understood why I could not read, except I must be stupid like they said.

I was 30 years old when I accidentally discovered I had Dyslexia and not stupid. I was taking a Test Measurements and Evaluations class in my Master's program. The professor needed a Guinea pig for the test, and I always learn best by doing, so I volunteered. When the demonstration was over, he asked me if I had known I was dyslexic. I told the professor, "No, and thank you." That experience and information gave a new name to what I had heard all my life. In third grade in 1956, the teachers had no idea about anything called Dyslexia. They told me that I was lazy, slow, unmotivated and not very smart, and that directly equated to being called "stupid" by my classmates, though few of them went unscathed for uttering that phrase to my face. From third grade on, I was put in the turtle group; becoming a gazelle was forever far out of my reach. My race car would never round the track the teacher had on the board in the front of the class to motivate us to great achievements. Instead of praise, that race track resulted in public shaming, teasing and humiliation. My friend Kevin and I stayed in the pits, never actually achieving anything of merit to get us into the race.

To our classmates, we became "them" rather than "us." Because we repeatedly failed to be motivated into academic achievement by the teacher's tactics as other students were, we were assigned endless sheets of dummy dittos—those photocopied worksheets where we were to connect the dots to make a picture. If the teacher was feeling a little more inspired to expand our education, we would be given pages of simple single digit addition or subtraction exercises to keep us busy while other students did their real work. I learned that if I finished the math dittos quickly, I would just be given another page with the same problems arranged differently. It was, after all, math hour and the teacher was occupied teaching math to the "us" students, the gazelles. It was not turtle time.

The process was my introduction to educators' methods of teaching students who learned differently. Do something to keep them busy. If they are not motivated, then do the same thing again and add shaming. Finally, do it again and add punishment of the loss of a desired activity. That will surely work. In my heart, I knew my teacher did not mean to harm me; I knew she was frustrated with my lack of learning. I began to understand that there must be something really wrong with me. She never understood that I was doing all I could, given the way she was "teaching" me. In the 50's, you were not instructed in mathematics or science until you first learned to read and write. The unspoken presumption was that Kevin and I were stupid, a little retarded. We were in the last two seats in the back of the class ready to be sent to the room at the end of the hall with the others who didn't fit in. I was beginning to believe that I really was stupid.

My salvation was recess. Over the years, I became very good at sports and learned that you don't have to spell "basket" to make two points or spell "fullback" to score touchdowns. What was required to win in a team sport was the ability to work together and to be able to see patterns develop in your opponent's offense or defense. Seeing patterns was the one place where I was "first." Dyslexia did not make any difference in my ability to run or throw a ball. I physically matured faster than others my age. I more than fit in; I was once again one of us and almost belonged. I was the team's first choice during recess but disappeared when recess was over. Opposing teams got to know my ability to see patterns emerging in the game and threw taunts in their frustrated attempts to distract me. Sometimes it worked, but mostly it did not, and they were left behind. We won.

They did not see life's rhythms as I did. They were not dyslexic and did not think in pictures and patterns. They were normal. In third grade, I was still learning about my differences and my skills. I learned to predict the teacher's moods to determine whether she would call on me to show my work on the board or make me read out loud even knowing that I could not. I'm sure the embarrassment she caused was intended to motivate me. Most students did not have to learn to recognize the many "I's" or aspects of ego that made up their teacher. I did.

"*I* just want you to learn," meant she felt inadequate because I did not learn using her techniques.

"*I* am so frustrated with you!" meant she knew I was not the "dunce" and that I could learn, but neither of us knew how to create the proper condition to do so.

"*I* think you would do better in a different classroom" meant she just wanted me out of the class so she could "devote her valuable time" to students who could learn, and stop feeling inadequate because she was not able to teach me.

Normal privileged students didn't have to know the precise moment to go to the bathroom or sharpen their pencil when the teacher was about to vent his or her frustration on them for being them. Perhaps it was not as important for them to learn what questions to ask to light up the teacher so they could see I was learning from her or getting her to extend the lecture so that board time was used up. Kevin had given up and sometimes asked why I still bothered. Why didn't I just give up like he had and learn to be quiet and invisible in the last seat on the last row just behind me? The teacher never called on him anymore. He had escaped into Kevin-land in his head. I was still present.

Unlike me, most of my fellow students were unable to find the path through the defense to be in the position where the defender was not, or where a defender was out of position or off balance. I saw it all. I thought in pictures and patterns as people with Dyslexia often do. In some ways, I guess I was fortunate to be able to think the way I did. I was thought of as the stupid kid, and every day I was afraid I would eventually be removed from the last two seats in the classroom.

Even more humiliating were the lectures about what "my problem" was. From time to time I was reminded that I was not learning like the other students, they thought I was not paying attention, not putting enough time into doing my homework. I was repeatedly told, "If you spent more time on your homework you would know this!" They didn't know I would go home, do my chores and my homework, then eat dinner and do more homework with my mother before going to bed while my sister watched TV. My sister never studied, she was smart. She could read and write with ease. Watching how my sister got through school convinced me that I must be dumb because she never spent any time studying, and she was an "A" student.

One time I made the mistake of responding honestly to the teacher in front of the whole classroom. I told her that in fact, I had studied. The silence in the classroom told me I had made a huge mistake. My teacher stood over me and from her injured "I" ego that wanted me out of her classroom came welling up, "You are wearing a Cub Scout uniform. Scouts don't lie. Scouts do their best. Scouts...." To this day, I do not remember the whole lecture, just the punch line: "You should not be in Scouts if you cannot tell the truth and you should not be in my classroom." She said it out loud for all to hear! I did not belong with them.

My grandfather was the Council Scout Master and had impressed upon me the importance of telling the truth. He told me that when I raised my right hand and recited the scout's oath, it was *not just words, but a life commitment, on my honor to do my best, to do my duty to God and my country, to be square and obey the law of the pack.* The oath was a lifelong obligation, and it had no exceptions. Other people's ability to trust me depended on my honor and truthfulness.

In her frustration with me at that moment, she had branded me as not only stupid but a liar. Essentially, she had said to all, "he does not belong with us." I learned a lot about people and life in school. In a social situation being "right" and telling "the truth" will not set you free; the truth will just piss people off.

My mother would write my school papers for me at night by listening to me tell her what I wanted to write but could not get out on paper. I felt like that was somehow cheating, but my father encouraged it.

My father was a 7th Grade Math and Science teacher who could not spell. He taught me scientific methods to solving problems. He taught me math and science on the weekends and taught me how to think. He told me that in his classroom he used pre-drawn outlines my mother had made for the overhead projector. He tried to soothe my injured self by telling me that spelling was not such a big deal, but I knew that it was. Every day I was told it was. All the love and support of my parents could not balance the humiliation of one day in school. My teacher nor I ever told my parents what happened there. Maybe because my father was a teacher she just assumed he understood her frustration. She didn't know that he could not spell either.

As a third grader, the only solution I could discover was to accept on some level that I was not like the other children, and that equated to not being as good as the others, and that meant not belonging. Part of me was self-assured and confident knowing I could physically do what most other could not. I also knew that I would never be acceptable by the "smart people"—whoever they were. I knew I could out-think and out-perform their best efforts, but I would always be the stupid kid in the corner, the "you're it," the idiot who could not read or spell. I would never feel like I belonged amongst them and they all made sure of it. From third grade on, it seemed that all of my teachers stole my integrity and my sense of belonging; they pushed me permanently outside their world. Maybe they were hopeful that excluding me would motivate me to work harder and to fight my way back into the group.

It did teach me to fight back. During recess, I physically beat up every kid who called me stupid and practiced their *I am better than you are stuff.* On some occasions, three of four at once got to eat grass. By the end of third grade, I had beat into silence every third, fourth, fifth and sixth grader. Never a younger child, but all my class mates and their older brothers. I also stood with my friends from the class room down the hall. They all learned from experience that if you picked on Bobby or anyone of the different ones, you got to deal with me. Eat grass, say, "I am sorry," make them cry and let them go.

My physical body had matured faster than my classmates. By the 6th grade, I was bigger and stronger than most of my class. My uncle, grandfather and father had a meeting with me during Christmas break. My father, the science teacher, brought out a board and had me punch it. It shattered into small pieces. I was proud for a moment. Then he said that the board was just as strong as my friend's jaw bone. If I ever hit one of them in anger, I could kill them. I had to stop all fighting and physical aggression immediately. My grandfather reminded me of the Old Testament commandment, "Thou shalt not kill" and they made me promise on my honor never to hit anyone with my fist again. Because I was honorable and respected the men of my family, I stopped punching those who taunted me. I could no longer use my fist to shut their mouths.

My tormentors didn't stop. Like horse flies on a bad canoe trip, they buzzed around me, distracting me, even stinging me. I knew from that day on I could either kill them or let them do their "Hey, stupid" taunt. I learned to feign deference, to endure silently and not respond, but not to submit. I never stopped paddling my canoe, seems like I was always attempting to get downstream away from the "horse flies" in my life. When one of my friends was in trouble, I came and would step in between them interrupting their words or releasing my friend from their grip. I stopped striking them with my fists, but I did not allow them access to subdue or belittle my friends. I physically released my friends, and we just walked away.

It was at this point in my life that my being stupid took hold. I stopped imagining that I could go to college someday. I abandoned my dream and began the acceptance of me as a damaged person. A person unworthy of lofty dreams for my future. My fear was that I would experience the same attitude in higher education that I did in grade school: you're *they* because your differences make you not as good as *us*. *It* never changed. *It* is the sometimes conscious, sometimes unconscious processes that gives permission to otherwise kind and well-intended people to talk about *those people, them* or *their kind* with prejudice. It is the entitlement every normal privileged person who fits in exercises when they judge, deride, tease, make fun of, condescend, belittle, pity and segregate those of *us* who are not their kind of person. Sometimes delivered in soft or subtle words with the pretense of protectiveness, sometimes loud and laughing, but always wounding. I had a teacher in the fifth-grade talk slowly and raise her voice thinking I would learn to spelled or read out loud if she just talked louder to me and spoke more slowly. Maybe I was deaf, not dumb. I don't know. On Sunday night as my sister watched the *Wonderful World of Disney* on my grandparent's TV, I was writing my misspelled spelling words 100 times each.

As a child, I was vulnerable to these processes because they were utilized by the people in my world who were supposed to teach and protect me. By adults. And when the adults in my social/educational world exercised their privilege, they gave permission and taught my classmates to practice on me and prepared the next generation of wounded/wounding adults to perpetuate prejudice (prejudging based on bias). I include wounded adults in this because prejudice imprisons the mind and strips away the humanity of both human beings involved. It is not an inconsequential act done to the "lesser among you." The act taints the soul of the perpetrator and wounds the soul of the recipient. Everyone involved pays the price with their lost humanity each time bias/prejudice leaks out onto another human being, both minds close off just a little bit. It is our educational process that produces narrow-minded even close-minded people.

On the playground, I supported my friends as they supported me. I never let them get picked on, teased or bullied. I learned about inclusion and exclusion. The other children who were really my friends were the kids who were released from their classroom at the end of the hallway and were allowed to join the normal ("us" group) for recess and occasionally came into our classroom. When they were allowed out of their special classroom and into ours, they would always come to my desk, and make me feel included and at those moments I felt like I was okay. These visits made me realize how alone I was among my own classmates.

I lost track of many of my friends when I went to junior high school. My father, the teacher, arranged for me to be included in a pilot program of what they called "unified team teaching." The class I was in moved as a unit between three teachers for all our subjects. No more spelling or reading out loud in class. I disappeared into the protection of not being called on ever.

High school returned me to education as usual. Thinking back to those experiences I am surprised that I was not removed from school or expelled as a behavior problem. When my English teacher asked me to read a poem out loud, I politely said no thank you. My history teacher was not willing to let me politely decline. She told me I could read or leave. I left. My English teacher heard about what had happened and took me aside and said, "You can't read can you." I confessed my failing. I told him when I must read out loud in front of anyone, I stutter. The words dance on the page. I still have to sound out words everyone else can just read. My ears start to ring. I break out in a cold sweat and feel like I want to throw up. That is why I refuse. Reading silently was little better—I did not feel sick, just stupid.

He smiled. I know now it is the smile someone gets when they have a unique idea they want to try. He talked to my parents and arranged for me to be in an Evelyn Wood Speed Reading class. I learned a method to get information in quickly. It is not like reading where the reader gets images and feels the emotion of the words. I learned to scan pages never reading single words. I still could not read out loud, and he could not fix my spelling. So, he made a deal with my other teachers. I would get two grades—one for ideas and one for presentation, spelling, punctuation and grammar. My grade point average was a 2.5—my ideas were given an A and my presentation bounced between a D and an F. The teachers who would not accept his suggestion I avoided. He even tried to convince me I was smart, but my old images were still too strong.

Because of my athletics (I had thought that was the basis), I was offered scholarships to go to a couple of traditional colleges. Brown University and Hope College. At Brown, I was also offered a job to turn on and off lights; it was a jock job. I found out one of my teachers had submitted an application and a reference for me. He was the one who knew I was very bright when I did not.

I went to Hope College in my home town. I was awarded two scholarships. One was really for football and one was awarded based on some competitive testing. When I arrived and classes started, my professors could not allow my level of spelling to be acceptable even if I was a "starter" football player/jock. I did what I could, but they came to the conclusion that I did not belong in college if I could not spell. It did not matter to them what ideas or concepts I was writing about, if there were any words misspelled, they would not accept my work. They said that it was just too distracting for them. My father had wanted me to join the service as he had in World War II instead of going to college. I had wanted to buy a BSA Hornet and ride the motorcycle until I ran out of road. I took a path in between. It was the middle of the Vietnam War, and I had taken an oath not to harm others. My father and I talked about my oath, and he said it did not apply to war. I believed the oath, my pledge and covenant given to all present and sworn to on the family Bible were not something I could be released from by him alone. I chose to do my service as a conscientious objector. I went through that process of appearing before the local draft board, was approved and moved to Colorado to work there for my two years of service. I was one of two young men allowed this designation from

Ottawa County. I talked my then girlfriend, Jetta, into marrying me and coming along.

The piece de resistance was my name, David Dick. Without blushing, I will let you imagine what the world did to me with that last name and why I learned deference as a child. You would think that after adolescence the plethora of "Dick" jokes and puns would finally stop. But, no, they just intensified and kept on right up to the day I changed my name to Winstrom so my son would not fall prey to the world's immaturity. I had friends who were disappointed they could no longer put the "Smartest Dick in Grand Haven" sign in my front yard when I finished my Ph.D. I received obscene phone calls from girls playing with their sexuality. The calls stopped when caller ID was installed.

David, It's Time to Come in from Recess

In 1971, when I was just 21 years old, I had the great good fortune to meet Dr. Westendorp when I was doing a summer job working at the county's youth program. I had just returned from Colorado living in Boulder. The year I was there doing my *service* I was a conscientious objector to the Vietnam war and "served" my country washing dishes in an Adventist hospital. That was the year California was scheduled to fall into the ocean, so *all* the hippies moved to "higher" ground in Boulder, Colorado. I mentioned this because I was around lots of people doing Acid (LSD) and other drugs, so volunteering in Holland, Michigan at a drop-in drug center was kind of a normal experience for me. It was very foreign to all of the more sheltered residents of Holland.

Dr. Westendorp was the director of the local community mental health program and was responsible for creating the services for troubled kids. He said he had watched me work and Dr. Westendorp offered me a job. I told him I was planning on becoming an art teacher some day and was not all that interested in working for mental health. He asked me to consider changing mediums and work with people to create conditions for them to come out of the State hospital. He believed that they could be returned to the community to live and did not require institutionalization. He was different too. I liked him right away and trusted him with my secret. I told him that I could not spell or write very well and so I probably could not work for him. He laughed and told me that was what a secretary could do. He told me the job would be to take a group of people with chronic schizophrenia out of the State hospital and integrate them back into their home community. I had no idea who he was telling me about as the term "chronic schizophrenia" had no meaning to me. He started to educate me by saying that someone with chronic schizophrenia has a thought disorder and a poor connection to reality. They hear voices sometimes and have visual hallucinations. We put them on medication to control their symptoms. He thought this basic information would help me understand my new job. It didn't.

I asked him again, "Who are the people you want to return to Holland, Michigan? Can you tell me about one of them, like Tom, the 45-year-old single man? What does he spend his day doing? What does he wants to do or be? You know, give me human being descriptions, please."

Dr. Westendorp laughed and said this was the reason he wanted to hire me. He told me that most of the people he wanted to return to Holland had "institutional egos" from years of being "treated" as a diagnostic formulation e.g. chronic schizophrenia and not as a unique human being. He told me that professionals often slip into depersonalizing people first by calling them patients and then by talking about them as a diagnosis like he just had. He explained that over time living as a label, isolated from one's community intensifies the difficulties and leads to the loss of relationships and ultimately to the person's loss of their own identity. He went on to explain that having a difference creates difficulties for a person, but it is being treated differently that causes the real damage. Being treated as sick or broken causes the withering of the person's sense of self.

That was why he wanted to hire me. He said I was therapeutic. My nature was to accept others without judgment, understand them and find ways to make a common connection. Hopefully, to repair the damage we have done to them by isolating them and separating them from their community.

He told he had watched me relate to the kids in the drop-in program. He said the kids I had been working with had their lives changed for the better. That was what he wanted me to do with adults. I trusted him, so I accepted the job.

We started the Creative Living Program, a day treatment program and an 18-bed unlocked residential treatment center for people diagnosed with chronic schizophrenia who had been in the State hospital for years. The first round of folks took six months to reintegrate. The second round took three months. The State of Michigan gave the program an award for being the most creative and innovative and then shut down the funding. When the State closed the program, our average stay was 21 days from deinstitutionalization to supported community inclusion.

Dr. Westendorp told me after the State closed the program that the reason I was hired was that I did not know it could not be done. He had been told by other professionals that his idea would never work. It would not be safe. It would be too difficult. The community would not accept the return of "those people." He said it was difficult to find professionals who would support his dream to bring people back into their community. Then he found me, and we made it work.

After the Creative Living Program had ended, Dr. Westendorp found an alternative college program for me and helped me get my bachelor's degree. It seemed like just when I found a place where I could fit in and where I was accepted and valued for who I was, it disappeared. For some reason, of all the 31 staff from the closed program, only myself and one other person were kept on and integrated into a clinic in another program.

It seemed like everything in my world was in an order I could belong in. Until Jetta wanted a baby. If not for her desire, I would never have become who I was intended to be. I would have remained socially withdrawn (happily) and continued to excel in my profession as a family therapist. Because of Jetta's new desire, I was compelled to reorganize and discover that my childhood experiences, the ones that I had thought were reasons not to have children, were my perfect preparation to be Adam's father. My father was correct; I was happy working where I most belonged. Creating conditions for the vulnerable better than anyone else could. I belonged where I was. In my world, I was respected. My difference in perception and ways of thinking was once more my strength; work was just like recess. I was better than most, so I belonged. I was hired by the Child Guidance Clinic to supervise and train family therapists. The people I trained said I made working with families look easy and natural. The folks I trained often asked me how did I learn to do this so well. I could have told them if only they were dyslexic they, too, would think in pictures and patterns and could instantly see the rhythms and progressions. What they were actually asking was, "what's the trick, why can't we do what you can?" I would tell them what I observed and how I made meaning out of what I observed. That was often not very useful as it furthered their belief in magic. What I learned to do was to create conditions for them to use their skills to understand other people. They could never get my way, but I could teach them how Dr. Westendorp or Jim would arrive at the same place I did by a different route. Dr. Westendorp had made me an excellent translator. I finally understood how the teacher felt trying to teach me to read. I never made them feel stupid for not seeing what was obvious to me. I tried to live by the principle of do unto others as you would have them do unto you, not like they did to you. I knew being shamed does not teach insight nor understanding. I changed my teaching style to fit my "students" so they could succeed.

Even with my "success" I was still very reluctant and afraid of bringing a child into this world because even with all my adaptations, education and training, the world I saw had not changed at all. Having a child would require me to deal with a society that did not respect difference, and I would be forced to become involved in systems I still observed as discriminatory, even hostile. It would also force me to be with the "smart people" from grade school. It was easier for me to relate to a combative, chronically mentally ill person than most of Jetta's friends. I could understand why the mentally ill person struck out, but I could never figure out why people who seemingly had everything they could possibly need could be so unkind to others. They were not my peer group or my place of belonging. I had become quite used to not having a peer group. Jetta and I had each other, and for me, that was enough. One person in the world who knew all of who I was. Who understood me and accepted me. That was all I needed or ever wanted.

It was my supervisor Richard who attempted to "normalize" me and redefined my difference as a skill and a gift. I could recognize my value in my work, but socially I still carried my dyslexic kros (cross). Richard gave me a new peer group of all fellow dyslexics: Leonardo da Vinci, Benjamin Franklin, the Wright brothers, Thomas Edison, Tesla and Albert Einstein. He told me that if I wanted to belong, I should pick a group where I would fit in. All of this was the bubbling stew of equal parts old septic crud and new accomplishments and perspectives. My wife had set in motion just the right friction to make it my time to grow. And that is why God gave me Jetta and then Adam—to water the seed that had been planted in fertile ground in me.

Princess Jetta

My lovely and loving wife, Jetta, grew up an adopted only child and was nicknamed "Princess." She won spelling bees, rode her own horse in equestrian competitions, and swam at the yacht club. Her aunt even took her to Disneyland for her birthday—by helicopter. She was the class Valedictorian. Jetta was a kind, compassionate, caring and completely lovely woman. There was no judgment in her about anyone who had a different experience of life. She was in many ways innocent and naïve, and she was a good woman.

We were married when we were just 20 years old. We had shared our childhood experiences with each other and decided to live our life without children. At least I thought "we" had decided together. When I proposed to Jetta, I told her I knew we were too young to really understand what making this kind of commitment meant, but...I knew she was the person I wanted to spend the rest of my life with. If she was willing, I promised her I would always work with her to solve any and all problems as they arose. That if we could be both patient and supportive of each other, I knew we could have an incredible life together. She had accepted.

Jetta had been a princess, but before that, she had been unwanted and abandoned by her mother. She never knew why her mother had given her away. Even with all the love her adoptive parents gave her, she had missed the attachment and bonding of the first moments of life connecting to her mother. Instinctively she did not trust connections. Being a very bright woman, she had found ways around her wound like I had around mine. She had always questioned if she could bond to another human being, especially a child and that was why she did not want to have children. I had found my way into her heart just as I had allowed her into mine. She had become free enough from her past to believe in herself and her ability to become a good mother.

As time passed, she changed and her instinctive desire to have children grew. She told me that we had no reason to doubt that we would have a child we would love and protect. She believed she was capable of making that connection and wanted to have our child. She believed I could get beyond my fears, too, and told me to trust her. She knew that having our own child could help me get beyond my old memories. She said that by becoming a father I could create a more accepting world for our child.

She knew that both of us would make great parents.

She convinced me that it was a new world in 1982 and that educational discrimination had been vanquished. Everybody she knew was fine. She knew that the archaic practices of institutionalizing children from the 50's were gone and it was the right time for me to let go of my distrust of other people's willingness to accept everyone equally. I wanted her to be right. I wanted to believe that what I saw in the world was just my distortion based on my old experiences. She was right, laws had made discrimination illegal, but it didn't seem that the law did much to stop prejudice—the sugar-coated, poisoned apple that kills the soul and steals ones' sense of belonging. My ghosts were screaming in my ears, you fool, you agreed to have a baby. I did agree, and by doing so, the work to release me from my old world view was set into motion.

My wife did not smoke. She did not drink. She took no drugs. She reminded me that I was a "Thalidomide Baby" (the popular drug given to pregnant mothers for morning sickness) and that the medical profession had changed. I am lucky that Thalidomide did not agree with my mother, so she did not take it very long. The research noted the drug's effect in the womb seemed totally random. The only effects I have from that drug are Dyslexia and a closed spina bifida with no physical or neurological symptoms; nothing like many children who were born without limbs.

Of course, she was right. She was like an ex-smoker filled with her self-assured zeal. She had freed herself from her fears that she would not be a good mother, not be able to complete the attachment and bonding connection. She never got to experience it with her mother and had always felt that disconnection all her life. No longer. She believed in her new possibility and our ability to change who we each were to become our better self. Her belief, like a snow plow, was clearing any and all obstacles. When I proposed I promised I would work with her as she changed. She changed. Now it was my turn. My turn to do my work. I could and should embrace my loving wife and her optimism. She was adamant that times had changed since I was a child and that professionals were more aware and more sensitive to differences in others. Still, I had doubts, but she reassured me that I had turned out just fine and that I would be a good father. After all, I was a therapist with 12 years of experience, a Master's Degree and was training a staff of 11 family therapists. She neutralized my two fears: that the educational system would harm our child and that I would not be a good enough father to protect our child. She convinced me that because I loved her and was a good, kind and patient husband that I would be just as good a father. So, I agreed.

Chapter 2
Hello, Adam!

As conception releases hope, anticipation, dreams and fears, birth is the pinnacle moment, the exhausted celebration of a new life's beginning. It is the defining moment when the dream is released, the fruition of nine long months of planning and enduring hormonal shifts. It is that moment that echoes on through time as one generation brings forth the next generation.

Planning Adam's Birth

We both thought we had prepared for this moment. Our child's arrival was Jetta's dream in the making. Jetta and I had spent months finding the right house in a nice neighborhood in the best school district. We sold our home on ten acres in the Allegan forest so we could move into town to be closer to her friends and those schools. She found her dream home, and I began remodeling her kitchen and putting in an upstairs bathroom and a nursery. We were in the right school district on a safe dead-end street just six blocks from the school—her dream was to walk our child to school someday.

We tried to time the conception of our child so she could deliver a month after her graduation with a Masters of Social Work from Michigan State University. Jetta had invested a year working with Julie, her therapist, on what had made her so afraid and reluctant to become a mother; now she had prepared herself to be a good mother. I began a private practice so I would have flexible hours. I had done my personal work with Richard to free myself from my ghosts and prepare myself to become the best father I could be. I put aside my ideas of a prejudiced world and added hope to my world view. We had thought of everything we could. Jetta was healthy and ready. She had put her world in order, and now it was her time to conceive.

Jetta loved being pregnant. She would tell me it was the happiest time in her life. She had no morning sickness and had a complete feeling of inner joy. She knew this was what she wanted—to have our child, to love and care for him or her and to make a home for her family. We talked to our soon-to-be child every night and played soothing music. She had visions of the future with other mothers getting together with their children and coming over to play in our backyard. Jetta's friends hosted a few baby showers for us and we received a crib, stroller, diaper service, and an assortment of clothes and names for both a boy and a girl. Jetta's friends were all excited and we were ready!

When Adam was born, I learned my personal mantra: I plan, God smiles, I am instructed. I learned that there is no way to get ready for life; there is life. The present moment is *everything*. Dreams are just that, dreams, and too often we mistake our dream life for our real life.

Adam Arriving

Jetta's labor started, and we were off to the hospital in Grand Rapids to meet our doctor Jeff. Having a child was no longer a dream! Being pregnant is real, but birthing a child is a life-altering experience. The moment of becoming completely responsible for another human being's existence; safety, security and future.

There is no experience that can equate to this transformation. From this day on I was responsible, no that is too weak, I was accountable for everything I did or did not do for this new person. Jetta shared this with me, but, when it was my time to meet my Creator, it would not be acceptable to say, "Well, I knew what was necessary, the right thing to do, but Jetta didn't do it." Now not only had I obligated myself to be what my friend, Dr. Larry Kennedy, had written about in his book

Becoming a Reliable Man, but I had accepted the obligation to be an impeccable father. We imagined we were ready.

Adam arrived after 16 hours of labor and did his best to participate in our exhausted celebration. It was clear to me during the process of his birth that something was different because the monitor Jeff, was looking at showed heart rate and respiration distress. Adam's life force was weak during labor. Jeff, the delivering doctor, was also our friend and reassured us that Adam would okay, but I could feel his concern. After 15 hours of labor, he suggested we induce Jetta so she could finish the delivery. She was tiring, and we could see Adam was in some distress. Even with the added medication to help Jetta push, at the end Jeff had to use forceps to help Adam into the world.

When he arrived, Jeff let me receive him and present him to Jetta. We were ecstatic. Through my smiles and with Adam in Jetta's arms, I cut and tied his cord. Jeff had done his job; Adam was a real, live baby boy! He turned us over to the pediatrician's nurse and said we were in good hands.

While the nurse took Adam away to clean him up, Jetta and I looked at each other, joyfully exhausted. We had a son! I could see Jetta's dreams come alive in her face. She wanted to have a child of her own to love and nurture, to read to and play games with. Today she was a mother! And soon the nurse would have Adam all cleaned up and in her arms again. It was the happiest moment of her life. Her joy filled the room.

The Kind but Injurious Doctor

Instead of the nurse bringing Adam back, the pediatrician came into the room, and Adam was not with him. That caused Jetta and I some concern. Without even introducing himself he said, "It is a shame you decided not to have an amniocentesis because we could have avoided this moment." And, without skipping a beat, he continued, "He could make a placement (no name used) at Pine Rest" (we knew this was a local institution for *special* children). As Jetta and I stared at him in shock, he continued, "You could try again. After all, the Apgar scores are very low and it will never talk, its tongue is too big. It will never have friends or be able to play with others, I've seen this too often. It will be a burden to you its entire life. We'll need your permission to do some genetic testing and will have the results back in 24 hours to decide how to proceed with your next pregnancy to avoid another retarded child." The *kind* doctor never gave a name to what was so terrible about our son that it would destroy all of our futures, but I knew he was talking about our son having Down syndrome. I also knew Jetta had no idea what he was saying anymore. He had matter-of-factly just shattered Jetta. I looked to her to share this moment, and there was no expression on her face not even a tear when moments before she had been elated. Later we realized that the doctor did not have Adam brought back to us so that we could make our decision before we became attached. He thought he was being kind.

That *kindness* from the doctor to spare Jetta the pain of raising a retarded child (his reference), deeply injured her. She was in shock and literally could not speak. He had stabbed her in her most vulnerable place and her weakest moment. How could he have known this was her Achilles heel?

I was also in shock listening to the doctor predict what our life would be that we must avoid. What was he suggesting? Return our son and try again for an improved model? Did he really say that if we keep this one, "it" will not have a life of "its'" own, and worse, "it" will destroy our life. Was this real? Were we being asked to choose; keep our child and surrender our life and future, or abandon him? He seemed so self-assured and all-knowing. He somehow knew our son would be better off someplace else, in a special facility for his kind. The doctor, who must know all, just told us what would be best. His words reopened all of Jetta's old wounds. Now she was being told to give up her son, just as her mother had given her up. Was he really implying "If you really loved him, you would take him to Pine Rest to be with his own kind." Jetta had collapsed. It seemed up to me. From my exhausted, numb lips all it would have taken in that moment would have been to say, "Okay," and Adam would no longer be our son.

On that August 26th day in 1984 in Grand Rapids, Michigan, it was clear we had not prepared for this moment. Jetta had never really considered anything but her dream…and, why should she? She had done everything she could to put her life in order, she thought. She had worked through her issues with her own mother abandoning her at birth. She still had a few remaining emotional scars, but she had worked hard to become completely vulnerable to this moment and her child. Instead, she was completely vulnerable to the kind doctors assault. No armor or protection. The *kind doctor* could not know he was attacking her through her worst nightmare. He was verifying her fear that she would not be a good enough mother and would, therefore, abandon her child just like her mother did with her. Her life had left her defenseless for this moment. Her dream of motherhood and physical state of exhaustion after 16 hours of labor had made her vulnerable. Two years of planning and nine months of pregnancy had just been destroyed in seven short sentences. The kind doctor had surgically amputated Jetta's life dream in a heartbeat and introduced a horror story in its place. How could she be prepared for his brand of *kindness*. Her exposure to people with differences was a visit to Coldwater State Institution in her senior psychology class where she saw children forced to stay in bed all day because they had Hydrocephalus and could not walk or talk or relate to others. And this is what the kind doctor just informed her was what her son would become. In her mind, the image of our son was systematically being erased and replaced with some kind of unacceptable creature.

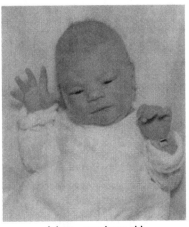

Adam—one hour old

The convergence of my childhood, my commitment to Jetta to have her dream and the doctor's words mixed with 16 hours of exhausting labor were just what was needed to ignite something dormant inside of me.

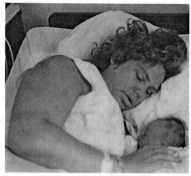 

Jetta and Adam bonding   David and Adam bonding

Standing at Jetta's bedside, I remembered my friend, Bobby, from grade school who had Down syndrome. I knew he was talking about Bobby. Bobby was referred to as mentally retarded and he was my friend. He talked to me and ran with me and we frequently played together. Today, "mental retardation" is an unacceptable term, but when I was growing up, I was told that it described the process of learning more slowly because to retard meant to slow down. My experience of that first friendship created a different normal for me and protected me (and saved Adam) from the doctor's *kindness*. As the doctor talked, he was describing my school friends, the children who were always there to comfort me. Something deep inside me understood that his self-assured point of view was born from professional ignorance and too much time playing God. Even with God's preparation of me over the years, I was in an emotional free fall; I just didn't see it. As we stood there listening to the doctor, it felt like hours were passing, but it was only moments.

We Choose Adam

The *kind* doctor turned his gaze to me expecting me to concur I imagine and rescue my now destroyed wife from a motherhood of unspeakable torments. What husband would not rally to her protection? But my reaction was not what he or I expected. He was unknowingly offering me an escape from my lifelong fears. I could accept his direction and forever pretend to be noble, the protector of my wife and one who made the tough choice to do the right thing and give our son his best hope for a good life.

Like the kids on the playground, at that moment I saw the doctor as just another bully. He was not kind. He was not protective. He was just pushing one of *them* out of the world intended only for only *us*. He had awakened that part of me that always stopped *them*. Like a bullet proof vest, my past protected me from his *kindness*. Jetta was in shock, but I knew she would agree with my next words, *"We are keeping Adam. Adam is our son, and we want him here with us now."* I spoke in a voice I did not recognize. Calm, clear, just forceful enough to disarm the kind doctor's self-assurance. It came from some authority beyond my capability.

I knew that this decision to keep Adam would change us more than anything we had ever done before. Adam was not just our new baby son but was our child who would forever be different. I was flooded with a cascade of memories and faces that brought me to make my covenant. I swore to do whatever was required for Adam. I swore I would become whatever I needed to become for Adam. I swore I would support Jetta in whatever way she needed. My covenant forged and sealed at that moment. Maybe I imagined myself as the fifth grader on the playground standing like a knight in opposition to all who would victimize those who were weaker and less capable than us. For nine months, I had worked to put my armor aside to live in Jetta's new kinder more inclusive world. Now I was putting it back on and it fit perfectly. At that moment, I made a stand: This far and no farther. This man who wanted my son was the first to experience being dismissed. *"We are keeping Adam."* I knew nothing could be more special than our home for him.

It was the kind doctors turn to be in shock. Our decision was not what the *kind* doctor was expecting, and he retreated without a word. The doctor's *kindness* remained after he walked away, it permeated the room consuming all of Jetta's joy, excitement and hope. Once Jetta and I were alone in the room she began to regain her bearings and come back from her stunned emptiness. Soon enough she had tears streaming down her cheeks. She hadn't said a word up to this point. Then she turned to me and said, "Yes, we keep Adam."

It took all Jetta had to return fully from the emotions resurrected by the doctor, but she wanted to be ready to meet Adam, and she was. Our baby, our son Adam, was returned to us all clean and looking and smelling like the cuddly baby he was and we kept him very close. He melted into Jetta, and they instantly made their lifelong connection even though breast feeding was slow. An incredible woman I found my wife to be. In only a few moments she put aside the agony of 16 hours of labor, forgave the doctor and the nightmares he introduced and connected with her son. We stayed together, Jetta, Adam and I, until both mother and son started to doze off. I had the nurse come back into the room they had put us in after Jeff delivered Adam to take our son to the nursery and Jetta to her room.

Adam was our son, we loved him, and the bond was complete.

My Friend Richard

We finally settled in and Adam was returned to the newborn room, and Jetta was sedated to sleep. Once I knew Adam was safe and Jetta was sleeping and I thought it was safe to leave them unguarded, I went to my friend Richard's house to catch a few hours of sleep myself. He was my clinical supervisor at that time and lived just a few blocks from the hospital. When I walked in, Richard looked a little concerned and asked, "How is it going?"

"Fine. I just need to close my eyes for a couple of hours."

He looked out the window and asked me again how I was doing, then pointed outside and said, "You just 'parked' your car in the middle of the street with the motor running and the door open." I recognized I was not fine and collected myself.

After I had moved my car, we sat for a few moments while I told him the story of the *kind* doctor recommending we abandon Adam to get a better child. Richard was an excellent therapist. As he listened, I got angry (finally), but he just smiled. When I was done, he poked fun at my car parking skills, told me to get some sleep and then come back up to the hospital. Just telling Richard what happened brought some healing to my raw emotions. I have since learned that telling one's story to each new person eventually brings a person (as it did me) back from the abyss, but it requires a lot from the listener. I encourage people to never shy away from actively listening when someone tells you their painful story because it may be the bridge to returning them to feeling human again. But please just listen, no comparisons to your life, not yet.

While I was sleeping, Richard went to the hospital and did what he thought was required to balance the handicapping process the system was using. I'm not sure how he did it, but Jetta told me that upon arriving he immediately went to the nursery and got Adam. Then he carried Adam through the halls loudly introducing him to every nurse and doctor on the floor, "Hey, this is Adam, isn't he a delight? He is such a gift!" I learned this process is intended to weave a new child into the tapestry of a new community. It is usually done by a Rabbi or Minister. But that was Richard's honor to do.

Jetta had Julie and Toby in her room and when she heard Richard coming down the hall loudly introducing Adam to everyone he saw, more tears, but now tears of joy. When Richard walked into the room, the drapes were closed, and the room was dark. Jetta's visitors, Julie (Richard's wife) and Toby (Jetta's friend), were sitting with hands folded quietly until Richard and Adam arrived. Richard handed Adam to Julie while he opened the drapes and let God's light shine in, bathing the room in love. Julie was grieving with Jetta about the *kind* doctor's words, but Richard came in and completely changed the atmosphere. He reinterpreted what had happened. The doctor was wrong, Adam belonged. Don't get caught in his imagined world.

When I arrived at the hospital three hours later, a couple of the nurses caught me before I got to Jetta's room and told me how unusual Richard was and how it seemed just right. It would have been great if the nurses had caught on to what Richard was doing, but they seemingly missed his statement that Adam was a new being to be loved and enjoyed, cherished and celebrated.

Punch Line

I learned later that after I left Jetta safe in her room, one of the nurses came in and with all kindness and compassion announced that she thought it would be best if we had our new parent's dinner celebration in our own room rather than in the community room with the other new parents. It would be more *special* this way. Perhaps she was trying to protect Jetta's feelings, but she had delivered a "poisoned apple" then smiled, closed the curtains and left Jetta with the full impact of the beginning of her *special* segregated life.

It was only our first day in the hospital, and we realized that the *kind* doctor had been correct about how difficult having Adam would make our lives. It was quite revealing that the *kind* doctor never understood that his attitudes and behavior were the reason our new life had become traumatic. Put bluntly, the difficulty wasn't with Adam; it was the doctor practicing his own brand of eugenics in an attempt to improve the genetic quality of the human population. That harmed Jetta. And, because he was a doctor, his attitudes were transmitted to the hospital staff all adding to the injury. Combined, it all made our life with our 10-hour-old son very difficult. Our interactions with misguided people made Jetta's 16 hours of labor and delivery the easiest part of our hospital experience.

While we were all still in Jetta's room celebrating Adam, there was a knock at the door, and she came in. The hospital had sent in a 25-year-old social worker fresh out of school with her Bachelor of Arts degree to help Jetta and I know how to handle Adam's birth. From the moment she walked into the room, we could see that there were things this social worker did not know and did not stop to find out. Jetta had a Master's Degree in Social Work and had 15 years' experience in the field. I held a Master's Degree in Family Therapy with the same tenure. Richard had his MSW (Masters in Social Work) and was a professor in social work and had been a medical social worker in Detroit and had privileges in this hospital. His wife, Julie, had her MSW as well. Jetta and I were surrounded by a great support system with a wealth of knowledge. And we were all sitting there telling Jetta how cute Adam was and by this time, she was feeling pretty good. She had not taken the time to understand how Jetta was feeling. She did no assessment so she could not take into account Jetta's mood, so her entrance and greeting was completely inappropriate; she did not even wait to be invited into our space.

The young social worker missed all kinds of information but started in on a speech that came from her perspective like it was some universal truth just like the *kind* doctor had done. "Oh, Mrs. Winstrom! I can't imagine how badly you must feel. It is often a hard adjustment when children like this are born unexpectedly. I'm here to help." Jetta, Richard, Julie, Toby and I physically recoiled at her words.

I suppose she had been told that another child with special needs was just delivered and she should talk to them and help them through their grieving. This social worker, the wanna-be grief counselor, was sent in to *help* Jetta begin the grieving process because she had a *special* child. But, she made the foolish error that helping professionals too often make and assumed she knew how Jetta must be feeling. It was a triple error. She was dead wrong about how Jetta felt. She was not connected to the world we were all in so she appeared foolish and alien. She had no regard for our privacy and did not show any respect for our boundaries as a family. The triple error disqualified her as a helpful person.

I reached my tipping point. I had no more patience for presumptions from *kind, sympathetic* professionals or their prejudices and foolishness in believing that they knew best. Neither did I have any more patience for people giving Jetta permission to feel bad about Adam. It was not this young woman's lack of experience and education; it was her arrogant intrusion into our lives with her fantasized belief that she was helping us.

Richard had done what he could to remind the world, nurses, and medical staff that we wanted to celebrate the birth of our son not mourn the loss of a fantasy future. This social worker had missed that lesson. Once more, the assault was on Jetta. It was momentarily effective, and Jetta was rendered speechless at this woman's invitation to feel bad about having a special baby. I reacted but quietly asked her to come with me as I walked her out of the room.

I softly began to rebuke her, "Who invited you to our son's birthday? What help could you possibly be? Can you change what the doctor said about how *it* would be a burden our entire lives? Can you make the nurses show up when Jetta wants to see Adam? Can they stop drawing the drapes closed in the middle of the day? Can you fix the harm done to my wife by the nurse who segregated her from the other mothers and did not allow her the dinner celebration for our son's birth? Can you find some sensitivity to our situation and consider whether or not we were better off before you came in? Why don't you go back to your office and think about how to fix your broken system—the one that systematically devalues people who are different? Then please come back, knock, wait to be invited in and listen to us before you begin to speak."

She never returned. She probably wrote me off as being angry with God and displacing it onto her, after all, she was trying to be *kind* and just wanted to *help*. The sad thing is, she really did want to help, but she didn't know what she was doing.

Evidently, my conversation in the hallway with the young woman wasn't as quiet as I thought because when I walked back in, Jetta asked if I had been kind to her. I replied that I thought I was very kind in how I handled that. All four MSW's in the room agreed that she needed supervision. She needed to change her style, and if I said nothing, she would just go on careening through people's lives thinking what she was doing was the best way to practice social work. Other families might not be able to interrupt her and suggest she become more observant and then come back better prepared to help.

Forgive Them Father

The real Adam at ten hours old, a newly born baby, was not very different from the other new born babies in the nursery. He slept and cried. He ate and pooped. He looked around and tried to focus on objects.

Adam was fine. No more effort was required to care for him than any of the other babies. Living through how the hospital responded to Adam gave Jetta a crash course in the world of being *special*. Those few hours in the system altered our lives in ways we did not imagine. Our son Adam did nothing more to change our lives than every other baby born that day did to his or her new parents. It was how the *kind* doctor and nurses responded to the knowledge that Adam was different that was life altering for us.

Jetta could see it for what it was—the doctors and nurses were inducting the three of us into the disabled world. Jetta was always the forgiving one. Her heart told her that they harmed without intention or understanding. And she was always willing to absorb all the emotional pain their unintended or purposeful behavior created.

I can see the *kind* doctor's prejudice and accept that his intention was to show us his truth about retarded children. He wanted us to accept as the only possible solution his imagined idea about the awful future our family was going to have. He even added the weight of our error into his formula by saying that since we declined the amniocentesis, we missed our opportunity to have an abortion; therefore, we must abandon our son to avoid a future of inconvenience before it even happened.

Adam was not even 12 hours old, and we were being told that our son would not talk or walk, would not be able to care for himself or have any friends. He would be a huge burden, would require a special school and would always be isolated and dependent on us his entire life. He would make our lives miserable. I identified him as the *kind* doctor because that is how he saw himself—protecting another family from the horror of raising a retarded child. His intention came from his prejudice, and his prejudice fueled his best intention to protect us from our *special* son. Being a doctor, he only saw Adam as having low Apgar test scores and categorized him as retarded and, therefore, incapable of developing into a functional human being.

He spoke to us in a manner of authority one might use to address children. His matter-of-fact style of talking about abandoning a child was disarming. It made his suggestions seem reasonable. He spoke to me as if he knew me and my deepest secrets and, therefore, knew what was best for me. He was so involved in his own words that he couldn't recognize who he was talking to, or maybe he really was that indifferent to my aspirations. I had not asked him to save me from my son. I had not asked him to determine the worth of Adam nor did I ask him to tell me how to live my life. And still, his feigned *kindness* rolled on almost hypnotically. It felt like looking into the black, empty eyes of a snake completely indifferent to who I really was. I was simply the object in front of him becoming mesmerized before he struck. But I knew him. I was surprised by what his suggestion brought out in me. All he could see were Adam's test scores and our son's outward appearance. He judged us and what he felt we must do based on his own bias. He made his decision based on his early exposure to eugenics and his belief that retarded children belonged in institutions.

He was wrong. He injured my wife by attempting to get us to abandon our son. The *kind* doctor had acted intentionally, separating Adam from us at the moment when bonding was critical so we would not attach to him, making it easier to let go of *it* (Adam). His intervention was strategic and wrong. As Jetta knew too well, the timing between the mother/child developing synchronicity that determines bonding and attachment is critical. Both must be emotionally available in those first shared moments. When the doctor disrupted our parent/child bonding by attempting to block Jetta's attachment to Adam, it was not just his interruption of time; in his *kindness*, he attempted to block Jetta's emotional availability. Had Jetta not done her work to repair the damage she had experienced when her mother was not there to bond with her, she might not have had the grit to come back from the *kind* doctor's assault. It was his prejudice, camouflaged as kindness and his intention to protect us for our own good that harmed both Adam and his mother. By grace, she, Adam and I made it beyond this first obstacle.

The nurses continued the induction into becoming a disabled family by deciding it would be better if we were not included with other newborn parents at the celebration dinner. I can only guess they thought they were protecting us. It felt more like they were protecting the other parents from us. Their prejudice determined their intended course of action for Jetta and me. They initiated the process of segregation—separate but equal. I wanted to forgive them because I wanted to believe they acted based on what they thought was right, but through their prejudice, they injured my wife. So today, I write about them all with respectful irony.

The social worker decided for Jetta that first day of my son's life and the first day of her motherhood that she must be feeling bad about having a child who was going to have special needs. The not-so-subtle implication was that Jetta and I had done something for which to feel bad—something morally reprehensible or inadequate. The social worker and nurses had been trained to help, but their prejudice or pre-judgment about how we should be, think and feel made them more like caricatures of helpful people. They imagined they *knew* what we needed and came into our room believing they belonged there because the system told them to help. Prejudice allowed them to disregard our boundaries, feelings, abilities and even our privacy.

It does not have to be this way. I did what I could to alter their perspective by rebuking the social worker I thought was correct, even kind. Dismissing her was also kind rather than have her stay and be instructed by all of us. We must all change the idea that being different is bad or shameful and, therefore, must be kept separated from the normal ones—from the *us*. We must examine and surrender our bias and prejudices about people who are different. Professionals must remember that their first responsibility is to *do no harm*.

When the little children tried to climb on Jesus' lap, His disciples tried to protect Him from them and Jesus admonished or rebuked them. When people try to protect the world from our different children, they forget their prime directive to *do no harm* and need to be rebuked and dismissed if necessary. Rebuke means to challenge what is wrong even when that wrong is done by a friend. Everyone has the responsibility to rebuke harmful or incorrect actions and to dismiss the person harming when necessary to protect all involved. Of course, this is not done out of anger but out of concern for families' well-being. Left unopposed, they could separate mothers from their children, fracture families and ultimately kill children.

Could This Have Been Better?

A child is a child is a child. All children are special in God's eyes. People look at the outward appearance, but God looks at the heart; He sees their beauty and their potential. We would do well to look into the essence of every child, see the possibilities for their future and make each child special in our eyes as well. If only they would have just accepted and welcomed Adam at birth. If the doctors and nurses could have held him and smiled at him and talked to him like Richard did, it would have been life altering. If any of us wants to make the world a better place and be intentionally thoughtful, do what our friend Richard did—embrace a family, person or child whose differences you are uncomfortable with and welcome them into your world. Please do not do what the *kind* doctor attempted by practicing his own special brand of eugenics. His intention was to surgically amputate my son's future, and I think that is wrong. It is crippling to steal someone's future, no matter how sharp the blade or precise the cut. This is especially true when you have no way of knowing what that future might be.

Let people have their dreams. They will awaken naturally and come to their own understanding when their dream hits mourning (not morning) light. Rushing in to make someone see the world as you see it is not helpful, respectful or acceptable. And it does not work.

Dear Social Worker

Dear social worker, the correct moment for you to be available to a family is when you are invited to do so. Attempts to induce your ideas of how someone must feel is futile. Remember that each person's life is theirs to live even if it is messy. Real life can be messy. Humans can solve real problems in real time with real support and information, so be respectful of their processes.

A professional announcement of *specialness* often triggers false mourning. There was no observable experience to trigger any real loss. It was only the doctor's words that crushed Jetta's dream of motherhood and emotionally removed her from herself. The *kind* doctor was Machiavellian in his delivery and timing. Where there was joy, he replaced it with horror. Where there was an expectation, he substituted fear. He took the fullness of Jetta's experience and created a black hole of despair and self-doubt. The picture his words painted of Adam's future life had no connection to who Adam really was or what his possible life might be. He spoke with authority about what he imagined. He invited us to live in his fantasy world and abandon our real child. To say, "sticks and stones will break my bones, but words will never harm me" is downright wrong. Sticks and stones wound the body, but words wound the soul. The doctor harmed the essence of Jetta's ability to be a mother, and we had to work together to clear the confusion that the kind doctor's prejudice created. The professionals ended up being the problem, not our son, Adam. He was fine. They were infected with their own prejudice.

If only the doctor had said something like, "Adam will have some differences as he grows up. We are not sure exactly what they will be or how those differences might affect him. Usually, we see some cognitive delays and muscle tone weakness. You will have all the support you need when you need it. Right now, he is just like every other baby who needs his mother and father."

If only the hospital staff would have come in, opened the curtains to let some light shine in the room and asked Jetta, "Where would you like to have your celebration dinner and would you like to invite anyone to join you?"

If only the social worker would have knocked and waited to be invited in then said, "I see you have visitors now but wanted to ask how you and Adam are doing. Giving birth is an intense, wonderful, confusing and life-changing experience and some parents find it useful to talk about it. Do you want to talk now? If not, I can come back later if you would like me to. All you have to do right now is be with your new son. Perhaps when you have settled in at home, could we stop over to visit. I will leave you my card. You may find that raising your son requires some additional support; remember, we will be here." But that didn't happen.

Adam was Fine

Adam did all the things a baby did including bonding and melting into his mother when he received love. Everyone around us was living on the edge of disaster, careening us toward an uncertain future as if the present moment never existed and the future was now. Departure from the natural flow of life into the professional world of the *as if* and treating *what will be* as if it was *happening now* distorts reality and creates a fantasized, disabled Adam.

Adam was fine.

Parents, trust yourself. Listen to the professionals, but never let them nullify what you know to be true. Their job is to support you, never to replace you as the final authority regarding what is best for you or your child. They are there to give you support and give you the information when you ask for it.

Adam was fine.

Adam was just one day old. All we needed then was to discover Adam and support Jetta by seeing to her needs and allowing her to rest so she could bond with him. When I looked into my son's eyes and saw the depth of his being, I loved him completely, and I know that he was available to receive that love from me. I had no reservation and needed no protection from what he might become. I knew that if I did not listen to their advice and protect myself or abandon him he would be just fine.

The real 24-hour old Adam was just fine.

And that was enough. Everything else was a distortion of time and created false, imaginary issues giving helping people who genuinely feel the need to do something a reason to unleash their concern. Adam required nothing from them that every other baby did not also need.

Except for his cellular anomalies, he was indistinguishable from the other babies.

Adam was fine.

Do Not Hinder Them

The hospital was not fine.

The kind doctor was not a bad person. The nurses were not bad people. The social worker was not a bad person. They did just what Matthew, Luke, Peter and the rest of the disciples who hindered the children from coming to Jesus did—they wanted to protect Jesus. They did not want Him distracted or interrupted by these children and their special needs. Our children are often still viewed as a distraction; they make life more difficult. The hospital staff wanted to save us from their imaginary idea that Adam represented a horrible future for himself and us. They all wanted to save us from our son. But we did not want to be saved, and that created a problem. Their fear blinded them to Adam's heart just like the disciples were blinded. It seemed like from Adam's beginning breath that we were invited to choose who we were with—our son or the *kind, caring professionals*. We chose Adam every time and forever.

Adam Would Be Fine

A golden rule just after *do no harm* is giving someone support must never make them weaker. The doctor presumed to take away our self-control and ability to decide by preemptively determining a horrible future and attempting to save us from the future he imagined our son would have. The nurses disabled and shunned Jetta by deciding for her where she belonged. Perhaps it was done in kindness and in the name of protection, but it was still shunning because they took away Jetta's right to decide where she belonged. The social worker repeated the error by disallowing Jetta to be wherever Jetta was emotionally. She unintentionally attempted to program Jetta to grieve.

If the hospital staff had not pushed us through their business-as-usual slot into their *special* category, then I would not be writing this book. The kernel in me might not ever have been ignited. I became planted as an obstacle to a world operating in the usual way. I was not to fight what was being done but to create a protective barrier or an obstacle that required the system to find a new path.

I live with the belief that all things come in their own time and for their own purpose. Nothing special please; just let me be different.

In recounting my 1984 experience with the *kind* doctor, I have used the language the *kind* doctor used at that time. He said my son was retarded and called him a retard. I recognize the term as derisive in today's context. I agree that the term is offensive and I use intentionally in context. Over the last 30 years, I have observed the language society utilizes to describe differences and change within a culture's awareness. For me, the terms special needs, handicap, and disabled are all seen as offensive. The word "handicap" comes from children in England begging with "cap in hand" from long ago. Special needs have also become unpopular and left behind as it implied some neediness other people do not have. As if no one else "needs" to be equally respected, included and adjusted to. I never liked the term disabled and B.A. (before Adam) I used to say they were children whose needs challenge the systems' ability to support everyone equally. I never personally felt disabled because I could not write although I did feel differently-abled. I guess this is because I could out-think everyone else. I think Adam also was differently-abled. Carol Gray from the Gray Institute coined the term neurotypical and neurologically unique, but that seems only to confuse folks.

Please do not be offended by the labels or terms used in my story; they are how people spoke at the time. I also hope I do not create any anger towards me or other people I talk about. Through telling this story, I have let go of most all of my hurt and anger and gained a clearer understanding of just how exceptional doing something normal really is. It is exceptional when we include each other in one community as our friends and our equals. The community Adam lived in brings hope to my heart and a smile on my lips.

Chapter 3
The Home Coming

Home and one's neighborhood are the second building blocks of belonging. Will our new son be welcomed into the neighborhood? Will all our neighbors and friends treat us like the hospital staff did, or will they continue to treat us as they had before and even share in our excitement and celebrate with us? I had cigars ready; after all, it's a boy. I hoped Jetta's friends were more like Richard and his wife, Julie than the *kind* doctor. I still held on to Jetta's hope that the world had grown up since I was a child. After all, Adam was just a baby, and there was nothing different about that.

No Balloons

On the day were to leave the hospital Jetta and I talked about what it would be like when we got home. To release herself from an experience she had not imagined possible, she said that what happened in the hospital surprised her, but she knew her friends would never treat her that way. So, Jetta was going to put the hospital experience behind her. The shock was wearing off, she was more rested, and she was determined to get back to her life, the one she had intended for her family all along. The one she held in what was left of her dream. She knew her friends would rally around her. Adam was our son, and we were going to become the family just like she intended. The neighbors would stop over and celebrate with us as we had with them. Adam would be different than other children, but that wouldn't necessarily change everything. Jetta was resilient, and she began crafting her new dream.

My wife had no experience with how fast the word *special* could get out into the community and the judgments that came from that label. The normal life of her dream was evaporating before it ever reached the light of day. There was nothing I could say or do to protect her or change the world quickly enough to avoid the collision I knew was coming. It was a collision that was inevitable, and it was happing in surreal time for me. I had already received the call, "How are you, David, I mean really, how are you?"

I put out the best fire breaks I knew how; I had to stop the special fire from engulfing Jetta's entire being. I communicated to all my friends and Jetta's friends, "It's a boy! Adam is our son, and we are thrilled! Yes, the hospital was difficult, but Jetta and Adam are fine, just tired." I suggested they could send Jetta a card of congratulations and welcome Adam to the world. Still, the *special cards* came. Even the staff where I worked put up a notice: "David and Jetta had a *special* son born 8/26/84. Adam Frank." When I returned to work, I took the sign down and replaced it with a new one: "We are happy to announce the addition of Adam into our family. Both Jetta and Adam are fine."

We thought we'd left *it* behind when we came home from the hospital, but *it* still followed us and began weaving its web of isolation in our real world. The friends she had moved into town to be more connected with did not show up. They did not know what to say, so they were uncomfortable and stayed away. Peoples' prejudices prevented them from doing normal life rituals with Jetta and Adam. Their discomfort made it difficult just to show up. Knock, come in and do the baby thing: "Can I see him? Aww, he's cute. May I hold him?" Then make stupid sounds and tell Jetta she looks good. It isn't rocket science. But *it* affects people's brains, and smart, caring people go stupid and thoughtless. The questions, "How should I act? What should I say? What should I do?" are all reasonable for a 2nd grader who has never been exposed to a new baby, except a 2nd grader would not ask; kids just do.

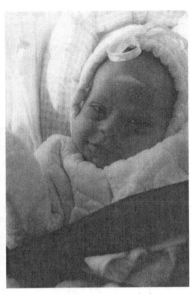

Home from the hospital

I could recognize the children who had received *special* instruction from their parents—hands behind their backs, quiet with a slow and restrained approach. The life and curiosity within them cinched in tight. They would look thoughtfully trying to see the mysterious *what* that was wrong. There were times I reached my tolerance level for accommodating the world's folly. At those moments when I could see the child's face after being puzzled by what they were trying to solve, I would say to them, "Can't find it, can you?" They would look at me quietly like I had caught them. I would say, "It's OK, can you see *it*?" And often they would shake their heads or say, "No." I would say to them, "*It's* not there. Adam is fine; he's just a baby. You can touch his hand and talk to him. It is an adult problem, that *special* thing; it has nothing to do with Adam." Then they would smile and laugh and treat Adam like every other baby they had ever seen. I wish adults were as simple to unlock and release as children are.

Don and Val were a breath of fresh air. The day we got home from the hospital our neighbor, Don, was standing outside waiting to catch me and talk. From my experience over the past few days, I was defensive, but I didn't want to be rude, so I said hello, and he came over and helped us unload the car. When Jetta and Adam were settled and we had emptied the car, Don hung around, and I had the impression he wanted to talk.

Don took me by surprise when he said, "David, I heard from our neighbors that Adam was special and I had no idea what they meant. I thought my new son, Jimmy, was special too, so I asked them, 'What the heck?' They told me that Adam was born with Down syndrome."

"Yes, Don, he was, but he's fine."

"Is it typical trisomy 21 or a mosaic?"

I found a genuine interest in Don's question, so I responded, "The genetic testing came back identifying that my son Adam was a typical trisomy 21, not a mosaic." I smiled and added, "He's not from Mongolia."

Don laughed a bit and added, "I can't believe term 'Mongolian Idiot' was still used in the books."

"Yeah, I know builders who still use lead pipes for drinking water," and he understood. Don was an architect and contractor. He knew that using lead piping for drinking water lines is toxic, but that some builders used them anyway because that was how it was always done.

Then, without any sympathy or pity, Don said, "My wife and I have read what we could find on Down syndrome to be better able to welcome Adam into the neighborhood. Is there anything we should read or do to support you and Jetta?"

"I wish people would just treat us all like normal, new parents and treat our son, Adam, whom we loved and wanted, like the one-week old baby he is. Later on, if all the neighborhood cats start to disappear and Adam's crib is lined with cat fur, we could all get to gather and decide what to do about Adam." Don laughed.

Don became my friend that day. He was so refreshingly normal and honestly and genuinely interested in Adam that I asked him to come in and meet our little son. He held Adam and smiled and laughed. Then he surprised me again and said, "My wife, Val, would love to come over anytime and give Jetta time to just chill."

I told him that we would probably take him up on that offer! I later learned that after our visit Don, he and Val talked to everyone in the neighborhood explaining our desire to continue just being ourselves and our desire to remove the word *special* from describing our son. They restated the greeting to: "Please welcome Jetta and David's son Adam whom they are celebrating!" God gave us another Richard to guard our flanks. Angels each, dispatched to make the way clear for our son's place in the world.

Filling the Holes of Reality

Jetta and I were learning to be parents; we no longer imagined what it would be like. Adam was our real son. His muscle tone was loose, his tongue was slightly enlarged and his energy was low, so he was slow to suck and nurse. He required stimulation, enough but not too much. All babies need to learn how to feed, but with Adam, it was more obvious. Typically, parents need to be sensitive to the moment their child has had enough attention, food, or awake time and stop stimulating their child and let them rest. Adam needed to be taken the smallest distance further. Too little stimulation and Adam would not get enough food (emotional or nutritional) and would withdraw.

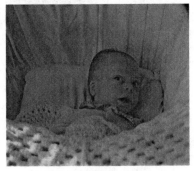

Adam, our gift from God

Too much stimulation and he would get fussy and cry perhaps blocking attachment and developing anxiety as he grew older. Jetta, sensitive to her son's timing, did that just fine.

Each day Jetta had to let go of one dream after another and fill that hole with her loving understanding of what was real. She imagined the perfect baby all new parents probably do. She imagined her friends stopping over, but they didn't. Why was never asked. I guess some just felt too awkward and bad for Jetta to come. The reason we sold our home in the forest and moved into the city was because of Jetta's dream—she imagined she would have visitors. Some did come. The *special* thing was out, and they would inevitably talk about their cousins' son who had Down syndrome and was doing well now in a group home. Another friend wondered if Adam would look like all the children with Downs syndrome when he grew up.

What we all imagined being a parent would be like and being a parent were two completely different things. The *special child* filter added an unnatural layer of imagination to their perception of Adam and our *situation*. No one would ask any other mother if their child

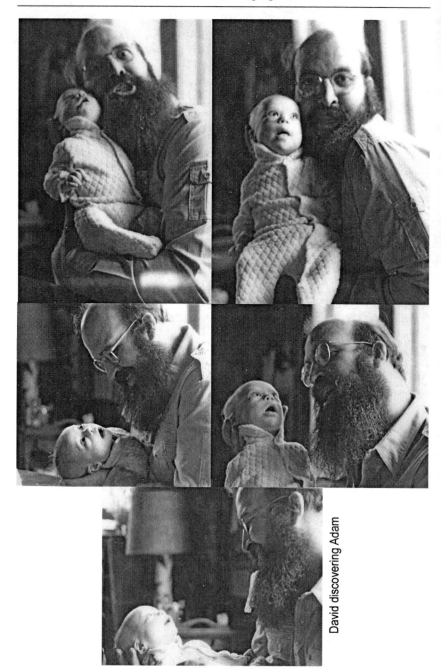

David discovering Adam

would have funny eyes when they grew up. Ignorance, awkwardness and anxiety weeded out most of Jetta's "friends."

We had the scars and scares the doctor had interjected. He had added an extra layer of uncertainty to every moment Jetta spent with our son. His kindness would forever gnaw at Jetta and undermine her belief that she could be enough of a mother for Adam to save him and her from the doctor's imagined future. His prediction festered and ever so slightly but forever imbalanced Jetta.

We learned that the process of letting go of what you imagine is essential so that you can connect with and love what was happening in the present moment. Jetta could have destroyed herself if she had incorporated into her being all the *special* noise, as I called it. A few friends remained, and some new ones entered our lives, but she let go of her social dream and accepted and loved our family as being complete. When the ghost of the kind doctor would appear, she would consciously set aside her fear, calmly take a deep breath and refocus on her son, Adam. She stopped all thoughts about the future and lived each day in the now focusing on what was real. Jetta, the real mother bonded with Adam, her real son. She was enough and she would proceed.

Jetta proceeded with nursing Adam even when she and Adam were tired, fussy or frustrated. Adam had difficulty suckling and sometimes even required extra encouragement to breast feed. When they both had no more to sustain them, Jetta would pump milk for the middle of the night, and I would tend to Adam to give her a break.

I confess I loved those middle of the night times with our son. When he woke up, I would get to spend time just with him. Sometimes when I went into his room, he just needed a diaper change and he was good to go back to sleep. Other times he was hungry, and I would get his bottle ready and sit in the rocking chair I put in his room and make up songs to sing to him as he sucked on his bottle. It didn't matter to him what we did, but for me, it was a special honor to sit in that rocking chair because my grandmother used to rock me to sleep in that same chair when I was a baby. Some nights Adam was ready to discover the

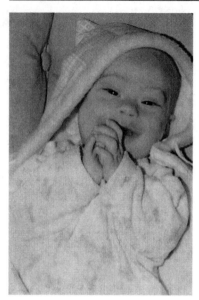

Adam making eye contact

world around him. I would carry him on an exploration around his room. What is this? What does it do? Look at the alphabet cards I put on the wall for you. Let's sing the phonetic alphabet! Our time together was never in order but always involved the senses of sight, touch and sound. Then he would fall asleep and I'd put him back in his crib. Maybe I just bored him to sleep, but it was a nice night for me with my son.

After a few weeks had passed, the three of us began to find our rhythm and started feeling like a family. Part of being new parents is going for the first follow up appointment with the doctor after the hospital. We chose our pediatrician. We had chosen Adam's pediatrician very carefully. He was a kind man, an excellent doctor and treated Adam like every other newborn and Jetta and I like every other new set of parents. He encouraged Jetta to continue to breast feed Adam and to pump milk so that I could feed Adam in the middle of the night and she could sleep and recover. He always took extra time with us, never foretelling the future but always assuring us that we were all doing just fine.

What he knew that we did not was that children with Down syndrome often have heart and neck problems. During our 6-month appointment, he told me he heard a slight clicking in Adam's heart. He asked me to listen, and I could hear it, too. He said it sounded like a mitral valve clicking and that sometimes the problem self-corrects. He suggested we see Don, a friend of his in Grand Rapids. Don turned out to be the best cardiologist in the area.

After listening, we took Adam to the appointment, and he listened to Adam's heart, then confirmed that a mitral valve problem would either self-correct or require surgery. He told us that it was not something to worry about; our pediatrician had an amazing ear, so we should just let him monitor it regularly and come back in six months. If Adam's heart was still clicking, he would correct it. What went unspoken was that if the mitral valve problem did not self-correct, he would require open heart surgery—and I knew that could be life threatening for an infant. We began to pray. Jetta never knew about the possibility of heart surgery; the doctor had not mentioned it. She didn't need to know about tomorrow, that discovery added another weight to the unknowable future, and she only needed to stay in this day with this son, Adam.

Adam's heart condition added regular doctor's visits, making it a little more challenging to be Adam and to be Adam's parents. While Jetta's role was being in the present moment with our son, a point of stability and predictability for Adam, my role was the scout. I began to read everything I could on the neurology and biology of Down syndrome and look at all possible futures to better understand and live in the present moment with Adam.

Professional Intervention

The County Early Intervention Program contacted Jetta to come for a visit when Adam was about two months old. Our hospital experience had taught Jetta and me that we needed to be together to withstand the *kind* people; now, we were faced with *helpful* people. It was challenging to be prepared but not be defensive. Jetta was very good at this, but I always wore my armor and had a hard time taking it off. Different from *kind* people, these folks made no pretense of being kind; their job was to *help* Adam in whatever way they deemed best. Once you let them into your world and signed their consent forms, they presumed the right to decide what was in Adam's best interest without any collaboration from us. They acted more like minor deities than angels of mercy. They were not like Richard or Don. They were not like our doctor, nor even the *kind* doctor; they were far more brutal.

I especially remember the first visit from the *helpful* people. We had only been home from the hospital for a few months and were still reeling from the *kind* doctor telling us that keeping Adam would ruin our lives. We were still in parental shell shock when she arrived and were not as prepared for the gravity of her visit as we thought we were. The detached, abrupt and self-assured professional woman who arrived not a minute late or a minute early, told us to sit in our living room. As Jetta held Adam, the *helpful* professional went into a monolog with no room for questions or interactions. She welcomed us to Ottawa County services for retarded children by saying, "By now you know you have a Down's child. I want to let you know what you can expect from the Ottawa Early Intervention Program. I will arrange for a physical therapist to come to your home once a week. The therapist is trained to work with the particular problems of Down's children like having an enlarged tongue that often protrudes like his tongue is protruding now." Adam's tongue was not in his mouth or sticking out, he was relaxed, and his tongue was just visible between his lips, but Jetta flinched when the *helpful* professional said, "like now" in a tone as if she had just seen gold. For Jetta, not being able to get her son to keep his tongue in his mouth was somehow another failure.

The *helpful* professional plowed on. "Some parents have decided to shorten their Down's children's tongues surgically. You will have to decide that, but if you want to have that done so his speech will be more understandable, you should do it soon. I will leave names of some of the local surgeons for you. I know this is a lot and he is not what you expected. Having a Down's child requires more decisions, and I will help you with them. Let me think…tongue, tongue surgery, oh, his upper body strength is what supports speech and we will show you exercises to do to support clear speech. Eating, how is feeding going?"

Jetta started talking about how breastfeeding was going, but the professional cut her off and said, "Your physician is the best one to talk with about that. We are getting more Down's children lately, and it is stretching our services, so talk with your pediatrician about that. Next is dietary supplements. I won't send out our dietitian, okay (rhetorically)? We have one that works through the Ottawa Area Center Program, and that is where you will go after we get you settled in and adjusted to all that has happened. We will wait to start speech therapy for a while and see what happens naturally, but probably you will get a speech therapist an hour or two a week. When the time comes for that, I will let you know. I know this is hard and not what you wanted, but it will be fine. We have a complete continuum of care. I will come back twice a week at first, okay? So, you will receive services three times a week as part of the early-on services and next you will be able to sign up for the Ottawa Area Center. That is a full day at school with trained professionals. They specialize in Down's children and Autism and physical handicaps. When you go there, it will be great. It is a special school where all the kids are safe and get to be with their own kind. The parents in Ottawa County wanted this program so their children would be safe. You know kids can be cruel. Okay, so he'll be at Ottawa Area Center until he is 26 and we stop being responsible for programming and you can start with mental health and be included in their day treatment or their sheltered workshop programs. And they have group homes, so you will be able to know your son is safe and you can have your life back."

She let us know what it felt like to be "special" in 1984. She did not mention it, but Jetta and I already knew the Ottawa Area Center required a two-hour bus ride to get there and another two-hour ride home. It would mean Adam would be placed in their lovely segregated facility in the middle of nowhere in Ottawa County. She told us that they had special staff there trained to work with Down's children. We knew the staff would work with Adam and he would be trained to eventually work at the Counties sheltered workshop for the "retarded" (a common term in 1985) until he was 26 and stopped being eligible for their "special" school. This was the *special* school the *kind* doctor predicted Adam would need. There is no real graduation from the Ottawa Area Center, only an exchange between government funding sources—their continuum of care. The school and mental health's creation of a community institution for lifelong support. She was actually smiling as she spoke to us about this quietly and almost in a sing-song style.

Jetta enjoying Adam
on one of our first
family outings.

I had been seated on the sofa next to Jetta who was holding Adam, and the professional had positioned herself in the arm chair across the room facing Jetta and me. Adam was in his mother's arms and out of the corner of my eye I could see Jetta singing to Adam and weeping over the loss of her dream as she often did when *kind* and *helpful* people explained the future Adam was entitled to by law. She wept as her future and her child's future was being erased by their all-knowing certainty of what was best for our Down's child. It seemed they were in a hurry to erase parent's unrealistic dreams and quickly replace them with ideas of what their future life as a retarded family would be. Gone forever were her storybook dreams of her baby and his childhood. She listened as the *helpful* professional painted a new picture of her predetermined world that she was entitled to by law. She wept because she knew their plan for her precious son was to train him to sit at an assembly table with his own kind.

Jetta and I already knew the students at Ottawa Area Center were divided into three classrooms: young children, middle children and older children. Our son would start out in the young group with some motor stimulation. Eventually, as he reached the middle group, he would learn to sort parts and count and record how many he had done. He would learn to do this very clearly and correctly. In the older group, he would learn appropriate behavior to go to "work" in a sheltered workshop. They claimed they were a job skill training program leading to employment. We knew it was a not-for-profit, segregated, "simulated" work environment funded cooperatively by Ottawa County Mental Health, Michigan Rehabilitation Services and donations. People were never placed into any jobs from there. It was a life sentence.

There was no physical assessment of Adam and what he really needed. There was no inquiry into what Jetta and I might want or need. The *helpful* professional just showed up punctually and proceeded blindly and off-handedly, pronouncing what our life would be. The professionals never considered that Jetta loved Adam and wanted to be his mother forever. Group homes were not part of her plan or mine. The *helpful* professional was talking about Jetta's life as a mother, a life that was not something she wanted to be rescued from. They never even considered that we valued Adam as a person and did not need to escape from *him*. She did not see that Adam, at two months old, had never disappointed Jetta. Jetta's friends had disappointed her. The hospital had disappointed her. Even this person in her living room by her off-handed dismissal of Adam's potential and worth was disappointing her.

Over time, the rumor developed among the *helpful* social workers that Jetta was depressed. They never directly said anything to us, why should they? They assumed all mothers of retarded children were depressed. They did not know her strength of character nor her actual mood. She was disappointed by their assault and their indifference. Every meeting with a social worker took away her son's future and erased him a little more like a real child—this was their idea of *help*. She wanted to nurture her son. She wanted to focus on him and love and support him in the moment, not look at what he may never be.

Prejudice and a positional sense of entitlement and/or obligation compelled the *helpful* professional to drone on with her 50-minute orientation to the rest of our Down child's life. What she could not understand was Jetta was not depressed, a clinical term for a chemical imbalance. She did not have a postpartum depression; she was depressing her own maternal instinct to dismember this insensitive alien in her home. Only a foolish person would imagine that it was proper to enter the home of a new mother and systematically devalue her child in the guise of *help*. Jetta's kind nature would not allow her to confront this person, but she was depressing her own natural instinct to defend Adam from the images the social worker's words created in her mind. It was painful, and she wept. Once more, Adam became an *it*. A Down's child and no longer her son. Any possible future for Adam was being preemptively erased in the 50-minute orientation to a Down's child's life in Ottawa County, Michigan. Period. The end. And thank you for your time. What we knew the whole time was that this *helpful* professional in our living room was taking us on a tour of what she imagined our next 30 years would look like.

Then she looked at her watch and came back to the present. She ended her visit by standing up and informing us that we would be receiving a call from a physical therapist in the next few weeks. She would also return for another visit, and then she walked herself out the door. Jetta and I and Adam were alone once more still sitting on the sofa. Just like the *kind* doctor, this *helpful* professional had managed to suck the life out of the room.

There was no assessment. We were now a retarded family with a Down's child. We were officially in the system with available service provisions in place, and every retarded family received what we were offered because that was just what they did. We found out that there were two approaches to every service provision. One, you get a little of everything because that is how we do it. Or, two, you don't need anything yet because your son is not developmentally out of the norm at only four weeks old. So, wait until there is a problem, then call us. Both approaches fail because neither involved an assessment of Adam. Jetta and I figured out how these people operated and learned to endure the *helpful* professionals' litanies because at the end we knew we might get something that would be useful. Jetta understood that they really did not know anything and said that we would be lucky to get their help. Eventually, she became better at not joining them emotionally as they annihilated her son's possible future. I could see her acquiring new armor after every visit from a professional.

It took the *helpful* professional a mere 50 minutes and the words "your Down's child" to take our son Adam and turn him into an *it* and tell us exactly what our lives would be like for the next 30 years. Because the professional saw him as a Down's child, she could predict with calculated certainty what each of the next 30 years of our son's life

Adam loved playing and learning

would entail. Where he would go to school. Where he would work. Where he would live. What his life would be like. What his potential would be. She made no mention of children coming over to play or horseback riding. There were no parties or girlfriends in the future she proclaimed our son deserved. And she did it all with a smile. The page in the manual that read, "Do no harm" had escaped her. We were well initiated into the *special* world now. We were treated impersonally as objects. She worked for a system that had removed the doors from the old institutions and simply spread the institution out into discrete compartments subtly segregating the Down's children and young adults into isolated groups. It was a perfect recreation of the lock step progressions of the old institutions. In her heart, it was still a separate-but-equal world view that she believed: being with his own kind and safely segregated was best. Our Down's child would have equal opportunity to experience school, work and live in a community; it was just a separate special community.

It seemed like we were always being taken out of the present moment into some future imaginary special world that the *helpful* professional was either going to prepare our Down's child for or guard him against. All of it was her helpful attempt to do what she could to support our Down's child's limitations and at least get him ready to live in a group home and work at a sheltered workshop with his own kind. And it was all delivered so calmly over tea that we did not have to worry because *help* was near. *Help* was here. And we were getting *helped*.

Jetta and I both knew this system. We were also helping professionals (before we were retarded parents) having worked in Ottawa County Mental Health Programs. At one time, I was the supervisor of all services to children. Jetta had worked with some of the group homes attempting to make them actual *homes* for people, but she knew the homes were a failure. We both did. She wept because she thought that was what was going to be done to her sweet son. Their creation would be his only possible future.

When the *helpful* professional left, I promised Jetta that that would never be Adam's future. I reminded her that it was 1984 and that Adam was our son. He was just a baby and was still too young to decide if he should go to Harvard or Yale. Despite her tears, she laughed.

She Could Have Done Better

What we received was a preprogrammed response to a diagnostic label released by the hospital to Ottawa County alerting the Intermediate School District that they were now responsible for providing support services to the Winstrom family. The helpful professional did not waste her time connecting with Adam because that was not the purpose of her visit. She was sent to our home by Ottawa County to tell us that we had a Down's child and what that reality was going to look like for him and for us. I didn't blame her for how she acted in our home, just as I didn't blame the doctor or nurses for their behavior. I did, however, hold them accountable and actively opposed their attitudes and style. They all acted out of their training, and their training was rooted in the American Eugenics Movement—the basis for what I called "normal privilege." I am doubtful that they were even aware of their foundational philosophy.

Adam was born into the social adjustment period between the eugenics philosophy and President Kennedy's and President Johnson's attempt to correct the remnants of the eugenics philosophy. The eugenics forces pushed for sterilization, institutionalization and euthanizing. Doctors were trained to refer mentally deficient children directly into institutions. People who believed in supporting normalization and inclusion focused on creating supports and improving services to promote acceptance of all forms of diversity into the American culture. The two philosophies were diametrically opposed and incompatible.

Social policy was at odds with the existing social norms. People were divided in their beliefs and localities reflected which side of these core beliefs they adhered to. Our county was still rooted in segregation, eugenics. Jetta and I saw the institutionalized segregation and knew about the changing laws. In 1896 in the court case Plessy vs. Ferguson, the Supreme Court of the USA determined that segregation was legal and did not violate the 14th amendment. "Separate but equal" was the law of the land until 1954. Segregation found "scientific" legitimacy in the eugenics philosophy that held that some people are superior. Those that are not superior are of lesser value. Each group belongs with its own kind. Mixing the groups genetically or even socially detracts from the aspirations and potential to succeed of those who are superior. Those who are inferior have less of a right to live and could/should be separated out of the culture and eliminated

In 1954 in the case Brown vs. Board of Education, the Supreme Court overturned the "separate-but-equal" doctrine. They wrote in their opinion that separate but equal was never equal, it was inherently unequal. The Justices went on to say that even if the building structures, supplies and teachers were completely equal, separation (segregation) itself created an inherently unequal setting. Their opinion made the aim of the eugenics movement to separate people by race, culture or IQ illegal. Jetta was correct that the laws had changed, but she did not see that for the last 30 years, the culture had not accepted the laws. Discrimination in the form of segregation was not good for anyone, and in 1954 the court ruled it was illegal. Kennedy had designed new supports for inclusion that, although identified in the law, had not yet become the culture in Ottawa County. The law requires inclusion and normalized not institutionalized living.

Eugenics was not an idea invented by Germany; its origin is the United States of America. It was not originally about white supremacy; it was equally supported by African Americans, intellectuals at Tuskegee University, Howard University and Hampton University. Eugenics received support and funding from Carnegie Institute, Rockefeller Foundation, Hamilton Railroad and even Kellogg. Eugenics was taught in all of the USA colleges and medical schools.

The ideas of eugenics are that being poor or disabled were equated to inferior genetics and moral turpitude, i.e. bad genes. Germany was

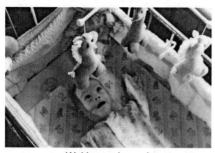

Waking up happy!

not alone nor first to exterminate those they deemed unfit. The American Eugenics Society had suggested the establishment of gas chambers in several geographic areas of the United States, but politicians decided the USA was not yet ready for that part of the solution.

Hitler's rise to power in Germany was the result of his populist appeal targeting the Gypsies, Jews and those thought to be feeble-minded as the reason Germany was no longer great. His divisive rhetoric prepared Germany to take the steps the United States was not yet ready to implement. Hitler instituted extermination as an acceptable solution by creating the public belief that to be great again, Germany had to solve her political problems. For Germany to be great again, the German culture needed to be cleansed. Hitler started by euthanizing the mentally deficient then the Jews and Gypsies in the German population.

In America, we also targeted the feeble-minded. Doctors institutionalized babies thought to be unfit at birth. Those institutions added live tuberculosis virus to the formula the babies were fed, and 30% died; the rest were carriers and, therefore, required institutionalization for life. Many of the adults were starved. In 1972, Willowbrook was exposed by reporter Geraldo Rivera.[1] He said that it smelled like death. Our hands are not clean.

Robert Kennedy visited Willowbrook at the President's recommendation. Kennedy did not want to blame the staff at the facility because they were also victims of a system that lacked imagination, adequate resources and support as well as the social will to do better. He called it a national disgrace. The institutions that were initially considered to be support systems rapidly became overcrowded,

---

[1] "Unforgotten: 25 Years After Willowbrook" (1997). Documentary Published Oct. 18, 2015.

warehousing 6,000 children in a facility designed to house 4,000. Staffing ratios were 40 to 1 and services were shameful. Willowbrook was not the only shameful institution, Pennhurst State Home in Pennsylvania[2] was equally as tragic for anyone unfortunate enough to be sent there. Every State had their hospitals, sanitoriums and child placement facilities. Michigan had many.

The resulting lag between changing laws and local attitudes created the situations we experienced with our own *helpful* professional. She was still implementing the old institutional model and could have done this better, but she did not understand the forces within herself and her origination that compelled her to see her own business-as-usual approach as helpful. That behavior we found repugnant.

This mindset was was devised also the cultural background for the *kind* doctor's ideas. The basis for his recommendation was rooted in the American Medical culture promoting courses in eugenics taught in most American Universities. It became the cultural norm. Doctors and ministers would grade better baby competitions at county fairs. A 1,000-point scale was devised, and the doctors would take measurements and sometimes the ministers would take histories and subtract points for deviation from their standards, like non-church attendance, family history of promiscuity by aunt Bessy or a business failure by great Uncle George. Points would be deducted for whatever the minister judged as social depravity. These were not unlike the quick Apgar Scale mental check that our *kind* doctor used to base his decision on that our son would be better off in a *special place with his own kind*–a phrase straight from eugenics philosophy. Straight from hell.

The *helpful* professional could have done better. I could have done better, too. Jetta's friends could have done better. Adam, being just a baby, was doing it just right. He had no idea all of this was being played out around him. And yet, these were the forces that we resisted to allow Adam to grow to his real potential in our community.

---

[2] "Suffer the Little Children" Pennhurst State Home. Retrieved from www.preserve-pennhurst.org.

Wolf Wolfensberger was a German-American academic whose ideas supporting normalization were in direct opposition to eugenics. His theory was rooted in an awareness of the normal rhythms of a life lived in community. To always be included in the normal conditions of life in one's own home, church, school and community. The Wolfensberger principle is based upon social and physical integration and dignity of risk rather than upon exclusion through the kind of special protections the helpful professional offered us.

His research supported Kenneth and Mamie Clark's 1954 work in the case of Brown vs. Board of Education[3] identifying segregation as harmful for all involved. That case changed the law. The research of Wolf Wolfensberger proved that inclusion was educationally and, equally importantly, financially better for everyone than the separate-but-equal special programs schools and institutions that, as Geraldo said, "smelled of death." Canadian education embraced Wolfensberger's model and verified this new philosophy. Canada transformed Canadian schools and had a noticeable impact on the Canadian culture that values diversity and inclusion to this day.

Despite these developments, the underlying instinctive attachment to eugenics still lived in the soul of the *kind* doctor and nurses, and I saw it again that day with the *helpful* professional. She could have done better had she understood Wolfensberger's work or just by listening to Jetta. I think she was influenced by the weight of eugenics and its belief in segregation and congregation—putting all the mentally deficient children together some place away from everyone else. Congregation lowered costs but increased isolation and precluded the possibility to observe and practice relating with typical students. They chose segregation over inclusion. These beliefs formed her and employer's instinctive responses and kept them all deaf and blind to what we knew to be the right path for our son.

---

[3] Clark, Kenneth B. and Clark, Mamie P. (1947). "Racial Identification and Preference Among Negro Children." In E. L. Hartley (Ed.) Readings in Social Psychology. New York: Holt, Rinehart, and Winston.

Chapter 4
Finding Our Way in the World

Learning How to Teach

It was clear that it was up to us to teach our son about both his world and the culture we wanted him to live in. All parents have this same obligation, but few parents have competition from helpful professionals who have a different plan in their minds for our child. That meant Jetta and I had to find the best ways to instruct Adam. The local methods that the county educators offered were routed in segregationist eugenics. If we went along with these helpful professionals, we would be supporting their eugenics based interventions. Their premise was, 1) Adam is the problem; 2) Solving the problem is best done in a segregated facility that specializes in instruction for retarded children; and 3) He would be taught appropriate behaviors to live in a group home and work in a sheltered workshop. The end-product would be a "separate-but-equal" life disconnected from the main culture. We choose not to follow their plan.

I began researching and found the best instructional methods and the best models for inclusion to teach us how to teach our son. One of those models was Temple Grandin. From her book, I learned that Temple Grandin was born in 1947, long before the Autism spectrum was invented. She wrote that:

> *...she didn't speak at all until after she turned three years old—and even then, her speech was idiosyncratic.*

Fortunately for Temple, her parents ignored doctors' recommendations to have her institutionalized as a response to her delayed development, temper tantrums and other issues—all of which earned her an Autism diagnosis.[4]

I attended a conference on inclusion in Washington, DC and listened to Temple Grandin talk about the differences in her perception and experience that Autism brought into her life. She talked about how the basic rhythms and rituals of life, everything she experiences was affected. She said she was different, not broken, sick or bad. She also talked about Tesla, Einstein and others she saw as having forms of Autism because their thinking process was unique like hers. Like her, they were all outcasts growing up because they all share unique mental processing, all of them were difficult for neurotypical (or normal) people to relate to. She described her struggles and said her differences were difficult but not insurmountable.

Other speakers, some with Down syndrome told their stories and talked passionately about not wanting to be transformed into something they were not. Each one said clearly and earnestly: I am not broken. I am not bad. I am different. I do not want your help to change me into you. I want your respect to be who I am. Accommodate my differences as I must accommodate yours. Please do not punish me or demand that I become like you. I cannot and I will not.

Temple Grandin said that she had

...read enough to know that there were still many parents, and yes, professionals too, who believe that once autistic, always autistic. This dictum has meant sad and sorry lives for many children diagnosed, as she was in early life, with Autism. To these people, it is incomprehensible that the characteristics of Autism can

---

[4] Grandin, Temple. *Emergence: Labeled Autistic.* Arlington, Texas: Future Horizons, 1996.

be modified and controlled. Then she added, "however, I feel strongly that I am living proof that they can." [5]

I listened, I learned. If the disabling expressions of Autism could be mediated for her, Jetta and I could do the same for our son. Temple was very clear: if Adam were to be included in the world of the typical people and not sentenced to live apart in the *special* world created for children with Down syndrome, he would have to learn the typical rhythms and rituals people commonly practiced. We had to teach Adam to recognize the rhythms of others but not force him into becoming someone he was not. It was clear he could not learn how typical kids behaved if he was in a *special*, segregated facility. Nor in separate, *special* programs in church or Sunday School classes. I understood the Bible to say that we are to teach our children in the way he or she should go and even when he or she was old, they would not depart from that way. To teach my son the way he should go, he had to be included. There are two essential elements to belonging. The first is to be physically present with the group you want to belong in. Temple said it was a hard, even painful process to learn to manage herself and to relate to others, but she had done it. She had learned how to deal with us and even live among us.

Timing, the rhythm of life, is the second essential element to becoming part of a group. It is the key that unlocks the doors of separation between people. It is possible to join another person in their world and their conversation if we can match their rhythm. **When we discover and share the other person's rhythm, it allows us to find each other, merge into the flow of life and begin our journey into belonging.** Both Temple Grandin and Wolf Wolfensberger were telling me this.

What Separates Us?

Neurotypical people (this describes most people) are governed by a collective circadian rhythm. They move through the world to the beat

---

5 Ibid.

of a similar drum because they have a normal brain so their instinctive, biological rhythm to life, their circadian rhythm, is pulsing at the same rate. People with neurological anomalies (the *them* group that includes myself and my son) are not governed by the same instinctive rhythm. Our interpretation of the basic rhythm of life is altered because the neurological structures (for instance basal ganglia and amygdala) that make meaning are altered. Essentially, we hear a different drummer. I see the world differently than you who can, with ease, read these words that I struggle to produce.

Adam also had a genetically unique perception of the world. As I had learned to live among the neurotypical, now I would teach my son. First, I knew that Adam would need to learn his own rhythm. Once he was secure in his own rhythm—his rhythm, we could teach him to find others and make a connection. I intended to teach Adam how to include other people who were different than he was.

We are biologically-driven, instinctive beings first. Pulsing to our circadian rhythms that, in turn, affect the basal ganglia. The basal ganglia are the part of the brain that regulates cognition, emotion, our rituals and if/how we learn from mistakes. Attention Deficit Hyperactivity Disorder (ADHD), Down syndrome, Autism, Bipolar Disorders, and Dyslexia all blossom up from the basal ganglia. They all share disordered timing and unique learning styles that impact all aspects of life.

The truth is that it is not our different biological rhythms that separate us in society. Differences are used to identify targets of opportunity. It was never Adam's unique timing that separated him from other children. Exclusion occurred because modern day disciples—people empowered by some authority—would not want Adam to bother others or distract the teacher. Jesus said we were not to hinder the children from coming to Him for the Kingdom of Heaven belongs to such as these. He stopped His disciples from *segregating* and keeping the children from *belonging* with Him.

What Brings Us Together

Natural inclusion is all the different rhythms finding their way to unify in play. If you want to observe life's rhythms unfolding and belonging rituals being developed, go to a children's playground and watch them play. It will show you exactly what Jesus meant when He said that unless you change and become like little children, you will never enter the Kingdom of Heaven. Heaven on earth comes from our sense of belonging to our group. Church, school, neighborhood, club, etc., are all vehicles to belonging—the experience of being someone to someone.

I think the best example of inclusion or belonging is the merry-go-round. Notice the children already on the merry-go-round spinning and laughing. Then watch as they encourage their friends to run up, jump on, and join them. When the timing of the spinning merry-go-round is just right, everyone gets on, laughs and spins around joyfully—everyone belongs on the ride. But sometimes the timing is not right. If the child trying to jump on does not connect with the rhythm of the spinning merry-go-round, they end up being dragged along in the gravel. They learned they had to match their friends' timing and their friends learned to accommodate them. Little girls are much better at this than boys.

Or, remember when you were older, and you were taking a family trip. You head down the freeway ramp to merge into traffic, but you cannot find an opening to enter. You pray something will happen so you can get into the flow on the freeway. If you did not match the flow of traffic and no one chose to accommodate you, you end up stuck on the shoulder.

Men use the ritual of shaking hands to establish a rhythm and synchrony between them. Not too fast not too slow. Not too hard not too soft. Not too long or too brief. Women often hug heart-to-heart to synchronize their rhythm. We make eye contact to recognize the other and allow them to recognize us, to briefly see into our collective soul. But not too long to threaten or too brief to seem untrustworthy.

Adam, like most people, would probably not be able to figure out why things happen socially. He would be an easy target for exclusion because he was different, and he would experience prejudice and discrimination without understanding why. That would wound his soul, and that was not acceptable to Jetta and me. Granted, including people who you see as like yourself is more natural because it lets you reinforce who you are. Including people who are different than yourself is more of a risk. By including people who are different, you are forced to expand your understanding of yourself. And that requires work.

Knowing all this meant we needed to support who Adam was so he would have a strong sense of himself and be secure. It also meant we needed to teach him how to recognize others' rhythms and make connections. If he could connect with them, perhaps they would find themselves in Adam. Temple said that it was painful at first, but it was worth it. Jetta and I would also have to become observant and selective about how Adam was inducted into different communities in order to engineer success and allow all involved to learn.

To begin this journey, first, we all needed to join the Winstrom clan, then the Grant Street neighborhood, then church and, finally, the neighborhood school to become a citizen of Grand Haven. It all hinged on becoming a Winstrom, being found by his mother and creating a bonding attachment to her and then connecting to me. Hopefully, he would decide we were okay to create a mutual bond with and share in our collective rhythm and our rituals.

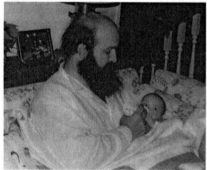

First Christmas

Lots of rituals. Bed time rituals. Morning rituals. Cooking, eating, clean up rituals...all ritualized behavior. Just how can this be done with an infant? As with all teaching, first you must find the student, then gain his trust, so he will accept your information. First, we had never defined them before, so Jetta and I had to make conscious our ways of operating—our personal rhythms and rituals.

Building Block Reinforcements

Each member of our little family had some old rituals and now some new ones to develop. As we developed our way of being the Winstrom family, we made sure that what we did we did *with* Adam not just *to* him. We were taking seriously the admonishment to "teach your children" not command them. But we did not start by creating intentional routines; we observed Adam and reinforced routines we could all live with. We became more observant and more in tune with natural rhythms.

All parents soon discover that they cannot make a baby sleep. They cannot make a baby eat. No one can make a baby love. Shared rituals develop out of the rhythms of life first observed and then reinforced so that they can continue and grow; if ignored, they will fade away. That is why giving complete attention and connecting emotionally during feeding and changing diapers are so important. When Jetta and Adam were both available to connect, they developed into the rhythms and rituals of family life.

When I changed Adam's diaper, it was language time—we named and touched body parts. We would sing, "Head and shoulders, knees and toes" and Adam would grin. Because of this shared experience, a strong attachment and bonding grew between us. Changing diapers was not done *to* Adam but was done *with* him. We used the time to increase our bond with him. It was an opportunity to assist Adam in his sensory integration and proprioceptive (body awareness and sensory integration) development. He connected with his own body. He learned to trust me and my touch. He connected with my attention and me with his. There is nothing automatic about human connections.

Attention, the awareness of one's self and others, offers millisecond opportunities of shared experience that connect us with another human being. I was there to meet Adam's inquiring gaze. His eyes would focus for a moment on me, and he would give me that brief opportunity to join him. They were golden moments. Momentary shared awareness is the first anchor for intimacy, relationship, turn taking and friendship. Because of the importance of these connections, Jetta and I chose to leave all distractions at the front door. We only considered bleeding, lack of breathing and poisoning as emergencies; everything else could be put off so we could connect with our son. If responded to, those milliseconds of shared attention grow; they decrease when interrupted by a phone call or a few distracted minutes on Facebook, and we didn't want to miss one opportunity. We learned that we must first fill our child's emotional tank with love and attention so that our child would have the confidence to become independent. We knew that withholding attention and early isolation or indifference could create an empty tank that always needs filing and we wanted Adam to instinctively know that we would always be there with him and for him.

These were the building blocks of the rest of our lives together. Mother and child bonding. Father and son bonding. Forming our family unit and establishing our unique rhythm and rituals. Understanding the systems that we would have to navigate with and for Adam. Including their rhythms and rituals, their prejudices and biases. Eventually, we began finding connections in a community of friends.

Jetta was an incredible mother. Just as I took my covenant seriously, so, too, did Jetta. She would not

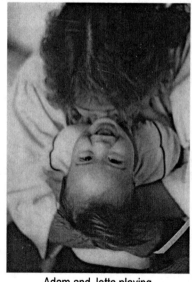

Adam and Jetta playing

accept the *kind* doctor's notion that she could not be a good enough mother for Adam. Her journals reflected her love and devotion to her son:

Breast feeding went well. Tongue and oral motor adequate if patient. Sees me and I love him!

September 6, 1984, grabbed Dad's beard. Good grip.

September 7 nursing better.

September 19, first tub bath. Loves water.

October 24, 1984, smiled at me, 8 lbs. 14 oz.

November 15, 1984, lots of cooing and smiles. Julie held him and he melted and slept.

December 28 ate cereal and napped in big bed with me.

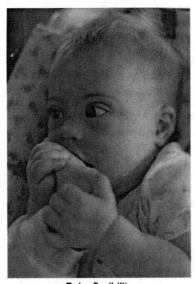

Baby flexibility

April, 1985, eats food in high chair.

May 15, 1985, keeps trying to stand up. Crawled to me for kiss.

These are just a sample of how Jetta dedicated herself to supporting and observing Adam during his first year. She wrote every day and shared the best moments with me. Adam was doing very well, and Jetta was loving being his mother.

When Adam was still an infant, our life was consumed by the typical

Jetta and Adam Time

adjustments all parents go through. We had new routines, lived on very little sleep and were isolated from our old world. But we also had the loss of support from Jetta's friends and the added "benefit" of the professional *helping* community. Like most families, we cocooned to figure out how life was going to work, but our cocooning lasted a little longer than usual because we had to filter through the well-intended and not-so-well-intended *helping* community to establish our Winstrom rhythm and rituals.

Every day I walked into and out of Adam-and-Jetta-time and thoroughly enjoyed watching them together. I was the addition. Most, if not all fathers, are there to support their wife and support the mother-child bonding. It is the natural order of life. Jetta and Adam connected just as she had dreamed they would. Just as words add nothing to the Mona Lisa smile, I found no words to describe the perfect union between Jetta and her child. She found Adam, and he accepted her into his world. I was there to support them.

Friends

The friends who chose to stay had to adapt to our world. One friend, Dr. Jim Piers who was a professor of social work, came to visit and wanted to hold Adam and celebrate our son with us. When Jetta handed 3-month-old Adam to Jim, he did not realize how loose Adam's muscle tone was and nearly lost his hold on Adam, first letting his neck flop backward and then losing hold of his legs. It scared Jim, but Jetta and I were used to it and just laughed. Even as Jetta shared her son with Jim, she kept a hand just where it was needed. For most of Adam's life, his uniqueness required people to pay attention and be present in the moment without any preconceived ideas of what being present would be like. I told Jim that Adam was still a little sloppy for his age, but he was doing just fine. I still kid him about trying to break Adam's neck, but the experience was good for Jim, and even today he credits his ability to remain present in new situations to that visit.

Ron, my partner in private practice, was a child psychiatrist and his wife, Mary Beth, was a pediatric trauma nurse. They came to our home to visit with us and told us that they would like to spend time with Adam a couple of nights a month so that Jetta and I could go out together and remember who we were. My defensiveness surfaced and I began my skillful redirection by saying that I was not sure that would be a good idea. Ron immediately cut me off and reminded me that they were our friends and were probably the two best people anywhere who could make sure our son was physically safe and who were capable to handle an emergency.

He was right. Jetta and I went out on a date together and remembered who we were and how we could better support each other. Those dates kept us from consuming ourselves with all the issues the system presented to us. We remained a team working together to raise Adam. When we went out we set some ground rules for those dates: we agreed to talk about what Adam needed for only the first ten minutes (although half an hour was more realistic). Even with all the world required of us as Adam's parents, Jetta and I found ways to stay connected and to support each other as much as we supported Adam. That was essential. The weight of the world's discrimination could have easily crushed Jetta or me, but not both of us working together.

Jetta and I were grateful for our friends in Grand Rapids and went to visit them often to remind ourselves that we were more than parents. They loved Adam and wanted him to be part of their family along with us. Sometimes Mary Beth would take Adam so that Jetta and I could just relax. It was a great comfort knowing we had friends who accepted our son.

Jetta and I were being transformed. What we kept was our love and respect for each other. What we kept was a sense of humor. What we kept was our faith. What we surrendered was the illusion that in 1984 the world was any different than it had always been. Privilege and discrimination were still the truth of our culture.

Chapter 5
Finding Our Winstrom Way

Forming Our Winstrom Rhythm

Each of us had our role in finding our Winstrom rhythm. Adam had to discover what it meant to be Adam Winstrom, our son. Jetta's role was to find and stay in the moment with Adam and allow him to join with her. She had to stay vigilant and available to Adam, matching his attention to the task at hand. Each human being has a limited amount of resources to bring to each moment. So much attention, so much curiosity, so much endurance and a limited amount of patience before competing distractions take over. She had to discover his rhythm and hop on his merry-go-round. Jetta had to support and connect with him to guide his random experiences and create conditions for him to develop his life rhythms and rituals in harmony with ours so that it would be possible to merge with us.

We began making sure that Adam's rhythm and our rhythm were synchronous by deliberately including Adam in each process. It was a simple matter of taking the extra moment to create shared attention by holding and making eye contact until a connection was established, then moving with Adam, never forcing him into physical postures to suit us. Adam was fine, but he was not typical; he was genetically unique. Jetta and I recognized that Adam had Down syndrome, but we never accepted he was or would become a Down's child. Temple Grandin had it right when she said that a diagnosis is a label of a current process, not a life sentence.

The Winstrom Family

As part of the Winstrom family, all our collective rhythms and rituals had to mesh. With typical children, this often occurs instinctively. It is better if parents can be thoughtful in this process, but often by accident, after some friction, a family's rhythm develops. Thoughtfully means that in each interaction a conscious choice is made to either support and give attention to or ignore and withhold attention. Because of his uniqueness, his rhythms were instinctively different. Jetta, and to a lesser degree I, had to find him before he would be able to connect with us. When I say "find Adam," I do mean that literally. We had to find where his body was positioned and face in the same direction. Was he attentive or tired of self-stimulation? Was he welcoming touch softly, more securely or not at all right now? Could we make eye contact for the moment with him? When we spoke, was he startled or soothed? All of these seemingly unimportant details were important to successfully join with our son. Once that rhythm was found, it was always a choice to know when to wait or when to introduce a new behavior to interrupt his ritual and create a condition for a different ritual that would better serve him based on her observation.

The rituals of eat, poop, eat, cookie, sleep, poop were the easy stages. As he developed, it took more thoughtful attention (focusing on Adam without distraction) to find him so he could connect with us and become a Winstrom, Adam Winstrom. One of the good doctors told us you don't choose the cards you are dealt, but you can choose how to play them. Adam's cards were not to be squandered as a throwaway. He needed our support to make a winning hand.

Creating A Boundary Around Our Family

My role was to filter the *helpful* system so that they would recognize and respect our rhythm and our rituals. I was the rock on the road, the speed bump that required the professionals to wake up and give

David connecting with Adam

thoughtful entrance. Jetta and I decided that all help would be filtered through me first so I could set the tone and rhythm of our guest. I was the buffer and reminded everyone who came through our door that first, we are a family and second, they are guests in our home. I created entrance rules. I had guests take off their shoes upon entering our home. It stopped them and changed their rhythm. It began their induction into

our rituals. I reminded them that Jetta was the only mother Adam had, and she was to be supported and respected. No professional ever took Adam away from Jetta in our home to "do" something. When physical therapy was needed, they were to teach Jetta how to do it and explain why it was needed to be done.

I watched one session as the therapist told Jetta that the objective was to strengthen Adam's chest and neck muscles. This was necessary to assist in developing a strong enough platform for speech to develop. In Down syndrome, muscle development is often delayed or underdeveloped and that often resulted in delayed or poor speech. The social worker instinctively reached for Adam, but Jetta very quietly and politely reminded her that we had decided it would be best if she instructed Jetta and let Jetta work with Adam.

What we did not tell her was that her timing was off. Her daily routines had clouded her awareness, and she no longer had the sensitivity required to connect with a child. Adam was not warmed up to being taken from his mother, nor changed from the position he was in. His attention and his focus had not been found by the helpful professional to enable Adam to engage in a new ritual. Her ritual of saying, "Hello Adam" then grabbing Adam and moving him into her lap was her normal way, her rhythm. She was a professional, and her time was valuable. Adam was just a baby, and it was okay to move him around; she did it all day. She could not see it was not good for Adam, she never took the two seconds to observe what she was doing, nor the consequence. It wasn't good for Adam, and it was not good for Jetta. She never understood us nor our ways.

Jetta would rock Adam into eye connection with her. Then she would tell him what we were going to do and starting with his feet say, "Today we are going to play with our arms and chest and neck to make you strong," as she touched each corresponding part of Adam. Adam now had shared attention with Jetta and experienced a connection with his own body and with her. Then Jetta did some lifting and relaxing with Adam's arms to get him to use that muscle group. Our way always took longer than the therapist had planned and inevitably she would look at her watch. Eventually, she would say, "Well my time is up, you will just have to do this without me." Jetta would graciously thank each

Learning to stand

one for their time and patience and for teaching her how to be a better mother for Adam. I would get up and thank them, then walk them slowly out of our home, keeping each one slowed to our rhythm.

Adam did develop and Jetta journaled and shared every detail with me.

May 21, 1985, Holds own bottle of juice.

June 26, 1985, swims in little pool.

August 4 1985, pulls himself to standing makes David nervous. Trying to child proof the world.

August 26, 1985, first birthday. Back in hospital surgery for tubes in ears. Went well. Sits in his high chair to eat.

Cattle Prods or Teaching

The day the therapist arrived to begin Adam's tongue instruction, I was home. Adam had grown enough to sit in his high chair. He was already able to smear food all over himself and his tray and drop multiple objects on to the floor to play the get-it-for-me game. The therapist was new, and as I greeted her at our door, she made her move to come in before I had talked about taking off her shoes. I made her dance with me as people do when they can't find the rhythm to move past each other. I apologized, although I thought she should have made the apology, and asked her to stop and remove her shoes. I held her briefcase as she complied. Then I asked her to follow me and seated her on the other side of Jetta in a place where she could not reach Adam.

I introduced her to Jetta as Adam's mother and once she connected with Jetta, she was soothed a bit by Jetta's grace and gentle voice. They talked for a few minutes, then Jetta asked her to explain what her plan had been, not what her plans were. Jetta, by implying permission to act but in the past tense, was effectively letting the therapist know that a change in plans had just occurred. Language is an incredible tool when

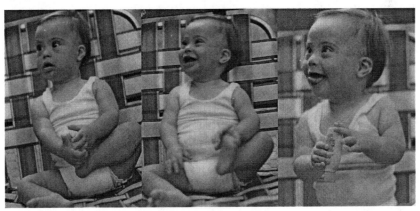

Lovable and adorable Adam

used intentionally. It organizes us and can even redirect a therapist without any friction.

The therapist began explaining what her plan was. She had a brush and an electric stimulator to teach Adam to keep his tongue in his mouth. The brush was to create a heightened awareness for Adam of his tongue. Then the electric stimulator would be used to teach him to retract his tongue when he relaxed it and it protruded out of his mouth. Jetta anticipated that I was just about to ask if she also had cattle prods in her bag and asked, "David, would you get Adam's toothbrush and a little toothpaste?" She had skillfully given me a time out and redirected me. I complied. Jetta was in charge. Jetta and I had agreed that whoever of us was in charge at the moment was always allowed to determine the flow of a situation. Discussions occurred later.

Teaching Adam

When I returned brush in hand, I was thanked and told I could join in. Jetta brushed Adam's tongue, and when he stuck it out, she stuck her tongue out and said, "Tongue in the mouth" as she slurped hers in. Adam mirrored her behavior.

The therapist watching with stimulator still in hand said, "That method would probably work also." Jetta repeated the exercise and Adam did the same thing; they slurped, and Adam laughed. There was no need to shock our son. There was no need to punish him when he could be taught. We felt it was a good rule to teach children, not antagonize them into anger or instill fear. I asked if I might try and Jetta agreed. Adam thought it was a great game. I asked the therapist, "Would straightening the tongue muscle help Adam keep his tongue in his mouth?"

"Sure, but I am not sure how you would do that."

"What about McDonald's thick milkshakes?"

Jetta rolled her eyes, and the therapist politely said, "Maybe."

When it was time for the therapist to go, Jetta thanked her and said she probably didn't need to reschedule us as we understood the technique. I showed her out. Then Jetta turned to me and said, "You have to be nice, thick shakes was over the edge for that poor therapist."

"But I never brought up cattle prods."

Milk Shakes and Community

Jetta slurped at home with Adam, and I took our son through the McDonald's drive-thru. The benefit of McDonald's thick shakes was a whole new social connection. We went every week for a shake and by the time Adam's fifth birthday came around, the staff gave him a McDonald's watch. It had a Ronald face on it and was one of their premium giveaways. He had announced his upcoming birthday to the woman at the drive-thru window the week before. We continued our weekly shakes, and the following year, the entire McDonald's staff chipped in and bought Adam a very nice watch. This one was from corporate headquarters and was a Timex with Ronald's hands telling the time. Adam had started to make his friendship circle.

All the therapists and all interventions were filtered in the same way—they were welcomed into the Winstrom ritual and rhythm. It was slower and more deliberate than most were accustomed to experiencing. Adam had Down syndrome, so it took a few extra milliseconds for his neurological processing to gear up and organize to share attention and focus. If we had let the *helpful* professional have her way, Jetta would have been disconnected from Adam. He would not have been able to get to a shared point of attention and would have returned to his own world to defend against this new person manipulating his body. It would have reinforced the idea that staying in

Jetta teaching Adam

your own world is better. He would have missed the condition created for him to join with another being and receive their attention. He would not have had the opportunity to gain language nor the satisfaction that comes with being with someone and feeling like you belong.

Teaching the Helpful Professional

Having a professional provide a service to Adam once or twice a week would not really have been an effective teaching model. I was the researcher scout for our family. I had found journal articles with positive outcome studies that supported the filial therapy model (a method of training parents to respond and interact therapeutically with their children that builds and enhances the parent–child relationship) when I was doing my research in my Master's program. Adam benefited the most from the training Jetta received from the professionals and then passed on to me so that Jetta and I could both support Adam just like the research identified. We modified the filial model routines to fit Adam better. We always did a warm up and established shared attention before going into a redirecting behavior. We worked the exercises into play routines as incidental experiences.

Reading with Dad

Too many times I heard of tired mothers getting a break from their child by giving them to the professional. So much is lost but could be gained if parents were supported to do the best for their children rather than be removed by a well-intentioned therapist.

Becoming a Psychologist

In 1987, Adam turned three and was beginning his new rhythm of life. I was becoming changed by him—he and Jetta were making me a better man. As our family had more contact with the Ottawa County Educational systems, it became clear to me that I had to get a degree in psychology to support our son. My early experiences with psychologists, professionally and personally, had convinced me that I did not want to be one of them. They all seemed too formal, judgmental, distant, almost condescending and they always ended up directing systems and not relating to the people in the systems. But for my son's sake, I could no longer let my bias keep me from becoming one of them, from becoming a psychologist. Psychologists would be the ones to determine *if* my son would be included in regular education classrooms. Psychologists were the ones to determine curriculum and behavioral management programming for my son. When I decided to get a Master's degree, I had decided to become a family therapist and not a psychologist or a social worker. That was a decision I had made before our son was born. It was clear that it was time to decide again.

I was still working as a family therapist, but I attended my first conference for psychologists. It was a conference by Byron Rourke, Ph.D., researcher and author of the book on Nonverbal Learning Disabilities (NVLD). When I attend conferences, it has been my good fortune to be invited often to meet with the presenter. This conference was no exception. I met Dr. Rourke on a break and asked if I could join him for lunch. He agreed as he knew no one and often just ate alone. I took the opportunity to first listen to him and what he was interested in, then I talked about my son and his growing nonverbal style. I mentioned I believed that I need to get a Ph.D. to deal with the

Family birthday celebration

systems. I'll never forget him looking directly at me and saying, "Just love him. Don't fix him because he is not broken, he is just different. Get a Ph.D. and fix the system, it is broken." He encouraged me to find a way to get a Ph.D. but not detract from my Adam time. We talked about NVLD and visual stimulation for Adam and he told me not to wait for his words to catch up. They may never catch up. As I listened, I knew I needed to find a way to stay connected to Adam, support Jetta and get the protection a Ph.D. would offer us.

When I returned home, I shared all I had learned from Dr. Rourke. Jetta and I started labeling everything in the house in large letters, STOVE, CHAIR, BED, etc. At night, I sang the phonetic alphabet to Adam as I carried him past each letter on the wall. I could teach Adam what I could not do, read. I would start looking for a way to get a Ph.D. and still stay connected to Adam and Jetta. As all parents do, I had hopes for my son. I wanted him to be able to read and spell, but more importantly, I hoped he would become a better person than I was in so many ways. Maybe he would even be able to move people out of their prejudices where I could not.

A growing boy

Learning to eat by himself

Chapter 6
Adam Changed His Rhythm

In Adam's third year of life, he began adding new wrinkles to our rhythms. At his three-year evaluation, the psychologist recommended that Adam start in the local pre-kindergarten. We enrolled him in the local preschool program and were impressed with both the teacher and the fact that they offered speech therapy. It started out well, but it seemed like every time I planned on something going a certain way and one of our rhythms or rituals continuing, God would smile, and I would be given a new understanding of what it meant to live life in the moment.

One morning I was called by the teacher who began the conversation with, "I don't want to alarm you, but Adam just stopped breathing." Before I could not be alarmed she added, "He's fine now." She told me that he had been sitting on the floor and slowly slumped over and when she checked on him he was not breathing.

I was the rock; why would I be alarmed? In a panic, I immediately called our pediatrician and made the first available appointment that day. Then I ran to the car and drove like a maniac to the school to pick Adam up.

The doctor examined Adam and could not find anything wrong. He wasn't overly concerned about his breathing but told me to watch him when he sleeps. I was very concerned. Jetta was better with this kind of thing than I was. Her time with Adam had made her better able to roll with these kinds of waves while I still thrashed about. Jetta had already accepted so much that she adopted the attitude that everything would work out. She had also begun going to church and was more willing to allow the world to be as it was. I was still caught up in what my fellow professionals suffer from—I had to

A furry friend

do something. When we put him to bed that night, I stayed up all night sitting by his bed and watching him to make sure he didn't stop breathing. The next morning everyone woke up refreshed and ready for a new day except me.

Don't Bite the Chiropractor

After the breathing incident, one of our friends told us about a chiropractor in town who was "very good." Jetta thought it might help with Adam's breathing, so we went. Adam, at three years old, did not want to sit in a waiting room or be physically touched or distracted from his mounting impatience. Here we all were waiting for the "very good" chiropractor to call us in. I was hoping he would call us very soon because I was running out of distractions and entertaining options and really did not want to begin our journey into this man's care by having to restrain Adam. If I did, then the chiropractor would have to work on my son in his most disagreeable state. Not the introduction I hoped for.

And he was good, very good. He asked for Adam, and instead of handing him over I started my explanation. He just smiled at me and picked Adam up. Suddenly, Adam bit him on the arm. My son bit the doctor! The chiropractor did not even pull away. All he said was, "Adam, that is not a very good way to make friends" as he gently pushed his arm into Adam's jaws. He told us that the instinct is to pull away, but if you hold still and press toward the teeth, children will release. Fortunately, Adam did.

As he listened to us tell how Adam stopped breathing at school he examined Adam's neck. Then he said, "It must have been a forceps delivery, right? The doctor had to assist Adam being born by turning him."

"Yes! That is exactly what happened," I responded.

As he held Adam against him and began to manipulate his neck he said, "with Down syndrome the neck, specifically the atlas axis joint, is a weak point. I suggest you come back once a week for a few weeks so I can continue adjusting him and make sure the adjustments are holding." Jetta immediately agreed. The good doctor continued, "Adam also needs to learn to come to my office and wait patiently for a few minutes, then come in and greet me in a friendly way. Adam will probably be seeing other doctors, and it would be good if he could learn how to be more comfortable with this kind of situation." I was thankful, relieved, and a bit in shock. Not only was he a very good chiropractor, but he was willing to support Adam and us.

Before we left the office, we set up the next appointment and prepared Adam to see Doc Brusveen again. Every week Adam sat in the waiting room and the very good doctor would observe us. At the right moment—just before Adam lost his ability to wait—he would come out and invite Adam into his office. It worked; Adam began looking forward to seeing Doc Brusveen and learned to wait patiently for him. I don't exactly know how it evolved, but Adam also managed to add the Mark Brusveen family to our circle of friends.

New Friends, New Churches

As our rhythms and rituals changed to include Adam, many of our friends no longer recognized us as belonging in their own rhythms and rituals. Friendships changed. Adam added to our world by creating a condition to move us out of our old circle of friends into a new circle. We avoided the *special* world of mother's groups and groups that accepted the parents of children with Down syndrome. There is a palpable difference between being included and being placed in social supports.

As Adam began to grow, we slowly became involved in two communities, and each had their own rhythms and rituals. With each visit to the chiropractor, we got to know Mark a little better. He was Lutheran and invited us to come to church with him. Jetta was raised as a Lutheran and wanted our family to belong in a church community, so we went. Naturally, Adam cried, and I couldn't get him to stop, so I got up and took him out of the service. One of the ushers followed me and suggested that "next time I could just start out in the *special* anti-room rather than disturb others. I would probably be more comfortable anyway." It made no sense to me to go to church and not be included as part of the body. The next week Jetta and I sat in the back, but I could tell I was not in the right place.

Jetta kept putting her hand on my knee because Adam and I were making noise. I told her I supported her going to church, but Adam and I would wait for her outside. Mark was an elder in the church and did what he could to influence the church community but found himself in opposition to the church's positions. When the church leadership didn't like Mark's approach, they told him that a committee was going to be formed to decide the best procedures to deal with a situation like ours. Forming a study committee is the typical response a system makes when it encounters opposition. Active disagreement is not a welcoming experience. Mark and his family remained our friends, but it was clear this church did not want *us*.

Richard and Julie as well as Mary Beth, another one of Jetta's friends from school, remained our friends. One day Jetta, Adam and I were visiting with Richard and Julie when Toby the Rabbi from the Temple just happened to come over. He came in and immediately walked over to Jetta and asked if he could hold Adam. Jetta handed Adam to Toby, and we all watched as he with gentleness and assurance looked Adam all over. Then he held Adam up and said, "HaShem...Adam, you are a perfect creation!" and danced Adam around the room. He did the same dance Richard had done with Adam in the hospital. Then Toby turned to me and asked, "Have you started blessing Adam every Friday evening. It is never too early to start, you know!"

He invited us to the Temple, and I choked out, "You know…we aren't…um…Jewish."

Just as I said "Jewish," he said, "members, it's okay everyone is always welcome." Then he added, "And if Adam makes noise…ahhh we can sing louder. Let him join in. If he needs to be bounced, bounce him. If you need to walk around, walk. We are 400 men and women; do you imagine we cannot find a way to include a baby? But you are not Jewish…Christian then?"

I said, "Yes."

"All Christians are Jewish first."

Jetta, Adam and I only went a few times, but the Rabbi was right when he said, "sit or walk during the service, but just come and be part of community." Sometimes Mary Beth would take Adam to church with her, but she said she never held Adam through the whole service because someone would always ask if they could please hold him. A community was affirming Adam. A community was wanting him to belong. A community was welcoming us, and it was not a program or technique; it was a fundamental knowing that all belong and all are welcome. I learned that I will always be a good Jew first and then a Christian. Jetta, Adam and I were always welcomed and had an open invitation to come to Temple, parties and gatherings. Good people found us. I began blessing Adam every Friday night, and I thanked HaShem for loaning me Adam, His perfect creation.

Jetta wanted a community in Grand Haven for her family. The Temple was in Grand Rapids and did not offer her the day-to-day experience she hungered for. She found a small church led by a preacher named Andy DeJong. She went to her new church in Grand Haven and Adam and I enjoyed what I called the Church of the Big Sky— nature. We would walk and see what God was doing today.

Eventually, Jetta's desire to include Adam and me in church culminated in a home visit from Pastor Andy. I liked him right away. He was bright and caring and had just the right edge of uncertainty to make any smug piety impossible. He told us Adam was welcome. Andy told us his brother also had Down syndrome and that we should come whenever we can and sit, stand or stay as needed. It was just what Jetta wanted to hear. She and Adam would go to the new church. Andy and I talked, and I explained to him that I found God in my Church of the Big Sky and would trust the safety and well-being of Jetta and Adam to him. And what an impact Adam had on that church.

Remembering Adam's First Sunday

The first time Adam showed up with his mother, Jetta, at church, there might have been some worshipers that Sunday who hoped it would be his last.

Music can be a very sensory experience. This is especially the case for a person with Autism like Adam. Although Covenant Life Church had already made the transition from more traditional hymnody to contemporary worship music, most worshipers kept their hands, arms and hips fairly disengaged, leaving the voice to do all the work of worship. That might have lasted for quite some time had Adam not shown up that memorable Sunday. The worship team had lined up some high-energy songs and Adam could not have been more pleased. Adam's arms were thrashing the air, his hips were gyrating and his voice was entirely discordant and loud. But it was authentic!

And that's really the point. Adam brought into our presence his authenticity. His free expression was unbridled by social or religious decorum, and his demeanor was always non-judgmental and his love unconditional. Adam incarnated so much of Christ's teaching and lifestyle and that it spooked some people in the church. It was almost too real this Christ-like presence.

After several weeks went by with what I perceived to be a growing discomfort with Adam's presence I decided through God's grace not to become upset with people and their negative responses to Adam. It was too tempting to say something from the pulpit and risk even further disturbance among our people. So, one morning, after the singing was finished I came forward to extend a welcome to everyone. I did this verbally. But then I walked off the raised platform, walked down the aisle in which Adam and Jetta were seated, put my hand on Adam's shoulder and said simply, "You are welcome here!" Adam jumped up and there, in that holy moment, we hugged each other as though we were long lost brothers who hadn't seen each other for far too long.

And that's all it took. Love not spoken but physically expressed.

It became the turning point for the church as well as for Adam and Jetta and eventually David to see all of us as belonging to the broken body of Christ where each person fulfills a necessary function for the body to thrive. I like to think of Adam as the heart. But if not that, he certainly was for us our rhythm, our de facto "spirit of soul."

Andy DeJong, Pastor

Losing Connection

Since Adam had been able to move his hands, he had always waved them in excitement, but between ages three and a half and four, what that waving meant to him seemed to change. He was not just being the bird man Jetta and I had smiled about. Now, his hand movements

Talking on the phone started early!

were not incidental as he walked but purposeful and were the focus of his attention more than being used for movement for balance. Or, as I had thought, perhaps it had more to do with motor strip bleeds—a term used when one's motor strip in the brain gives instruction to fire to more than the discrete muscle group. It seems that walking required his whole body to be stimulated. At three and a half years old, his walking was not yet flat-footed. He did not really play with toys, but he enjoyed spinning things

like the wheels on a truck. At his preschool, he would cover his ears when the music was on but would stand right next to the record player (yes, this was before 8-tracks or CDs). He started talking on the play phone but stopped talking directly to anyone. He lost eye contact and seemed to withdraw, get frustrated and fall into tantrums more often.

Added to Adam's journey, Jetta developed kidney stones. They did not pass, and she had to have them surgically removed. When Jetta went into the hospital for the kidney stone removal, they performed a partial nephrectomy. The doctor had to remove part of Jetta's right kidney. Adam and I spent a lot of time in the waiting room playing dancing sun rays. I observed him letting the sun shine on his face and waving his fingers in front of his eyes (known as hand flapping). He seemed very calm and peaceful when the sun light was being reflected, but he was no longer with me.

Jetta's recovery was slow so I asked for a second opinion and found out the doctor had nicked her lung during surgery and it collapsed and needed to be inflated. The original surgeon had thought her difficulty breathing was the result of his removing part of her rib so he could more easily get to her kidney—another detail he had not mentioned. We changed her care to the second surgeon, and she began to improve. All this extended her time in the hospital and slowed her recovery and her ability to hold Adam close.

When Jetta got home from the hospital, Adam was less connected to her and not as connected to me either. We guessed it was just a minor bump from being separated from him while she was in the hospital. But we were unpleasantly surprised to see Adam continuing to withdraw from both of us. Hand flapping became a highlight of his day.

When Jetta tried to pick him up, Adam would sometimes arch his back and flail about clearly indicating that he didn't want to be held. I would come home from work and find Adam on the couch in his own little world and Jetta in tears. When I leaned toward her to kiss her hello, she would say, "I need to take a walk." I would sit with Adam. I could find him, but it took a while and was not a direct route.

Quiet reading time

She would return from her walk to find Adam on my lap reading a book. I thought I was making our home better by finding Adam and then reconnecting them when he became available, but my help only served to accelerate her feelings that she was losing her connection with Adam even more. The times he would accept her attention became fewer and fewer. She had tried to give him room. She would give him a few moments of non-stimulation so he could regroup and then she could return her attention to Adam, but it was just not the same. He was not the same anymore. He seemed to experience touch,

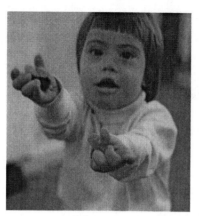

Learning to share

even her touch as uncomfortable. Her embrace no longer seemed to sooth him. He was not melting as he had before she went into the hospital. We both thought the three days she spent in the hospital had thrown Adam's rhythm off and that he would connect again soon. When I would come home from work I saw the Mona Lisa smile fading from Jetta's face and being replaced by fear, searching, and longing for her son.

Jetta did all she could to find Adam. She would try to get his attention before touching him. She would wait to approach him. But nothing seemed to be working for her with her son the way it used to. She did not give up but kept trying different ways to approach her son. Sometimes successful but it was becoming more difficult and her success more intermittent. She was doing all she could, and I was doing all I knew how to do to support her efforts.

Chapter 7

How a Family Fractures

One Saturday morning when we were eating breakfast, all Adam wanted was to get down from the table. He was frustrated about something, moved too fast, fell off the chair and started to cry. Being the good mother that she was, Jetta swooped him up only to have Adam arch his back, bite and claw at her until she put him down again. I waited until Adam was available and picked him up and held him tight until he melted.

But I had not solved the problem; I made it worse. I had done what so many helpful professionals had done—I unintentionally demonstrated to my wonderful wife that she was a bad mother. I imagined I was being helpful in quieting Adam and then bringing him to his mother. But that is not how Jetta saw it.

From her hurt and fear that had accumulated over the past three years she looked at me and said, "I want a divorce. You are just too perfect. I'm obviously a bad mother, and I want out of this insanity! I've lost my friends. I've given up my job. I feel isolated. I feel like a failure. All that would be worth it if Adam wanted me to be his mother, but he doesn't. I can't even comfort my son; he only wants you!"

My world came to a screeching halt. I knew Jetta was frustrated, but I do not think either of us know the depth of it. We were both surprised and just a little shaken. I agreed to her request on the condition that she would have full custody based on Adam's age and his developmental need for his mother and said, "I am sure the court would agree, but I will take Adam on Wednesday nights and every other weekend."

It worked. She started to cry, then pouted, then finally laughed. She was flooded with her feelings and fears of not being able to be a good mother for Adam. Watching Adam let me into his world convinced her that Adam would be better off without her. Her heart broke and crushed her faith in herself about being Adam's mother.

Not all mothers recover, and not all families survive the intensity that parenting requires. The *kind* doctor would say that Adam caused this. Jetta believed she was responsible for her son having such a struggle. At that moment, I was oblivious to my wife's vulnerability and just solved what I perceived as the problem of Adam in need of comforting.

Wrong problem identification often leads to family fracturing, but we didn't. Jetta said she felt like she had just thrown up and was feeling better after getting rid of all the junk she had been holding in. I could see that she was struggling, but when I asked how she was, she would just tell me it was a long day, and she would be fine. I just thought she was still recovering from her kidney surgery and was tired. So, I tried to do more with Adam and give her a break. What I did not see was that I was breaking their bond.

We were able to regroup with Adam on her lap and began asking a different question. What is the best way to organize our family to be the most functional for everyone? No one needed to be a martyr or a hero. That question allowed us to eliminate identifying a problem person and let us each offer only our best attribute to solve the puzzle. We skipped the step that a problem of this magnitude must be someone's fault and went directly to what would work best. We decided that I would start being at home with Adam more since I seemed to get his timing a little easier. Jetta was a very good social worker and could get a job to pay the bills. She would return to being a professional. We decided to switch roles.

I was lucky to have such an amazing wife. Adam was even luckier to have such a good mother. Jetta was able to come to terms with what she could and could not do, and we figured out how to change our family structure to accommodate both Adam and Jetta. It took an incredible woman to put aside her dream of being home with her son, and not injure her ego, so she could create the best possible conditions for her son to grow. It wasn't long before Jetta would come home from work and tell me that just working and only having to solve one problem at a time was like a vacation. Jetta was very skilled at supporting emotionally overwhelmed children and teachers and resolving conflicts.

I confess that I didn't thoroughly think through all the social adjustments that would be needed or all the new skill sets I would have to develop. It wasn't long before I was banned from doing laundry after I didn't separate the colored clothes from the white ones and Jetta's work clothes and my white shirt soon became an odd shade of blue. I learned to pay more attention to household details, but I was doing a bang-up job being Adam's father, and to me, that was the best deal.

The new way of being the Winstrom family worked out quite well. She reconnected with adults and was given lots of reinforcement for being such a good social worker. I also caught the "house husband, gigolo, living off my wife stuff," and other side comments. Once again, the culture reacted as I expected, but I no longer cared. I was Adam's father and Jetta's husband. That was more than enough for me. It was an unusual shift for the culture of Grand Haven, but we tried it out. I would stay home with Adam to be his companion/father and hopefully his bridge.

Moments of stress are often the point when families fracture, and everybody loses. From the beginning, being Adam challenged our family system. Later on, who Adam grew into and ultimately became changed the culture and challenged the flexibility of everyone—friends, extended family, churches and schools.

Autism: BOO!

The word Autism unnerves most people. It might not be quite as bad as cancer, but it gets the runner-up prize. After Jetta and I had switched places, I was the one with Adam for his therapy sessions working on core strength and balance. Before she left Jetta told me twice to watch and listen to what they would teach. When they arrived, the *helpful* professionals just began the physical therapy work with Adam. They said they were going to work on balance and trunk strength. They had Adam walk. He was walking on his toes, and they said he must learn to walk more normally. They began to force Adam to walk with his feet flat by pushing down on his feet and then adding their weight to his shoulders. The word "No!" was loudly and liberally used as they worked with Adam. I watched and could see the frustration building in Adam and in them. This created an overstimulating experience that reaqched a tipping point resulting in the need to pick him up, use the basket hold for physical restraint and put him in a safe time out. The entire experience was far from helpful. That one "demonstration" was sufficient for me, and I was just about to stop them and invited them to come back much later when I remembered what Jetta had branded on my being that day, "Watch and listen to what they want to teach you… just once please!" I witnessed their best instruction.

As I observed Adam in this therapy session, it provided me with that moment to detach and observe. I was not to interact per Jetta and as they wished, but it became clear to me that something new was emerging in my son. The session concluded with Adam being tired and frustrated. I did as Jetta asked, thanked them and showed them out the door.

As time passed over the next weeks, Adam was talking less. This retreat had begun in preschool and increased after Jetta's surgery. I read that oral language and sign language was the best for our son, so Jetta and I had been consistently using it with Adam and had total communication. As the weeks passed and Adam talked less and less, we eventually could only sign with him. When his back was toward me, I had to stomp on the floor to create vibrations in order to connect with him because my words failed to reach him. We decided to have his hearing checked and were told that his hearing was perfect, yet my words were no longer reaching him. Touching and holding Adam required critical timing to succeed. The other people who worked with and knew Adam from preschool also said something was different. He was fascinated by spinning objects and dancing sun rays but less and less in people.

It felt to me like my son was showing the signs of Autism. I wanted to know for sure, so I called a child psychiatrist I knew and scheduled a visit for Adam and me. Dr. Van Volkenburg confirmed my observation and told me that Autism and Down syndrome often coexist, but most people miss the duality. He told me that treating children like they only have Down syndrome and failing to see the difference in timing and sensory complications creates aggression in children. It was a mouthful of truth to absorb. He said I was a very good diagnostician and an extremely challenged father. He told me Adam was lucky to have me as his father. In life, you don't choose the cards you're dealt, but you can choose how to play them, and he knew I played very well.

I went home and told Jetta that Adam was distancing himself from us, not just from her. She was a good mother. She was warm, caring and loving. Adam had Autism, and that was the game changer. Jetta and I agreed that for now, we had made the best decision in switching roles to accommodate Adams' shift and continue being a family.

Fortunately, Dr. Van Volkenburg warned me that the *helpful* professionals would continue their attempt to physically control Adam unless I stopped them and that is exactly what happened. At our next physical therapy session, even before I could share with them Dr. Van Volkenburg's diagnosis, they engaged Adam, and when he got overstimulated, they began using their basket hold on him again, but I interrupted them. The *helpful* professionals seemed excited (maybe it was anxiety or confusion I am not sure) when I told them that Dr. Van Volkenburg diagnosed Adam with Autism and indicated that this methodology of restraint was no longer acceptable. They just started talking faster and were more animated. With their most somber faces, they asked me if I understood what that diagnosis indicated. As I smiled at them, I thought to myself, *I live with Adam and have seen his new processes, you have not.* I could see the changes and the differences in his rhythm, timing and intensity. They just dropped into our life for an hour every week bringing their own sense of timing, but they never took the time to observe Adam at all. He was nearly four years old, and I knew all too well his new hypersensitivity to sound, light and touch and his diminished interest in the world. I could still find him in his new world, but it required intense effort on my part. Their assumption that I didn't know what Autism meant brought on a smile and I laughed. It was not the laugh of a happy man, not even smug; it was the anxious laugh of a father who finds himself surrounded by fools. I felt alone seeing these professionals clueless about who my son was and how Autism might change his development. It was clearly my journey to find and then keep a connection to my son. What else could I do?

The *helpful* people went on and on about all the things Adam would not do, could never accomplish, how he could no longer care about others and how he would always treat people as objects. They tried to teach me about Pennington's theory of the mind. It was an Autism 101 lecture that included Kanner's definition of Autism. For me it was their "holy sh-t, now what!" dog and pony show. They seemed oddly accelerated at the prospect of "sharing" more information to help educate me about my child who they now considered an autistic, Down syndrome child. At least for the moment, they had forgotten about putting Adam in a basket hold, and he was moving freely around the room with my eye on him, not theirs. They were full of important information they wanted to share with me now.

And sharing this kind of important information inevitably continued in every other area of Adam's life. Friends we told all had ideas about what to do now. The school had to arrange a meeting with their psychologist and us to approve the new information. The psychologist, who had just completed his three-year evaluation of Adam and had not seen this process, took a parting shot at being an expert and told Jetta and I that Autism was the result of "refrigerator Moms" (lack of maternal warmth). Why kind and helpful professionals continued to target my sweet, loving wife I still do not know. They did not know that it was only the compassionate Jetta who stood between them and the 9-year-old knight inside me who instinctively wanted to draw his sword and cut off their tongues to silence them so they could no longer harm her. As I would rise in reaction, she would touch my hand and say quietly, "Be nice." So, I moved to release us from the meeting, thanked him and said, "I think we are finished here." I could see that the psychologist was warming up to deliver another jab, so I added, "Please stop. Thank you for explaining to us the process of what it is like to live with a child with Autism."

He replied correcting me, "You mean an autistic child."

I thought to myself, No, I mean a child with Autism but only said, "I will certainly consider all your suggestions. Have a good day and thank you for your time" as Jetta, Adam and I left. It was not a useful meeting for us.

Autism Blossoming–Learning to Relate All Over Again

A little voice reminded me that, "if Muhammad will not go to the mountain, the mountain will go to Muhammad." I also remembered something Richard Gottlieb and Jim McDowell had taught me when I was a clinician: Never attack someone's difference in thought or behavior. Forced change always creates opposition and solidifies the difference. It will drive the person further into their world and away from any shared world you are working at creating. Remember, they create their world from their experience and for their protection, not to create a problem for you. To connect, they must recognize you as the door to the world as they experience it, then they may invite you to join them in their world and, in turn, they may try your world. This may be obvious and polite, but it is rarely done by professionals. The professionals usually punished to make contact then inserted their own rules. It was a demanding and overpowering style.

Years before Adam was born, when I was as foolish as the hospital social worker who just walked into another person's world, Richard began training me. It is, I think, the error of youth and youthful folly believing that one's intention to help is enough. Richard was a movie buff and used them as instructional aids. He had me watch *Son-Rise*. A movie about how Barry and Samahria Kaufman had used modified play therapy to join in their son's world when he withdrew into his own world, just like Adam was beginning to do. His movie reference was doubly helpful—it had helped me be a better therapist, and now it was a key to being a better Dad and provided a path into my own son's way of experiencing the world.

I was trained to understand that what we call mental illness is the result of unique perception often based on unique brain structures and powerful experiences that shape how a person makes meaning out of their environment experienced. Adam experienced the day-to-day occurrences in a unique way. He did not have the ability to incorporate the understanding of his environment most children gain by inferential instruction. Children learn which bits of the 10,000 bits of information that each person processes every second that must be attended to because they are the ones the culture values and calls real. It is the process Piaget and Pennington call "theory of the mind." It is their explanation of how a child is enculturated into our common shared perception and shared understanding of the world around us. I was taught by Floyd that it is not the only way to make meaning out of our environment. Maybe not even the best. Floyd pointed out it was not how I arrived at my understanding of this world. Floyd taught me to value and respect all paths to understanding and making meaning. All of my prior learning paid off. I was able to respect and honor Adam's way and he, in turn, was able to connect with me and allow me to connect with him.

The training I received from Dr. Westendorp, Jim McDowell, MSW and Richard Gotlieb, MSW was diametrically opposed to the direction the *helpful* professionals wanted me to follow. The professionals would tell me I was the adult and Adam was supposed to follow and listen to me. They had never heard of Kaufman's way of connecting. They did not have time to learn about Adam; they were there to teach him their way!

The professionals were equally convinced that I was ruining Adam because I did not say, "No" to Adam, I only said, "No, thank you" to them. To Adam, I would say, "Please stop. Look and think. Is this your best choice?" Adam's mantra became, "Is this your best choice?" I was taught that *no* is not an instruction. It has no actual meaning as most parents apply it. We ask our children to interpret our parenting, but how can a two- or three-year-old learn what *no* means? Oh, how we create the opposition of the terrible twos by making our children think abstractly and decode higher order meaning. Formally, *no* really means to refuse or resist. So, linguistically we are telling our children to refuse or resist us and when they do we blame them for doing it. Dr. Aaron T. Beck published articles addressing learned helplessness (iatrogenic illness) and differentiated that from instrumental helplessness (organic deficits). But the *helpful* professionals had not heard of Beck either. Wolfensberger writes about the deep wounding inflicted upon families and their disabled children. But they had not heard of Wolfensberger. Overpowering children with neurological differences to force compliance is at the root of the wounding.

Adam and I were encircled by people who thought power was a solution and external control was the aim. They believed that I had to control Adam so that when he got older, society would be able to take over and control him. I wanted my son to control himself and be his best self and thoughtfully relate to others. I wanted more for him than creating a controllable Down's person. I wanted him to be aware of himself and his surroundings, exercise self-judgment and adapt his behavior to each situation. I expected Adam to grow to be a respectful, thoughtful, compassionate man. I wanted him to be a better human being than the *helpful* professionals were. I wanted him to learn to be in charge of his own life. They never considered that as a possibility.

Making Children Mind, Ha Ha!

For ten years as a family therapist, I listened patiently to parents tell me with varying degrees of frustration how their children suddenly started saying *no* to everything. I always reminded them that adults and children learn mostly by experience and immediate consequences, not by insight or thoughtful reflection. When adults act like big children and shout *no* in a multitude of situations, little children must create conditions to understand what this power word really means. I learned to be a good parent from all the failed efforts that other families shared with me. I knew very well what did not work. We force our children into saying *no* to us in every new situation so that they can discover what we mean by *no!*

I also patiently listened to parents say, "My child does not mind me." Imagine you are new to the English language and someone screams *No!* every time you try to explore your new world and connect meaning to activity and learn communication. Imagine a grown-up person occasionally running up and grabbing you and saying, "I said 'No!' and I meant 'No.' You need to mind me. You get a time out so you will learn to mind me." We infer, but we fail to instruct. Then we punish them because we confused them with our ambiguous parenting instructions. Often, what is wrong with them is us.

Observing these parents say *no* to their children from across the room I noticed how they did not use proximity to communicate with them. Their child would sometimes stop what they were doing to look up, but then they would continue. For the child, the questions are many: Did you say something to me? Do you mean stop? Do you want me to do something different? Was this a warning and is it okay for me to do this for a few more minutes? Many variations followed. Sometimes "No!" was yelled, usually without eliciting any change in behavior. Sometimes they would say, "I am your father/mother, and I am in charge. You must listen to me." Afterward, they would often sigh and then ignore the child. You can guess what the child learned. Sometimes the father/mother would say, "Wait until (variation here) I get you home (or until your father gets home)…you'll be sorry then."

When I was meeting with a family, I would ask if I could demonstrate a different way to communicate with their child. They were the parents, and I respected them and honored their position in front of their child. When they agreed, I would stand up and walk over to the child. I would interrupt their child and say, "Your father/mother wants you to stop what you are doing. It is time to stop." If they tried to turn away, I would say, "I will help you learn to listen to your parents. Do you know what they are telling you?" If the child kept on with the unwanted behavior, I would say, "I am here to teach you how your parents want you to behave. Your father/mother said *no* but what they wanted was for you to stop touching/playing with this." I would put my hands on their hands and stop them. It rarely got to hand-on-hand instruction, but sometimes it did. Then I would say, "Good job, you stopped touching it, thank you." Then I would ask them to touch it again and have their parent ask them to stop touching the object (my substitution phrase for *no*). I would repeat this at least three times; then I would have their parent get up and do the same exercise. The process of doing something over and over is called over-learning.

The lesson to the parents was not to give commands that they did not intend to enforce. It is better to ignore an unwanted behavior than to have your child learn to ignore you. Children need rules and require active sometimes hands on instruction. Be in close enough proximity to your child to guide them through the desired behavior if necessary. Work with them to learn how to be cooperative companions who will develop good judgment and self-control. Clear rules and enforcement by parents make children feel safe and secure.

In the beginning, I would say to Adam, "Please stop, look and think." Then I would add, "Is this your best choice?" At first, he only responded to the first part of the command, *stop*, but I wanted him to hear the whole sequence and fill in his Schema card (outline of a plan) with the complete instruction. Piaget used this phrase to describe how children store and organize information to make sense out of the world and develop their sense of consciousness. A Schema card is much like a file folder on a computer. Information that is of a similar nature all goes into one folder (Schema card). In the beginning when you decide how to organize information these file folders are established and are semi-permanent. With Adam, his file folders (Schema cards) were much more permanent than in a typical child's brain, and I helped him organize his information.

Adam would try out *stop*, and I would reinforce it by saying, "Yes, stop, and we are stopped, what do we do now?" often followed by "is this our best choice?" At first, I wanted us to be in this together, but eventually, it became "is this *your* best choice?" When I had his attention, I told Adam what I wanted him to do. I did it with him, we both stopped. Then we both did the next thing.

Before my instructions could be accepted, I had to join his world, find his rhythm and respect his emerging rituals. My job at first was to create the environment for us to explore safely. In a safe environment, I could learn how to be a fellow traveler: join first, learn, and respect the rules and meaning of the other person's behavior. To accomplish this, all you have to do is not interfere. Be present and quiet. Then participate in parallel. When I was accurate in my parallel behavior, it felt for Adam like he was looking in a mirror. He recognized me in/ with him, and I was included as a fellow traveler. Then you start your next journey together. Once you are recognized, reinforce all adaptive behaviors. Be the sun warming their world. When you can follow and are recognized as a meaningful part of their world, ignore the behavior you are required to change. I know this is counter intuitive, but when dealing with neurologically altered perception, understanding their perspective is the only place to start. It is foolish and arrogant to attempt to change another human being until you know the function and meaning attached to their way of doing things or their behavior. Much of the other person's rhythms and rituals are counter intuitive to your own. Once you understand their way of being, you can find other behaviors of theirs to reinforce a competing behavior (when it occurs). The more the competing behavior is practiced, the less the target behavior (the one you did not want) can occur. This way to teach adaptive behavior is not quick, but it will change the behavior even when you are not present. Lastly, interrupt and redirect only for safety reasons. Simple, right?

One day Adam began trying to pluck out his eye. In the conference on non-aversive behavior management, I remembered seeing videos of self-mutilating behaviors by some individuals who were autistic. In the movie, the solution was punishment for the behavior. There was no understanding or joining the other person, just shock until they stopped. The method was rated as "sometimes successful," and now my son was trying to mutilate himself. I knew I had to interrupt and redirect this behavior quickly and "Stop!" was not going to work. He was too invested in what he was doing and with his high pain threshold, he could conceivably pull his eye out. Others in the movies had. I had to interrupt his train of thought and behavior. So, I yelled very loudly (and I rarely yelled) "Do not pull on your ears!!!" I was across the table from him and would not have reached him before he had accomplished his intent. My yelling something novel had the desired effect. It startled Adam and bought me the three seconds I needed. I stood up moving toward him grabbing my ears yelling at him never to do this. He immediately let go of his eye and grabbed his ears. In two strides, I was next to him, grabbed him and said, "Don't you do this!" Then I began to laugh, and soon we were both laughing and pulling on our ears. His eyes would be fine. His earlobes, over time, became mildly elongated, but this technique of interruption and redirection worked. I knew "No" would not save his eye. Just raising my voice would have accelerated the behavior I wanted to eliminate.

Psychologists call it "extinction bursting." It is the increase of a behavior that has been identified as needing to be challenged. It occurs because reinforcement is reinforcement and you will never get rid of a behavior by reinforcing it. I chose earlobe pulling as a form of redirection because I really did not care if he pulled his ears. But, Adam did not know that. It was not damaging and gave him a tool to begin learning self-control and a way to oppose me safely. I could never really stop him from grabbing his ears anyway; he could always move two steps away from me and pull his ears. And pulling on his ears gave him a means to safely self-stimulate. As Adam got older pulling his ears was sometimes used to oppose my instructions. He would look at me and pull his ear when he did not want to do what I asked inviting me into a power struggle with him. The behaviors we do not want our children to do are filled with power. Swearing and sticking out our tongues are both power moves. Be wise about what you add power to. I chose ear pulling.

To this day, I thank all the families who shared their lives with me before I had Adam. I observed that "No" didn't accomplish what they intended—to teach a different behavior. "No" would not teach Adam to stop doing something, but the word "Stop" was exactly right— it meant "stop what you're doing and stand still." I learned to teach Adam how to be safe and compliant by telling him what I wanted and reinforcing his "good" behaviors. I would never instruct my son in behavior I did not want him to do. I found that with Adam it was best to ignore behaviors I didn't want and reinforce behaviors I did want. The word "stop" interrupted behavior that, in the moment, was dangerous or markedly incorrect so that I could redirect his actions to more constructive behaviors. When natural consequences are not too dangerous, let them teach what is real.

After working with families, the other path I knew not to take was using vague instructions like, "Don't do...." Don't and do both reinforce and create the condition for the behavior to occur more often. "Don't touch that, it's hot!" generally accelerates the probability of a burned hand, especially if yelled in fear because you add energy and momentum to the behavior you intended to stop. Kids told me that if their parents got excited and yelled about something, it must be important to learn about. It must have power. The fellow who thought up behavior modification, Dr. B. F. Skinner, said both positive reinforcement and negative reinforcement accelerate the probability behavior will occur. That is why they are both identified as reinforcement.

At our next session with the *helpful* professionals, they were prepared to teach me their other technique for managing Adam's behavior—the time out. For them, putting a child into time out was punishment.

Often it was suggested that if Adam did not mind them or me, he should be told he was being bad, physically picked up and put into time out. This technique had so much inaccurate information.

The spot or place where the behavior occurs is the anchoring point of the behavior. We code memory as where we were when this happened. The physical location is always paired with the event. Your first kiss, proposing marriage or for people my age, where you were when you found out President Kennedy had been shot. Picking a child up is a show of force/power, demonstrating someone else can control their body. Their focus turns from exploring the environment and learning into first protecting themselves, then feeling helpless. It is domination, not discipline. Their process was actually punishment. That was the reason to pick up and remove the child. Time out is classically defined as a neutral moment or an interruption in reinforcement. Ignoring someone is a classical time out. According to B.F. Skinner, both positive and negative reinforcements will cause a person to do more of something. The best parenting is done at the place where the issue is discovered. Children are anchored to the environment for context. To first ignore, give a time out, then to reinforce the beginning of any behavior you want to compete with the one you do not like, and lastly, if required actively interrupt the behavior and redirect it to a different behavior then over-learn the new behavior. Parenting to me meant teaching my son to explore and learn how to best learn from and be safe in his environment. He had to make mistakes and do retakes or do-overs to learn the best behavior for each situation. There was no teleporting him into another zone before he learned his lessons where he was. Adam and I were fine.

The professionals said Adam had to learn "turn taking." In my language, this meant finding a mutual rhythm to share the moment and become intimate with others. They insisted that I had to teach Adam to follow my instruction because I was the adult, but what they were really talking about was controlling another human being. When I was at my best, as Jetta instructed me, I thanked them, and they went away. When I was not at my best, I would tell them that "adult" had two root words—addled (unable to think clearly; confused) and dolt (a stupid person). Then I would add that there was no need to force Adam to comply with unclear instructions when he would happily follow clear invitations to belong and be involved with me.

I used my time with Adam to go into his world. One of his favorite activities was spinning things, so we spun plates for an hour at a time and laughed, and eventually, he noticed my plate. We flapped our hands in the sun light and laughed together. We walked on our toes and called it dancing. Then we would jump. This required his feet to be flat and spring up. His own weight pushed his feet flat on the ground, and it was fun, so he repeated it over and over. I could not shake my head back and forth like he did because it would make me sick, but I mirrored his actions, pace and intensity as best I could until I "got it" and then would add just a little to it.

Silent expressions

Adam's judgment was different than other children, so my job was to allow him to explore and keep him safe—physically safe from harm, emotionally safe from professional, *helpful* people and intellectually safe from disappearing into his own solitary world. I did this by accompanying him into his world and leaving bread crumbs that lead back to our home. This means remembering how you got to where you are. For example, we did this, then this, then this. Returning just meant undoing the same path.

He enjoyed spinning things. If he found something to spin he would sit and spin it. If he decided to spin a small glass plate, I would substitute another object to spin. I always had 50 cent pieces in my pocket. We could spin them more safely. His curiosity and attraction to strong stimulation were stronger than his survival instinct. I choose not to let him get hit by a car to learn that streets were dangerous. I preempted that lesson by teaching street safety very early. Stop. Look for cars. Look again. When you see that there are no cars close, take my hand and help Dad across the street.

When I found Adam's timing, and he recognized me, I had lived in his world enough to be a companion on his journey to make sense or meaning out of his environment. It was in 1988 when I learned that for most people, reality was based on their own perceptions. Rather than being based on real, fixed truths, reality depended on the neurology of the observer. In 2012, Oliver Sacks wrote a book entitled *Hallucinations* that looked into altered or different perceptions not necessarily damaged perceptions. It confirmed my observations with Adam. I think going with Adam into his world prevented Adam from complete detachment and was equally a grand gift to me, one of many I received by being his father and fellow traveler. I was able through sharing his experience to see the world differently than I was accustomed to seeing it. I saw things I would never have noticed, unique ways of putting things together to make meaning out of a sequence of events.

Adam's oral language during the day decreased as the genetics of Autism blossomed. Expressive Aphasia (an inability to find the word to express an idea) often accompanies Autism. It is different from elective mutism (an unwillingness to talk). He would sign with me as Dr. Rourke had indicated Adam would. Every night I would rock him until he seemed relaxed and sleepy then I would tuck him into bed. After I left the room, I would sit outside his door and listen as he would tell the story of his day in the dark, alone and undistracted. From 6:30 am to 8:00 pm he would go through every event: "First, we do this, then we do this, then we do this." When we were going to do something, anything, I would go through the steps out loud to get from where we were to where we were going. From beginning to end, he repeated all the voices in his day's choir. His memory was quite impressive, and he rarely missed one participant. It confirmed to me that he was often so stimulated in our world that he could not talk, but it was clear that Adam had not lost his language skills. It was also clear that he was internalizing what I was trying to teach him.

The Real Divide Between the *Helpful* Professionals and Me

The truth most adults forget is that children are doing their best in every situation to thrive. They take what *we* have taught them and practice what they understand we want. They are learning language and the meaning of our words. They are learning about new environments, smells, textures, shapes and tastes. They are learning safety rules. They are expending massive amounts of energy attempting to make meaning out of our seemingly random world. Their bodies and brains are physically changing every day, and that takes much of their available energy. And then they must make sense of us—unclear, distracted, short tempered and "in charge."

The real divide between the *helpful* professionals and me was that I looked at Adam's behavior as his best effort to do what I had taught him and comply with my request. They saw Adams behavior as "noncompliant" or disobedient, and that meant Adam had to be disciplined or punished. I always tried to first fix my errors in parenting instruction and found, most of the time, that Adam would adapt. People who live in cold climates will get this example. When it is below freezing outside, you do not just get into your car, start it and drive away because the car will buck and miss and often stall. Instead, you let the car warm up so you can drive it safely smoothly. My parenting errors were often similar. If I did not warm Adam up to an idea but just pushed him, he would act just like my car and buck and stall. All I needed to do to avoid a struggle was to let Adam know what I had in mind. "Adam, it will be time to go to the store in three minutes. Let's get ready. The first thing is to finish what we are doing. Next, we will get what we need to go outside to the store...." I named each step in the process. Then we did the process. Then we said, "Good job, we did it!" Some things took more time to warm up to do than others. Some things took more time to finish before we could do our organization to prepare for our next thing. When parents rush the process, children resist. Dr. Vander Woude was one of my clinical supervisors. He made me read the book. *Don't Push the River: It Flows By Itself* by Barry Stevens. Dr. Vander Woude, like Jim McDowell, Dr. Westendorp and Richard were all fanatics about respecting personal process and timing. Pushing people only creates resistance. Find their timing, warm the car up and eliminate most of the conflicts between people.

Adam was not yet invested in being right or wrong. Good or bad. His way or my way. For Adam, it was all investigation, exploration and trying to make meaning out of my instructions in his world. I think the biggest difference between our approaches was they believed I had to control Adam. I believed Adam had to learn to control himself and be responsible for his own life.

One of the *helpful* professionals told me that if I did not start disciplining Adam, he would never learn appropriate adaptive behaviors. This was professional jargon for letting others control Adam. He went on to quote what he thought came from the Bible and said, "spare the rod and spoil the child." My smile was his only warning. I told him that quote came from a poem entitled *Hudibras* written by Samuel Butler in 1664[6]. It was not a quote from the Bible.

I did not stop there; discipline does not mean "punish" as he seemed to think, it means to *teach* as in tell, show and support our children in the way we want them to go. Discipline, as I understood it, came from the Hebrew word *nynwn* meaning bidding and from the Greek word *paideusis* referring to the rearing and education of the ideal member of a body of citizens. Both are considered acts of love and have to do with instruction to correct willful disobedience. To chastise or rebuke. Punishment comes from the Greek *kolasis* meaning correction and is used to deal with the criminals for penial infractions; it was not meant for our children. I often disciplined Adam through instruction but never through punishment. I reminded the helpful professional,

---

[6]http://www.thisdayinquotes.com/2010/11/spare-rod-and-spoil-child-is-not-in.html.

now quiet and maybe feeling a little bit trapped, that if punishment really worked, then the children who were wards of the court because their parents abusively punished them would be the best behaved and happiest of children because they were often severely punished.

He was probably referring to Proverbs 13:24, "He who spares the rod hates his son, but one that loves him is careful to discipline him." His rod in this context is translated from *shebbe it* is the shepherd's rod, figurative of divine guidance and care and love. Also found in the passage "Thy rod and Thy staff, they comfort me" (Psalm 23:4). Punishment was never intended but discipline through love was. That ended his sessions with us.

I told Jetta about my conversation when she got home, and she said, "You were just showing off. Did you make a new friend? Or were you just letting the poor counselor know how smart you are? You could have just said that we do not think punishment teaches new behavior as quickly as reinforcement and over-learning does." She always protected them, and she was almost always correct.

Most people in the world danced to waltz music while Adam played jazz in a slightly different key. I enjoyed it. Each form of music has its rules and structure, but a waltz played by a good jazz player is still the same yet very different. Then I made a discovery: most people could not transpose the music, did not know how to waltz and were not musical.

Just as Wolfensberger wrote, our pendulum swung between protecting Adam from the world and protecting the world from Adam. Jetta and I protected some very good people who had the heart but not the skills to create safe conditions for Adam. Normalization is not just treating unique children just like everyone else. I wish this were true as it would make life so much easier. It begins with treating all children as the same, but even parents with twins know every child is also unique and requires a little different treatment to support their success. It is a moving target, not a fixed point. All children with Down syndrome are not the same. It required Jetta and me to create social conditions and events to naturally include Adam in birthdays, Christmas, going out to eat at other people's homes, etc....always with escape plans to avoid over-stimulation.

Learning Is More Important Than Knowing

Einstein said imagination is more important than knowledge. He was alone and had to imagine a different way of being. I had a guide so that I could experience and learn. I did not need to imagine, Adam did that part for me. Away from them and being Adam's full-time parent from the time he was three years old on was fantastic! With Adam, I was allowed to see the world I had known for 30 some years in a whole new perspective. Adam's sense of being connected to the natural flow of life and divergent from the social rules made perfect sense to me.

- Do not stay in situations that are hurting you.
- Yes, you can just get up and move away from a bad situation.
- No, you do not have to tell others what you see as bad or wrong, it only pisses them off. Smile and move on.
- Find a spot and regain your internal balance. Observe the situation and return when you can join in productively with the flow.
- Being kind and polite feels good.
- Every moment is there to observe and to gain new information and experiences. Use every moment to explore the world.
- See all the ways each object and each interaction can add to what you understand.

Adam did all of these things instinctively and organically. If I suspended my cognitive knowing of how everything already worked, I was allowed to see another possibility for my life. For Adam, life was not simply an intellectual quest to gain knowledge; it was a quest to discover meaning and to know the world inside and out. Through his experience, he acquired what it meant to be alive rather than definitions made up by systems. He discovered through experience and showed me that learning is more important than knowing. Every time I learned something new what I had known to be true changed.

The *kind* doctor was correct, having Adam as my son made life difficult, but not because Adam was being difficult.

We were fine.

Jetta always emphasized that every teacher and fellow professional had studied to learn to help others, not harm them. She believed that I should forgive them because they were not intentionally doing anything to hurt and harm us. I never told her it was their lack of intention and attention that made them dangerous and frustrated me the most. They were the sleep walkers, preprogrammed to continue the world of eugenics as it had been. Had they been awake, they could have discovered a new way to teach and learn.

Chapter 8
Our Many Epiphanies

Epiphany of Natural Inclusion

One day Jetta and I were sitting with Adam in a little park in Grand Haven, Michigan. We had been talking about how to best go about arranging for Adam to have some playtime with other children and how to teach him proper behavior in those situations when a little girl came up and sat down next to Adam. Adam started flapping his hands and shaking his head back and forth, initial signs of being over stimulated. The little girl did the same, flapping her hands, shaking her head and laughing. They both stopped, and she asked Adam, "What's your name?" Adam didn't say anything. Before Jetta or I could even find words to explain Adam to this little girl, she said, "So you don't talk much, okay." I told her that his name was Adam and she looked into Adam and asked, "Do you want to come play over here with me? You don't need to talk. I can talk for both of us." She lightly touched his hand, and Adam got up and walked off with her as she engaged him in a one-sided conversation about the day and making new friends. Over her shoulder, she said to us, "It's okay, we will be right here."

That day Jetta and I experienced child-to-child inclusion. It was easy, and it was incredible. But not all children, certainly not all people, were so good at it. Little girls, usually two years older than Adam were, for the most part, a perfect match. Their energy, order and instinctive drive for fairness and inclusion were natural. Girls wanted to promote everyone participating in communication and relationships. Boys were erratic, tumultuous, and tended to be rough and aggressive. They seemed fully occupied in the pursuit of winning. Adults lived in their heads rather than energetically connecting on a heart-to-heart or being-to-being level. They were generally distracted and had their own internal dialog going on that prevented them from fully sharing in the moment, especially a moment with a child.

Changing Places and Meaning Making

The next two and a half years were a blur for me. I was in Adam time mostly—reinforcing his adaptive behaviors, learning about him and teaching him meaning making. Meaning making is the process of how a person construes, understands or makes sense out of life events. In retrospect, I was always shown God's highest way for Adam and our family, but sometimes I could not it see it at the moment because I thought I had to solve every problem myself. It was not so much ego as misplaced responsibility. I had already been given everything Adam, Jetta and I needed. It was up to me to use the gifts I was given wisely. How could I ask for more?

During those years I lived bridging Adam's world with Jetta's world (any other world being too elusive). I am, by nature, adaptive

Helping gather fall leaves

and free and although Adam and I had been working together for five years, he still required rhythm, ritual, routine and constant guided redirection. From 6:30 am when he naturally woke up until 7:00 pm when I started his night routine, I knew what was going to occur every 15 minutes so that I could offer him assurance with every activity. By 8:00 pm he was asleep.

We had a specific bedtime routine. Every night at 7:00 pm he would find Jetta to be hugged and told he was loved and sent off to bed. Then we went upstairs, and I would sing the phonetic alphabet as we walked by each letter. After brushing our teeth, we sat in the rocking chair for more songs and rocking. I made songs up about parables and lessons in life. Once Adam fell asleep, I would put him in his bed and sit outside his door until I knew he was sleeping soundly. That was the point he had redone his day and put it into his order. This nightly recapping was something he had started when he was younger, and it continued. By 9:00 pm I would go downstairs to visit with Jetta.

Adam, is opening the door your best choice?

Adam required an environment that was safe and also predictable. Adam needed to connect with another person, me. He also needed to discover cause and effect and time binding, so he could learn to sequence, so he could begin to put order into his life. He played with light switches turning them on and off, on and off, on and off to see cause and effect until my patience was thoroughly tested. All children initially live only in this moment, now. Children, as their neurological structures mature (Basel Ganglion), naturally understand that time can be divided into something before this present moment. What they did, the past. What they are doing, their present moment. What they will be doing next, what they intend to do. Because the genetics of Autism is a unique developmental sequence, not a developmental delay, like Down syndrome the two divergent genetically driven developmental progressions were a challenge and my gift to observe. The challenge for me was to discern between ritualized behavior and establishing rituals to learn to master his environment. Both outward behaviors are the same, but the difference is intensity, frequency and duration. For instance, he loved remote controls. He would click the TV remote, and the world changed right before his eyes. He would press the garage door opener and watch the door repeatedly open and close. This elicited such joy and excitement that it would be followed by hand flapping and head twisting back and forth. I accompanied his exploration by adding the narrative. Light on. Light off. Garage door open. Garage door closed. Turn the water on. Turn the water in the sink off. Shoes on. Shoes off.

Adam needed to develop upper body strength so he could talk. I learned that the chest muscles are the platform that supports speech. We made up our physical work out routines to develop core and upper body strength and worked on getting strong.

Adam needed to learn how to make meaning out of the larger world he lived in, not just his internal world. We learned what wrapped boxes meant...presents! We learned to unwrap presents and smile and say, "Thank you." When I realized that I had forgotten to build in the momentary pause to look at and admire the gift, we had to back the lesson up a bit. But it didn't take Adam long to learn the meaning of gifts!

I taught him what was funny and how to laugh about the world around him. We practiced laughing—big belly laughing. If I were authentically laughing from the souls of my feet, Adam would get infected and that, in turn, infected me with more laughter. It was fun. He taught me that everything is funny and he taught me the pleasure of just being.

I taught him how to move around people and find their pace. He taught me how to experience the moment more completely and experience the space between people as being just as real as the space people occupied. The space between people is an expression or reflection of their confidence, comfort levels, need for privacy, control and intimacy. Adam revealed the natural flow of being. I taught him all the constructs humans have devised to create identity and meaning separated from the natural flow of life. I taught him all the constructs humans have devised to create identity and meaning separated from the natural flow of life.

We would go for walks and sit and watch people interact, and I would tell Adam what they were doing. Adam mostly liked to watch men working with machines and tools. He never developed an interest in toys but was very drawn to tools, especially hammers, saws, and screwdrivers. What we called play time others would call work. We would vacuum and clean counter tops. We did "wax on, wax off" on everything because Montessori had discovered that wiping table tops was the precursor to handwriting. We sorted the silverware and then put it away and would clean out and organize drawers and eventually closets. One day we tacked the entire garage. Adam loved that project!

Categorization is the foundation of abstract thinking. Doing work together allowed me to create a behavior chain. This means: What comes first? Then what? And finally, how do you know when you are done? All tasks have a planning, first step, doing, concluding and evaluation process. This could be taught abstractly or as I did with Adam, it was just how we worked.

Working with Dad

Years later, people were amazed by Adam and would ask me how a 16-year-old ever learned to do that. I would say, "Well, at four years old when we organized the garage..." and they would stop listening because their child was 20 and didn't know how to do that. They were hopeful that their young adult could also learn Adam's social competencies and organizational skills. No one had helped them understand the necessity for inclusion. Their children had missed some critical developmental skills because they were taken out of the normal flow of development and educated in a special environment. Their young adult had missed being exposed to and missed staying connected to typical growth and development. Their child had been placed in *special* programs and cheated out of the exposure to typical demands of living. Like Temple Grandin had told me, it took hard work starting when she was young to stay connected to the real world. It made me sad to see that, as a family, they had been handicapped, shunned and removed from the possibility to practice and gain peer support to master the survival skills that other children learn in their everyday environment. It was as though they had been pulled out of the mainstream and placed in a special deep freeze now thawed out at age 26 and expected to fit in. Don't misunderstand me please, it is always time to learn, but learning is a sequence of experiences that build upon prior experiences. It is very difficult to skip so many steps.

The foundation of all learning comes early when we show our children the first how to. From the beginning, Adam learned how to be by being with me. I knew that when he became a teenager, he would have input from his friends about why he and I did as we did and would have to decide if what we learned together still fit for him. My privilege and obligation as his father was to clearly and faithfully demonstrate the path to walk as a man. I made a conscious choice never to use the "do as I say, not as I do" approach to parenting but to demonstrate for him my best possibility in everything I did. Every moment we had together was used to learn, fully experience and develop skill sets for the next challenge in life.

While we worked, I tried playing classical music in the background in the hope that he would become interested in the unique rhythms. He liked the record spinning more than the music, however. It turned out that he liked the rhythm of Freddie Mercury singing "We Are the Champions." He also liked Guns and Roses. Thank you, inclusion, and I mean this both tongue-in-cheek and earnestly. I was always hopeful my son would enjoy classical music. I presented it to him when he was younger, but his friends had more sway and influence regarding his musical choices. My Brahms was relegated to only me. The joy of inclusion is double-edged. There were some things Adam learned that I wish he had not. Every child on his or her way to becoming a man or woman has to learn the difference between right and wrong, good and evil. It comes from experience, not just fatherly words and advice. Adam learned with his friends.

The Day Adam Stood Still

Adam was always in motion. He was exploration personified. One day as I followed him through his exploration of cause and effect using the TV remote, he repeatedly hit buttons until Sesame Street popped up on the screen. Adam paused, stared at the TV, then looked at me. He was enthralled with the show, and Sesame Street became part of his path into a larger world. I videotaped Sesame Street and when he did his, "Hello, TV" (Adam greeted people and objects equally and taught me that everything deserves respect and a focused attention to meet and begin interacting), he would stop his exploring and stand in front of the TV as if he was greeting it and waited for it to give him his show. I noticed his interest as a window into another kind of learning for him. Sesame Street would appear just where he left it, and soon we began watching Sesame Street forwas no light and there were glassminutes, then 11 minutes, then longer.

What I learned about life from Sesame Street was what I called the Sesame Street progression. On Monday, the show is new. On Tuesday, the show revisits Monday's themes and adds some new content. On Wednesday, the content from Monday and Tuesday is refined and reinforced, and some new content is added. Thursday and Friday followed suit until Monday began a new theme. They would introduce information then reinforce that information until one mastered the information/behavior/process, then start over again. TV became one of our best learning activities. Everything else was exploration on the move. Adam could sit in my lap and learn the comfort of another person while he watched Sesame Street. He learned by watching and then by doing.

"Adam Winstrom: This Is Your Life" Show

Adam taught me so much about perception, how people learn, and how we derive meaning from the random experiences in life. As I learned from Adam, I also learned from the best academic minds I could find. One local source of wisdom was Carol Gray, our school advocate. She was devoted to children who had Autism and taught me about social stories, a technique she developed to present information to children who had Autism in such a way that they could internalize it. I thought of the technique as new parables, kind of like a written form of Sesame Street.

She would take an issue and look at the back chain of how it developed, then write a story with a different progression, being careful to include enough of the original to let the child identify with the story and internalize the message. She was writing modern day parables for children and, of course, it worked. I learned from Carol, but Adam did not yet have the capacity to internalize what he read, so Adam and I used video. She was writing modern day parables for children. Of course, it worked.

We would set the camera up and do life in front of it. Then we would watch parts of the video and learn. "Was this your best choice?" "What would you do differently?" (Autistic/Down syndrome talk, for lack of a better term. "I" or "you" often confused the meaning for Adam.) Then we would do it again and record the "redoing" in the best way we could that day. Adam learned to enjoy watching himself. He learned from redoing and over-learning. We discovered the best way for Adam to learn and we practiced it over and over laughing at every take. There's never a wrong or bad behavior, but sometimes a mistake or a "miss take" requires more practice and a do-over.

Affinity for Technology

Adam's new speech therapist told me there was an articulation problem because of his incorrect "phoneme formation of his graphemes." In plain English, that meant he was not connecting sounds with images or symbols in his mind. This information took Adam and me into Macintosh land. We played on the Macintosh computer speaking into the microphone and making sonograms or visual graphing of the recorded speech. It visually showed the sounds and symbols he was connecting. I discovered that Adam was doubling his sounds, not that he did not know the sound to make. Adam and I began playing match the graph games and using the computer program I removed the extra sounds, so he heard his own voice saying the sound correctly. And he saw it. He was a visual learner. Because his hearing was genetically unique, it was better teaching to match the pattern. He was able to create a visual map to match the correct sound of the word, undoubled.

Fascination with Computers

Adam loved computers. He had had an Apple computer since he was two years old. When Peal Software first came out, it was designed specifically for neurologically atypical children, so I called and talked with the designer. The day she accepted my call, a CBS News film crew was there to feature her work. She graciously made them wait to talk with me about Adam and her software. We got one of the first copies of the software CD when he was three and a half. As she made the film crew wait, I could hear her saying that the children she had designed the software for were more important than the film crew's time. She was a caregiver.

I built on her concepts and found two computer programmers that were out of work and hungry. Together we created *Adam and Abby*, an interactive computer program with a K to 12 curricula that could be easily modified. It recorded what each user did and had simulated choices built into the game that reinforced "is this your best choice?" I named it after Adam and one of his first baby sitters, Abby. Her parents had nicknamed her "*Pickles*," and Adam just laughed every time they came

Adam's computer game

to pick up Pickles. It was the beginning of a lot of silly names in Adam's life. He talked about Pickles and even called himself Adam "Pickles" and laughed. It struck him as very funny.

Adam's affinity for technology was unique like all of him, and by three years old he was frequently on my computer with me. By four and a half, he had conquered the Adam and Abby computer games and had found "back doors" or short cuts that us programmers had built into the programs to allow back-end access. I made the error of using a back door into the program code to put in a fix. What happened next should not have been any surprise. Out of the corner of his perception, Adam had seen me change the code, so when I left him to play for just one moment, he went in and changed all the codes. Adam helped by crashing the program in every way possible to help us get the bugs out. Macintosh computers and Adam's brain were too closely linked.

Adam enjoyed using his computer. He could type things he could not say. His expressive aphasia was oral; mine was haptic expressive also

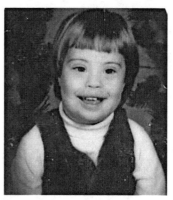

Adam in preschool

called Dyslexia affecting writing. What a team we were. He had difficulty finding the words he wanted to say out loud but could read, write and spell. I had difficulty finding the words to write, had had difficulty learning to read and could not spell as well as my son could. The perfect odd couple. Happy, sad, glad, or mad Adam never threw a computer or harmed it in any way. "We don't hurt tools because we made a mistake" was our mantra.

The Fake Phone: Real Communication

From sitting outside Adam's bedroom door at night listening to him talk through his day to his affinity for talking to the Mac computer and his wonderful new speech therapist, one of Adam's lifelong addictions began—the phone.

At first, the speech therapist made pretend phones then used old house phones. The fake phone became an amazing tool for Adam. Not having to look at a person when talking to them freed Adam from being overwhelmed with having to process too much information and trying to talk at the same time.

I remember being on a flight to Mexico with Adam and we were in some turbulence. Adam got out his fake phone and started talking. The stewardess immediately came down the aisle and said, "all cell phones must be turned off!" I told her all cell phones are turned off. Without skipping a beat, she repeated that he had to turn his cell phone off. I turned to Adam and asked if the stewardess could talk on his phone just for a minute because she was scared, too. She put the fake phone to her ear said, "Hello!" then gave it back to Adam who was excitedly flapping his hands and shaking his head. In the midst of the turbulence, Adam talked to God on the fake phone for a while longer then went to sleep on my shoulder. His cell phone was a "normalizing prop" that he used to do his "self-talk" and not appear to be a crazy person talking to himself. And it worked very well.

Eventually, I got him a real, live cell phone and unleashed him upon the world. Talking on the phone gave him the same freedom that talking to himself at night in his bed with the lights off did. Without the over stimulation of the other person's face, Adam could chat it up pretty good. I set up voice dialing so he would have to speak clearly to call a certain person. He would often call me and get refueled. When he really got overwhelmed, he would give himself time outs by stepping out of the world and pretending to talk on the phone.

Doing Our Best

Jetta, Adam and I worked and played through the next couple of years. The helpful professionals would help us identify the issues we were encountering, and we would all work together to develop the supports for Adam. Eventually, we found the bridge between Adam and Jetta so that they could each give and receive the love they needed to share.

During those few years, Adam and I created a bridge and a connection strong enough for both of us to travel on. There is a Latin proverb that says, "by teaching, we learn." By teaching Adam about life, I was forced to observe life in the moment, absent of filtered interpretation. Just life. And that was one of the gifts I received. By teaching Adam, I learned who I was intended to be. By teaching him manners, I learned to be polite to the most arrogant of helping professionals and was reminded that they, too, were doing their best every day.

Summers were the best of times. Adam was developing routines and rituals that Jetta could join him in. Jetta loved water, and so did Adam. We tried going the beach, but it was too much for both of them, so I put a pool in our back yard, and the two fish were happy. Often one or two neighborhood children would come over, and Adam would learn to interact with them socially.

Understanding IQs

I had already started working on my Ph.D. with a dual major in Clinical Psychology and Educational Psychology, Inclusion, Curriculum Development and School Law. My advisor, Byron Rourke, encouraged me to dedicate my daytimes to Adam until he slept, then connect with Jetta. At night, when she slept, I did research and wrote papers to complete my core requirements for my Ph.D., then I would sleep for four hours and return to being Adam's father in the morning. Our nap time was sacred, maybe more for me, but we napped one hour every day.

After the first year of our new family structure, our lives together were going well enough that I could go away for three or four days for some dedicated research time or to take an intensive class. When I traveled, Adam would call just before he went to bed. When I answered, I would hear, "Hello." Then he would say, "Blah. Blah. Blah. Goodbye" and hang up. We did this every night, and it always made me smile. Jetta and I talked after Adam was asleep.

I always seemed to always come back to "it"—prejudice of some form: Dyslexia, Down syndrome, Autism. It kept cropping up in our lives. One of the deans of my doctoral program told me, "People with Dyslexia like you have no business attempting to be involved in higher education." What he meant was, "*I* don't want you in my classroom, you don't belong." One of the post-doctoral fellowship placements that I applied to focused on Dyslexia informed me that they do not consider people with Dyslexia as researchers in their program, just subjects. Once again, I was told that I did not belong with the smart people. I just kept on writing and got my Ph.D. in Clinical Psychology with a cognate in Educational Psychology.

I called and wrote to the best in the field that I was currently studying. I discovered that being a doctoral student opened doors that being a parent did not. As a student, I corresponded via the Internet with people who were on the cutting edge of inclusion. Most were very happy to share their ideas with me. For those who were reluctant to talk with me, I told them about Adam and the reason I was a student, and they often opened up.

The motivation for continuing my education was to protect Adam from the helpful school psychologists. My Test Measurements and Evaluations class was particularly useful. In it I learned about IQ tests. Dr. Wechler, the author of the Wechsler Intelligence Test, instructed all who used his test to note that it is important not to attribute low performance on the Wechsler Intelligence Test, when, in fact, it may be attributable to physical, language, or sensory difficulties. This was important because it meant my son's tested IQ of 40 was not an accurate assessment of his potential to learn. By now I knew that, but the school still wanted to use it to restrict Adam's exposure and inclusion in their educational process.

I found an expert assessor who had experience with children with Autism and Down syndrome. I kept the results to myself in case I ever needed them. Just like the letter from Dr. Van Volkenburg with his diagnostic formulation of Autism, this test was important to us. Adam's newly assessed IQ was between 70 and 75 with expressive aphasia (the neurologically based inability to express oral language sometimes called Broca's aphasia). That difference in IQ scores was important legally because it meant the public school owed him an education, not just to be trained to work at Kandu.

The joke, at least *I* thought it was funny, was that I also took an IQ test. I found out I was much smarter than the people who called me a stupid dunce. I took an IQ test so one of my fellow students could practice test administration and scored in the top 2%. That meant my IQ was higher than 98% of the people in the world. Jetta did not think it was funny on many levels. She always knew, like her friends and most of the world, that they were smarter than I was. When normal privilege and the accompanying prejudices are involved, one's accomplishments have no meaning. Ironically, they were not as intelligent as I was, but still, they shunned me as the dumb one. When Jetta found out that her IQ could not hold a candle to mine, there was a moment of silence never

Jetta and Adam after church

to be mentioned again. I found out there was an organization called Mensa (Latin for round table) for (*us*) really smart people and I joined. Jetta just rolled her eyes.

Mensa is for people whose IQ is in the top 2%; it is a round-table society where race, color, creed, national origin, age, politics, education or social background are irrelevant. We are different. Brighter than 98% of the rest of the people, and we do not discriminate or judge each other's differences like normal people seem to have the need to do. In Mensa, they regard IQ as an accident of birth. It is viewed as an obligation not an entitlement. Most of the folks I met in Mensa were less arrogant than my grade school classmates. They understood IQ is nothing to be ashamed of or proud of. It was like having blond hair or blue eyes. Most were also outcasts, folks who never quite fit into normal society. They joined to find others to converse with who could understand their uniqueness. Meeting these very bright people let me see that being smart does not assure success or happiness. They all agreed that Adam did not need to be bright to be happy and successful because it was not really such a gift. I used the Mensa logo and my title of Dr. to combat and neutralize normal privilege when it arose, but my son's friends never knew I was a member or that I had a Ph.D. In the inclusive world Adam lived in, I was just Adam's dad. A nice guy who rode a Harley. And that was just the way I liked it.

Chapter 9
Preparing School

School is the third test of belonging. How successful a child is in school has a significant influence on how they see themselves fitting in as adults. Erik Erikson's research and writings including *Childhood and Society* (1993) demonstrated the powerful influence the first years in school have over the entire life of a child. Wolfensberger's research demonstrated how full inclusion benefits *every* child. Without taking anything away from the brightest students, inclusion had a positive impact on them as well as on the average students and the least able students. The bottom line is that each student improved by learning together.

Adam had made it past the first test of belonging: Does Adam belong in our family or in an institution? We decided he belonged in our family and made that a successful process. Adam passed the second test: Does Adam belong in our church or does he belong in the anteroom for *special* people? The church that *included* Adam and Jetta within the body of Christ rather than forcing them to be outside looking in was where we belonged. That took the minister leading the way. Most church members wanted to do the right thing; they just did not know what that was. It took prayer groups within the church asking God for guidance. It took Andy, the minister, creating conditions and preaching God's word about including everyone at the "table." It took Jetta's gentle hand leading people away from *special* classes and *special* places into receiving Adam as God presented him. As the Rabbi said "Adam, God's perfect creation."

Now the third challenge: Does Adam belong in his neighborhood school or in a separate but "equal" *special* facility?

Erikson in his book *Childhood and Society* (1993) identifies social, emotional and academic work done from kindergarten through sixth grade as industry vs. inferiority. The reason inclusion is critical in school is that being included and feeling successful at that stage determines their sense of belonging and adequacy for the rest of their life. Separate but "equal" will create a lifetime condition of feeling separate and not as good as others. Inclusion determines an individual's comfort level and confidence to either be part of the world or to seek separate, sheltered situations. Wolfensberger's studies proved that every minute a child spent in full inclusion saved time spent in the social system and dollars spent supporting children with differences when they got older. Not only is it the right, morally correct thing to do, but it is the best financial investment for society. Being excluded as a child was the worst part of my life, and I determined that Adam was not going to have the same experience.

I always felt an affinity for Martin Luther King, Jr. and felt that I owed a debt to him and the Civil Rights movement. That struggle and the resulting landmark Supreme Court decision of Brown vs. the Board of Education (1954) proved "separate but equal" is harmful and is never equal. His life's work to be free from what I called "it" or prejudice, he called discrimination. He also recognized it as evil. His life work gave me and other parents court precedence to free our children from *special* separate-but-equal facilities and separate-but-equal instruction within the regular school buildings. He had to deal with white privilege. I had to deal with normal privilege. Dr. King had written about how people who are accustomed to privilege felt oppressed when they experienced equality. I found that I could verify his words.

Discrimination had been outlawed, but prejudice was still alive and thriving. It just operated behind a softer voice. A smile. It had benevolence to protect, but the naïve, sometimes unintended arrogance of normal privilege lived on.

Preparing School for Adam

Jetta and I agreed the school transition was my area. Adam was fast approaching five years old, and the issue of school was on the horizon. The helpful professionals had assumed all along that we would put Adam in their Ottawa Area Center, the school for *special* children in our area. I went to the Intermediate School District Board meeting when Adam was born (they were the central coordinators for special children in Ottawa County) and told them that I was new to their system but wanted to inform them that, though I appreciated all they were doing for special children in Ottawa County, my son would be going to Mary A. White Elementary School and Grand Haven Middle and High Schools and would never go to their Ottawa Area Center. I told them my visit was a courtesy, so they had time to put in place the supports for full inclusion that Adam was entitled to by law. I thanked them for their time and left.

When Adam was three, I went to my local school district to inform them that when my son was five, he would be attending Mary A. White for kindergarten and that I would let them figure out how to work out accommodations but would be happy to meet with them at their convenience. Initially, I used Wolfensberger's institutionalization pendulum of protection to try and protect Adam and others. Wolfensberger wrote about an imaginary pendulum that swings through society. On one end were the people who said it is important to protect the "mentally impaired" people from society so that they are not victimized. To protect them, society builds institutions for the mentally impaired for their protection. Funding for these safe havens is always reduced, and supportive services are removed, and people languish. Then the social pendulum swings back and the mentally impaired are viewed as dangerous, and society once again sends the mentally impaired into the institutions, which are again underfunded.

Both sides of institutionalization pendulum—one to protect the individual and other to protect society—are evil.

Still, I fell victim to the illusion of protection. The illusion was that you can learn without making mistakes—that somehow you could learn to ride a bike without falling down. Impossible. I had read Wolfensberger's ideas about the dignity of risk and the right to fail and learn. His ideas made perfect sense, but what parent wants to let their child fall down so they can learn to balance and walk even if it is an essential part of growing up.

Protection is seductive. It promises learning without experiencing discomfort if you go slow enough in a safe, specially designed environment. Eventually, it comes to the critical moment when we learn by our experience—actually doing what we are trying to learn and master. It is the only and best time to learn. Facing fear in the moment with the people who are afraid is the only true protection from living in fear, anxiety, confusion and anger.

The helpful professionals who had come to our home all said Mary A. White Elementary School would never do. They all, as a choir, recommended Ottawa Area Center and wanted to help us arrange the two-hour bus rides. We had tried Grand Haven Preschool busing for two weeks during which Adam had learned to spit, bite, pinch and push. The over-stimulation was too much too soon, and Adam noticeably withdrew into his own world. It took me six weeks to get rid of the spitting and biting. At four years old, riding a school bus with a bus load of typical children for 30 minutes let alone a group of children with emotional impairments for two hours seemed a recipe for disaster.

When Adam was four, I contacted Mary A. White again and informed them that next year Adam would be attending. I contacted Bill O'Neal, the Director of...drum roll...Special Education, to let him know Adam would be fully included. While Adam was taking his afternoon nap, I had done my research homework on education alternatives and talked with Marsha Forest in Canada. She suggested I come up to visit her and see the Canadian schools. Jetta agreed, so I went.

Canada: Eyes Opened to Educational Possibility

The four days I spent with Marsha Forest in the Canadian school system changed me. I was treated to spending my days in classrooms and my nights in community or "Circles of Friends" as they called it. Circles of Friends is a meeting with non-neurotypical people and their neurotypical friends. They chose not to call themselves normal and abnormal or normal and special, handicapped, disabled or any other designations that society used to identify them as less than normal. In the Circles of Friends gathering, everyone shared their collective experience of their day and made plans to create better conditions for the next day. Marsha introduced me to Robert Perske, the author of *Circles of Friends* and another pioneer in this new inclusive world.

The quality of life I observed in everyone around me made me want to move to Canada. They all worked together and included everyone. The teachers had met every morning before the school opened for students and shared strategies. At one meeting, I asked how they had negotiated this time into their contract. They explained that in Canada it was not a contractual requirement to come to school early, it was a professional decision. Their Principal would sometimes be there and sometimes not. At that meeting, coffee and sometimes breakfasts were served, and every teacher shared frustrations and solutions for daily issues along with their understanding of a child and their school environment. It was a community process.

When I was visiting the grade school, the students would walk with me to their class. They asked who I was and why I had come to their school. They told me I was welcome to sit in their classroom. I watched and listened. No bullying or disrespectful behavior. All the children interacted to support each other. If a student had a problem, they were given time to sort it out. If they seemed unable to sort it out, the students who sat around the student experiencing the difficulty would offer their support. If all failed, the teacher would be summoned. Teachers taught, and students learned not only factual data but how to learn and, more importantly, how to learn to live and work together.

I talked to grade school students who could not understand why I would be concerned about my son going to school. One class told me that if Adam's school would not accept him, we should move there and they would make sure he was safe and learned and had friends. I melted and wept. I had seen inclusion working. I felt what inclusion was and now I experienced what it was like to have my son not just accommodated but wanted, accepted, welcomed and allowed to be with normal people. It was the opposite of my experience as a child. It was the opposite of my experience as a parent. It was heaven on earth. It was Canada.

All the students, teachers, administrators and parents were convinced that this was the way it must be. Wow! I also learned that it did not happen overnight. But it happened. I could see that inclusion really worked and experienced it in action. I knew this was the way I wanted my son educated. This was the kind of community I hoped to belong to with Adam.

In Canada, inclusion was the normal state in their school systems. I was high on this experience. I saw that it worked for everyone including children, teachers, parents and the financial system. Surely this would be an easy transition in Grand Rapids. I felt like I was bringing fire back to my tribe.

The Soul of Education

I remember asking the Principal in Canada how inclusion happened. How did he move his staff from their old perceptions to this reality? He explained the difference between education in the U.S. and Canada. In 1977, the Canadian Ministry of Community and Social Services implemented Wolfensberger's theories as law. They instituted mainstreaming or integration of exceptional children into the common flow of the educational system. Mainstreaming sought to end segregated classrooms for *special* children and make available to all people with intellectual disabilities patterns of life and conditions of everyday living that were as close as possible to the regular circumstances and ways of life in society. He told me that inclusion, as he referred to it, was universally adopted in all Canadian schools. He said that in the U.S., prospective teachers are trained to work with curriculum that the State approves not set goals for learning. Your student teachers practice methods of implementing curriculum, not crating their own curriculum nor developing adaptive instructional methods. The U.S. focuses on classroom management while Canada focuses on creating a cooperative learning environment. You are obsessed with achievement, but don't understand how to teach students to achieve. You teach to the mind and hope the heart is good. Your teachers may accept inclusion because it is a new law, but they will not really support it for quite a while. They will worry about neglecting their brighter students. We have seen our brightest students excel in our inclusive classrooms. He said they were more fortunate in Canada because the government decided to support the Catholic School system instead of creating a separate State system. Canadian teachers are taught to make their curriculum not use the only one the State imposes. Individual achievement is not their method. They support academic competition, but to compete, the playing field must be equal, and participants must cooperate. Achievement in the U.S. is too often at the expense of others. It is based on beating others not on being your best. In achievement, the bar standard is set, and some always fail (like me). In their brand of competition, everyone learns and improves. He said the real difference was that in the U.S. teachers did not support inclusion because they thought it interfered with achievement. In Canada, they had read Wolfensberger research that proves that in school where there is full inclusion, every student benefits. And for them, inclusion was not the result of a government law, they understood it as the best practices and as being biblically correct. No one worried about being sued by a parent for not including their child under ADA (American Disabilities Act), or 504, or 94142...they all had read Matthew 25:40. The teachers and administrators believed it was their eternal soul that would be in peril if all the children were not allowed to come to school. I began to have some respect for Christians. This group of teachers did not just pray, they acted.

I returned home and told Jetta about heaven. I was ready to move. I really wanted her to experience a world where our son was wanted. She, the wiser of us, wanted to improve the schools in Grand Haven. She reminded me of the little girl in the park who wanted to play with Adam. If we were in Canada, the young girl in the park would have missed that experience.

Inclusion was possible. I loved her and I loved Adam. We would stay in Grand Haven and make it a better place. I knew that would mean causing friction. I understood that I would become the school's pariah and their salvation. It was my calling to be Adam's father and remove discrimination, so my son could live in my community. We stayed, and I prepared to support my local school.

The Director of the Intermediate School District in Ottawa County had become aware of my different approaches to teaching Adam and my intention to have Adam fully included in our local school. He invited me to meet with him and to join a committee to study the feasibility of inclusion. I met with him and listened, as Jetta had instructed (more imprinted on) me to do. I asked why his staff was still working to create a parallel special system within the regular education buildings. It was no longer a best practice to deliver their services in that way. He told me they had years of experience and were very invested in the model they had developed over the years with parents (and he stressed *with parents)* who wanted their children protected. They were all working very hard now and really did not have time to look for new fads. After all, I could not expect them to take the time to look at new ways to program, they were overwhelmed just responding to all the children like Adam that the county had to deal with. Most parents in the county were grateful for the level of support the ISD (Intermediate School District) offered. What I heard was: "What you are talking about is an unproven fad. We, the care takers, are already over worked public servants. You are asking too much and should be grateful for what we give you." He was a class act, smooth and self-assured. I reminded him that "separate but equal" was not supported by the law any longer. In fact, "separate but equal" was a violation of the law. Without skipping a beat, his response was, "unless parents specifically ask for it." I reminded him that I was asking.

The Director implied that my son could, of course, attend his neighborhood school. But if I did not want him in "special education" he doubted it would work very well. He told me that the county had invested a lot of time and money into creating and refining their "system within a system" as he referred to their model. In every building, there were at least two "resource rooms" where kids like Adam would spend most of their day. The rest of their day could be taken up by speech therapy, physical therapy, gym and art. It was a well-organized, safe alternative to just dumping Adam in a classroom.

From his perspective, special education was a set of physical structures and class rooms. From my perspective, special education was an administrative structure in a district that was responsible for assessing, creating and implementing appropriate individualized supports in the least restrictive environment. It was individual programs of support vs. clustered classrooms of places where every child with a difference goes, is contained and helped.

They were holding onto their 1954 "separate-but-equal" system. Spouting eugenics as a rationale and shaming parents who asked for more.

The ideas behind full inclusion were the result of Wolf Wolfensberger's normalization theory. According to Wikipedia, the normalization principle means "making available to all people with disabilities patterns of life and conditions of everyday living which are as close as possible to the regular circumstances and ways of life or society." Temple Grandin had convinced me that this was essential. Normalization does not mean making people "normal" e.g. does not mean forcing them to conform to societal norms. Normalization does not support "dumping" people into the community or schools without support. Support services are services, not physical structures. The principle of normalization is congruent with "community integration" and has been described by educators as supporting early mainstreaming in community life. Wolfensberger himself emphasized in 1980 that the environment, not the person, is what is normalized. This has been known for decades as a person-environment interaction.

I told the Director that my son would be requesting special education supportive services but would be in regular education. Get ready.

Chapter 10
Grade School

Enrolling in Kindergarten

On our first visit to Mary A. White Elementary School, I knew what the school's question would be before they even asked: "Is Adam really ready for kindergarten?" There were many obstacles and no obstacles, really. Where they wanted the discussion to go was toward questions like, "Could Adam adapt to their system?" "Could Adam fit into their school routines (rhythms and rituals)?" "Is Adam really (really was often used in their thought process and expressed in their speech in hopes that I might vacillate and give them any equivocal opening for their intended problem identification and solution) ready to be part of us?" (What was not said out loud was, "We do not think he is.") And, finally, their punch line, "Would he be better educated with his own kind?" (a phrase that always raised a huge red flag for me). It was another reorganizational point in Adam's development. I had to choose to follow their direction and put him in their institution "for Adam's own good" or find a way through that obstacle. There were many obstacles, and they created most of them.

None of these questions came from the perspective of, "Do we want to welcome people who are different from us in our group as the law required?" They were a little surprised when I asked, "Are you ready for Adam? How will you accommodate Adam's new rhythms and rituals in what you seem to consider your group, which is also my neighborhood public school?" It was a moment of inevitable friction.

The school system, still based ideologically on the 1869 "separate-but-equal" doctrine, by encountering Adam and I was being required to understand and practice the 1954 Supreme Court's doctrine that still required inclusion 30 years later. Just how long did they need to prepare to follow the laws of the U.S.? This really wasn't even an obstacle. The only true obstacle was the school system.

Like church, Adam's and my involvement compelled these systems to examine what their purpose really was. Is church a place where people go to sit quietly and separately to listen to music and be told about who Jesus used to be and how God is unknowable? Or, is church a place where people come together to affirm their relationship with Jesus and to experience God's grace through collective submission and affirmation that we are one body, one people? Is it the one place where everyone belongs?

Adam's kindergarten school was compelled to come to terms with their purpose, their reason for being. Was it solely to teach children the three R's—to read, write and do arithmetic? Or were they, more importantly, intended to create conditions for our children to learn to live together, work together and solve problems together? Their first answer would be, "We do the 3R's." That is the reason the American education system is ranked 25th out of 34 comparable nations. Asian countries that also focus solely on academic achievement ranked 18th. Canada, which ranks number 2, focuses on both how to work together and how to learn.

We got Adam enrolled in kindergarten. I wanted to tell them how lucky they were going to be because Adam would create a condition for them to reorganize their system and move from their current U.S. style of instruction producing the bottom 1/3 of achievement in the world to a Canadian style creating a condition for children in Grand Haven to excel to the number two ranking in the world. But I did not. And they could not hear me had I even bothered to say this to them. They were already overworked and underfunded, and Adam's presence would require more of them. It was America, not Canada, and they were required by law not to discriminate, but they would keep their prejudice. They could no longer say, "We do not accept retarded children in our *regular* schools" because that was discrimination. What they could say was, "We think Adam would be better served in our *special* facility with its *special* teachers and its *special* programs where he would be safer and more comfortable *with his own kind.* You know, sometimes children can be cruel to children like Adam. Sometimes kiddos like to start fights because they get too frustrated and we want to protect Adam from them." This last tag line was intended to move the conversation into their direction, but it also carried the underlying message of segregating Adam so he wouldn't get angry and hurt other children. It was difficult for me to believe that they thought they were being kind or acting concerned for my son, but I said, "Thank you for creating such a wonderful place for Adam in your *special* facility, but when do we start preparing for Adam to go to school here? Will special teachers come and help the school adapt?" I did not want to create friction or make them uncomfortable, but I had seen and experienced what inclusion looks and feels like and I knew my son deserved nothing less. It was better for everyone (except maybe some of the teachers). I saw differences being celebrated and welcomed in Canada and I was hungry for that in Grand Haven, Michigan. But, I did not live in Canada; I lived where differences were too often experienced as a problem to be contained not solved. The "problem" people were grouped together and separated from the mainstream.

Regrettably, in 1989, few schools took the time or even had an opportunity to observe themselves and reorganize their way of doing things so that they could become better. In fairness, they had never done what I was asking: "allow" (their words) or "welcome" (my words) a child with Adam's neurological anomalies into their lives. Martin Luther King, Jr. said that we fear the unknown and those we are not familiar with. Adam and I were their first, and so we scared them. We were many peoples' first encounter with inclusion, and often it was uncomfortable for them. Adam and I just kept playing through.

After I had returned from my first trip to Canada, Jetta suggested I share my experience with the school. She was a school social worker and knew the district special education services was having a retreat to talk about new educational paradigms. She still held her optimism, or more likely, she wanted to introduce new ideas to them but not have them come from her. I was already their pariah.

I went and, of course, they were not interested. I thought I was invited to share my experience in Canada, but they did not want to hear that inclusion was working. I explained what I had seen and what the students and teachers had shared. They said it would not work in Ottawa County and asked if I could teach them the techniques necessary to guarantee success. What were they supposed to do when students became aggressive? Could I guarantee other students would not lose valuable instruction time? Why should they change the services they had developed and abandon their new center-based program that cost millions of dollars? After all, the building was only six years old, and they built it so parents would feel comfortable that their child was safe. I smiled. I understood how they thought and they confirmed that I did not belong among them.

When it was over and Jetta and I were alone, she said, "Be nice" and laughed. I laughed with her and said, "None so deaf as those who will not hear. None so blind as those who will not see." In the end, she had succeeded in introducing them to what was coming, not to change them really. She knew it would take more than current research and best practices shared with them. As Jetta and I had agreed, I would be the bad guy.

Mary A. White Elementary School

For three hours every day, Adam went to kindergarten. He went to school with his own kind—the kids from his neighborhood. But doing normal things was not seen as normal at all. Although they offered to pick Adam up early to and from school in the special education bus to avoid problems, we walked to school so that he would not be isolated from the normal comings and goings. Adam needed to learn how to manage the typical chaos. His teacher also had an additional aide in the class room.

Bill O'Neal, the Special Education Director, and I had become friends by now and he called me one day and told me that I was expecting a lot from the teachers and staff. They had to work very hard to relate to Adam and to help other students relate to him. After all, his IQ was so much lower than theirs (40 points).

I confess, it was probably my old childhood experience of wearing the dunce cap and sitting in the corner that made it impossible for me even to listen (as Jetta had instructed), but I lost my patience. All the *kind* doctors, nurses and professionals stood out in my mind, and I just could not muster sympathy for the helpful professionals and how difficult their life was. Nor could I keep my mouth shut. Why should I be thankful and grateful that they were willing to deal with my son?

Because Bill was my friend I wanted him to understand my perception. I began my litany: "You and his teachers are 40 IQ points brighter than Adam. Given this superiority, I would expect all of you to find a way to relate to him." It was the tone in my voice that alerted Bill that something was coming. I have been told my tone is unsettling. I speak more slowly, articulate more clearly and just a little softer than my typical conversational volume. I have been told they seem like they

Adam in kindergarten at Mary A. White Elementary School

come from my toes and though they are not spoken forcefully, it is clear there is a force within me that is their origin.

Bill got defensive, he said, "We are finding ways to reach Adam, but it is a lot of work."

I asked Bill, "Is it not the same work I have to do every day?" In an effort to console me, Bill said, "I know it's difficult being Adam's father." He had misjudged the origin of my frustrated efforts. He assumed I was being challenged by my son and was frustrated, but it was his moment to see the world from another perspective: "No, Adam is easy! I am 40 IQ points brighter than you and his teachers. The difficulty is having to wait patiently for you to get the point. The difficulty is having to smile and reinforce your reluctant efforts without condescension or sarcasm, to wade through their tediously concrete thought processes and excuses for just being slow and unmotivated and seemingly unwilling to think beyond what they have always done. Their intellectual limitations and condescending attitudes are without merit, and I am tired of having to take care of them, spoon feed them ideas, tell them about how Canada did it every day and all to deaf ears and closed minds. I am restrained by Jetta to keep from reminding you have had 30 years to prepare for this moment I had none. As for Adam, Dr. Temple Grandin wrote about her struggle to belong and how difficult and painful it was for her. Adam equally has to struggle. He is forced to sort through their jumbled emotional states, lack of clarity of instruction and general distractedness. Adam and I volunteer to do our work; it is their *job*, they get paid."

I spoke the unvarnished truth, but I could see the pain in my friend's face. Bill was a caregiver, but his special training weighed heavily on him and kept him more restrained in his thinking about inclusion than he or I wanted. He wanted to embrace this new perspective but he had the weight of 20 years of how it was always done and a staff fearful they would fail. Additionally, he had an entire special education staff afraid they would lose their jobs. He wanted to let go of his old perspective, but did not expect to have it torn from his person by me.

Bill physically winced, moved back noticeably and said, "Please do not to talk with any of the teachers about how cripplingly slow and plodding you experience their thinking." Then he added, "It might be a good time to include Jetta in our discussion." I agreed.

When I told Jetta about my failure to be kind, she started to lecture me then simply said, "You forgot to be nice." Bill, to his credit, had recovered and even recognized how the pity he expressed to me burned my soul as much as my response had burned his. We had enough respect for each other to continue being real in spite of our frustrations, but not let them move us away from what was best for Adam.

And this process was not about my being nice. It was about our son, Adam, getting what he needed and what the system owed him according to the law and according to God. I assured Jetta that I would play nice, but I would not sacrifice Adam for the sake of his teachers. This was about creating conditions for our son to learn to get along and to belong in the common culture. Jetta responded by adding my own phrase, "Yes, but *do no harm.* Whatever you do for Adam has to be done without hurting anyone else or transforming environments beyond their limits. Being smarter, more informed and more able is an obligation, not an entitlement." She was very good at reminding me of my own words. And she was good at compelling me to act impeccably, not just talk about it.

This was another growth point for me. The end of any idea of sides—*we* and *they* thinking—had to disappear. It was not something to beat Bill over the head with. I could no more force the lesser among us to comply with *my* truth than they could be allowed to use force to overpower our son. Ouch!

By the time Jetta joined Bill and me, we had already both refocused on Adam and let go of any offense but had gained some new understanding. Bill finally got that Adam was not a burden for me. Jetta, Bill and I met, and she reminded us that we were all responsible to take care of both Adam and the teachers. It could not be either/or ever again. No one could suffer or we were not doing our respective jobs. My first reaction to her statement was defensive: Why is it my responsibility to take care of the caretakers!? (I have since discovered that there are caretakers and caregivers. The Canadian teachers were caregivers.) Her answer was obvious: Because we are asking them to take care of our son. Knowing I must always lead by example with compassion and patience if I also wanted them to lead my son well, part of me wondered if had acted incorrectly in my conversation with Bill. It is so difficult to know how to create a condition for an entire system to move from away from an ideological position where it has always been. Jetta was correct, if it were not a cooperative solution, it would fail. I think I was also correct to give my friend Bill, the Director of Special Education, a shock. He and I knew my words were true. He also knew I intended him no harm. Active resistance is not passive, and when experienced in the moment, it may not always seem kind. I knew I must seek the path of cooperation, but I also knew I was clearing a path littered with intentionally placed obstacles that required me to remove them for my son and for other children, too.

This experience gave me some idea of how difficult it was for God to watch His Son suffer at the hands of fools. And what great compassion He had for them and for us to allow that. Jetta was more capable of that kind compassion than I was. I probably would have sent in a second flood with my tears and never started over again. What a piece of work is man.

It was a final transition point for me. Jetta reminded me of how she had felt the times when I moved too quickly to solve Adam's problem. She was left feeling inadequate. She asked me, or rather instructed me, to work with the teacher at the teacher's pace so the teacher could learn to trust me and could feel empowered. Bill agreed.

Bill arranged for me to meet with Jenna, Adam's teacher and I listened to her as I would listen to Adam. I was present with my full attention and respect. My defensiveness and impatience were left in my backpack. I discovered she was a very good person and a good teacher for typical children. She had been systematically excluded from *special* children in her education and by the school district. She had never taken any classes in her school preparation about children with neurological differences. She had never even had a non-typical child in her classroom in all the years she had been a teacher. She wanted Adam in her classroom and thinking about him kept her up nights trying to find a path for both him and for all of her other students.

We talked about over-stimulation in *all* kindergarten children. The special education consultant had talked about time out or telling the child to go and sit on a chair until they could be good. From my own experience, I knew that punishment for being neurologically different only teaches contempt and hostility. It not only fails to teach or correct our children, but it injures the spirit. Punishment had taught me contempt for my teachers and to be ever vigilant for their next attack. Dr. Westendorp had worked with me to soften and even redirect my defense to assist others in unlocking themselves. As a therapist, I was quite good at this. As a father, I was quite good with Adam. Back in the environment where I first had to learn to defend myself and now having to defend my son, it was hard work! I was not always successful. Bill had had a small sample of the hard side of me. When Adam was present, and I would start, he would tell me to "be nice" (he learned well from his mother).

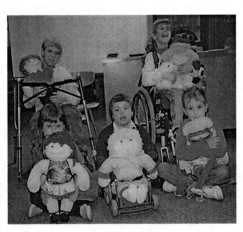

Teaching others about being different and the same.

Adam's kindergarten teacher and I decided on a different strategy. She rearranged her classroom into work stations. Student work groups would move from station to station and learn together. She combined cooperative learning and work stations beautifully. When she noticed any student getting overstimulated or too fatigued to relate, they were offered a refueling station—

always with a buddy. It was a quiet place in the room to give them the opportunity to refuel. It would also be a place where kids could go if they were finished ahead of others. She made a couple of refueling stations with adaptive ideas and manipulatives intended just for Adam. The community of kindergarteners was encouraged to invite a friend to refuel if they thought that was needed. The teacher just had to nod her approval. Everybody gained.

When Jenna, Adam's teacher, would be concerned about Adam in the classroom, I asked her to videotape so we could watch and learn. Every weekend we would watch the Adam Winstrom show after Sesame Street. We would watch and see what his best choices would be in each situation and I would reinforce him with, "Good job, good job!" until I could see the beginning of his path toward his best behavior in the moment. I would say, "Oh my! Is this Adam's best choice to do (and name the action he was involved in)?"

We would play "what else could Adam have done?" and play act through the more productive (beneficial, fun, most productive) behavior he or I could think of. Again, it was my adaptation of Carol Gray's "social story" idea. By doing this every Monday, Adam's behaviors were more akin to others in his classroom. It was a delicate balance between being Adam and blending in. She allowed videotaping so Adam could do his behavioral homework. Interestingly enough, she said letting the other children know that they were teaching Adam how to fit in with them allowed many to risk connecting with Adam. It went well with everyone showing their best behavior.

Through my studies, I came across a fellow in Florida with a Ph.D. who wrote about how classroom management and behavioral management were really curriculum issues and not a sub-specialty of how to make students behave. His bottom line solution was too easy: reinforce positive behaviors. He said all children like to learn and feel what it is like to succeed. He told me that for his research he made curriculum adjustments in the school and it eliminated classroom behavioral problems. Talking with him was very instructive. I shared some ideas with Adam's kindergarten teacher and helped her implement her version of what I had learned.

Although I knew what worked in Florida and Canada, when I introduced Adam's teachers after kindergarten to this concept, it often created friction. They felt blamed. They were not bad people. They were not stupid people. They were not uncaring. They were well-educated people who, like the rest of us, had no idea about what they did not know. Their behavior told me that what they could not imagine or and had never experienced was invisible to them and without great effort was unknowable, or worse yet, was something to be feared. The teachers had many years of experience in seeing segregated special education. They had no experience with inclusion. They did not want it and until I entered their lives most parents they dealt with did not want it. They all preferred the safety of the Center. Like Adam, they needed bridges to this new perception. They were all in the process of discovering the best ways to make friends, get along, learn and live together in a new environment, just like Adam. The difference between them and Adam is that Adam did not have to unlearn as many unproductive behaviors as they did.

Jenna, his kindergarten teacher, got it. Jazz was allowed in her classroom. She even played a little. My euphemism for living with a person with an obviously different rhythm for life is like taking a ballroom dancer into a jazz dance studio and letting them experience a new style of movement.

Today, if I could bring Adam back to visit Mary A. White, maybe they could understand why their position was so repugnant to me and so potentially harmful to my son.

Meltdowns

A meltdown, as I called them, occurred when Adam could no longer manage the stimulation he was experiencing. Neurologically it is caused by a cascade effect that occurs when the brain gets flooded by too much neural activity and shuts down the higher cortical functions to lower the stimulation. It was like a temporal lobe seizure and was an organic survival mechanism for Adam. Reason and logic are not available because the higher cortical functions are flooded and not available. They have been short circuited. Human brains are physical structures that function based on chemical balance and electrical balance. If either is off, behavior is more unique. If he was balanced, he was fine. For Adam, it was the electrical balance that caused the meltdowns. Too much stimulus would shut down his rational mind and only his more primitive neurological functions were available. The fight or flight level of operation of the brain stem, the Basal Ganglia, kicked in and until his brain could discharge the excess stimulation through that fight or flight mechanism, he was in survival mode. He did not want to be touched or talked to. It was unpleasant and chaotic to experience as an observer/companion to Adam. It could completely disrupt the environment.

I learned that I could not eliminate the meltdowns until I taught Adam to have a greater capacity to process stimulation. I had to create conditions to expose him to less stimulation until his brain could manage the activity better. It was not willful opposition; it was organic survival. Forcing him to stay in overstimulating conditions would only habituate the meltdowns. Punishing him or getting excited only added fuel to the meltdown.

Temple Grandin wrote about how her parents would pop a bag to make a loud noise to shock her into discharging her excess energy and returning to her own self-control. I had read about the old (and discontinued) practice of slapping seizure patients to interrupt a grand mal seizure. I preferred the gentle teaching model of nonphysical management. Moving with Adam or physically accompanying him but without touching or restraining is called non-aversive behavior management. I called it herding cats.

Behavior–An Attempt to Communicate

The summer Adam graduated from kindergarten I was invited to another non-aversive behavior management conference in San Diego and from there asked to spend two weeks at the Attachment and Bonding Center in Golden Colorado affiliated with Foster Cline. I also received an invitation to come to the Rocky Mountain Non-Aversive Behavior Management Center to learn non-aversive methods and to listen to Temple Grandin. I attended all three events and found all the approaches on behavior useful at different times.

The basket hold is a method of physical restraint that the school suggested I use when Adam had a meltdown. The person who had told me to try this added that I should be careful Adam didn't break my nose as he panicked and struggled. It knew this technique didn't work very well and it certainly didn't appeal to me, so I never did that to my son.

It wasn't until Temple Grandin told what a meltdown was—a loss of all security and containment—that I began to understand how useless words were in a meltdown. "No!," "Don't!," even my "Stop" ricocheted off Adam when he was "gone." Temple wrote about how her parents would pop a bag behind her and sometimes the startle response would reset and reconnect her. Sometimes a slap would work. I had read about both techniques working to interrupt an epileptic seizure, but to me, they seemed as wrong as the basket hold. Temple had invented a squeeze machine for her cattle to hold them and calm them and she said it also worked for her.

This all seemed to support the Attachment and Bonding Center's approach of the holding therapy. It was like Temple's squeeze machine but also vaguely resembled the methods that A. R. Luria used with his Russian soldiers with brain damage and had some similarities with and yet was very different than their basket hold. Holding therapy, attachment therapy or the Evergreen model was not complete restraint, but it was complete immobilization. It is holding until the child "melts into soothing." Adam and I did this together when I was too slow or simply unable to anticipate the world enough to create the conditions for Adam to explore but not get overwhelmed. Meltdowns came from emotional overloading. I learned that once the dominoes had fallen, it was too late to anticipate; all I could do was protect Adam and learn to anticipate better next time.

One fine and sunny day Adam and I went for a walk to learn about the world around our Grand Haven home. About three blocks out we were on the corner by the hospital when an ambulance took off with sirens blaring, lights flashing and at whoosh speed. Instant meltdown. With hands flailing and legs wanting to run, I had no chance to get Adam home. I grabbed him and sat down on the corner, well knowing that once one begins holding therapy, time disappears as the measure of life. You hold until they melt, hours if necessary. And hours it was. So long, in fact, that the police were called. I had been sitting for an hour with my legs crossed over Adam's. My arm was around his back pinning one of his arms down and holding his other hand. I cradled his head with my other hand and calmly told him over and over that I would hold him until he felt safe. Safe meant not resisting and melting.

The police came, lights flashing, voices excited, wanting (demanding) to know what was going on. They were there to *help*. I told them, "This is my son. He has Autism. He has been terrified by the ambulance, and I am making sure he feels safe and loved."

"Well, shouldn't you let him go?"

"Only if you want to try to catch him before he runs into the street or wherever he heads. I'm Dr. Winstrom if that helps you feel any better about what you see."

"What can we do to help?"

"Turning off your flashing lights would be a big help. And if you want to stay, you could hold Adam."

They left. After another hour he finally melted. We both got up and walked home, exhausted.

The difference between a basket hold and holding therapy is simple. A basket hold is intended to restrain. There is no eye contact, and you put the child in a bear hug from behind. When they stop struggling, you release them. It is hard to know if they have melted or you have just held them too tightly and stopped their breathing. Children have died in this restraint.

The holding therapy places the child on your lap and a little at your side. You make eye contact and can stroke and reassure the child. When I had to hold Adam this way, he would still be struggling and would yell "Go," short for "let me go," and I kept stroking Adam's chin and repeating "I want to let you go, but only when you are safe. You have to let me know when you feel safe and when I feel safe, too, we can go on." Adam could always move some and there was never any pressure on his chest to reduce his breath. He always knew I was there with him all the way. I was not the enemy holding him down; I was the shield protecting him until he felt safe. With opposition, it is best to agree to what the other person wants, but *only* when you are sure they are safe. They demonstrate their readiness by their relaxed body and calm mood.

While holding Adam on that street corner, I should have whistled Kenny Roger's song,

You've got to know when to hold 'em
Know when to fold 'em
Know when to walk away
And know when to run

Sometimes I would hold Adam, other times I could let him work it out of his system. Sometimes I knew we could "dance" together with a non-aversive kind of touch and release. There is no right way every time. After every meltdown, I would do a functional analysis to help me understand what happened. What was his behavior trying to tell me that I had missed? What could I have done differently? What skills did Adam lack to make it through those moments? What skills did I lack to support him? Then I would learn those skills and that resulted in us regrouping together. The more technical name for this process is functional analysis, sometimes called ABA (Applied Behavioral

Analysis). Both are structured ways for answering questions such as: What just happened? What was going on before this happened? Does this happen a lot? Does this behavior always occur? Does it occur in different situations? It is a way of understanding someone's physical communication (behavior) and is intended to assist professionals to get away from the "whose fault is it—punish them" approach to improve communication, so a meltdown does not have to be repeated.

First Grade PTA Invitation

I thought I might breathe again. My Ph.D. was completed, a dual major in Clinical Psychology and School Psychology, quite an accomplishment for someone with severe Dyslexia. Adam was in his local school. Jetta was a school social worker in Holland, Michigan, a job she loved. Just when I thought I might breathe freely, I received an invitation from the Parent-Teacher Association (PTA) of Mary A. White Elementary School.

When I arrived, I discovered this was not a "come join us as a new parent" invitation. It was "come be part of a discussion." The discussion was a motion to have Adam go to school with his own kind. And there was a 50/50 split. Half the parents wanted their child in Adam's classroom, and half wanted him out of the school. After all, Mary A. White was one of the top grade schools in Grand Haven—the very reason Jetta and I bought the house we did so Adam could go to the best school. The indirect suggestion of half of the parents was that if Adam had to go to an elementary school in Grand Haven and not attend the Ottawa Area Center as all the others did, then he should at least go to Central School. Central was in the poorest part of town with lots of transient students and difficulties. The other half wanted Adam to stay and wanted their children in a class with Adam. Half of the parents apologized for having this meeting, and the other half wanted an answer.

Remembering Jetta's words, I thanked them all for letting me know of their concerns. I agreed to talk with Bill O'Neal the Director of Special Education that week and left. When I got home, Jetta asked how it went and what the meeting was about. I told her they were concerned about the quality of education and that I would do my best to assist them. The school was my job, not hers, and I was nice.

First Grade—Adam is 7

The desks were all in a row, and it was quiet time when I went to visit Adam's classroom. He was in the back of the room with his aide attached to him. That day he had been pulled out for speech therapy, physical therapy and occupational therapy before I got there. The school had implemented a new math curriculum where the students would all take their chairs into the hallway, and the entire school did the math together. Those who achieved good grades moved up to the honorable chairs near the teacher. The race track on the board from my childhood was again made real to me. I could see that jazz would not be recognized as an allowable form of expression in this ballroom and that Adam would not do well in this setting. It was loud and confusing and blew Adam out. Adam's teacher had a good heart but had no idea how to create an inclusive environment for him that would allow him to succeed in his own way.

"Every teacher must learn how to teach every new student," were Jetta's words to me. Jetta had been a school social worker and had to support many teachers while they learned how to relate to new students every new school year. This was one of the most difficult processes for me. But, Adam and his teacher had to find their way together. I did not want anything more special for Adam than I would want for the rest of his classmates, and knowing this style is not useful for anyone's learning style made me a lot more kind and patient as the failures began to occur.

The first-grade classroom, recess and gym did not go as well as kindergarten either. Adam was scheduled for speech and physical therapy that both removed him from his classroom. In the classroom, the teacher and aid were not receptive to me; they were getting their support from the special education consultant who knew it would be better if Adam were with his own kind.

I had a conversation with the gym teacher who said Adam was failing gym. He would be able to participate in the class for about ten minutes before he would run to the end of the gym and go behind the wall mats. She was frustrated. After all, she had allowed him into her class and treated him just like everybody else. She said she was doing just what I had made them do, put him in regular classes and treat him like a normal student and it just was not working. She was giving off the subtle message that he would be better off with his own kind. I asked her if she saw a pattern in his behavior during gym, hoping we could share ideas about what to do to improve Adam's performance. I asked if she would she consider adding ear muffs, so the sound was not so overwhelming. She said, "No," then she got a serious look on her face and said quietly, "I think he would be better off with his own kind."

"His own kind?" I asked.

In a whisper, she said, "I am afraid so."

And I asked just as quietly, "Where is the school for children of bald psychologist Mensa member's sons?" Her reaction was like the *kind* doctor—she made a silent retreat back into her gym.

They all liked Jetta best. I could have handled that better, but sometimes I just couldn't, and frankly, when I did it better, nothing changed. My observation was that once someone has decided on a course of action or has invested a lifetime developing a belief system, change only occurs as the result of a disorienting shock.

Adam's teacher wrote me a note a few days later saying Adam was pushing in line. I wrote back asking if she had instructed Adam how to stand in line. Then I asked her what time of day? What line? What happened before he pushed? Who did he push? What happened after he pushed in line? I needed to do a full functional analysis to know why Adam was pushing in line now and what his behavior was communicating.

She wrote back that she didn't know the answer to any of these questions but would tell Adam to stop pushing in line.

I wrote back, "Sure thing, right away" then I went in to talk with her. The thing about behavior is it happens for a reason. It is not random. It is communication. It is learned.

A few days later, Adam's teacher told me that the pushing was happening during the outside recess line. So, I went to school at recess time and watched Adam. I was far enough away that he not noticed me. When it was time to line up to come back into the classroom, Adam was invited to line up by some kids in his class. Then, as more kids came to line up, some lined up behind him, and others cut in front. I could see a couple of children reacting to the squeeze effect and when the line began to move and compressed in anticipation of entering the building. I watched Adam push the child in front of him. It seemed to me Adam was being included by some of his classmates, mostly girls. He was being challenged by some of the boys. This is normal as boys often are working on their power and control issues and girls are working on their inclusion/exclusion issues. But Adam was my son. Adam was the different one. It did not matter what other boys were doing, Adam was being noticed by the adults. I learned when I was playing football that it is usually the second guy to throw the punch that gets flagged. Adam would never understand that tactic of boy behavior. I preferred he learn cooperation and inclusion, typically girl behaviors, along with kindness, compassion and being polite. Girls would like him more, and he would have more friends on this path.

I met with Adam's teacher after school when I came to pick him up. We talked with Adam, but I had the impression Adam was not really taking in the instruction. I said to Adam's teacher, "How about putting Adam first in line? Then there would be no one to push."

She thought my suggestion rewarded Adam by making him first. She preferred he was last, so he would not get squeezed. Out loud I quietly said, "and the last shall be first," and knew this was not the place to press that point.

She thought for a moment then said, "You're right, he should be first." Then she added, "I'll talk to the whole class about how I want them to line up for recess and have them practice lining up in the class room before we go outside." It worked.

She surprised me. She had let go of Adam "getting away with something" and solved the problem. And she added instruction. That was a good day! She surprised me again when she came up to say hello to Adam and me in church a week later and let me know that her special education consultant had not agreed with our solution, but it was working. I did not know she went to the same church as Adam. I also surprised myself. I rarely quote Scripture, and that verse had just come out.

Overall, it was not a very good year in school. Too many "pull outs" for speech and physical therapy instead of being included in the regular classroom activities and almost always at the worst times, but Adam was included in hallway math, gym and recess.

At home, with security and routines, our family grew together. With the amount of continual effort that I had to put into getting the school to include Adam, I was about to give up by the end of the first-grade school year. Then Adam's teacher asked to come to our home. She wanted Jetta and Adam there, not just me. She was tearful, and Adam got her a Kleenex. She said this was the worst year teaching she had ever had. She had never not been able to relate to a student. She had asked the Principal if she could teach second grade and have Adam again. This time it would be different. She would have stations

School friends

in the classroom for speech therapy, occupational therapy and physical therapy with student support. It took a year of suffering through to come to this and honestly, I didn't have much hope for change, but Jetta always had hope and said, "Yes." As the teacher and Jetta chatted on, Adam and I left.

Second Grade—Adam is 8

The following year, the PTA had not resolved anything about wanting to move Adam to a different school, and I was tempted to not return to Mary A. White, but we really wanted Adam at that school, so we stayed. I thought it was their fight, not mine. Half of the parents wanted Adam to be there, and the other half did not. There was nothing I could add because I was Adam's father. I had sent Bill a note offering to hire a consultant whom I had met in Colorado at their State inclusion conference. Rosemary had worked in Michigan before she moved to Colorado and knew Jetta and Adam. Bill knew her as well and agreed that it would be a good option to have her come in and meet with the PTA. She agreed to come in for a week of meetings with teachers and the PTA.

The first special PTA meeting she attended she talked about inclusion and its benefits. She observed that there was a split in the parents—those who wanted to compromise and those who wanted Adam in a special school with his own kind or at least at Central School, which was more suited to who he was. The consultant observed that most of the staff were interested in having Adam gone. It weighs on one's soul to know one's child is unwanted. I had to focus on the glass being half full of those who wanted Adam to be with their children. The staff would be the tipping point. If they continued to work to get Adam out of Mary A. White, that would collapse the system and create too much difficulty for Adam.

Although Adam's second-grade class was filled with kids who wanted to be with him, there was still the majority of teachers who did not want Adam in their school for his sake or for the other children's sake. Once again, Wolfensberger's institutional model was alive and well in Grand

Haven. The special educational consultant found a way to "get to" Adam. She set up a computer class where he would do very well.

The prior 15 years before Adam arrived, I had lived my life nonviolently as Gandhi had intended. I leaned toward a passive approach to conflict. I had worked in hospitals doing alternate service, helping the sick and injured instead of shooting the enemy. But ever since Adam was born, I was in one struggle after another. I did not enjoy taking others apart, but I learned that I was very good at it. My ability to recognize the different "I's" inside another human being and to connect with each one of them allowed me to clarify and unify their fractured selves. As a therapist, my ability to take people apart was appreciated. But doctors, nurses, social workers and especially teachers did not like it.

Bowling

The best part of second grade was bowling. I was informed that the "in thing" was a bowling party and that Adam would be invited. I thanked the little bird for letting me know. Bowling, like gym class and basketball games, was held in a large non-acoustical shell. The large room was incredibly noisy and chaotic and made for a guaranteed meltdown environment. So, we started preparing using the Sesame Street model. We drove by the bowling alley. We walked in and walked out of the building. We walked in and stayed and had a snack. Eventually, we spent quite a long time in the bowling building and started thinking of the sounds as joyful noises. Then we learned to bowl. I hired the local pro to teach Adam every day for an hour after school. By the time he was invited to a party, he was a very good bowler. His genetic differences gave him the gift of repetitive motion—the bowling ritual. And the unintended consequences of being a regular at the bowling alley were the girls.

Girls at that age are practicing their relationship skills. They descend in packs for protection and practice flirting and mothering. It is innocent, but it did capture Adam's attention. Adam was clueless about how to respond. His first attempts were loud noises, a typical male testosterone response. He got attention, but not the kind he wanted. He asked me, "Dad...girls...meet them?" I told Adam I was too old and not old enough to get girls for him.

I did teach my son how to meet girls—quietly and respectfully and to support their best selves. I taught him to be polite and listen more than talk, to compliment them and give them room to come as close as they were comfortable but never to crowd or pursue them. He learned the joy of friendship and connection. We dedicated a lot of time and practice on encouragement. It is useful as a connection to boys and girls. It took him a long time, but he got it. He really mastered encouragement.

Caretaker, a "Special" Trap

The special computer class was just before lunch. It was taught by the special education consultant. I should have known better. Bells and loud noises were difficult for Adam. Fire drills were always avoided. Adam was in her class, and I got a call to show up immediately because Adam was out of control! I was at the school in five minutes and ran in and asked where Adam was. She told me he was in a safe place, but we needed to talk. I asked again where my son was and she took me to her closet and opened the door. There was no light, and there were glass cups and dishes on the shelves and Adam was shaking his head back and forth and flapping his hands in an autistic meltdown. She had managed to drive Adam so far into his own world that in his mind he no longer was in the closet; he was in Adam land. It took me 20 minutes to reconnect with my son. I got Adam calmed down, and we left. I promised her I would return.

The next day I found her in her preparation time and asked her to tell me what had happened. She said Adam was out of control and she had to lock him up. I asked again for a step by step recount of what happened. She told me Adam was at his computer, then he just got up and slammed the door to the room and yelled, "Shut up!" and went back to his computer. She thought he was going to destroy the computer, so she grabbed him, and he struggled, and she locked him in the closet.

Adam playing with his classmates

What happened next was not my proudest moment. I repeated her story but added some details I had been told by a couple of parents who had called me the night before and told me what their children said: "Adam was at his computer, and the lunch bell went off, and the classroom door into the hallway was left open. The sound was intense, so Adam got up, said, 'Shut up!' and closed the door. Then he returned to his work. He did not in any way actually do anything to the computer but type. Next, you grabbed him forcefully, and he resisted. You locked a child in a closet without proper safety measures and in total disregard for his well-being."

She responded, "The problem with Adam is that you never punish him!"

My reply was the not correct side of me, and it is burned into my memory, "My son was not violent or aggressive. He was scared. You were the aggressive one and inflicted harm on a child. Although my son is not violent, *I am!* This will never happen again, ever. The Principal should give you an extended time out."

I should not have told her I was a violent man, but that was my instinctive response to a bully.

The Caretakers Revenge

It was a week later when I was again called to the school in another emergency for alleged violent behavior. She was building her case. This time it was in Adam's regular class. The accusation was he had stabbed a little girl. The special education consultant was not around but had filed the report.

This time Adam was still in his seat, and the girl was talking to him. My rebuke to the special education teacher had half of my desired outcome—at least no one had grabbed Adam or locked him in a closet.

When I got to the classroom, I heard Adam's friend saying, "I know you didn't mean to hurt me." I asked the teacher to join me to listen to the little girl. The school, afraid of my filing a possible lawsuit for assaulting my son, allowed me in the classrooms to deal with him. I asked the girl to show me what happened—I would be Adam, and she would tell me what to do. She told me to get up out of my seat and go to the pencil sharpener with my pencil. I did what she instructed and started putting the pencil in the sharpener when she said, "No, the other way. Pencil point out, not eraser end out. This is why I stopped Adam." Then she showed me she had reached for the pencil and the point of it had punctured her finger.

I showed her my scar on the first finger of my left hand from 3rd grade when I had done the same thing to Bobby, a classmate with Down syndrome. We had matching pencil punctures. By now, Adam was curious and was listening. He said "twins" and went back to work at his desk.

The teacher said she would remove the caretaker's report of Adam being "violent" and I talked to the class with Adam there. We talked about being helpful and how to support Adam rather than physically direct him—to invite him but not pull him. We talked about how if Adam seemed upset to step back first and wait ten seconds before they approached him so he could be done with his hurt and ready to connect to a friend. Adam's meltdowns were intense but momentary. The kids always got it better than the teachers because the kids wanted Adam to be with them.

It was okay, but it was not over. I knew that.

Jetta and I had a meeting with Bill to try to figure the best way to address the growing concerns of his staff, parents in the PTA and

what was in Adam's best interest. The moral and legal issues were clear: Adam belonged at Mary A. White. Bill agreed completely, but the issue was how to bring his "special educators" and the vocal 40% of the parents into that reality and into accepting Adam in his rightful place among all children.

Inclusion was working as each day more children were connecting with Adam in just the way we had hoped. The kids were playing basketball and enjoying outdoor time. That was working. In the classroom, the staff was slowly learning, but there was strong resistance within some of the staff, and parent notes and meetings were occurring with the aim of getting Adam out. It was not an issue of good vs. evil or right vs. wrong; it was the price in human suffering that social change costs. This was something I had not recognized. Letting go of one's sense of how the world is in terms of values, morals, status and belonging does not shift because the Supreme Court orders the transformation. It occurs from exposure and support from the pulpit and the PTA and from neighborhoods where all children play together. It had not happened before in Grand Haven. My naïve expectation that having God and the court on our side would allow that change to occur. It did with the children but not with the adults. They were frozen in 1954.

Bill did not want to see Adam pushed into becoming a "behavior problem" locked in closets or pulled out of classes, and he could not change his staff's thinking, so he asked to meet with us. It was not an easy meeting to consider changing schools. None of us wanted that to happen, but between the three of us, no one knew how to stop it. I had heard of a Montessori school in Spring Lake and was hope filled that it would be a possibility. For Adam and all the children and parents who supported us, I was and still am eternally grateful because Adam made some friends for life at Mary A. White. I told Adam he was graduating to a new school. He was always happy to meet new kids. We made the change at the close of the school year.

Chapter 11
Changing Schools

Out of the Frying Pan

I remembered from my research in Educational Psychology that Maria Montessori was a strong proponent for educating children with disabilities and that she initiated educational reform in the treatment and education of "mentally handicapped" children. The roots of Montessori education came from her observations and education of children with disabilities when she was a co-Director of the school for children with mental challenges. She had developed her curriculum with children like my son, so I thought a Montessori school would be just the place for Adam. No more endless questions or challenges to my son's belonging. No more questions from teachers asking how to teach Adam. Here was a curriculum designed with him in mind.

But the Montessori model of learning had been moved on to typical kids and was forgotten as a viable way to teach children like Adam. In Michigan, Cruickshank developed special education programs for students with a learning disability by practicing with children with Down syndrome and then utilized the perfected techniques for gifted and talented children. But, the public school no longer utilized these methods for children with Down syndrome. They were simply used as guinea pigs but never got to benefit from a better teaching model. Even so, knowing that Montessori was designed with Adam in mind, Adam and I would try it. Bill agreed. Jetta agreed. The switch was all set to occur over the summer.

I contacted the local Montessori school to see if we could work together. They told me their Montessori school was in danger of losing their building and would have to close. I made them a deal they couldn't refuse. I bought their building so Adam would have a school to go to and charged them a fair rent that we traded for tuition. The first year went okay, and Adam made some lifelong friends like Hanna there.

Hanna's First Memories

My first memory of Adam was at Walden Green. He was chasing everyone on the playground and attempting to pinch them. I ran until I couldn't run anymore, my adrenaline was pumping, I was pinned to the fence and bracing myself for the incoming pain. As he ran up to me, fingers in pinching position, I looked at him and said, "Stop." He stopped, looked at me, and then I grabbed his hand, and we ran around the playground. He never pinched me again after that fateful day, and we never stopped being friends from that day forward. I remember numerous birthday parties, pie fights, trips to the bowling alley, swimming everywhere we could, spinning in the blue chair in your living room while watching Wheel of Fortune. I remember feeling intense jealousy when he first started hanging out with Taylor because I felt like she was stealing my best friend. There were so many nights that I would cry thinking that Adam was going to choose her to be his best friend and we wouldn't be friends anymore. All I knew was that Adam was one of my friends just like any other student there. He sat by me during circle time, we played outside at recess, he attended all my birthday parties, and we hung out a lot after school and on the weekends. There was a learning curve for both of us at the beginning of our friendship, but that is the natural progression of any relationship—learning about one another. Adam was my friend. Then, I grew up to realize that Adam was everyone's best friend, and he made everyone feel like that. It didn't matter how much time passed between visits; he would embrace you and carry on as if you were the only person in the world who mattered. I don't know another person in my life with that skill.

Hanna was one of many people who, out of frustration or fear, made a direct connection in the moment. The other kids on the playground were playing their version of keep away. Adam was trying to connect in the only way he had figured out to get a reaction. If he pinched, he was recognized and his behavior forced interaction. It was not what I taught him. It was not what I wanted. He did not pinch at home. The "catch me, pinch me" ritual evolved at school. The running and loud response was much more reinforcing than a lecture would interrupt. I had asked the school to teach what they thought was appropriate playground behavior. They told me it was recess, free time from instruction. They told me the kids all figured it out on their own.

Except for kids with Autism who do not initially generalize behavior from one physical setting to another. What Adam learned on the playground with me at Mary A. White would not likely be what he did at Walden Green. And it wasn't. Before Hanna naturally found a solution for her and Adam, the school had called and told me that Adam was chasing the other kids around the playground and pinching them. They told me to tell Adam to stop chasing kids on the playground and *no* pinching. If he didn't stop, he would lose recess privileges. It is easy to teach a new behavior. It is difficult to stop a behavior once it is ingrained, especially if it has become a ritual. Chasing and pinching were already a ritual by the time I was called. I suggested the school tell the other children to stop running and have them tell Adam to stop when he approached them. Then take his hand gently and have Adam join them in an alternate behavior than chasing and pinching. My typical dilemma with systems was that they would not create conditions to teach what was appropriate behavior for their environment but would waste no time punishing children who did not follow the rules that they did not teach.

Hanna instinctively did what was exactly right in the moment. Perfect. Some might say, "See, it all works out naturally." But the problems with this philosophy are many. If Hanna had not been exhausted from running and out of desperation was inspired to act in this way, she like many of the kids would have grown up being afraid of the Adam's in the world. Hanna gained a lifelong friend through the experience. A friendship that she shaped and that shaped who she became as an adult. Hanna now has her Masters in Social Work and works primarily with children. Taylor and many other kids became Adam's best friends.

Systematic Purging

That was Adam's first year at the Montessori school. The second year was a disaster. The owners of the school applied and got a charter school designation. That meant they were no longer dependent on private tuition because they received public funding. They decided it would be easier if they got rid of all the unique children. They began systematically purging all the unique students and recruiting new more normal students.

It got ugly. Parents of the children being moved out invited me to one of their meetings. They were not sure I could be trusted because I had been on the old school board until I resigned. They asked me why their children were being targeted now? Why now was it so important for their children to be moved into "special schools"? Walden Green was now a Michigan charter school and, like most charter schools, it was choosing not to provide support services. That was the reason to send their children off, back to their local districts. Many of the parents had interviewed this school like I had, when their local districts had failed their children. The other parents, like Jetta and I, had come to Walden Green because of their inclusive program. But now Walden

Green was a publicly funded school, and it would have to test every student and the level of achievement would reflect on Walden Green. The kids who did not test well had to go.

Walden Green was caught between their own mission statement to be a Montessori school where all are welcomed and a chartered public school where test scores determine funding and if they could keep their charter. That was why it was getting ugly. Walden Green's solution was to return the children whom they had welcomed back to their local districts "separate-but-equal" schools. Most choose to endure silently and leave. I had already "moved on once" and decided to stay and hold the school accountable to follow the law. I did not accept their idea for educating Adam after they began excluding him from other students and school activities. They relabeled him as emotionally impaired, not autistic or educationally mentally impaired. That shift allowed them to punish Adam and not instruct him. They could suspend him for inappropriate behavior (like hand flapping and shaking his head back and forth) that they considered disruptive to the educational environment. It was a setup. They had changed Adam's educational status without a proper Individual Education Planning Committee (IEPC) meeting.

IEPs at Walden Green Montessori

I requested an IEPC because they had improperly changed Adam's educational designation and his educational program. Tommy, their nepotistic administrator (with no degree and no experience) informed me that the school belonged to them. The IEPC process belonged to them, and that was it. He began making up rules and policies, none of which were written down. It was power without maturity.

In their environment, no one sat at desks; children moved freely within the building working on projects. Adam had an assistant, but they wanted her removed to encourage me to want Adam out of their school. They excluded him from ski club. They kept him from recess. They eventually separated him to a back room. I disagreed with everything including their educational reclassification. I told them that

Autism and Down syndrome do not just disappear. I informed them that their process was not correct or legal. I challenged their correctness and process of reclassifying Adam as having an emotional impairment. Had I allowed their change, Adam would have left their system without the protections he needed as he entered the next system I could find.

They informed me that the IEPC was their process and they could do as they choose to do. They told me I did not know anything about Autism and that they knew better. When prejudice is front and center, reason fails. It felt like I was back at the beginning when Adam was in second grade dealing with all the problem statements about what was wrong with Adam. "Adam can't...Adam won't...." I could agree with them that Adam was different, but they only focused on what he could *not* do. Systems use their power to limit possibilities and put people into categories that they created or established. It was not an IEP (Individualized Educational Plan) for Adam Winstrom; it was their convenient plan to move Adam out. The Montessori staff had decided that now that they had public funding, all the *Adam's* they had welcomed to build tuition should be back with their own kind in a special school. They no longer needed nor were charging tuition. The Walden Green staff were intentionally defining Adam's problems so that the solution would be special education in a special facility, not in their school.

Parallel Play

I did not support their new direction, their return to the special systems, still I offered them my support when they moved in any direction that supported my son. Adam had been exposed to downhill skiing since he was five years old. Jetta and I loved skiing and had hoped Adam would too. I had been a ski instructor and a National Ski Patrol. Jetta and I first met skiing. We had arranged for Adam to be exposed through the Challenged Ski Association when he was just five, and he liked it.

When the Montessori school excluded Adam from their school ski club because they thought the bus ride would be too much, I objected.

The club left school around noon and everyone went off together to ski. To get them to agree to include Adam, I offered to drive him to the ski area. Once there, I had expected them to do what they did for all the other students. He rejoined his classmates, and they all got skis on. I went to the lodge to let Adam be with his friends and was looking out at the beginner skiers expecting the group to be flailing about on the beginner's bowl with an instructor. But that was not what was happening. The aid which the school had sent along was directing Adam away from the group and toward the rope tow. I got up and started out anticipating what would happen next. Just as I got out of the door, I heard her yell, "Just grab it and hold on!" Adam had gotten into position and was letting the rope slide through his hands, just as he had learned before. He was not grabbing hold tight and quickly, the completely wrong way to get on a rope tow until she yelled at him and he did so. Adam was picked up and dragged out of his skis and up the hill until he did a full face-plant in the snow. There was no attendant on duty to stop the lift, and by the time I reached Adam, the rope was running over his back, and the aid was yelling, "Adam, what would Jesus do?" Adam was yelling, "STOP!" but nothing was stopping. No one was stopping the rope from running over him or stopping the aid from yelling, "What would Jesus do?" I got the rope off Adam and let it run on my back, so he did not get a rope burn and got him up on his feet. I dropped the rope back down on the snow and said, "Did you see what I did? That is what Jesus would have done." Adam was upset and looked ready for a meltdown. I asked Adam, "Ski or hot chocolate?" It took him a moment to regroup, and the hot chocolate won out. We gathered up his stuff, left the aid and went into the lodge. Later, I took Adam to the ski instructors area and asked about private lessons. The fellow behind the desk said he would be happy to arrange a lesson, but no instructors were here that day because a school was there and said they did not need any instructions. But Canonsburg Ski Area had a very good challenged ski program and instead of $35 an hour it was $5 if I made arrangements ahead of time. I set Adam up for lessons at the next school ski club outing.

As Adam and I sat in the lodge drinking our hot chocolate, we watched other kids being dragged by the rope tow. I kept thinking, WWJD? What kind of a response is that? There were no instructors and the kids' knit mittens were being shredded by the rope as they fell face forward in the snow and the rope ran over the top of them. From the safety of the lodge, I talked to Adam about how to get on the rope tow. The next week, I took him and gave him to the instructor. Adam really did like skiing. He also liked Cindy, the challenged ski instructor I had arranged lessons with. For his first class, I brought my own skis and we had a good time. I was even able to help some of Adam's friends learn their snow plow. Adam enjoyed skiing well enough that he and I skied Breckenridge in Colorado the next year while Jetta was working.

Being included was not always perfect. This was one of the times I chose to have Adam do parallel play and be in the same place as his friends but do a little different activity.

The Beginning of the End at Walden Green

I offered no support for any of their ideas that limited Adam's inclusion. I would not support Adam being systematically excluded, being kept in from recess or not be allowed to use computers like the other students. They had arranged to block Adam having access to Carol Gray the Academic Intervention (AI) Teacher Consultant assigned in Adam's IEPC. How they explained their keeping Carol out of their school was truly evil at work. They decided that Carol Gray was assigned to them and not to Adam. Even though Adam was the only student identified as AI and Carol Gray was the AI Teacher Consultant. They said they did not need her. Therefore, she would not be called to the school to observe Adam and make recommendations to improve their educational services to Adam. This topic was just one more of the many hearing issues.

When the Montessori charter school attempted to force services on us that would isolate Adam, I would listen and smile but would not sign their contract for services agreement. They would inevitably attempt to define the problem as Adam: Adam can't or Adam will not or Adam will be hurt or Adam will hurt others. All this led to their desired conclusion: put Adam with his own kind where he belongs!

When I would not agree with their plan, their reaction was, "We can have a formal hearing." So, I accepted their invitation to a couple of due process hearings. The hearing was a 4-month process. I had done my homework to prepare during my doctoral program and I attended a week-long training in Chapel Hill, North Carolina, one of the national centers researching Autism. They were also the place that created the best curriculum development based on their assessments such as the Treatment and Education of Autistic and Related Communication Handicapped Children assessment tool. That training week had the bonus of a weekend conference attached to it. Dr. Pennington, author of *Executive Function Deficits in High-Functioning Autistic Individuals: Relationship to Theory of Mind*, Dr. Byron Rourke, a researcher into Nonverbal Learning Disabilities and a research group from Harvard working with brain researchers at the University of Utah on early diagnosis and etiology of Autism were presenting. It was the perfect condition for me to have the most current information from the best national sources. It also gave me the opportunity to have dinner with Sir Byron Rourke (he had just received notification that he had been honored with a knighthood). I told him about Adam and the school, and he reminded me that culture in the United States had not embraced unique individuals as Canada had. To stay in my country and raise my son here would place me at odds with the culture I lived in. All the truth I may have about what would be most correct would only anger the systems I needed to depend on for my son's education. He was happy I had listened to my instinct and just loved my son rather than force him to be institutionalized. I returned to Ottawa County and the culture that did not support unique individuals.

My way of rebuking was to present the data through the due process hearing. The school engaged their attorney after I filed 26 complaints, each one a separate violation with the Michigan Department of Education as the first step in the process. The Department of Education conducted its investigation and made recommendations. The school did not accept the Department of Education's findings and requested a hearing. I was very specific with my complaints because the hearing officer can only address issues identified in the initial filing and I wanted everything included. The school hired their attorney, and I had to hire an attorney who specialized in school law. The next three months was the process of fact finding allegations and development of proofs. The Department of Education's investigation was very useful and provided my attorney with most of what he needed. Adam was to "stay put" while the hearing process was underway. That meant he had to stay at the Montessori school and they were ordered to provide the correct services.

In an effort to force Adam out of their school, they accused him of being destructive and breaking a computer keyboard. A few students who had become Adam's friends told me who really broke the keyboard and when that news got out, that phony charge soon disappeared. But it was quickly replaced with another lie. They were caught in their own web of deception. The hearing officer agreed with me and ordered them to pay for summer school to make up for not providing adequate educational programming during the school year. They were ordered to comply with the law allowing Adam full inclusion in the school. His educational designation was returned to Autistically Impaired (AI) and Educable Mentally Impaired (EMI).

The school had changed from an open, inclusive style back to segregation that systematically retards children because they were excluding them from natural learning environments. The old system was very good at producing young adults with institutionalized behaviors. Mastery-based instruction equally retards learning. Most curricula for children with cognitive challenges were based on scoring 85% on tests before any new information would be introduced. Like the Dummy Ditto's I had in grade school, there were no incentives to aspire to beyond the material to be mastered. It was the same system of instruction that made my third-grade friend, Kevin, give up and made me think that I was dumb. Typical learners are given instructional material two levels above their mastery as Soviet psychologist Lev Vygotsky recommended. Both Vygotsky and Wolfensberger proved that only inclusion in typical educational and social environments with supports that recognize a student's right to fail and learn were supported by best practices models.

The right to fail (Wolf Wolfensberger in An Overview of Social Role Valorization Theory by Joe Osborn) is sometimes a difficult concept to understand. In special curriculum, children master specific areas of information before any new information is added. It was called errorless learning introduced by B.F. Skinner. The truth is that what humans remember most are the mistakes they made that they corrected. Errorless learning does not allow mistakes to occur. The overlaying of mastery based and errorless learning were and still are a mistake. Holding back information until mastery occurs retards (slows down) the possibility to learn. When errorless learning is coupled with isolation, the next level of achievement cannot be observed, and the result is systematic retardation. The hearing officer understood or at least was more familiar with the Wolfensberger model more than the schools were. After the Montessori school, the problem was isolation and punitive behaviors.

Adam and I never lost either of our due process hearings. That is the reason, or at least what I imagine was the reason, that after the hearings, the school system identified me as the problem instead of Adam. They were fearful of losing again. They knew that I would not be silent about their practices that violated Adam's civil rights.

Still, they did not comply with the IEPC goals and continued systematically to isolate Adam. The last straw was a field trip to Chicago. They took him assuring me that he would be fine and would call if he was not doing well. He broke his foot the first day when he stepped off a curb in Chicago. They would not let him call home even though he was complaining of pain and did not believe his foot was really hurt. They felt he just wanted attention, so they ignored him. When I picked Adam up from the field trip, they told me how they had decided to deal with my son's attention seeking. On the way home Adam was still complaining that his foot hurt, so I took him to urgent care. They x-rayed his foot and put it in a cast.

At both the Mary A. White and the Montessori schools I had done what I could to support the schools. I had found consultants to train the staff and teach at the school and paid for the staff to attend training. The problem was their core belief system. Their hearts would not allow them to change their attitudes. Adam stayed home from school from that point on. It was dangerous for him to be with them and I reopened the due process hearing. They would not change. The hearing officer agreed that withdrawing Adam from the Montessori school was the best solution. He agreed that Adam would not receive the correct services there. He also agreed that it was not safe for him there and awarded us a money settlement instead of supervised school adaptation.

During the second phase of the due process hearing, Jetta and I had to shut the ringer on the phone off so Adam would not answer it and hear things like, "You belong with your own kind, not at our school." "Go back to where you came from; we don't want you." After a few more of those calls, I rerouted our phone number to an answering service to keep our son, who was very inquisitive and already drawn to the phone, from hearing their toxic messages. Some parents wrote editorials in the local paper wanting Adam in the school; others wrote letters about not wanting him. It was the same experience we had at Mary A. White all over again, only harshly public. At least the parents from Mary A. White were respectful of Adam even in their desire to have him go to another school. The parents from the Montessori school were not; they forced me to rebuke them, take my money and leave. They did not like me, and they did not want Adam to be in the school. No one likes the guy who tells everyone that the emperor has no clothes and I was exposing the school system's prejudice at every turn. They wanted me to just let Adam be a child with Autism and Down syndrome, and it would all go just like the helping professionals had told me: Ottawa Area School, Kandu, and later a group home. I just could not allow that to happen to my son. The charter school would never comply with the hearing officers ordered behaviors. I really wanted to go to Canada. I did not want to be a political or social cause; I just wanted to live and work in a community that welcomed diverse people, and I wanted our son to be included. The cost of social change was getting to be too much. The sad part of this collision was for the kids like Hanna. They could feel something was not right. Some could hear their parents talking about their good friend Adam. Hanna wrote:

> *I totally get that things were not how they should have been for Adam, and a lot of it I was oblivious to- due to my age & understanding of the world. If I could go back & change things for him, I would. I wish I could have changed things for him at that age, and I lived in ignorant bliss of it all. I just wish I would have been older & wiser when all of that stuff was going on so I could have been more of a friend & protected him. As a kid, you don't see that stuff or understand it the same way. But honestly, I didn't see Adam as any different than my other friends. He just needed to be shown how to play with us just like any kid learning a new game or in a new environment, and man, when he picked up how to be gentle & be a good friend, he perfected it & showed the rest of us how it was truly to be done.*

It is through Hannah's eyes and words that I know inclusion, even what I considered failed attempts, were not complete failures. On the child-to-child level, it was a huge success. On the adult level, it was not. That made the environment dangerous for my son.

Finding Our Way

Winning a battle is a victory, but not a solution. It was mid-year, and no public school would take Adam because the suit might get appealed, and Adam was still in "stay put" mode for the rest of the year. We were a potential problem for any school who accepted our son because we wanted him educated in accordance with the law—God's law and the law of the land. Both authorities agreed with what Jetta and I wanted for our son. The educational systems did not agree and wanted us to use their special system. Illegal, immoral segregation was their one offering. The school system did not appeal the settlement, but they kept the suit open until school was done. It was their last bit of power.

I home schooled Adam with a tutor for the remaining five months of the school year. Over the winter and spring, his academic achievement went from a 2nd-grade level to a fifth-grade level. He could read and spell better than I could, but he kept telling me that he wanted to be with other kids. My son with Autism wanted to connect. He wanted to sit in classes. He wanted to learn to deal with the confusion. He wanted teachable moments available to him to learn about being in the normal world—one filled with hate and limitations as well as love and possibility. He saw love and possibility in the world just as his mother did.

Temple Grandin's words were ever present with me during this time. Being neurologically autistic and socially autistic did not have to go together. She had found her own way to live with typical people, something people with Autism are not supposed to want. Temple said it would be difficult, even painful, for social systems and her to be together and I was prepared for that struggle. I was having difficulty even getting Adam into situations so he could do his painful work to learn how to belong. After prolonged exposure to neurotypical (normal) people, he would often break down and cry because it was such an emotionally overwhelming process. But he wanted to do the work. If the system would just let him.

I did my best and remembering the Christian schools in Canada, tried a Christian school in Grand Haven. I offered to have Adam's tutor accompany him to help him during classes. I offered to pay full tuition if Adam and his tutor could just use the library and attend for a partial day in selected classes like gym and art. They said "No." It was clear to me that Canadian Christians and Grand Haven Christians were not the same Christians.

That weekend I was to be a co-presenter at the Rocky Mountain State Inclusion Conference in Denver, Colorado. After one of my workshops, I had two different job offers, both in Oregon. I called Jetta, and we agreed that I would look. Perhaps Oregon would be open to having Adam included in their school system. Two weeks later, I was in Oregon interviewing and both jobs were offered. I began looking at houses in Klamath Falls, Oregon and found a 10-acre mini ranch on the top of a mountain. I checked out some schools, and they had been talking about moving toward a curriculum of inclusion. The whole process was moving fast. Jetta and I flew out two weeks later, leaving Adam with my parents, fingers crossed. When we got there, we found out that the realtor I had worked with had committed suicide and there was no record of where the ranch was. In addition, the school had decided to abandon inclusion and was moving back to a center-based program, and Klamath Falls had had their first and only earthquake. Wow! This was obviously not the answer.

We were at a loss and flew back home. All I knew was that I was not solving the problem. I did not know how to get beyond segregated systems. I was frustrated by an educational system that affixed blame, punished by withholding one's sense of belonging, failed to teach new behaviors, were blind to insight in any new situations that arose and never solved the problems. Kids don't drop out of school; they are pushed out by an educational process that numbs their minds and damages their spirit, a rigid system that leaves no room for alternative learning methods. It systematically underestimates potential and cultivates institutional adaptation leading to an undervalued lifestyle. It was 1994, and after ten years of pushing, pulling, prodding, supporting and suing the educational system, it was unchanged. I was ready to surrender and move to Canada.

We are instructed by our heavenly Father to teach our children well. The Bible talks to fathers about not aggravating or provoking their children or they will become discouraged. Canada got it. We in the US fail to listen. Our systems are set up on sand, not the rock of truth. Estranged from any core value, we punish our children for not learning and this is not teaching. Punishment provokes our children into failure. I regret I was as guilty as they as I punished the system for punishing children. I made my efforts to teach, but when I was not received, I ended up turning over the tables in frustration and pointing out that they were just into education for their personal profit. We went our separate ways.

A Well Pleasing Son

Adam and I volunteered as janitors in the church every Friday after school as our way of serving. When we would clean the sanctuary, I would hold Adam high and say, "This is my son in whom I am well pleased. I thank You for giving him to me." It was my way of affirming Adam and being thankful to God for the gift of my son. I also blessed Adam every Friday night at our family dinner.

One day when Adam and I were doing our janitor thing at church, Pastor Andy had observed me in the sanctuary blessing my son and thanking God for all He had done for us. Andy stopped me and asked, "Do you ask God to solve your problems or to make the world a better place?" I responded by saying that I thought that making the world a better place was up to me. Andy thought a minute then challenged me by saying that my faith was strong, but my surrender was weak because I did not ask God to make the world a better place for myself, my wife or for Adam. Adam and I loved and respected Andy, so I really thought about that. And no, I never asked God to fix the world. I never asked God to fix Adam because he was made just right. I figured He had made the world this way for a reason and who was I to ask Him to change the world for me? I also believed He had already answered any prayer I could think of, so I was always grateful. It was not my way to ask God for more than He had already given me.

Intellectually, I trusted God, but I believed I was responsible for how I lived my life. It was up to me to make a way for Adam to be included in school, that was my obligation, I just couldn't see how to do that very well yet. What I did not confess to Andy nor really recognize was that I did not *experience* God. I was still seeking that connection. I knew about God; I just felt like we never really met. He was in heaven, I was here, and the distance between us felt immense. I had my moments when I felt connected to everything, but those experiences were fleeting and never lasted. I experienced my connection to Jetta and Adam, and I knew we were connected.

Jim Kruis wrote a book entitled *Christ Without a Church,* and in it, I found simple truths to things that I was wrestling with. Jim wrote that God exists in a special way in that God is existence. God is one in a special way in that God is unity of all things. God blesses in a special way in that God does not bestow blessings on people for their actions or chooses who and when to bless. God is blessing all the time, and the closer one gets to God, the more blessing is experienced. Blessing is not earned or bestowed; it flows through His existence and the oneness of everything. It fit with my belief that God had already given me everything, and I understood why I did not yet receive the keys to solve my life puzzles.

My seeking had taken me far away from this truth. I had moved away from God looking so hard trying to find Him. Albert Einstein said men worship the servant, not the master. He was observing that we marvel and celebrate our own logic and reasoning, the tools he called the servants. Through our ego and our self-importance, we worship our tools and lose sight of the master, the consciousness, that it all comes from. Einstein wanted to know God's thoughts on how He created this world, He was not as interested in all the separate phenomenon and stated that those were less interesting details.

I had gotten caught up in the details believing that was the way to solve problems. I had worshiped the servant, not the master. I read and studied. I looked for God in church when I was younger but did not see any trace of a living God. I left organized religion, and I was looking within myself. I experienced no presence, so I had accepted that God had created me in His image and expected me to carry on. It was my obligation to reshape the culture to allow all people equal access. I imagined that I had to make the world better.

What I had to do was allow myself to be. I had to stop seeking with my mind and use Adam's way of first the experience, then make meaning. Just surrender my ego and my self-importance and observe what was already there for me. To accept I was the created, not the Creator. I had to trust I was not alone. I had to trust others and the world around me to offer the best condition necessary for every situation. What was required of me was greater observation and attention to the possibilities already created and to accept the blessings that were already there. All I had to do was move closer to my own impeccability and observe my existence as a microcosm, a fractal of my Creator and experience that relationship.

Adam's 10th birthday

Chapter 12
Zeeland Christian School

Surrender

That week I stopped seeking and creating, I surrendered my self-given assignment to fix the world. I got in my car and just started driving around and talking to God. I was not angry and not really praying—I was just having a simple conversation with God. "Okay, now what? I really don't know what to do. I thought I was doing my part in faith to honor You, but maybe I am missing Your point. I will stop focusing on my will and start listening and looking more." We talked like this for a couple of hours. He never spoke to me but was quiet and present. It was a complete unburdening. I talked and talked. I just never shut up long enough for Him to get a word in. I don't think I really expected God to answer my questions or solve my problem for me. I just aimlessly drove all over Ottawa County having what seemed like a one-way conversation.

It was time for me to stop and listen, so I pulled my car over to the curb. I closed my eyes and shut my mouth. I stopped my thinking. When I looked around I recognized where I was, I was in front of Zeeland Christian School. It really wasn't my intention to go there, but I had asked God, "Okay, now what?" and here I was. I had to do a little self-talking to accept that I might have been given an answer. I got out of my car, went in and asked to talk to the Principal. No appointment. No introduction. I was not really sure who the Principal was. His secretary just announced that someone wanted to talk to him. Then she said, "Mr. Van Dyk will see you now."

The Principal introduced himself as Bill Van Dyk. He asked me to sit down and then asked what I wanted to talk with him about. I told him about Adam. I told him about Jetta. I told him a shortened version of my story of our educational experiences. I told him about the schools in Canada and their Principal telling me that all children belonged. He never interrupted me. He never seemed impatient. He had closed his door, and it was as though nothing else existed for him but me and my story about my son, Adam. It was the first time someone listened to me without their own agenda. Well, except for the conversation I had just had with God. It was certainly the first time I felt like I was being listened to by a school principal. He didn't judge me for my attempts. He didn't judge other schools for their attempts. He did not judge the Christian school in Grand Haven. He just listened.

When I stopped, I realized I had been talking for more than an hour. Then Bill said that he believed in the same things I had experienced in Canada. What he did not say was that his classes were already full. He did not say that Zeeland Christian School served the Zeeland area and did not accept students from Grand Haven because there was a Christian school there. I found that all out later. Evidently, he believed that part in Matthew 25:40 and 25:45—the part the Christian school in Grand Haven had missed. He asked when would it be a good time to meet Adam and where would Adam feel most comfortable having Barb Newman and Jan DeJonge, his student support specialists, observe him doing some school work? I told him that the best place would be at Adam's tutor's home and gave him the time and contact number. After I left, he immediately made arrangements to visit Adam at his next tutoring session to evaluate what he needed and where he would fit into the Zeeland Christian community.

I confess that I did not doubt God, but I had a hard time believing what was happening. And after my experience with the Christian school in Grand Haven, I had little faith in Christians. Bill Van Dyk was different. Barb and Jan were different, and they asked different questions about Adam: "When is he most comfortable?" "What does he most like to do?" "How does he learn? By exploring, watching, or maybe reading about something?" "When he is afraid, how do you get him to relax and feel safe?" "When he is upset, what is the best way to approach him?"

I had always been very good at understanding others, seeing their problem and creating conditions to solve the problem. I could do this for others, but not for my son in school. For my own son, I could not create conditions for him to be successful. The educators did not allow me to help develop, modify or implement a plan. As Adam's father, I was not considered an asset and my ideas were routinely refused. Until now. Bill, Barb and Jan invited me to create a plan for Adam with them. Finally!!

A quick review of my record with the public schools showed that I was not batting 1000. I could see what was wrong, but I was never allowed to work with them. Even getting my Ph.D. so that I could write IEPC goals did not assure compliance. In the public school, there were always the special education consultants in the system who "knew it was best for Adam to be with his own kind" and they were always working for that purpose. It was painfully clear that if the school system does not want something to work, it will not work.

Dr. Grant, a professor at Grand Valley University I had studied under, once told me that public educational systems only change because of lawsuits, rarely because of a best practices model. He was right. I had tried to change them and ended up with money awarded from winning those lawsuits and a reputation as someone to be avoided—neither of which I wanted and neither of which helped Adam become successful in a school. I caused systems trouble because I knew school law and what Adam had a right to. All I really wanted was a community and an education for my son without a hearing officer ordering them to do the right thing. All they wanted was for Adam to be with his own kind in their "special community" and for me to go away.

After that day in Bill's office, I was different. After that day, everything was different. Pastor Andy once told me, "If you were not so invested in seeking, maybe you would discover that God is with you. If you were not so intent on making a path, you might discover that the path that was already laid out before you." At the time he said all that, I thought he was just saying some Rabbi paradox like "be still and know." I thought, know what? That the folks I was interacting with did not want my son to be included? I knew that was true in Grand Haven where Adam was shunned, but this time that was not what was happening. Until this moment, not belonging and being unwanted was the truth I had been told and was shown and quietly observed.

It took listening to Jim's understanding of God and having everything I had initiated fail. I thought I had been still but was like the man who looks everywhere for his glasses until he finally sits down and discovers he is already wearing them. I was always looking past God's presence in the moment. I had imagined that I couldn't see and was amazed at how clear the path was. Zeeland Christian School was the path laid out for my son.

I had known about Zeeland Christian since it began when Bill Van Dyk interviewed to be their first Principal. I was present at his interview representing the ARC (Association for Retarded Citizens until we changed the name to Advocacy and Resource Center), but I did not see it as a place for my son. Maybe it was because I lived 20 miles away in another city. More likely I was just blinded by wanting our local public school to be the place for our son. I think it was the result of the decision Jetta and I had made to stay in Grand Haven and work with the local schools to support their efforts to provide inclusion. It was clear that Zeeland Christian was the place I had been seeking but did not see. Bill and Barb and Jan, as well as all the other teachers and children, saw inclusion as their path. All I had to do was trust them. Maybe because it was based on their faith, but more importantly, inclusion had become their experience. Because of their experience, inclusion flowed unstoppable from their soul. It was their *normal*, who they were and what they believed in. Outside this island of belonging, inclusion was still new and untried in Ottawa County.

In the 40 years since the federal law had mandated inclusion, "it" (prejudice) had suppressed the implementation of the law. It was clear that the parents and staff at Mary A. White experienced being required to educate Adam in "their public school" with all the other kids as an assault on their rights. Adam and I were, by reputation, seen as problems, but the real problem was never understood as their own lack of heart. Their failure to want to include and having their sense of privilege challenged made them feel like I was oppressing them, forcing them to give up something that they believed belonged to them. Their right to *lovingly* segregate. After all, if what I had told them about inclusion and asked them to do was correct, then their monument to *kindness and protection for the retarded kids* or segregation in their sparkling new special school was no longer something they could point to with pride. It would represent a huge financial mistake and a moral failure.

Bill never talked about what he heard about me nor about what his board said to him. He welcomed Adam and Jetta and me. Everyone loved Jetta, that came easily. Adam had learned to wear down any resistance to his belonging. He was learning my best ways and had no scars. I was amazed, grateful and relieved by our welcome at Zeeland Christian. I was relieved of my self-imposed burden to create. Now, I only had to accept and support the right thing.

Canada in Michigan, Zeeland Christian School

Adam entered a school system that wanted him. They took a risk, and I took a risk. Historically, school administrators and staff knew me as either their best friend or their worst nightmare. At Zeeland Christian, they let me be their best friend. They made every attempt to teach Adam to get along with others and to educate him. It was not perfect, but it was a perfect effort. Because they really wanted Adam to succeed, I relaxed. It was like when Adam went to kindergarten, and his teacher wanted Adam to be successful. We trusted each other. That disappeared after kindergarten. Now, here, once more, they wanted

Adam to belong and succeed. They offered Adam all I ever expected, and he found a place to become part of a community. He made friends. It was third grade, not fifth grade, but it was a perfect fit.

Bill had suggested that Adam would do the best in his third-grade class, not in the fifth. I was reluctant to agree, but I trusted Bill. Bill was matching the community of the third-grade class and the best teacher personality to build community around Adam more than straight academics. I found out later that he only wanted Adam to have to be challenged socially as Adam had mastered third-grade curriculum. I also learned to trust Barb and Jan as they also created conditions for Adam to succeed.

Within his first week of school, there was an incident of an older student trying to bully Adam. In any confrontations, I had taught Adam to 1. Walk away; 2. Find a teacher to get help; and if those didn't work, 3. Solve the problem—punch the person once very hard in the face, then walk away. Bill called to tell me that Adam had punched someone and began telling me what happened. I got defensive and interrupted him, "I taught Adam to do that as his third option, not his first!"

Bill never flinched; he just continued his story and then said, "The boy's mother wanted me to thank you and Adam. She had told her son not to act that way, and he learned a good lesson. I looked into it, and Adam did walk away. He also talked to a teacher. Evidently, neither of those actions kept the boy from bullying Adam, so he punched the boy once and walked away. So, if Adam talks to you about this, it is all okay." This was such a different experience than confrontations at other schools!

I was grateful for Zeeland Christian School. The fact that Bill just accepted us. I found out later that he believed that God had directed me there. I didn't have to fight his systems to have Adam included and accepted, that was more than significant for me. I could see that God already solved the problem better than any of my past attempts had and certainly better than my attempt in Klamath Falls, Oregon.

Zeeland Christian had been available to Adam always, I just did not see that truth.

I was now able to see opportunity presented and no longer needed to create or manufacture the situation. I do not think I can really explain how this changed for me. I thought I had to "make things happen." To be responsible for my life and for my son. To act in the best way I knew, and teach Adam that same principle. That was still true but. But I discovered that I had to see in each situation the different potentially and naturally occurring possibility that would best work to create the best condition for everyone. I saw clearly that in every moment we have hundreds of choices to go down hundreds of possible paths. Each one is already there, but we do have to choose it and not another. I found my synchrony with life. All the solutions, always presented, if only I could see them clearly and choose to follow them honestly. I had made many right actions, but I was adding my energy and focus in the wrong part of solving the problem. I was trying to push Grand Haven to transform themselves 30 years overnight. I was demanding, by my presence, that they change their separate-but-equal educational system as the court ordered in 1954. But they had not really changed from their idea of education in 1954.

I had taken the position to redirect the flow of their entire system. I had been putting all my energy into keeping Adam in their regular education system with "special education supports." They had been putting their energy into convincing me that special education was a parallel system and that their separate-but-equal system within a system was the correct path. It was never a dialog. I was forced into a protecting mode. Another one of my many epiphanies. If the problem is identified as "Is inclusion correct?" Then it allows for the possibility that inclusion is not correct and may be abandoned when things get messy. If the problem is identified as how do we all learn to live and learn together? Then when things get messy, we all search for solutions that support everyone. No more scape goats. As King wrote, "No one is free until everyone is free." For me, this meant that no one can really belong until we all belong. If John can be removed from the community, then who is next? To believe that our lives will be better off if we eliminate one kind of person soon leads directly back to the eugenics idea that because I am superior you are all expendable and I may use you for my gain.

The faculty at Zeeland Christian treated Adam very respectfully. He even got on their track team as a shot-putter. Lars Dreger came down from the high school to help out and taught Adam how to shot put. Lars was good and even taught me. It really was a community for Adam. Lars was third in the Dreger family to connect with Adam. Lars' two older sisters had taken care of Adam so Jetta and I could go for walks or out to dinner occasionally. As his sisters got older and went off to college, Lars had asked if he could be our child care provider for Adam. Lars came into our lives at just the right time. Adam needed a guy to run with, and I was already showing the signs of my football knees and motorcycle crashes. Adam loved to wrestle in the pool and Lars was a varsity wrestler; it was perfect. Jetta had read studies that athletics was a door into inclusion and belonging. It had worked for me, and now Jetta was engineering conditions for Adam to be skilled enough to be one of the guys on a track team or bowling or swimming and golf. Lars and his family were strong Christians, and that also mattered to Jetta.

Adam Knowing God

The community of Zeeland Christian School was a great gift to Adam, Jetta and me. Adam's faith was nurtured. His desire to pray about a problem, as I had taught him, was respected at Zeeland Christian. In public school, I had had to call Adam's praying a time out rather than a prayer. I liked calling what Adam was doing prayer because he was not just interrupting his own behavior to take a break, he was seeking guidance and support to improve his behavior. In the public school, I had had to describe this as self-talk. Zeeland Christian allowed prayer.

In both the public school and the charter school I had asked that Adam learn to read the Bible. They had reluctantly agreed because I had written it into Adam's IEPC that reading the Bible and complying with those morals would be his behavior modification base. That might have been a little devious, but it was true. However, at Zeeland Christian, it was everyone's baseline.

I was able to remind one of Adam's teachers at Zeeland of the power of prayer. If Adam began to develop a behavior they did not like, I asked them to try my way of dealing with it. First, ignore it by giving him a time out meaning not look at him or respond to him. Second, find a competing behavior and reinforce it. Third, interrupt and redirect the behavior by finding two popular students, a girl and a boy, to pray with Adam that he would learn to follow Christ-like behavior and do the competing behavior (whatever that was) or ask Adam if in his prayer he had found his better way to act. All students would benefit from a behavior modification base approach of, "Stop, we need to pray about this." If the child needed to gain insight, it is simple to ask if they understand what we need to pray about. Then let them identify their error and determine their better path. My question to Adam about his behavior was always, "Is this your best choice?" Prayer is a request for direct and divine intervention so we can discover our best choices. Amen?

Our Sense of Church Community Grew

As Adam got older, I began to attend regularly, and it became *our* church. More Adam's than mine, really. I walked less and sat happily next to my son as he grew in God's grace. As long as Andy was the minister, no committee was ever formed to discuss inclusion; Adam was just part of the body of Christ. Adam and I would come and go during the service from the front row. Andy told me some members asked him if it bothered him that we would leave the sanctuary, sometimes in the middle of the sermon. He replied, "I'm surprised others don't do the same!" When Jetta joined the church, Adam joined with her, but I did not. My attendance was intermittent.

One day Andy asked if I would allow Adam to come and stand with him when the last hymn was being played. He was wise in the ways of organized church life and thought it would be a good thing. He knew that because some people were beginning to question how Adam was fitting into the church, a little more support was necessary. I agreed. A few more Sundays passed with Adam standing next to Andy before Andy went back up on the stage for the traditional blessing and closing.

Adam blessing the church

The next Sunday Andy talked about how God uses the least to instruct the wise. He led the church into inclusion. This time as Andy left his place in the congregation to return to the center of the stage to recite the blessing of departure, Adam followed him up and stood with Andy, raised his hands and blessed everyone just as Andy was doing. Andy announced that everyone's week would certainly go well as they were doubly blessed. Adam was an unofficial assistant from then on. Always going up front to stand next to Andy when the last hymn was being sung. Most Sundays he let Adam go up to the pulpit alone to close the service.

Andy had a gift for including everyone. When Adam wanted to take communion, there were, again, some concerned (prejudiced) Christians who were not sure Adam really understood the miracle of communion. Adam said he liked communion because it meant he belonged to Jesus and belonged to the church and to the people. That was good enough for Andy to affirm Adam and assure his right to belong. I told Andy (with Jetta tapping on my knee) that I was doubtful most of the Christians even understood Christ or community or how to become like children, like Adam, to get into the Kingdom of Heaven. Jetta and Adam had a church community because Andy was a good minister (I called him Rabbi) teaching his flock God's real words about everyone belonging in the body of Christ. Andy was an imperfect man and the perfect teacher and Pastor for our church and my family. The people in Covenant Life Church were real people. Some adored Adam. Some wanted Adam to be there. Some were not so sure. They were all normal people.

One Sunday, Adam, age nine, decided to sing and from the bottom of his toes released sounds he heard as music. There was not one note or rhythmic similarity to the music being played. I had been listening to a woman in front of us because she had a pitch perfect voice that could melt the polar ice cap. She never flinched. When church was over, I started to explain my son to her, and she interrupted me and said, "We choose to sit in front of Adam because when he sings, it is from the depth of his soul to God's glory, and we cherish each note he shares." I never knew just what response I would get, but it was usually strongly one-sided, adoring my son's presence or wanting him gone.

Travel—the Cure for a Seasonal Affective Disorder

Adam flourished in this environment. He made friends. He learned how to relate to other kids and match their rhythm. For the most part. When he could no longer adapt to their way of being, because of their relationship developed with Adam, they adapted to him. It was a mutually enriching community. No one was always the recipient of support. All received support as they became in need. When Jan noticed Adam's pattern of having difficulty starting after Christmas, we figured out he had a seasonal affective disorder (SAD). His doctor suggested a low dose of an antidepressant. I convinced Jetta to try Disneyland instead: sunshine, and lots of it, and M-i-c-k-e-y-M-o-u-s-e!

During every Christmas vacation from school, we traveled to a sunny location to recharge Adam. Travel was not easy, but it was worth it. Planning the trip was essential. We began by telling Adam when and where and how so that some part of him was familiar with the novel situation that we would face. His mother and I showed him the hotel brochure so he would see where we were going. He saw pictures of the pool and of the city. We watched travel logs about Puerto Vallarta.

We played Mexican music. We talked about what to do in situations. How to stand in line at the customs desk. How to show your passport and always how to say *gracias*. And then we went and did our best.

On one trip to Florida when Adam was young, we stayed in a home that,

Jetta and Adam enjoying the ocean

like most places with warm weather, have tile floors and Adam was reluctant to walk on tile floors and would never walk barefooted. He was reluctant to pass through a new doorway even if it was open. His routines anchored him, and in new environments, many of his old behaviors would return. My salvation was that dealing with old behaviors was easier because we had already figured the shortest path to return balance.

My loving, wonderful wife was the more adventurous of the two of us. She would regularly break routines when we were traveling. She wanted all of us to stay up past Adam's 8:00 pm bedtime routine. She would sleep in and miss breakfast, but Adam would wake up at 7:00 am and start his day. And breakfast was at 8:00 am. She would overstimulate Adam and change routines and then go shopping or to the pool and let me enjoy my son. And that was our contract. She loved and enjoyed Adam; my job was to juggle the world and create conditions for Adam to thrive. She believed stirring the pot, as I called it, was an essential part of Adam's growth and her obligation to do. She was wise. It took both of us to create the best conditions for Adam.

I cannot say I recommend travel with a child with Autism, but it did benefit Adam. He always returned stronger and just a little bit more flexible. After each vacation, I was exhausted and in need of a parent vacation, but that never happened.

Zeeland Christian from Barb Newman's Perspective

I had been involved in working for the Christian Learning Center (CLC) since 1985. CLC was a center in Grand Rapids, Michigan that offered Christian education for children with intellectual disabilities. It was a segregated option as were most offerings in the 1980s. R.H. "Bear" Berends was the Director of CLC and heard about something new happening at a Catholic high school in Kitchener, Canada. At the time, it was called Supported Education and was being championed by Marsha Forest. Bear paid a visit to Kitchener and came back eager to think about how CLC could shut down the segregated model and have children with intellectual disabilities attend their local Christian schools with their siblings. Zeeland Christian School was the first to agree, and I was eager to join the adventure. We transferred a few students who lived in Ottawa County and attended CLC in Grand Rapids and tried to create an option that only existed at a high school in Canada at that time. There was no pattern book or model that we knew of. If any existed, it would be found in the I Corinthians 12 portion of Scripture that talks about each part of the body of Christ being gifted and important to the functioning of the whole body. That was God's picture of inclusiveness that we wanted to follow.

Since 1989, Zeeland Christian School (ZCS), in partnership and under the direction of CLC Network, had placed the welcome mat out for families who wanted a Christian education for their children, all of their children. So when David Winstrom first stopped at the curb of Zeeland Christian School and walked into Bill's office, there were many other students in the building with varied abilities. I remember the trip Jan and I took to meet Adam for the first time. We didn't know the path that David and Jetta had traveled with Adam, but we did meet a robust child who was working very hard

Winstrom family

with his tutor. His tutor talked to us about Adam's curriculum and some of his unique behaviors, and we knew he would fit in well at ZCS.

As Adam joined his new classmates at school, we started to learn more and more of David and Jetta's path. We understood why David would meet us at the beginning and end of every day to give us a report of how Adam was doing before school and to get a report of his day after school. As we walked together with the Winstroms, we tried to get them to delight in the fact that it was not parent vs. the school but parent partnering with the school. So many parents had come to us having had to fight for what they wanted in school, but in a Christian school, we are partners with parents, working together for the best for their child. Eventually, David shortened his daily visits. I imagine there was some relief in not having to gear up for battle every day.

David didn't plan this, God smiled, David was instructed.

Adam was fondly remembered as a student with personality plus. He was boisterous and happy most *of the time. Yes, most of the time. When Adam found life a bit too cluttered or unpredictable around him, he would show his frustration by getting even louder and calling out a few choice words that most of the children at Zeeland Christian had never heard before. A most memorable day was when Adam found the 30 extra visitors in his classroom on Grandparent's Day a tad too cluttered and unpredictable. He demonstrated his frustration by loudly calling out a word the grandparents wished their grandchildren did not know. All eyes were now focused on Adam. Thankfully, part of living life together at Zeeland Christian meant that peers knew exactly what was happening with Adam. They quickly explained to their grandparents what Adam was frustrated about, and life moved on. Adam and his special visitor that day took a short tour of the school so he could find that "happy place" once again. Thankfully, Grandparent's Day is only once a year.*

Adam grew so much in the time he was at ZCS. His growth reminded me of the words that were spoken about Jesus at the end of Luke 2:52. It says that Jesus grew "in wisdom, in stature, and in favor with God and man." Adam did the same. He developed wise coping strategies, a muscular build from doing hard work with and for people, prayed meaningful prayers that expressed his love for Jesus, and he was well-loved by students and teachers.

While Adam was growing as a student, we started to see that the ideas David would give us to try with Adam were often so different from what we had used with some of our other students. As new and complex situations would arise, David was willing to meet with us and brainstorm new ideas. Jan and I would say many times that God brought such a gift to us in the form of Adam's Dad. He had the ability to see things from a slightly different angle, and that perspective would often allow a student to grow and move.

Even after Adam graduated and moved with his friends to Holland Christian High School, David continued to stay connected with us at ZCS. He mentioned several times that we had such a unique student body, and he willingly gave us his time and ideas. When I became interested in supporting congregations so they could better include individuals with disabilities, David read my book manuscripts and gave suggestions and encouragement. To this day, whether it's for the CLC Network Church Services work or another beautifully wired child, handcrafted by God with a pattern we have not yet seen at ZCS, I continue to learn from this man who God clearly led to the doors of Zeeland Christian School. God had a plan that none of us could have imagined at that point in time.

Barb Newman

Zeeland Christian from the Principal's Perspective

I believe in inclusive education with all my heart and soul. When David Winstrom first walked into my office and told me about Adam, it was hard to believe his story. I was then warned by colleagues in the public school to stay far away from the good doctor because of his history of wanting what's best for his son and stopping at nothing to get it. This included a willingness to get lawyers involved which make school systems very nervous, especially because he won all his suits. In spite of these warnings, I felt that what David was asking for was exactly what I believed and what Zeeland Christian School was doing.

Our first encounter was the beginning of a very warm and fruitful friendship that was a huge blessing for me. There were definitely a few bumps in the road like the Grandparents Day when Adam was upset by the busy-ness and the lack of predictability that all the grandparents brought to the school. Adam expressed his displeasure very clearly by swearing out loud and throwing a chair. Seeing the shock on all the grandparents' faces, I thought I might lose my job, but that fear was quickly replaced but my admiration for the fifth-grade students who clearly explain to the adults why Adam was upset. When they understood, the grandparents expressed great admiration for their grandchildren, Adam and the entire school system.

So, who benefited more from Adams presents ZCS? Was it David Winstrom, Adam Winstrom, the students, the teaching staff, the parents or me? The clear answer to this trick question is all of us benefited in amazing ways and we grew together.

Jesus said let the little children come unto me. That is exactly what we did with Adam and every other student for whom parents wanted a Christian education. Students like Adam changed the culture of ZCS from a school that was pretty self-centered to a school that truly loved others as much as they love themselves.

In addition to the incredible blessing that it was to have Adam in school, it was also an incredible blessing to have David Winstrom's creative approach to working with students with special needs. David's professional knowledge and his experiences with Adam gave him amazing insights and very creative solutions that met students' needs in unique new ways.

So, the bottom line for me is incredible gratitude that God brought the Winstrom family to Zeeland Christian School.

Bill Van Dyk, Principal
Zeeland Christian School

Graduation from Zeeland Christian

During Adam's time at ZCS, he learned to touch people's hearts. He made friends. And his life experiences were expanded. He rode a Harley Davidson with me. He skied the mountains of Colorado. He swam in the Pacific Ocean in Mexico. Someone once asked Jetta if we did all these things with Adam to make him normal. Her response was very, very clear, "Adam was perfect just as he was, we did these things with him because they were fun and so he would have normal things to talk about." Adam and I did them because we liked to.

Eventually, all good things come to an end and Adam's class was graduating. Zeeland Christian did a very nice transition for their students. At the end of the day before the evening ceremony, all of the teachers went to the entrance are and knelt down. All of the graduating students gathered in front of them and one at a time sat in a chair in front of the teacher. The teacher had them take off their shoes and the teacher repeated a blessing as the teacher washed their graduating student's

8th Grade Banquet

Dear David and Jetta

Thank you for allowing us to be a part of Adam's life for the past 4 years. We will never forget his smiles, laughter, love of motorcycles and telephones, and his enthusiasm for life. He has touched the lives of every 8th grade student and teacher here at ZCS. May God continue to bless Adam and you as you move on to ZCS.

Love, Jan and staff

feet. Each student was given some one thing from their teacher to carry forward in their life. That night, Zeeland Christian had an evening graduation ceremony All of the graduating

Adam's 11th birthday

students and their parents came together and had a small meal and took pictures. All the young adults dressed up in formal wear rather than school clothes. There were all moving on from their place as children into becoming young adults.

I had expected graduation to be our goodbye to this wonderful chapter in our lives and we would then have to find another condition for Adam. I did not know what would be next. The high school was different than Zeeland Christian. They had not embraced full inclusion yet and I was not inspired by the meetings we had had. It felt too much like *helpful* people. I had started to look for work situations that could be his entry into a more adult world.

After they had gathered together for their last class picture, Adam's class and many of their parents gathered around our family. They said they wanted Adam to come with them to Holland Christian High School. They would make sure Adam was okay. WOW! They created the condition for our family to continue on with them. An army 60 strong was headed to Holland Christian and they had an aim—to include Adam. No matter what the high school had planned, it would have to adapt to Adam's community.

Graduation from Life

Adam's grandmother, Jetta's mother, died of cancer when Adam was five years old. He had brushed her hair and held her hands and loved her. Jetta's mother wanted no ceremonies, so Adam only knew she disappeared. I tried to talk with Adam but he would say she was gone and stop talking. He was not upset, but he was done talking and would get up and disappear into a project or start a new conversation. He was too young for the conversation I had considered. At five years old, the truth of death is that she is here one day and gone the next. Period.

His first year at Zeeland Christian, my mother died from cancer. During our visits with her, Adam would brush her hair and hold her hands. He loved her. When my mother died, Adam and I were more prepared to work through this together. My mother's faith was her own. It was not very demonstrative, but she was very willing to let Adam pray for her. We talked about death as a passage into the next place God had prepared for us. When the body died, the soul was released back to God. It was clear that talking with Adam was helpful for my mother. The church minister who came by did so out of duty and obligation. Adam spoke from his heart. His prayers were a dialog, not a canned speech. He did not read the 23rd Psalm without inflection or in the "voice" that he and I identified as the television evangelistic salvation sellers. Adam spoke, and his comfort and relationship with God soothed my mother and assuaged her fear and awkwardness. They could join in prayer without being self-conscious. *Kavanah* in Hebrew means to open one's heart to God and feel each word as if it was the first time ever spoken and that was Adam's way. He had personal chats with God. Adam was never self-conscious about his prayers, he was conscious only of God's presence in each moment with him. My mother found both comfort and peace in her own faith praying with Adam.

Adam and I did the rituals that became our family tradition with death. We would visit and pray, laugh and tell stories and brush women's hair. When their body stopped working and their spirit returned to God, we were happy for them. We cleaned their house, went to a celebration of their life, looked at the body they left behind and went to the cemetery to bury them. With my mother, Adam's grandmother, the cemetery workers were not sure what we were doing as we stayed by the grave. Adam and I eventually went to where they were and asked for shovels to fill in the grave. This was new for them, but they learned.

When Adam's Grandfather died a few years later, the cemetery workers were there with extra shovels. Adam knew as surely as the body went into the ground that the soul went to heaven. He could see the end of the operation concretely. The body abandoned by the soul, without life and buried in the ground—the shell of what had been someone. At my father's funeral, Adam had an empty seat next to him and told me that Grampa liked the service. Some say they thought they saw an old man sitting next to Adam. Maybe he could see both sides.

Adam arrived at Holland Christian with me, loud and proud. This was his idea of an entrance into high school culture.

Loud and proud Adam on
Harley black soft tail standard

Chapter 13
Holland Christian High School

Adam was 18 as a freshman. Bill's suggestion to put Adam in the third grade instead of the fifth grade had paid off, and his slowed development had eventually synchronized with his peers. He was an adolescent, exploring *all* the wonders of a fully included world. Adam was becoming his own person. What he believed in, what he supported and how he thought he should behave were all clearly developing. He was developing his own internal control and discovering how he wanted to fit into the world. He was becoming a responsible young man. That journey meant he had to make his mistakes and learn for himself what was right and what has wrong. All aspects of becoming a good man including life and death as well as relationships and disappointments occurred as he passed through Holland Christian School. During this time sweet Jetta, Adam's mother, discovered she had cancer.

Football—Building Community

I had played sports all my life and understood the value of being part of a group or team with clear goals and routines. When Adam was entering Holland Christian High School, I went to meet the football coach, Tim Lont. He was an anomaly as a coach. He told me his aim was to build community and character and develop the potential in every player. His aim was to develop Christian men who played football, not football players who attended church. Amen. That was just where I wanted Adam to be. I knew that **with Downs syndrome**

Adam's spinal cord was a weak point and one good helmet hit could snap his neck. I considered teaching Adam to be a place kicker, and he would have been very good but not good enough to possibly die for. I told Mr. Lont that if he would allow Adam to be part of the team as a trainer, I would provide a consultant to work with Adam to do his job well and work with the team to create a condition where everyone would benefit. Mr. Lont agreed, and Adam became the team trainer.

The benefit of belonging to the team combined with his friends who wanted him to come to Holland Christian High School from Zeeland Christian allowed Adam to expand his possibilities in high school. What that looked like was transforming for everyone, and because of football practices he was already part of the main community by the time school started.

Holland Christian was much more traditional than Zeeland Christian. They ran a segregated program within a traditional high school. Adam started his year in the special classroom at the end of the hall with its own entrance and exit. I guessed it was set up that way to protect the special students from the general education students. But this is where Adam's inclusion in Zeeland Christian paid off. He had his built-in protection that the school did not recognize—the group of students who came with him from Zeeland Christian. And he had his new peer group of the football players. He was safely included in the general school community. I only heard about a few of the solutions that his friends came up with to help Adam through rough spots with other students. In the first weeks of school, some students had decided to bully Adam. The members of his football team observed it and placed the bully in a locker for a period of time, saying to the bully that "no one messes with Adam." Amen to the power of community.

Coach Adam: Team Trainer

The football team expanded Adam's community. One of the players had gone to a movie called *Radio*, about an individual with Autism and a fascination for radios. He made the rest of the team and the coaches all go to the movie together. They considered calling Adam "Cell Phone" because he was

Adam leading team prayer

just as attached to cell phones as the actor in the movie was attached to his radio, but they decided just to call Adam by his real name. When I heard about that team outing, it warmed my heart.

The depth of Adam's belonging and being part of the team so quickly and so completely surprised me that I was energized to talk with Adam's self-contained classroom teacher (with *special* training) about how he would fit into the mainstream of Holland Christian. I told her that for the first semester I understood her need to have Adam in her special classroom with his main assignment being collecting pop cans from all the other classes as a way to teach Adam the layout of Holland Christian, but that was not an acceptable long-term education for him. She was surprised. I was seeing Wolfensberger's pendulum again. She was sure Adam needed protection from what might happen in the regular population or to protect them from what Adam might do. Wolfensberger model states that segregating people to protect them is the aim but the pendulum swings between who needs protection and never rests in the middle where inclusion is protective of all. I assured her that his teammates and his community from Zeeland Christian would take care of that. And they did. It wasn't long before Adam broke out of the end room for the *special* students and attended regular classes. He infected more of the Holland Christian community with his friendship. Others from his *special* class eventually were released and joined the Holland Christian community.

At the end of each football game, the coach had the whole team gather at midfield and the coach or team captain would pray. I do not know how it happened, but Adam began leading the prayer. I talked to Coach Lont and said I could try to keep Adam from doing that but he said, "No, don't. Just let Adam be Adam. We love him." The gathering began to grow, and parents and cheerleaders eventually began to assemble with the football players at midfield. As Coach Lont had said, Adam grew in faith, friendship and community as did every other player on that team.

Adam's birthday happened to fall on the night of the first game of his junior year. When the game was over, no one left the stadium. The team went into the center of the field with Adam, and everyone sang happy birthday to him. If only the kind doctor could have seen how alone and friendless Adam was in that moment with his happy birthday chorus a thousand strong, maybe he would understand the depth of his error.

I don't think I can overstate the point that separate but equal is not okay because it is not equal. It steals possibilities for learning from everyone. It fosters fear and separation. Adam was included. If he had gone to the Ottawa Area Center as the professionals had planned, everyone would have missed this moment. All 1,000 faculty, students and parents would have been cheated out of the possibility of friendship with Adam. Had he grown up in Pine Rest and been released into the world after 18 years of separation, he would always have been afraid of all he had been cheated out of being exposed to. He could never have withstood the roar of love from the crowd; it would have paralyzed him if he had not had years to prepare for just this moment. The 1,000 people gathered would not have had the possibility to know someone as unique as Adam and would have, as human beings regrettably do, been afraid of the guy who looked different than they did and talked differently than they did. They would never have felt the depth of love and friendship that they had been year by year exposed to by knowing Adam. This pinnacle moment could not have occurred without all the years of accumulated momentum from association and letting go of prejudice and privilege until the moment in time when everyone could celebrate their best friend, Adam, on his 21st birthday.

Being Late for Class

Adam was beginning to be chronically late for one of his classes. The school's solution was to make him come in early as punishment to fix his tardiness. I complied twice then asked to meet with the Principal. I explained to him that Adam loved being in school, so the punishment was more of a reward and that my wife and I did not think it a useful tool to educate people or to change their behavior, at least not a change for the better. So, I prayed with the Principal that we could find a solution to what the Principal identified as Adam's perceived lack of education about punctuality and his lack of respect for their time. I knew Adam had more respect for time than the principal did; he had kept me waiting for 15 minutes before our appointment, but I did not raise that point. Part of the neurology of Autism is a need to follow rules strictly. So, if something was causing Adam to not follow the rule about time, it was stronger than his own instinct. After we had prayed, I suggested we look at what the real problem was and not the symptom of being late. I asked to have someone follow Adam from class to class to see what the problem was.

A few days later, I met with the Principal to discuss the findings. Again, he was late. Evidently, men who run organizations are often late because something interferes with their intention to be on time, but I did not hold that mirror up as he would only have become embarrassed and defensive. Instead, we stuck to our focus on Adam.

The person following Adam reported that when the bell rang, he got up like everyone else and entered the hallway to get to the next class. He would do an interesting dart and weave pattern down the hallway until he got to the bathroom. Then he would go into a stall and hide until it was quiet enough for him to go back into the hallway and get to

Adam and some school buddies

class. I talked with the Principal about what Adam's behavior meant and defined the problem differently than being late. The issue was that Adam was getting overstimulated in the hallways and needed to find a safe place to hide and refuel until he could go back into the world and continue on with his day without a meltdown.

I again asked to have a short prayer of gratitude to find a clear solution to this issue. On the one hand, the Principal's solution was correct to reinforce Adam's good judgment by allowing him more time in school. Adam really liked coming in early before the whole school erupted in the controlled chaos of a high school. But the current "solution" of coming to school early each day would do nothing to address his being late for class in the middle of the day when he was more vulnerable and tired. In fact, it might exacerbate the situation bringing fatigue on earlier in the day from the extended exposure.

I suggested four options. First, to just let Adam get to class a few minutes late as he had found his own solution to handling the overstimulation. Second, we could let Adam out early from class so he could get through the hallways before his dart and weave overstimulated behavior took over and indicated he needed a safe place to refuel. Or third, keep him in his class until the hallway cleared and quieted so he could get to class, again he might be a few minutes late. Fourth, find a few students headed the same way and hook Adam up with them, and they could walk together to teach Adam how to get to class safely.

We settled on Adam leaving early. The problem was not that Adam did not respect time, he did. The issue was his genetic lack of filters to protect him from all the noise and confusion that made the trip from one end of school to the other too daunting causing Adam to give himself a time out to better handle it. A very good choice, I thought.

After that bump, I began walking in the shopping mall with Adam to teach him how to navigate what seemed like chaos to him. He would rev up and start his dart and weave and then need to seclude for a few minutes. It was amazing to see and experience his understanding of us neurotypical people. As I observed the undulating mass of the mall crowd, moving within it were the strikers—they were the hurry-up people who darted in and out, weaving through the mass of people as Adam had attempted to do. Adam had chosen them to model his behavior because he did not want to be *late*. It took us holding hands, wearing ear muffs and slowly walking through the mall to find our comfortable path. No more streaking. Then we tried it without ear muffs. Then we tried it not holding hands. It took time to walk with Adam and first see the world as he saw it, then understand his solution. Next, we added safeguards so that he felt safe enough to try my way. Teach your children well; do not exasperate them into bitterness, discouragement or anger.

Just the physical act of walking through the noise, confusion, chaos and physical overstimulation was punishment, but it was a punishment he chose to endure to be part of the community. Had I agreed with the system that more punishment was the solution to "Adam's problem" and applied force to make him mind by adding shame every time he could not get to his class "on time," he eventually would have had a meltdown in the crowded hallway and possibly scared others and humiliated and possibly harmed himself. Typical children, when pushed too far beyond their ability to cope become "cutters," commit suicide or take drugs to get numb. For too many years as a therapist, I treated them in their woundedness and mended broken spirits in children and young adults who were punished for doing the best they could. How could I not support my son's best effort? How could I not encourage him? How could others not see that he was doing all he could to do his work and trusting us to do ours?

Learning to Swear Really Well

Holland Christian had a zero tolerance for swearing and Adam was learning to be good at it. This time the Principal was ready. Knowing that Adam liked school, he suggested that he stay home from school for an hour each time he swore. For some reason, he never understood my concept that punishment was not an educational tool. I told the Principal that I also had a zero tolerance for swearing and that neither his mother nor I had ever sworn in front of our son. We intentionally had not. But I couldn't allow the problem to be defined as simply as Adam is swearing in school nor could I accept the Principal's logic that people who swear cannot be in school. So, I met with the Principal as I had when Adam was late and told him that I understood his logic of removing Adam from school if he swore but told him I saw the problem differently.

Schools are intended to teach. Sometimes students learn unintended information. Adam was learning a great deal in school and was being instructed in the art of swearing by the "bad boys" in the Learning Disabilities classroom. They were responsible for teaching him to act in unacceptable ways. I told the principal that I had noticed Adam muttering at home and had asked what he was saying and it was, "F**k you." He said the guys were teaching him how to swear. Oh, the joy of inclusion with adolescents! And since my son was being instructed at school in this new behavior, I held them responsible for fixing his newly learned behavior in the place he learned it. At every offering from Adam of the unwanted word choice we decided that Adam would not be held out of school but that the school would develop an educational protocol to assist him in returning his language to what we all agreed was proper and back to the word choices Adam learned at home before his Christian education had expanded and *enriched* his vocabulary.

I introduced the Principal to my style of working with Adam. Our conversations went something like this, and each time we made a little more progress in changing Adam's behavior:

"Adam, when you swear, what are you trying to say? What do you want me to know? Swearing at another man means you want to fight. Do you want to fight?"

"No," Adam would mutter.

"Swearing at a woman means you want to humiliate her, make her feel worthless. Is that what you want?"

Adam would always answer, "No."

"Do you think swearing is a good thing to do?"

And he would answer, "No, it was bad."

"Do you want to be bad?"

Whatever bad was, he did not want to be that, so Adam would say, "No!"

"Are you swearing to be like your friends?"

And he would often say, "Yes."

"Let's try something for a week. When one of your friends swears, ask him to please not do that, it is not nice." Then Adam and I prayed about it, asking God to help Adam find a better way to talk that did not offend others.

The process took more time than yelling, "No!" or "Don't do that!" or "You can›t say that" (obviously he had said it) or being threatened with some future plight of losing an hour of school or being sent to the Principal's office to be expelled. These interventions seemed to escalate the behavior and would teach my son that he could use power words with other people to externalize his discomfort as everyone else does. Don't deal with it, pass it on. I always wanted Adam to solve his own issues. I wanted him to act morally because that was the path he most wanted to walk not out of fear or shame but because it was what he knew in his heart was the correct path for him no matter what anybody else did.

My way took longer but had the benefit of actually working. And the Principal got my meaning that if the students were teaching my son improper behavior at school, the school was the place we would correct their error. Additionally, to interrupt a behavior and redirect it required in-the-moment interruption. Techniques like "we are going to deal with this when your Dad comes home," etc. do not work well. Teachable moment interventions require cognitive retraining after you have interrupted and redirected the behavior. They do not happen through punishment especially if anger or emotionally charged words are involved.

The other piece of information I shared with the Principal after we had prayed that this would work was a training video I had seen in Colorado. They showed a therapist working with a young child with Autism. The child was swearing, and the therapist determined that the child chose to swear as his method of rebellion/defiance mostly because his father was a minister and would be mortified by his son's use of the profane in front of parishioners. The therapist had chosen "implosive therapy" to address the issue. He had the father and son sit together and swear. They repeated the F-bomb over and over and over until it had no meaning. The therapist asked each one if they would like to try a new word. Eventually, they did, and the child's swearing lost power and meaning and stopped. I assured the Principal that I was not planning on showing up at school to desensitize his environment to words. Nor would I come in screaming to demonstrate that all noise is noise. If screaming can be ignored, it will stop. For today, we would stick to teaching Adam that what he learned here in school was a mistake and we wanted him to talk better. And we wanted him to teach his friends to talk better. Adam was summoned to the Principal's office, and we told him of the plan to help him relearn his respectful ways to communicate. Adam agreed.

A Teachable Moment Flat on His Back

All I have said about force and physical management do not mean I never physically interrupted my son. Like my father before me I never struck, spanked, slapped or hurt my son. I did hold him tightly when we were by the hospital, and the police asked if I needed assistance. I had held my son in a supermarket when he was younger until he could relax and regain his internal control. But Adam was much smaller then. One day my 5'5," 180-pound son tried out being a man as I had in my youth and that was that moment when an opposite reaction seemed to fit the situation. And this day came like it had come once between my father and me when I was 16 years old.

Adam and I came home, and Jetta was upset and began chiding Adam about something just as we came in the door. Adam had had a long day of school and football and was not his best self. His filters were exhausted. He had no real idea what his mother said, he just experienced her being upset and could not deal with one more thing. Out popped clear as a blue sky on a summer day, *"F**k you, Bitch."*

I remember spinning around catching Adam under the chin, picking him up off his feet and placing all 180 pounds of him on his back on the floor with my knee on his chest. He was 20 and had executed his oration with clarity, proper tone, pitch and timing. I equally surprised him, Jetta and myself with the grace of my chin lift and gentle placement of our young adult son on his back. He was not thrown down but gracefully elevated with my one hand and supported to the floor with the other. It was especially surprising to me because being

Adam 11th Grade

physical was not my chosen style with my son. I remember looking into my son's eyes and saying very calmly, "Adam, 'F**k you, Bitch' is an invitation to fight. Is this what you want?" I remember raising my hand up over my head with my pointer finger in the air—the signal Jetta and I had agreed on that if she or I were in the middle of some teachable moment, the other person would not interfere. And she said nothing other than a gasp that escaped her lips. It was a quiet moment with both of them in shock.

While Adam was lying flat on his back, I remember telling him that I loved him and was so surprised he had wanted to fight with me or hurt his mother's feelings. She was obviously already upset about something and needed her own time out, not an insult from her son. She needed someone to be kind to her in the face of her frustration, not someone to make it worse. He was completely unharmed but shaken by the experience. I invited him to get up and come outside and talk nice with me and then we could come back in, and he could talk to his mother. We did. I never yelled or was angry, but I used the experience as a teachable moment. As my father had done with me, I removed my son's inflated idea of his entitlement to act with indifference to others. His consideration returned immediately, and he and his mother greeted in their usual loving way. She had taken her own time out and was as remorseful for her part as was my son. We all agreed coming home was to be a welcoming experience, and we used the unfortunate circumstance to learn and grow.

Jetta had done very well living with cancer, but there were moments, like the moment Adam and I walked into our home when she was overwhelmed the conditions cancer had created. The doctors had recommended a partial then a full thyroidectomy (surgical removal of the thyroid gland). That was followed by ingesting radioactive iodine to destroy the any and all residual thyroid tissue. The non-intended consequence of that procedure destroyed some of Jetta's memory and her orientation to both where she was physically in the world (she could get lost driving home) and how to do some of the things she loved such as cooking. She never complained, but there were moments when she had real difficulty managing herself, which is what Adam sensed full bore as he walked in. The frustration was more than Jetta could manage to conceal and more than Adam could process. He popped first. I had missed all of this as I walked in focused on getting Adam to take his backpack upstairs and get cleaned up to eat. What Jetta had said to Adam was not the issue. It was all the undercurrents she had to deal with within herself that Adam also experienced. There was no fault. It was another perfect storm moment. Positive, negative and neutral energies coming together creating a discharge and clarity. When anyone entered our home from then on, we entered with patience, love and support or we waited outside the door until we were able to do so. Every person entering was greeted with that same intention or greeted with I'm having a hard time, but it is not about you, and I do love you. When cancer collided with Autism, we developed rituals to manage our lives.

When Adam and I reentered, Adam made it a point to greet his mother as he usually did with a "Hi, Mom!" and a smile and a hug. She did as she usually did and said, "I'm glad you're home! How was your day?" When we had all recovered I got a Jetta-look, and as she gave me a hug she whispered in my ear, "Did you hurt your back lifting him up like and placing him so softly on the floor?" Jetta realized that maneuver could have easily blown out my back again. I had already had corrective surgery for three ruptured disks. "No dear, he was lifted light as a feather." We ate and reminded each other how we most like to be greeted as we come home. And we practiced again after dinner. Going out and coming in and hugging and laughing. We all learned from that moment how fragile and how strong relationships are. We also learned how quickly and without intention we can shred someone we love.

Interrupting and redirecting behavior can be accomplished in many different ways. Sometimes it can be as simple as removing attention by turning one's head away from someone and then turning back with a new thought. It can also be as disquieting as I had just done. Simple behavior modification always involves three steps: 1. Ignore behavior you do not wish to have continue; 2. Reinforce behaviors you want to continue, especially those that compete with behaviors you want to get rid of; and 3. Interrupt and redirect behavior. I had interrupted and redirected Adam's behavior then talking quietly and calmly about what behavior I would like instead. I asked that the school to do the same by stopping Adam when he was swearing. My interruption was more dramatic than a school could provide, but it was the same principle.

My father never struck me and only spanked me one time. I was about 15 years old, and he came into my room to tell me to go to bed and say good night. I am not sure exactly what sparked in my testosterone-enriched brain, but I made some derogatory comment about him and that he could not tell me what to do. He somehow picked me up out of my bed, turned me over and spanked me twice and put me back in my bed and gently placed the covers around my chin. Then he said that he did not ever want to have to do that again, but I was his son, and I would listen when he required that of me. From that day on with my father I wanted to be more respectful not because I was afraid of him but because I could see on his face that I had injured him with my thoughtlessness. I instinctively knew how sons relate to fathers and never mistook him for one of the guys, even though we would do things together as I did with the guys. He was my father.

My instinctive response to Adam that day reminded me of my father. A correction needed to occur not out of anger or to punish but some primordial point of father/son respect and clarity. Adam also seemed to be more thoughtful of me and physically helpful to me. My son was not afraid of me as I never feared my father. We added words and rituals to the event, but what happened was instinctive and never repeated. Like my father before me, I rarely went over what did not work or what went wrong. The question was how could we have done this better. And then do that.

The Bird in Church

Along with their classes on swearing, Adam's guy friends had dedicated some time to teach him to "flip the bird." All of my efforts to teach Adam dexterity and to move his fingers individually, including piano lessons and even a piano recital really paid off that day. Jetta, Adam and I were in church and Adam, in the middle of Andy's sermon, raised his hand high overhead and with great dexterity, flipped the bird. It was Adam's first unveiling of this new skill. I am not exactly sure what moved Adam to express himself this way, but I did not think it was the time or place nor would it have been useful to say, "Don't do that," or ask, "Do you know what that means?" or any other non-redirecting verbal or physical behavior. I choose to see it as an emotional expression that required some recalibration to be more functional within the church culture. So I immediately raised my own hand and told Adam that the full hand with all fingers raised was better and then raised my other hand and said, "Yes!" Adam did the same. We became the first responsive worshipers in our church. Inclusion... praise be! Adam was not flipping off Andy. Adam was not flipping off God. I think he was trying a new power gesture to see what would happen. Maybe his friends told him that it was what you do when you are overwhelmed.

Church for Adam had always been close to "too much" stimulation. I had understood my son's quivering and even sweating in church at times as his neural physiological reaction to all the people and noise. I

Learning to shoot a bow. Patience. Focus. Breath. Release.

assumed it was a sensory overload thing. Jim Kristen reminded me that Adam experienced the world differently. I see the people, the congestion and noise, but Adam may be having a completely different experience. Jim said that where two or more are gathered in My name, there am I. I had to allow for the possibility that Adam could experience God in His unfiltered presence and be filled to overflowing or be overwhelmed in a different way. I think Jim might have been correct. I had taught Adam to retreat from situations that were overwhelming and go to his safe place to unstress himself and then return when he was able. But that day in church, Adam was filled with energy and showed no interest in retreating.

I found out the boys at Holland Christian had tried to introduce Adam to being cool. They "flipped each other off" in response to feeling a strong emotion. They wanted Adam to "fit in" and "F**k you" and flipping each other off was done in jest, for fun and just because. I had an idea where it came from, like swearing, and just worked with Adam on a better idea of when to use such expressions such as only with those friends. I voted that he never use these expressions, but I was not hanging out with them.

Adam continued to raise his hands in church when he was moved to do so. He seemed to raise his hands to touch someone near, and I was okay with his decision to respond to feeling something that compelled him with full hands extended.

Cheerleaders

Another issue arose as the year went on. Adam was part of the football team, and home games were fine, but away games on the bus with tired and emotional football players seemed like a disaster waiting to happen. On the bus on the way to the game the players were focused and prayerful. Coming home with the players after a game loss might have included tears or anger or injury—all too much for Adam to integrate, I thought. The coach wanted Adam to be at the away games as did the players. The football coach talked to the cheerleading coach, and it was decided that Adam would ride home with them. What a perfect solution. Except, the cheerleaders were all very beautiful young women, and Adam was an almost 18-year-old male. The issue could be reduced to one word—testosterone. Fortunately, no one did anything wrong, but a natural evolution started, and Adam became distracted by female breasts and could not stop staring at them. His team mates did not discourage it because they all had the same fixation. Adult women ignored his behavior but noticed it. Even Jetta's friends were subjects of this fixation. I did my coming-of-age talk #47, but it was a glancing blow at best. My son was having an innocent instinctive response and was becoming entangled in adolescent sexuality, and all I could do was talk to him. Logic was not the answer. He could tell me just how he was supposed to act but was not acting that way. My corrections only would reinforce, or worse, be experienced

Adam in High School

instinctively as another male exerting dominance. I found a solution I was comfortable with but did not tell Jetta. This was guy stuff.

I went to Hooters, introduced myself and asked the waitresses for a favor. Twenty dollars each for every waitress that would come over to hang out by my son when I came in with him. Every waitress was to smile at Adam and say, "Adam look at my face, not at my breasts" when his eyes wandered. "Tell me what color my eyes are. What color is my hair? Tell me I am pretty and nice. I like that when you do that. I don't like it when you just stare at my breasts. Look at my face." I think they enjoyed helping me with my son and doing it loud enough that other tables could hear. Adam learned. He

Learning to make eye contact

learned how to make connections with women. He told them how beautiful they were. What nice eyes they had. How nice their smile was. That they were a strong and powerful woman. He learned he could hold hands if he was respectful. As one of his friends described him, he became a chick magnet. No longer did Adam gawk or undress women with his eyes.

Jetta noticed the difference and said my talking with Adam was really paying off. I told her about Hooters. She was happier thinking that our father/son talks were the magic. I think our father/son talks in the bowling alley in third grade gave my son a good foundation, but the women at Hooters were the best instruction at the moment. It worked.

The bumps in his road were the normal developmental bumps amplified through his genetic anomalies that all aided in his development into an incredibly sensitive young man and a very good friend to many people. These were two things he never outgrew. When I would pick him up after he was with his friends or at an event, he would cry on the way home. He was able to hold himself together all the time he was with his friends, but it was still overwhelming to experience all the chaos being around neurotypical people. He was always willing to melt into me. From the time I got back into his world when he was four until the time he died, he found comfort, safety and support in my arms. Autism never separated us.

Internet Porn

Inclusion is such a joy; it creates the condition for so much incidental learning. Along with swearing, shooting the bird, and women's breasts, Adam's friends introduced him to computer porn. He loved to spend time on the computer, and I always monitored his computer history and explorations, so when I noticed some sites he was visiting, I talked with him about it. I should say more accurately that we talked and looked together. I told him I had seen some of the sites he had visited like F**k.com and pulled one up. His first response was embarrassment. "I learned this from my friends, and they told me not to tell my Dad." I sat with my son and watched porn. His first response was that it was bad and he should not see sex. I told him I thought sex was really quite wonderful but this was not sex. And it would be sad if he got the two confused. This stuff was fantasy and empty of love and caring. How could he experience tenderness from a computer screen? We watched some more, then he had had enough (and me, too). Internet porn is boring, and if you are watching it with your father, it is embarrassing. I tried to be a fill-in for Adam's heavenly Father reminding Adam that He is always with him and I did not know how except by example I could have gotten that across.

I asked him how he found the stuff and he told me bad words dot com was the key. So, he showed me the bad words he knew. That was quite eye opening. I did not know how sheltered I was. I will not describe the videos he found, but they were complete with fetishes. We watched and talked about how the videos were not real life. We touched the screen, and it did not feel like holding a girlfriend's hand.

We talked about holding his real girlfriends hand, how that made him feel happy and good. I asked him how the bad words dot com made him feel. He said, "Excited but bad, so sex must be bad."

I talked about how sex was wonderful and how I hoped someday he might get married and enjoy being intimate. But being intimate is not possible with a computer. We talked about how porn is not real; it is make believe. He did not know the girls, and he had to pretend to make feelings. And I told him it was not even close to how great being intimate with his wife would be. I kept getting the invitation from him to reinforce his idea that sex was wrong and bad. I didn't. I told him over and over that sex was good, and a woman's body was beautiful—a real woman, not a TV screen picture. And we talked about how to become more intimate with a woman and what being sexual was all about. I told him that he could watch bad words dot com as much as he wanted as long as I watched it with him. That was our agreement. If he wanted to discover something, we would find a way together. We also agreed that would be the rule for learning new things with his

Kayak adventure

friends—we would do it with me present. If he and they were comfortable, we would discover the meaning in it together.

I always intended for my son to make moral judgments from his heart without fear. I believed, and still do, that each of us instinctively knows right from wrong. I raised my son to focus on internal control, believing he was responsible for his own decisions and life choices. He was not responsible for his friends. I taught him that God was within him and if he just listened, he would know.

Learning to Support Others

Adam could read people very well. All the time we had spent learning to make meaning out of life paid off. Adam also benefited from the many people who had hired me to work with their families. But my professional life had to have firm boundaries because I was Adam's father. I explained to all who wanted to hire me that I would be 100% with them during our time together, but I could not offer after hours' counseling over the phone unless they understood that my son would listen to our phone conversations. Adam wanted to know what I did, and he wanted to understand people, so every phone call was a teachable moment for him. He answered the phone at our house properly, "Hello, this is Adam Winstrom. Who would you like to talk to?" If it was for me, he would run to the other phone and quietly listen whether it was the lumber company calling about a delivery or the garage mechanic calling about fixing the car or a patient wanting to talk. Eventually and unintentionally, Adam would do what he observed and would ask them how they were doing, and a conversation would begin. Sometimes they were happier talking with Adam. His genetics made him unfiltered and wide open. I had dedicated years developing my gift to be able to do what he did naturally.

Adam put a lot of work into surviving his gift of not having filters between himself and others. Because Autism left him emotionally unfiltered and unprotected, it took a long time for him to not feel everything from everyone all at once and to learn to emotionally separate from them far enough to properly relate to them. In the beginning, he was overwhelmed by others' thoughts and feelings. We had spent years

First motorcycle - David & Adam put new front forks on it

building our bridge of trust, and it had become strong enough for others to cross and for Adam to meet them safely. It was even strong enough to let 1000 people sing happy birthday to him on his 21st birthday.

The many people who called me and had these 3-way phone conversations found the best of me in my son. He was kind and completely patient. He was dedicated to connecting and was supportive. Sometimes they would call when I wasn't available and would have a good talk with Adam. In the conversations, he would always come around to one question: What could they do to create the best solution for themselves? What he could do—supportive listening—he did, and if he sensed that wasn't enough, he would ask, "Do you want to talk to Dr. Winstrom?" A few people did, but many found his support enough. I never knew until my next appointment. I told them if they really wanted to talk to me to just tell Adam to get me and he would. They said they knew that but sometimes just needed to have someone listen and care about them, and let them solve their situation from that supported position. It seemed to work.

Kirk Cousins, one of the Holland Christian Quarterbacks, was an intense competitor and would come off the field frustrated with his own performance. Many of the other team members were also strong competitors in the infancy of the Holland Christian Football program and would be upset at not making a play. When they were upset, Adam would get excited and upset. He and I had many talks about his job. His job was to encourage them—tell them, "You did your best. You played well. Focus on the game. Focus on the team and work together." One night Kirk was having a difficult game and was on the sidelines by himself. Adam went over to him and put his arm around him and then began drawing plays on his clipboard to encourage the quarterback to keep trying. The coach came over and told Adam to leave Kirk alone so he could concentrate. Kirk told me that he told the coach to let Adam do what he was doing—it helped him keep perspective, kept him real and got his head back into the game.

One of the last incidents the school called me about was a request to pay for a computer keyboard that Adam had allegedly broken that belonged to another student. It was the end of an ongoing situation involving one of Adam's girlfriends. A young man had been following Brea around calling her a whore, bitch, etc. The report from Brea and others was that Adam had told the young man to stop and be nice. Adam then walked with Brea, telling her to ignore the other fellow. He talked to a couple of teachers and then my training combined with his new learning at Holland Christian took hold. When the kid would not stop harassing Brea, Adam stuffed the kid in his own locker for a period of time. The young man's locker was full of books and his keyboard, but Adam made it all fit.

My response to the school was that I would gladly replace the keyboard when the young man apologized to Brea and to Adam. I asked the school and his parents to let me know what corrective action they would be undergoing to assure that he and all other young men were respectful toward all the young women so that Adam was not required to act as a social policeman. The only message I got was from the young lady thanking me for Adam.

Weekends with Friends

Adam developed many friends. One group I referred to as the Bad Boys Club. They loved Adam and even protected him from being bullied or teased. Adam would hang out with them on Saturday afternoons and play video games and do guy stuff. These were the friends who did not want Adam to be too much of a goody-goody kid. They were also the guys who helped Adam learn to flip the bird and to swear. It was how they spoke when adults were not around. It is how most young adults talk. They were both irreverent and respectful as well as responsible. They were guys trying out being young adults. They taught Adam to shoot a gun. I had gone over gun safety rules, but I never took Adam shooting. They did, and they explained the entire outing to me when they came back. They were a little edgy for Jetta, but I knew them, and

I knew they loved Adam and would not harm him or do something too stupid.

One afternoon it got late, and Adam called me to tell me he would be home soon so I would not worry. When they arrived, I went out to

Class reunion after two years

greet them as I always did. I could smell the beer. Adam was 21, but they were not. Fortunately, the driver was clear enough and was not drunk at all. Adam being older was an extra benefit to his friendship with them. I only told them once to please have Adam drink O'Doul's (a non-alcohol beer) and don't be stupid and buy too much. The joy of inclusion! They never came back smelling like beer. His friends were being normal and trying out different behaviors. And Adam, being their friend, discovered the world right along with them.

Learning To Be a Good Date

High School was the best of times. Adam had become very good friends with Brett Kuipers, one of the football players. Brett and Adam would hang out, and Brett had a younger sister. As time passed, Adam began to ask Katy out. Katy worked all through high school, so her time to go out was limited. One time when I was dropping Adam off we bumped into Katy and Adam asked her out again. Katy seemed genuine in her telling Adam she would like to but had to work, so maybe another time. I asked Katy if she was okay with Adam asking her to go out or if I needed to interrupt his behavior. She said, and I believed her, that she liked Adam and would go out with him when she had the time. I asked her to consider doing Adam a big favor.

If she went out with him, would she also take a friend so Adam could enjoy going out and not get overly invested? I also asked if she would teach Adam how to be the perfect date—to be polite, to open doors, pull out chairs and be a gentleman. I told her that I thought women always trained men how to behave, but I would appreciate if she would be very thoughtful about it this one

Date night with Katy and Darlene

time. Would she pick the nicest place she could think of and let Adam take her and her friend out? She and Darlene and Adam went out to one of the nicest restaurants in Holland. It was a sport coat kind of place and they had a wonderful time together.

After that evening, Adam got to practice how to be a good date a number of times. I say practice because initial dating is a learning experience about how to behave and what to expect. I wanted Adam to understand that going on a date was not the first step to marrying that girl. Dating was a way to relate to young women as friends and to learn to enjoy being with each person and to let them enjoy your company.

Hot Chicks

"Hot Chick" was a phrase given to Adam by an adult friend, a woman, who thought it was cute. I was not comfortable with it, and Jetta did not like it at all, but Adam really did. On one occasion, he addressed Mrs. Kuipers, Brett's mother, as a Hot Chick and as I started to correct Adam, she laughed and said it was okay. Something in Adam's heart allowed him to use this phrase and make girls and adult women smile.

While on vacation in Mexico, Adam and I were headed down to the pool for breakfast when a lovely woman in a perfectly fitting bikini walked by. Adam looked her in the eye, smiled and said "Mmmm,

A lovely evening of dancing

Hot Chick!" I looked at the woman and apologized for my son's remark. She said, "He's cute, but you watch it." He was an innocent who had learned from his father that women are beautiful and if you smile and look into their eyes and tell them that, it is okay. Apparently, I had not practiced what I had taught because I wasn't really looking her in the eye; I think I had been noticing her bikini.

By the time Adam was a Senior in High School he had had many wonderful experiences. He had flown airplanes, skied Colorado mountains, swam in the ocean in Florida, California and Mexico. He had water fights with dolphins until the dolphin surrendered. He had made incredible lifelong friends and had over 100 girlfriends whose hands he could hold.

Cleaning an Angel's Motorcycles

One summer during High School Adam and I took a road trip vacation riding a Harley Road King. We had stopped for the night at a cabin in northern California. We got up early the next day to hit the road and saw that the bike was full of dew and sap from the trees. Adam got a wet rag and two dry towels and cleaned off the bike as I

went in to get our gear. When I came out, he had started on some real biker's bikes who had pulled in later than us. These were not rental Harleys with chrome. These were serious road bikes. There is a rule among bikers—you never touch another person's bike. I

Road trip

mean no offense here but a common saying is, "you can ride my wife but stay off my bike." Adam's heart told him to clean off their seats and tanks before the sap dried. As I opened my mouth to tell Adam quietly to please stop, a couple of the bikers came out of the cabins to address us, I thought. Adam and I were wearing our leathers that said Harley Davidson on a crest. The colors they sported read HELLS ANGELS, Oakland Chapter. As they came closer, Adam said, "Nice ride, clean it off." I was ready to get shredded as I apologized. But they just looked at Adam, and I think they said, "Solid, thanks." Then they looked at me and said, "Back off, he's okay." I did and Adam happily cleaned off the five angel's bikes.

He was coming into his own way to relate to the world, and the world accepted him.

Sunset Grand Haven Beach

One beautiful summer night with a perfect painted sky I drove with Adam to the beach to watch the sunset. Adam and I were quietly sitting together in the car with the windows down having a reflective time witnessing God's glory when another car pulled up beside us. They, too, wanted to enjoy the moment. We all were sitting looking at a magnificent sunset when Adam leaned out the window and announced to the couple sitting quietly in their car, "Hi, nice night. Pretty." Once again, my attempts to contain my son were useless, and my need to protect Adam was dissolving. They began talking with Adam and soon exchanged phone numbers.

He was secure in himself, he was safe, and he was accepted because his heart was more visible than his physical features. If only I would respect the man he was becoming just a little more. I needed Jetta's bravery and willingness to stir the pot and see what would happen to keep pace with Adam's maturing.

Compassionate Heart Ministry

Donna Bunce created a place for community to happen and named it "Compassionate Heart Ministry." Over the course of ten years, it became organized and defined. Their mission is to be a Christ-centered drop-in program for teens and young adults with mild to moderate disabilities in order to build inclusive friendships in Christ through peer and mentor relationships. Adam found this place when they were just a few blocks from Zeeland Christian School. Back then, Donna's focus was on kids with different kinds of mental and physical disabilities. Adam wanted to go there one night a week and hang out. I was initially not very supportive of his idea because Donna was creating a place for the "special" kids to come together. I wanted Adam to be involved in more inclusive activities, but he convinced me, as did his mother, that it was his right to choose where he wanted to be. He had lots of activities with typical kids, and maybe he needed to meet more kids who were differently abled.

Adam's friend, Chris, went there and so did a few of Adam's other friends from Zeeland Christian, some as participants and some as mentors. Adam knew them all. Kids would go there to do their homework, to hang out and to meet and make friends. Adam was already pretty good at making friends and loved Donna and the

Compassionate Heart Ministries

whole collection of folks. The distinction between "mentors" and "participants" blurred quite quickly. Everybody formed a community together, and some of Adam's best friends came from that community.

Serve Camp

Contributing to their community, Donna sponsored a Summer Serve camp. The camp was an opportunity for young people with disabilities to be paired up with a peer-mentor for one week and participate in a week of service-oriented projects in the Holland/Zeeland community. She modeled it after a national program in which youth come together to worship and to play, but most importantly to engage in work projects to improve the community. Adam loved work and play and worship. He participated in Serve camp every year and worked on projects such as painting someone's home who desperately needed the work done but could not afford it or manage the project on their own. They did landscaping for folks who were too old or unable to take care of their property. Crews would go out to work sites with the mentors working alongside the participants on the projects. This added so much joy to Adam's summers. He was proud of the help he could give to his community. And every Serve camp ended up with Adam meeting a new best friend to go out with. Many would call and explain that they had met Adam at Serve camp and wondered if

Summer Serve Camp

they could pick him up and go hang out with him, or go to dinner, or a movie, or.... Adam made many great friends, and his summers were full of fun activities such as Harley rides, convertible car rides, horseback riding, fishing, swimming and more.

Chapter 14
Graduation, Another Transition

Graduation, A Pinnacle Moment

The auditorium was packed. All students, parents, grandparents and friends were instructed to hold all applause until the end of the ceremony when every student had walked across the stage and received their diploma. But when Adam Winstrom walked across the stage to get his, everyone stood and applauded. Adam was in their hearts. He was not a mascot or a *special* person who was allowed to be there through Christian charity. Everyone really loved him. He knew them all by name and knew the football players by name and number. Everyone had his phone number, and he had theirs. An amazing student community had developed.

Immediately after graduation was the all-night lock-in celebration at an entertainment center in Grand Rapids and everyone was going. The school had provided buses to transport the students. Adam's good friends, Travis, C.J. and Gus had gotten together the

High School Graduation

week before and told me they would look out for Adam so I would not worry. It was an event not to be missed. Adam was excited, and his friends were excited to have him join in the fun. They had made plans together talking about what they had planned to do on this celebration of their last night together.

Then "It" Showed Up

After the graduation ceremony and the tears of joy and the pictures and hugs, I went with Adam to make sure he connected with his friends on one of the six buses heading for Grand Rapids and high school heaven—their all-night reward for four years of hard work. Adam really did not need me, but I wanted to be sure he found his friends. In every bus he looked into, he received a, "Hey, Adam! Come on, ride with us," but he told them he had already made plans with the guys. When Adam found the bus that his friends were on, he got on, said goodbye to me and the doors closed. It was their night.

I started back to meet Jetta knowing that Adam was secure with his friends, safe and included. Imagine my surprise when two teachers approached me and said, "We are sorry, but Adam cannot come on this trip. It wouldn't be safe. For his protection, we just can't let him come to the lock-in because we don't have enough staff to supervise him." I explained that Travis and Brett and Gus and P.J. had all stepped forward and said they would make sure Adam was fine, but the adults said no. No. No. No. Adam, who had just been cheered across the stage, included in the hearts of all assembled, really did not belong. It had escaped me that even at Holland Christian there were still those who did not think people like Adam would be safe in a group of normal folks. They were not a majority, but they could and were exercising their power in this situation. They were saying, "Not on their bus."

As I stood there, I had a moment of déjà vu. The year before, when the school had their Junior-Senior Prom night, all the typical students had their parents' cars and drove to the event. Before the event, they all met at a local park to take pictures and show off their evening clothes.

As this event was coming up during Adam's junior year, I asked his student support home room teacher how they had this event set up. Did I drive Adam or was there some other arrangement the school made? She explained that the special education class had never been included in this event because they had no transportation. Adam was an anomaly for Holland Christian. He had an IEPC and was *registered* as a special education student so he could remain qualified for any needed supportive services, but Adam was completely included in regular education classes.

When Jetta and I heard that all the kids in Adam's home room, the special education support class room were not included, we decided to hire a limo service for his class and some of Adam's friends went with his junior class as chaperons. His class arrived in class—a stretch limo. Jetta wanted to get pictures at the park, and we were given directions. When we got to the designated park, only Adam's class was there with his special education teacher and some parents. She had *her* students taken to a different park, one that was quieter and more manageable. Separate-but-equal treatment, unintentional exclusion. Stunned, Jetta put Adam in our car, and we drove to the other park to get pictures of Adam with all his friends, then drove back in time for Adam to get in the limo and go off to the event. The next year, I rented the limo again, only I gave the driver the correct coordinates to the park everyone else went to, just in case.

I thought we were through with this habitual foolishness, but on Adam's last big moment on the eve of graduation, it returned, and it was always "for his own good." I smiled at the two teachers and said, "Okay. I'll follow the bus in my car and will be happy to supervise Adam to assure he joins in at the party safely." It was an offer they could not refuse, or it would have been too obviously evil and too blatantly discriminatory.

Cell phone at the ready, I called Jetta and told her I was invited to the all-night party with Adam and just could not refuse. Could she get a ride home with her friends? She was rightfully confused. We had planned our own graduation party for that night and friends were coming over, some from out of town. I told her it was the only way Adam could go to his party and be with his friends. I told her that I loved her and that we would be home tomorrow morning sometime. She said she could get a ride and knew how much fun I would have all night. That evening was really a gift. I was allowed to observe the blossoming of my son in his world of young adults.

When we arrived and were locked in, I told Adam that I would be fine without him, but if he ever wanted to visit me, I would always be near and that he was free to enjoy his friends. My son and his friends told me it would be okay for me to hang out with them, but I knew and they knew it was not my night. It was for them.

Adam went with his friends and what that looked like was incredible. He moved smoothly between different clusters of young adults. He was always welcomed and often sought after to join another group. Food, young ladies and dancing seemed to be his interest. As he was with a group of young ladies, his male friends would wander in and join his party. They were dancing, playing basketball and just hanging out. All the ghosts of doctor's past statements and all the self-appointed, unnecessary safety patrols whose images danced in my brain were evaporating before this unfolding all-night party. I could see with my own eyes just what real inclusion looked like. This front row seat in life's live performance showing that night of my son safely in his community, loving and loved was the gift the teachers gave me when they intended to exclude Adam. I was filled with so much joy seeing that my son was just hanging out and that hanging out was noticeably filled with laughter and smiles and hugs and kids wanting to be together. Nothing special was what all the kids were doing, and that was so very special to me. In those moments, everything our family had gone through was worth it. Adam knew how to be a friend. He knew how to enjoy life. He cared about others, and they equally cared about him.

He had fun. His friends had fun, and they all included him. The teachers were free from any obligation, and Adam liked it. I lost a full night sleep but smiled and laughed as I was reminded again about my making plans. God smiled, too.

By 5:30 a.m. Adam was done, as were most of his friends and I was invited to sit and chill, eat some chips and drink some Mountain Dew. I found some coffee, and when I returned to the table, Adam was saying to a friend, "Okay, good Crats (his nickname), time to go. Call me." We found a real supervisor who released us and Adam moved me out the door. He slept all the way home from Grand Rapids to Grand Haven and once home went to his room to sleep some more. My day had just started, and Jetta had to hear it *all!* How did Adam do? How did he get along with the other kids? Did he stay close to the food all night or stay connected to with Travis and Guss? Listening to her ache to experience what I had just been forced to do helped me realize the gift I had received. I had been there to see our son in his community.

Graduation Parties on a Harley

For all three years that Adam attended Holland Christian School, he was invited to every graduation party. I would do the rounds with him on our Harley Davidson. I had started riding a bike with Adam when his physical therapist had suggested riding would help his balance and I was more than happy to do this for my son! Riding a Harley was a point of notoriety for him. I remember his first football practice as we rode in on our bike and all the instant testosterone in the air as the team wanted to know who this kid was. It was an ice breaker and later became an identity.

Going to graduation parties on the Harley

We would ride on our Harley Davidson and hit eight parties a day on weekends and some nights, and every time he was always greeted with a, "Hey, Adam!" I would leave for 20 minutes and ride around, then return and wait. I put 7,000 miles on my bike the first year and the local Harley mechanic, a real biker, said, "I guess you aren't a RUB after all." A RUB is a Rich Urban Biker whose leathers are spotless and who rides 30 miles a weekend to be seen. RUBs are disdained by real bikers. The following year when Adam was a junior, after he and I made our own modifications to the bike and

Adam with Brittany Van Byssum

put on a new front end, new head light, gas tank, pipes and juiced up the suspension, we got the honor of hanging out with "the guys." I found that the hard-core bikers were the most tender hearted, patient and (sometimes regrettably) instructive folks. They were a solid community for Adam. No matter where we rode on our Harley, other Harley riders treated us like family. It did not matter whether we were riding our smaller Harley Standard or if we had moved up to a Road King, we were always given the same greeting because we were family.

David securing Adam's motorcycle helmet

Adam Loved Parties

The first party Adam had at our house was when he was in the 8th grade at Zeeland Christian. He invited ten friends, and the invitation included maps and offers to transport. Ten friends showed up—all young ladies and all in their bikini swimsuits to enjoy the day celebrating Adam and enjoying our pool. Jetta wanted me to take pictures, but I suggested strongly that she was the one to do that and I would cook.

It was a great party with wonderful friends. The young ladies really enjoyed having Adam to themselves with no other guys to have to deal with. It was the talk of the school, and his parties were considered a must-attend.

Adam and some of his girlfriends

Adam's Graduation Party

Adam wanted to have a graduation party like all his Holland Christian friends had. The tradition at HCHS was to pass out invitations the last week of school. Jetta and I made up 100 invitations for his party. But knew that was no indication of how many friends would show up. We had prepared supplies for 300 just in case. We served tacos, rice and beans, salad, bottled water and some pop and of course cake, lots of cake. Just in case, I parked my car at a neighbor's house so I could get out and get more supplies if needed.

It was incredible! More than 500 people came. I had talked with (warned) and also invited our neighbors. We lived on a private road that was about a ½ mile long off the main road. Parking could be on one side, and we roped off the other. One neighbor, Bob, Adam's snowball buddy, offered and mowed the field between our house and his for extra parking. This party was our way of thanking everyone who included Adam. Some kids came six in a car, others were dropped off, and some guys came on motorcycles. Kids from the special classroom where Adam started his school days came, too. Football players by the carloads came. And girls, lots of young ladies. There were high school teachers and teachers from Zeeland Christian Middle School there. His minister and half of the congregation came, and most of our neighbors showed up. There were people I had never met before, but Adam knew them all by name and greeted each and every one. It was a most diverse collection of people all connected by their friendship with Adam.

They were not coming for *special* Adam or cell phone Adam or biker Adam or Christian Adam. There were there just for Adam, their friend. It was a very long but incredible day. A fairy tale in real life kind of day for Jetta and me. Here was Adam, the kid who I was told would never have any friends and who would be a burden to us his entire life, the center of attention of 500 friends. I should have invited the pediatrician, but I didn't think of it. I think Adam probably had more friends than he did. As for being a burden, yes, feeding 500 was a budget buster, but it was okay; it was a welcomed burden.

A number of Adam's friends talked with me that day about how thankful they were that they had had the opportunity to know him. Knowing Adam had changed their life as much as Adam knowing them had shaped his life. Many of them told me that because of Adam they were going to be teachers and get special education training so they could make sure everyone could have the same opportunities they had. They saw the joys, struggles and benefits of diversity that day. They were going into special ed to stop the segregation and isolation that the separate-but-equal notion had created. They were world changers let loose on an unsuspecting special education system. They were going to reshape *special* into exceptional and separate but equal into included. They all thought of Adam in a very special way—they all loved him.

I had resisted *special* Adam's entire life, but after seeing things from their perspective, maybe the next generation could embrace *special* without fear. Maybe the next generation of parents and their children would be able to experience a transformed special education, one that was there supporting them and their families rather than segregating them. All of these young folks were sure that having Adam included was one of the best parts of their high school experience. That was a "game changer" to borrow a phrase from Kirk Cousins. I did not work to have Adam included to change the world. Jetta and I did this to allow Adam to reach his potential. Adam brought all of his friends along with him to find their potential to make the world a better place.

The party from invitation was from 2:00 p.m. until 6:00 p.m. and by 10:00 p.m. most all of Adam's friends were safely on their way home. They had a blast.

Learning to Drive

Teaching Adam to drive my stick shift was hard on my neck. We found some deserted stretches of road in the country and began our lessons. In the beginning, it was like riding a bucking bronco, but eventually, he got the hang of it. I would drive home, put the car in park at the mailbox to get the mail and he would move into the driver's seat. Like a king, he would drive up our quarter-mile driveway home while I sat in the passenger seat pretending to be relaxed and reading the mail. Jetta did not approve, but he was so very pleased with himself for driving. He took his new responsibility *very* seriously with full attention on the road. Seated in the driver's seat with sweat rolling off his forehead, hands at 11 and 3 and smoothly maneuvering through the corners and into the driveway and a hard stop. Then the horn and cheers. He always exited the car on his kingly cushion of air floating on his pride.

I wanted him to know how just in case something happened to Jetta or me and he was the only one around. Driving was also something I thought a guy should know. I never intended to have him get a license, not because he could not master driving, but because I knew other typical drivers would not follow the rules and that would cause problems for Adam. He could stay in his lane and not pull out in front

Learning to drive a stick shift car

of others. Although he could learn to drive, that would not make him safe from others' road rage.

Adam Winstrom Day

Jetta Adam and I were not sure what was next for Adam. Work, volunteering, or what? Adam had been exposed to many possible futures during high school and worked at different kinds of places. At Zeeland Christian, they had done exposure to employment. They had in their program an on-the-job exploration with different businesses in the community. Every semester, Adam would go with an aide to a job site. Once he sorted parts and inventory for the local John Deere dealership (he loved the big tractors). They were surprised and amazed that after a week of sorting parts in their parts department, he had memorized where each one was and its coded number. When a customer of an in-house mechanic came to the window to get a part, Adam would take the "real" parts employee to the correct spot to retrieve the part.

He also worked in food prep and washing dishes at a restaurant. Another time, he worked in a nursery caring for the plants. Adam loved to work and enjoyed every experience. In high school, Adam had focused more on academics: How to sit in a class and take notes. How to find the main point of the lecture. How to find information. He learned how to learn.

Adam had slowly been exposed to staying with other people by spending the night with Jim and working a job with Jim Kruis.

Adam had had the benefit of spending every Wednesday evening with Jim Kruis for what he called "Adam Winstrom Day." Jim reminded me how this all started.

> *One day, I bumped into Adam's father, Dr. Winstrom as I knew him before Adam came into my life. We were both waiting to get out cars fixed. He was just talking about his son and how Adam wanted a job. Adam was interested in working part time. I was winding down a building maintenance company and owned a*

few rental properties. The way he talked about his son made me curious. I told him, sure, I knew of a part time job cleaning offices. He asked, "Where?" With me. I thought a part time job working for me was possible.

He made the arrangements, and I met Adam at Zeeland Christian Junior High. I liked Adam right away. He had big eyes, direct eye contact, a broad smile, and a firm handshake. He topped it off with a robust, "Hi, I'm Adam." (I found out later that Adam was looking between my eyes, not into my eyes. David and Jetta trained him to make nose contact, not eye contact. Apparently, direct eye contact is often difficult for people with Autism.) Still, he fooled me.

I offered Adam a job, and we cleaned offices one afternoon/evening a week. Initially David joined us but eventually, it was just Adam and I. Usually, I picked Adam up at school about 3, then we would go to work.

The friendship between Jim and Adam grew and lasted 12 years. I had wanted Adam to learn to work, to be productive and Jim had owned a cleaning service that he had retired from. He reopened his business enough for Adam to clean three offices on Wednesday night and Saturday mornings. That evolved into Jim inviting Adam to spend every Wednesday night with him and returning him to school or back home in the morning. It was great for Adam, and Jim said it was great for him. It was also great for Jetta and me as we had some time alone on Wednesdays. Jim wanted to understand Adam, and Adam wanted to understand everyone, including Jim.

His time with Jim was a great benefit because Adam became comfortable staying with friends for additional "Adam Winstrom Days," as his time away from our home began to be called.

As cancer progressed in Jetta, we had to make trips to the University of Michigan Hospital in Ann Arbor for surgery or a procedure. We invited Adam to join us, but he wanted to stay home or do sleep-overs. On this particular weekend of Jetta's treatment cycle, he had chosen to stay with Gayle, one of Jetta's friends. When we got home, Gayle told us that Adam got up early Saturday morning and made her breakfast. He then went out and moved everything out of her garage, cleaned the floor of the garage and had her come out and organize it with him. He even set up a chair for her to supervise his organization. He really loved to work. Gayle said he could come back anytime, of course.

Adam Decided

I had come to understand life as an adventure, a journey into the unknown and being Adam's father allowed me (compelled me) to see the world as possibilities without definition. Wherever Adam went, how that place functioned and what people accepted as normal, was always altered.

As Adam and I visited his friend's graduation parties and even at his own graduation party, what was next after high school always came up in discussions. Adam had not said anything about what he wanted to do after high school. We had been waiting to discover Adam's next adventure, and I think he was waiting for Jetta and me to make suggestions. The problem was Jetta and I were more distracted by her having cancer than either of us could see. We were so focused on Adam getting through high school we lost focus for a while.

As the cancer in Jetta progressed, Adam also progressed in his independence and comfort moving around in the world. Jetta and I had dreamed of our son having friends and going to high school. When cancer was introduced into our lives, we got distracted even though we tried to resist that. Here we were dazed after graduation; the effort to get here had consumed our total vision and what we worked for had happened. Adam was safe in his communities because of all the people he knew. He had strong connections. Adam was using his potential and his ability to begin to create his own condition for independence; our dream was real. What would come next had to depend on Adam.

Around July 4th, we were at a friend's house, and all the kids and their friends were in the pool playing games. When they came in, one of Adam's friends said how cool it was that Adam was going to go to college. Adam had started to talk about what he wanted, and this made it easy. My part in the conversation was to help him remember all the different things he had done and what those experiences of work, volunteering and school had prepared him to do. Adam said that most of his friends were going to college and that was what he wanted, too.

We had done our best to prepare him to be in charge of his own life and imagined that he would need a support system but not 24-hour-a-day containment. In our distractedness, Adam had found his own focus and his own voice. Now instead of two people making plans for Adam's life, there was one person—Adam. When Adam chose college, it made sense to us. Jetta and I took a moment to reflect and enjoy all that Adam had become and then began talking with him about what college might look like. We both laughed, remembering the *helpful* professional's stark response to my suggesting college could be a possible future for our son way back when he was three years old. Now, it seemed like a very practical next step.

Some of Adam's friends were going to Western Michigan University, Michigan State or Calvin College and others were headed for Hope College. I don't think Jetta or I were ready to let Adam go too far off to college and try living in a college dorm, even with assistance. That seemed to be too big of a step. Jim Kruis had prepared Adam well to spend a few nights away from us, but we did not think Adam was ready for a full semester. Calvin College was in Grand Rapids, and there was a program called "Ready for Life" run by the Christian Learning Center (CLC Network) to give young adults a college experience with some support. It was a possibility, but it was 40 miles away in Grand Rapids. I seriously considered working as a therapist in Grand Rapids to make sense out of driving Adam there every day like I had done to get Adam into Zeeland Christian and Holland Christian. It was possible, but

Jetta did not think Grand Rapids would be a very good community for Adam and I agreed because Grand Rapids would probably not be his community after he graduated from college. That meant Calvin, Western and Michigan State were not the right choices for Adam.

The First "Ready for Life" Class in College

I was more in favor making something happen at Hope College right in Grand Haven. I imagined it had to be easier than grade school for a college to accept Adam. I considered having Adam enroll as a lifelong learner at Hope College. Hope was a smallish religious school with a campus in Holland, Michigan. That academic year 4300 students put in their early application to attend Hope and of those most received an invitation to pursue full admittance. There was only room for 810 freshmen, and the students who applied early with their 3.5 GPA and high national test scores based on their written essays were selected first. Adam did not fit their selection profile, but I thought it would be good for Hope and good for Adam, so we proceeded.

Jetta and I decided to create something at Hope College for Adam. Adam did not have to be an accepted, degree-seeking freshman. We could just pay the tuition for their lifelong learners' courses, and Adam could attend a couple of classes. It would require some effort but wasn't impossible. It would mean finding a study buddy, learning the campus with Adam, talking to professors and driving back and forth from Grand Haven to Holland...a piece of cake, right?

Hope had already created a reduced tuition for people who wanted to take a class or two without the expectation of graduating with a degree from Hope. This was a way we could let him enjoy college life. Our friend, Jim Piers (the same friend who, shortly after Adam was born had not held Adam tightly enough and almost lost him, causing him to worry that he had harmed Adam's neck), was a professor at Hope and was willing to give it a go.

My father had graduated from Hope. I had gone there and played football my first year after high school. I had also been a guest lecturer there to expose students to Neuropsychology. I knew a little about the campus culture and many of the professors. Hope was a top-ranked school that many of Adam's friends were attending that focused on academics, social work and pre-med. Adam's prior inclusion would mean he would have some connections as he walked through campus. I imagined because I had played football there and my father had been a player/coach there that maybe I could connect Adam with their football program as I had at Holland Christian. It all seemed worth the effort to explore.

Professor Jim Piers and I started meeting to plan this new adventure. After a couple of meetings, Jim came across the start-up project by the Christian Learning Center they were calling RFL or Ready for Life, the same group that provided supports services to Zeeland Christian and Holland Christian for Adam when he was a student there. It was intended to provide typical college experiences for young adults with developmental disabilities, and they were attempting to add a Hope College experience to their continuum of services. They were in their beginning processes, and it seemed to me the path was laid out before me once again.

Jetta and I also discovered that the Ottawa County Intermediate School District (the county-wide special education support and coordination Agency for K-12 who supervised all programs in the public Schools in Ottawa County) had a Community Based Instruction program (CBI), that was working with Hope Colleges partner school Western Seminary through their new Friendship House. The two campuses adjoined and shared classes. Friendship House was a portion of Western Seminary housing where seminary students would live alongside persons with disabilities for the benefit of all involved. It was a two- story building on the border between the two campuses that had four apartments intended for two seminary students and one learner with developmental disabilities to an apartment. CBI provided assistance through instruction for each learner to become familiar and safe in the Holland community around campus.

Jetta and I took from all the possibilities available to us. Through my association with Hope College and my friendship with Professor Jim Piers, we worked with other professors to open up their classrooms to Adam. Through the Ready for Life program, we enrolled Adam in college and helped them get their program up and running at Hope College. We enrolled Adam in the Community Based Instruction program so they could teach him how to use public transportation to navigate the city of Holland, their program aim. He would also participate in their supervised exploration discovering the social outlets and housing possibilities available in the Holland area for him. All of these created the best condition for Adam to continue his development toward supported independence. All these internal and external support resources were the reason we choose Hope College. They all wanted the same thing Jetta and I did for Adam.

Jetta and I had read old educational studies that said inclusion was nice, but it had little effect after middle school and often disappeared after high school. We were observing and validating how wrong these studies were. Adam was as forever changed by his inclusive community as were they. It had supported him through high school and now into college. I imagined that many of Adam's friends would be future business owners and that would open up doors for employment for Adam and many others. Inclusion had forever altered Adam's sense of belonging. He was more comfortable in new situations than I was. I still carried my dummy scars, but not my son. He was free. I could put on my Dr. Winstrom costume and manage any situation. Adam could find the common relational ties and connect with the people naturally. Adam and I were living proof that studies were wrong.

That is how it came to be that Adam and five of his friends were the first class in the RFL program at Hope College.

When Adam's friends found out he would be going to Hope, they were excited, and they all wanted him to continue to be part of their lives and attend their classes. His full inclusion in Zeeland Christian and Holland Christian paid off.

Chapter 15
Hope College

Not as Smooth As I'd Hoped

My perception of the world is different than most people. I process information differently because I am dyslexic and faster because my brain organically works faster than most. I accept my world view. I see systems flowing and information coming to me in images and concepts, not as bits of information needing to be found, added up, organized and interpreted. It is my problem that I see solutions to other's questions as fast as others see problems. It leads me to see how a system *can* work where others see only how it will *not* work.

Paul Watzlawick wrote some very good books on change theory. When I first met him, I felt like I found someone who spoke my language. His premise was that people work for and talk about change. But what they are really talking about is reorganizing information, not change. We laughed about the years I had worked in Ottawa County Mental Health, and each new director would come in and pick a "new direction" with which to fix the system, yet the system never got fixed. It was just reordered from centralized services, the institutional model to decentralized services with lots of small satellite offices in the community, the community-based model. What was lacking was any transformative change. How the providers thought about themselves, their unique services and the people they supported never changed, just their parking lots. Decentralized services have fewer administrators and therefore more places to park.

Paul had affirmed my observations about systems and the people in charge of them. Most systems were formed organically to address one set of problems. Once those problems were solved, the system did not disperse. It continued and attempted to address situations and issues that it was not suited to address. Old solutions were constantly applied to new problems. When the old solutions did not bring the desired results, the system redefined the issue then doubled its effort, applying twice as much of what did not work to solve the problem. Even knowing this about myself and the world around me, I was still surprised by what other people considered successful.

Separate but Equal One More Time

When Adam entered Holland Christian, the administrator's definition of including him in high school was having him in the building and having tutors come into the special education home room at the end of the hall. The people designing the system thought including a special class room in the general education building was inclusive enough. They never understood the social forces that kept the special ed students segregated in their classroom. They never noticed that all the other students moved easily throughout the facility and the special education students *never left their room.* They imagined their one-way valve of having regular education students visit the special education classroom would be enough, but that was not inclusion. These same people were the architects who were creating the "college experience" for my son.

Christian Learning Center was partnered with Zeeland Christian, Holland Christian, and now also with the new RFL program at Hope College. Adam and I had assisted them in modifying their concepts so Adam could attend regular classes at Holland Christian. Yes, Adam's class work was a little different. His job was to sit quietly in the classroom and take notes. His job was to pay attention to the teacher and tell me from his notes what he learned in each class. It was his job to find the one or two main ideas for that day. He learned how to learn and attended regular classes and was included. He was recognized as belonging in the class. Different but belonging.

The RFL program was initially an extension of the separate-but-equal concept of eugenics and conflicted with the ideas of inclusion and normalization. While Christian Learning Center's role was to help organizations change direction to full inclusion, changing the direction of existing organizations regrettably was proceeding just the way Paul Watzlawick had described. The RFL program took their central facility programming out of the centralized facility and placed it on the Hope College campus. By placing it in a geographic position, they were able to say that they were on Hope's campus, but that did not assure students being able to move freely throughout the campus. The RFL students would stay in the classroom initially allotted to them by Hope College, in the basement of the last structure on Hope's campus.

The world had been given 30 years to come to terms with the Supreme Court Brown vs. Board of Education ruling, but Adam only had *now*. He could not wait another 40 years for normal privilege powered by eugenics to die out. We had taken Holland Christian from 1954 to 2004; now we would do the same at Hope College RFL before the program could develop self-limiting structures and rituals supported by the separate-but-equal philosophy.

As I had been instructed by my wife, first I had to accept them and their ideas as they were. Their idea of a college experience was going on scavenger hunts on Hope's campus conducted by Hope students, the students who wanted to go into special education, leading the way. The Hope students were the Seniors and the crop of the soon-to-be special education teachers. The Ready for Life program was housed in the basement of a building one block off campus, an extension of the idea of the last classroom in the building at Holland Christian intended to provide less confusion to the students. With less stimulation and less mixing into the culture of the campus, there was less chance of a problem. And from my point of view, no chance for inclusion. The floor above the designated basement overflow class rooms was the Hope College financial administration offices. Above them on the second floor was Morgan Stanley Financial offices. One adjunct professor had one class there two days a week. Almost no Hope student traffic came to this building; it was a social dead zone for inclusion.

I am amazed how ingrained separate but equal is planted in the minds of educators, even 60 years after Brown vs. the Board of Education Supreme Court ruling (347 U.S. 483 (1954)). I supported the RFL staff efforts to provide a "college" experience but not their separate-but-equal philosophy. I supported Hope students becoming exposed to the unique people they would eventually be instructing. I also supported *all* of Hope's students being exposed to the possibility of making new friends that I hoped they would eventually live in community with. I did not support the classroom location RFL had chosen—the basement of the business school almost off campus. This was not the experience Jetta and I had desired for Adam. The Provost utilized Professor Piers and me to update the RFL concepts into 2005. We all worked together to stretch their vision.

The first year RFL opened its doors on Hope campus and Adam began his college experience, the new freshman class had been on campus for three weeks and had started classes. RFL staff had thought it best to allow the freshmen students to settle into their academic year before adding contact with the RFL program. I had hoped Adam and the other young men and women could have been part of freshmen orientation. That was the time everybody was equally disorganized and all learning how to be a freshman class. The first week, all students were given tours of the campus in small groups. By the second week, all the freshmen buy their Hope College hoodies, which were all gone by the time Adam arrived on campus. The RFL staff were segregationists and didn't even know it. The staff never considered having the RFL students and the Hope College Freshman class integrate and jointly participate in the Hope College sponsored freshman orientation meetings. They never considered it important or appropriate.

The RFL staff were busy organizing their special classroom for their special students so that the future special education teachers could come to this special class room and work with these special students in the way only special education trained teachers can. (Jetta would have scolded me for writing this last paragraph.) All I could say was, "Father, forgive them, for they know not what they do." They all believed they were doing something *really* good. These were the "good" people, and they were unable to understand that what they were doing was not the best thing for Adam.

The first part of Adam's first semester was scavenger hunts on campus. Playing the card game Uno and walks across campus with upcoming special education students. They also went out for coffee with the new special education student teachers so that everybody was comfortable.

When I discovered that Adam was allowed to do some vacuuming in the lunch hall at Hope as a way to be included, I arranged a chat with his teacher. Jetta had instructed me to let them get comfortable and begin their program, but after four weeks, I thought I had waited long enough, maybe too long. I went in and met with Adam's teacher. When she explained what they had my son doing, I told them I was not able to support their current curriculum, and I would be happy to help them expand their possibilities. That meeting was stopped abruptly, and the next day I was invited to meet with the Director of the RFL for Calvin and Hope College. I explained my vision. I explained my avenues of support. They brought up the value of their approach. I listened, and I smiled....

They said, "having Adam vacuum the Phelps Hall Commissary was a very good activity. We felt it was a safe way for him to be in the crowded and confusing area filled with noise and laughter and it gives him a purpose. We have him wear ear muffs to deaden the sound. He's learning a skill for future employment and was...." I stopped them.

I asked, "What brought you to the conclusion that Adam needed employment training? I had thought he had enrolled in RFL for a college experience, not OJT (on-the-job training). Has Adam raised employment concerns?"

She told me, "OJT is just what we do; it is a central part of our curriculum."

"How did you come to consider vacuuming as part of Adam's college experience? Do you think he might aspire to vacuum for a living?"

She responded, "Well, it is a skill everyone should have. And we know from experience that people like Adam like repetitive jobs and one day he could be employed as a janitor's assistant. Lots of people like Adam did that and he could, too!"

I asked, "Did he do this task alone or was there a staff member assigned to vacuum also?"

"No, our staff does not vacuum, but Adam was doing a good job on his own. He is a very good worker, fast and thorough."

I asked, "How much was Adam going to get paid for vacuuming?" As she became less and less cordial, I stopped and just made my point. "Paying you for the privilege of having my son vacuum at Hope College was not money well spent on a college experience. If you had asked me, I would have said 'no, thank you,' because Adam already has this 'skill.' Had you asked what his skills were instead of assuming he was a person with Down's with no skills, you would have gained a different perspective of him."

I gave her a moment to think then asked, "What do you make per hour?" When she balked, I told her that the program's funding was public record and she responded that she made $15 an hour and her supervisor made $20. I explained that Adam made $35 an hour cleaning offices every weekend and used his money to pay them for his college experience, so please don't waste his time and money making him vacuum for free. I added that I used to work for Ottawa County Mental Health and they used to "teach skills" by having their clients clean up their facilities. After being challenged in court about this, the State of Michigan had written an administrative rule that patients/clients (folks like my son) doing work without pay was akin to slavery.

I waited for the impact of the awkward moment to settle, then continued. "So, could we all agree that from now on unless you want to pay Adam $35 an hour, his usual wage, you must stop enslaving him, stealing his time and must begin his 'college' experiences?"

After 25 years of dealing with well-intentioned people, I still did not know how to take them from 1954 to 2005 in a gentle way. I had determined it would be worth the shock to open them up to a different perspective.

His teacher said that she never thought of what she was doing as enslaving Adam and that she.... I cut her off and finished her sentence... "never intended to harm Adam." She never thought what she was doing was taking advantage of him or anyone else. I told her I knew it was not her intention, but it was the outcome of her actions. I apologized if my words seemed harsh, but like her, my intention was to move her beyond her old understanding of what she thought was in my son's best interest and open her eyes to what would best serve Adam as gently as I could. I told her that I hoped we could move past any thought of blame and into solutions. She agreed.

She told me that they might not be able to stop the vacuuming activity right away because they had agreed to vacuum that area for the semester. I told her that I understood and hoped she also understood that she would have to take over the vacuuming responsibility. I volunteered to take Adam with me for that period and begin his college experience. We would be going to the Kletz, the Hope College coffee shop, and hanging out. Other times we would be off to Skyles Bar, another college hang out, to have a pizza. They agreed.

When I had told Jetta that I was going to meet with Adam's teacher, she was concerned for them and for Adam. Afterward, when I told her how the meeting had gone, she said the slavery part was a bit heavy. I reminded her about the ruling that came down from the State office when she had worked at mental health, but, yes, I could have wrapped it in sugar and didn't because I thought the shock would open them up to 2005 inclusion.

Adam became their trail blazer and the first to enroll in a Hope class. I suggested/chose Hope's freshman orientation class. A psychologist I knew was teaching the introduction to that class to orient freshmen students. Adam could still get because it was right before drop/add week for class redistribution. The class curriculum included health (eating and exercise); resisting peer pressure; how to meet people; and concluded with the development of a "life plan" for their four years at Hope. RFL asked me not to contact the professor as they wanted to do that. They allowed Adam into the class. Brittney, a girlfriend from Holland Christian and a fellow freshman, heard about Adam joining the class and volunteered to be Adam's tutor. It was the ice breaker for all the kids in RFL to become more included in Hope classes. It changed RFL at Hope into a more inclusive experience although the program at Calvin remained a separate-but-equal experience.

Hangin'

I remember one day when I went to pick up Adam after class. He was waiting with Chris who had expected to see his ride, but it had not arrived yet. I could see Chris was uneasy in this new place. There were people he did not know, and he was end-of-the-day tired. Adam was also tired and his plan was to get in the car, go home and eat. I asked them both if they knew how to hang out? I received two puzzled looks and a, "No." I invited them to sit in the grass with me, and they reluctantly did. I told them the first step in hanging out was to relax. So, we took a couple of deep breaths. I explained that the second step in relaxing was to look around and see what the day was like. Sunny? Warm? Windy? Blue sky? Just look and see. (I thought to myself since I was winging this, I needed a moment to come up with step 3). Next look at the people and watch what they were doing.

Chris said, "My ride is late."

I responded, "Chris, this is important, and I don't know if I will be able to do this later. Take another breath and just relax and look. Now, tell me what you see?"

"People."

"Good. What kind of people? Tall? Short? Girls?"

Chris and Adam described all the people to me.

"Great, and now what are they doing?"

Adam said, "Sitting reading."

"Yup, that is one way to hang out. What else?"

"Talking together."

"Yup, that's another way."

Chris noticed someone playing a game of throwing a bean bag. "Great! Do any of them look like they are afraid? No? Good. So, there is nothing to be afraid of right now. Are they happy and laughing?"

"Yes."

"And you, right now, are you warm sitting in the sun?"

"Yes."

"Are you with a friend?"

"Yes," in unison.

"I want you to practice hanging out right here at Hope with all these people hanging out. Five minutes, OK?"

The two young men sat with me *hangin'* out talking about classes, girls and what they were going to do later until Chris' ride showed up. I told them I was really proud of them learning to hang out at college like this. Adam got good at the *hangin'* out stuff. Chris's ride thanked Adam and me for waiting and I told them we were not waiting for anything really, we were busy *hangin'* out.

Adam also developed his own skills to include himself

Reading the paper in the Commons

in college life, and to me, it appeared that God gave him his path to promote fellowship. Adam was a natural community builder, and it was observable. Adam had been included in so many different situations from grade school to college, including church, work and travel, that he naturally made friends all over campus. Adam was often joined on his path by Chris, his friend from Zeeland Christian. Chris was small for his age but frankly, brighter than Adam. Chris was just a little shy, and Adam was confident. They made an incredible team navigating Hope's campus.

Developing Inclusion Once Again

Once Adam was in the freshman orientation class, he began attending other freshmen classes. I talked with Adam's professor at mid-terms and discovered that he knew nothing about Adam—the RFL staff had not made the bridge I had hoped for. I shared Adam's background and learning style with the professor and let her know that Brittney was supporting Adam every day. They would get together at JP's coffee shop, hang out and study. The professor suggested I get RFL to make portfolios about each student and let other professors know what was expected. I passed the message. After that, I decided I would initiate contacts for my son.

I put on my old Hope College letter jacket and made an appointment with the head of the Athletic Department. I introduced myself and did the alumni sort of thing. He probably wondered what in the world a nearly 40-year-old ex-jock was doing sitting in his office. I asked about the coaches I had played under, and they were gone. I told him about my family tradition of supporting Hope football. My father had gone to almost every home game until he died. I was relieved that this fellow remembered my father. I told him what I wanted for Adam. To take physical education classes like swimming and weight training. I asked if it were possible for Adam to also be part of the Hope football team as a trainer. He told me he could open up all the physical education classes to Adam, but football was going to have to wait. The team had 70 students on it and was in its ninth year of a losing streak. The meeting I had walked past on the way to his office was a reorganizational meeting and staff realignment. There was too much chaos to introduce my son into. He did open up weight lifting and swimming classes to RFL students. Adam and Chris were in like fish the next semester's swimming class.

I did my Dad part to support my son, but Adam did his own inclusion work. He found out that his friend Brittney was the chairwoman of the student services board. She made it possible for him to make his way onto the student services board and made sure Adam was included. The students organized other students into community work groups to do volunteer projects in the neighborhoods around Hope College and the Holland downtown area. It was just like Serve camp for Adam, and he loved it. After the first outing, he was given the Guy in Charge badge because he kept the freshmen Hope students focused and working. He always worked harder than his crews did, so they followed him.

The projects were usually on Saturday mornings so we would get up early to pick up his crew and then drop them off or meet them at the job site and work would start. He would call me when he was done so I could come pick him up. His favorite project was collecting food for the food pantries in town. The team he was on broke up into pairs and went door to door around Hope College asking for donations. He went with two girls as I had taught him to do, donned their brown FEED ME t-shirts with turkeys on them and harvested four big bags of food. They had to stop because they had a hard time carrying the food. Adam loved the t-shirt and wore it often.

That first year at Hope College, Adam infected lots of fellow students with his friendship. He was living in a much larger world and added lots of phone numbers to his cell phone that year. He had so many people to say good night to each evening and to wake up for classes the next morning. He also had lots of people to pray for during exams. He had so many lunch dates with friends that he had to buy a bigger pair of pants.

My experience with inclusion at Holland Christian had taught me some of the normal opportunities to expect. It was a Christian college, and for many students, it was their first experience away from their parents' control. I had already had the introduction into "drugs, sex, and rock 'n roll" from the bad boyz at Holland Christian, so this time I thought I would get a little ahead of the game.

I had attended Hope College as had my father and I knew that the most popular student hangout was a family run bar just off campus. I took Adam there and introduced him to the bartender/owner. I asked her if she ever forgot a face, and she smiled and asked, "Is this your son?" I introduced Adam to her, we talked, and I ordered two beers.

One O'Doul's and one Bud. I asked her if she would remember to always serve my son his favorite beer, then turned to Adam and said, "Right Adam?" He nodded his head, and she smiled again. He was 22 years old, and I let Adam pay for the beer and show his ID that he was so proud of. I told Adam to always tip this bartender the price of his beer. Adam trusted me, but the bartender said it was not necessary, she would look out for him. We left, and I thought I had done what I could before I released the world to Adam. The bad boys from Holland Christian had always ordered O'Douls and Becks nonalcoholic beers for Adam when they went out. They had noticed that one regular beer made Adam drunk, which made him tired and zoned out in an hour's time. After one nonalcoholic beer, Adam was the life of the party, drunk on fun and on life, and they liked that Adam.

Navigating the Bus System

Through the Community Based Instruction program, Adam was introduced to the city of Holland, Michigan. He learned how to ride the mass transit system. I was pleasantly surprised to discover that Holland was very ADA compliant. They had a trainer available free of charge to teach folks who qualified under ADA to learn how to use their system.

I was surprised because we lived in Grand Haven and when I needed to find transportation home from the Montessori school one day a week, there was only a cab service, and I had to do my own training. I had to talk to the cab company and get one cab driver assigned to get Adam every Wednesday after school. I had created a problem by scheduling therapy sessions on Wednesday afternoon while Adam was in school. Even when I left myself an hour to get from Holland to the Montessori school in Spring Lake, if one of my clients had a crisis that required more of my time, I had to choose between my obligation to Adam or them. I choose both. That was the impetus to expand Adam's world and the world of the cab company. So, we practiced. We met the cab driver. We visited his cab and sat in it. I came to get Adam at school in the cab. The cab driver went to get Adam after school, and I followed them home. Adam went in the cab by himself. Adam and the cab driver became lifelong friends.

Adam and the Holland city bus driver also became friends. He would wave at his driver when he passed him on his route as Adam walked to his classes and would ride the bus home at the end of the class day at Hope. He also rode the bus twice a week from Hope to Compassionate Heart Ministries in Zeeland.

I learned about a miscommunication in the bus system from Chris. He thought it was okay, but I heard him talking with Adam about how they had to stick together at the train station. I asked Chris what he was talking about and both boys told me that the new ride they were getting from Hope to Zeeland was no longer a nonstop ride. They were being dropped off at the train station in town and were told to wait a half hour for their next bus to come and get them. Holland, Michigan is not like Chicago, but any train station is not a good place to hang out. I knew from growing up in Holland that the hobo camp was just down the tracks and around the corner. I knew from my work with gangs in Holland that the train station was a boundary line between two groups. And the train from Chicago came into town about the same time Chris and Adam were hanging out there. It was not safe to hang out there like it was on Hope's campus. I met with the bus scheduler and explained the possible problems that might arise with dropping Adam and Chris off unattended there. Chris and Adam both had their Americans With Disabilities (ADA) card that obligated the transportation system to provide supervision or to return to providing a nonstop ride for them. It was an oversight and a scheduling adjustment they had made without considering the possible non-intended consequences. It was an easy adjustment but necessary I thought, and they agreed.

In college, Adam learned to hang out and to study, and get across campus and around Holland. Lee DeWitt, the Director of CBI who had taken responsibility for teaching Adam how to navigate the city of Holland that bordered Hope's campus told me that he had walked Adam through the best route to come from his class at Hope and get to the CBI program two blocks from campus. It was through downtown Holland and offered distractions and street crossings to navigate. He had talked Adam through the route as he had walked with Adam to teach him the way. He retaught Adam to cross streets. I had trained Adam, as had his mother and Jim, but Lee, being the professional he was, wanted to make sure for himself that all was in order. Lee told me that the day he let Adam go by himself, with Lee playing 007 just out of sight behind Adam, that my son did it perfectly. He even talked out loud to himself repeating Lee's instructions. Over time, Adam began to say hello to people on his way. He told me he would say, "Hi, I'm Adam. I am going to CBI just around the corner." His class was the end of the day, and eventually, Adam knew all the store owners he passed well enough to smile and wave and remember their names. He was so well known that when a friend of mine from out of town accompanied Adam to the Farmer's Market, she was politely stopped, after people greeted Adam, and asked how she knew Adam. He was safe in the city of Holland and Zeeland.

I think it was while Adam was attending Zeeland Christian that I had lost my professional identity—I became known as Adam's father, no longer Dr. Winstrom. That was okay with me. What Jetta and I had started, dreamed about and worked for Adam was creating. He went to dances at Hope College with his friends, some new and some from his old high school. It was his community, and he was safe. He was wrapped in the protective blanket of inclusion.

Adam was not yet concerned about what he would do after he finished at Hope. He had only been there two years, and knew from his friends that college usually takes four or five years to complete. But Jetta's clock was ticking.

Jetta Wants to Know

Jetta was concerned about Adam's future and what he would do after he finished Hope College. RFL had not set the parameters for how long they would support a college experience. There was not a one, two, or four-year schedule. Still, Jetta, like every mother, wanted to know that Adam was established and safe in living his full life involved in his own community. Unlike most mothers, she knew she would be dead soon. Her time as Adam's mother was just about used up. The type of cancer she had was untreatable. The prognosis was four years and we received that when Adam was still at Holland Christian High School four years ago. She wanted to go to her grave knowing what could not be known—the future—for her own peace of mind.

David, Jetta and Adam

Adam, being his mother's son, began making comments about his future. When I grow up, I will...live...be...do. My experience with plans is that they, by their nature, create limitations more than they create freedom. I felt they held no sway or meaning yet Jetta wanted to know there was a plan, so it was given to me to develop it.

"What next" began unfolding this way. Adam and I began talking about possibilities on our ride home from Hope one day. Really, I began talking about what Adam might do after college, and he listened. It was not in his nature to talk about his distant future. Adam focused on today and tonight, maybe tomorrow. Next week and next month were not his concern. To think about what would happen next after Hope College was not on his mind; he was still going to Hope College and would do the next thing when the next thing was in front of him. That made talking about what would happen after Hope College seem unimportant. The elephant in the room was what happens after his mother dies. It was Jetta's intent that Adam and I make "our" plan without her involvement. I started talking about what his friends might be doing or what I thought he might like to try after he graduated. As with many of my talks with Adam, I did a lot of priming the pump. It would go something like this.

"Are your friends thinking about what they will do after college?" If there were no response, I would tell Adam a story about a friend of mine who was not sure what he would do after he finished school. My fictitious friend did not have a serious girlfriend and was not sure where he wanted to live or what kind of job he wanted. He was not ever sure which city he wanted to live in. He decided to try out different things. I rattled on unless Adam got on his cell phone or wanted it quiet—his way of saying, "I've had enough." My aim was to introduce possibilities and keep him open to all that the world might offer.

I also talked about his mother going with God soon. I told him I did not know exactly when but probably sometime in the next year. It would not hurt, but her body would stop working, and she would close her eyes and leave her body behind, kind of like going to sleep except when she woke up she would be in heaven. Adam listened and then talked on his cell phone. I knew he was listening as he always listened to me but he had not organized the coming events yet. It was a work in progress.

One fall day on our drive home from Hope College in Holland to our home in Grand Haven he told me that he would stay with me until Mom died and a little while longer to make sure I was okay, then he wanted to move out and get a place of his own. Maybe get married. Okay then. That was what was next. Adam's next thing was to make sure I was okay then do what his friends were doing: graduate from college, get a job and get married. His plan was to have his own home, a job and maybe find the next Mrs. Winstrom. I told him we would start working on finding his own home now and then a job when he finished at Hope because it took a while to find the right home just for him. Having a wife also needed some more work, I thought, before we created that possibility. He agreed. When we got home, Adam told his mother his plan. She liked it. She felt like she could start her own plans now.

Adam and I talked about when he wanted to finish at Hope, and his response was, "Later." I translated that into not now, and when it was time, I would know. From that day on, it seemed that Adam began organizing his life differently.

Adam decided he wanted to lose weight. His health classes had given him information about being overweight, and he was asking for some assistance, but not ready to really change. Jetta made an appointment with our family doctor to talk to him about Adam's weight. Our doctor asked her who bought the groceries? And who cooked the food? Jetta said she did. Our doctor said Adam's weight and mine were the results of the food in the house and the meals we ate, meaning it was up to Jetta to change what she did and that would control my and Adam's weight.

My friend Jim Kruis had the same idea. Just tell Adam he can't eat certain foods and can't drink certain beverages and that will fix his weight problem. I did not agree. It was once more the debate between internal and external control. Which is correct? Have Adam control himself or have others control Adam *for his own good!* Jim and our doctor said Adam's health was at stake and he needed to be protected. I thought his life was at stake and he needed to manage his health better and protect his freedom. Jetta wanted the problem solved, but she also wanted to have a "small" bowl of pretzels with Adam every night before he went to bed saying "it made him sleep better." We needed change, not transformation and fewer pretzels.

My solution was to support Adam making better decisions about food, and that was the path our family took. Adam took the freshman orientation class three times until he integrated nutrition and exercise into his way of thinking. I asked Jim Kruis to exert "control" by asking Adam when he wanted a pop or ice cream, "Is this your best choice?" After a year and a half Adam had integrated health into his way of being. He lost 50 pounds and was making his best choices most of the time. When he went out with friends, he used portion size control and would save half of his meal for later. At home, he and I would eat half the serving. Adam was developing more control than Jetta in this area.

Adam needed to learn to manage his own life with simple supports from his friends. The question was always, "Is this your best choice?"

and letting Adam decide. I asked his teachers to support Adam's desire to understand health and weight. They reported that they told Adam he was eating too much, but that did not seem to help. It was frustrating watching the way people wanted to "support" Adam by punishing him and telling him he was doing it wrong. I asked if they would help him preplan his meals at school by getting the menu ahead of time and talk with Adam about what would be his best choices for lunch, then support his good choices when he went with them at lunch time. All the teacher said was, "Yes, I eat with the students, but that that did not work during lunch."

Adam and I went on line the night before and found the lunch menu and planned his lunch for the following day. He liked the planning and the time we spent talking about his best choice, but without my being there he made a different decision when the food was in front of him. I was convinced that eventually, Adam would integrate what we talked about and that it would just take time and persistence. But I also enlisted his girlfriends. I asked all his female friends to support Adam making good food choices. And 20-year-old women were the secret weapon. They were supportive as they were also working on this issue for themselves while 20-year-old guys just eat. It took Adam almost a year to get eating healthy, but he got it and mastered his weight.

Adam was doing well at Hope and was not quite ready to move on, but it was Jetta's time to go.

Chapter 16
To Know the Unknowable

Jetta's End Game

I think Jetta asking me to assist Adam to plan for his future was Jetta's way to make sure Adam was working on his acceptance that she would die and that he would be okay. It was her mother's way to encourage her son and me not to be stopped by her death as so many people are and are unable to move forward. She wanted Adam to have his future. That was the source of Jetta's need to know that Adam had a plan in place for his future after Hope College. She could tell she was about to leave and with the assurance from Adam of his plan to get his own home, she had less concern. She told me as much that dying did not really concern her, living with the certainty that her life was to be short was the challenge. She was completely at peace with who she was and how she lived her life. She felt already God's grace touching her and was comforted by His presence. She told me she was going to be fine.

What she did worry about was what would happen to the world with no one to tap me on the knee. One night after Adam was asleep, she said that to me. I told her not to be concerned because Adam had her knee tapping down. He even had her tone of voice. Jetta also worried about me. We had looked after each other for 40 years. We had grown up together and grown together. I was formed into me by my 40-year relationship with her. Who Adam had become was a team effort, and the job was not yet complete. She told me, warned me really, that many of her friends would offer their ideas about how to raise Adam and that I should be kind, but only do what we would do. She reminded me that based on our support and guidance our son had become an incredible, unique person balanced with his own faith.

We always came to a joint decision about every important aspect of our son's life. (Well, maybe not teaching Adam to drive my little stick shift sports car or one of the motorcycles, but in the important things we were always together.) She warned me that after she was gone, I would have to find a new way to deflect well-intended friends who believed they had earned some right to have a voice in our son's future. She knew her friends and that they would think they should step into her position for Adam's sake. And she knew Adam. He had made every one of her friends feel like the most important person in his life. She smiled and said, "For years we agreed that you would be the bad guy. Soon, you will have to be both the good guy and the bad guy. Make sure Adam continues to grow in the way we know is best for him. People may tell you I gave them instructions. I have not. Some of my sisters have told me of their concerns, and I have listened and smiled. They may think that smile was my agreement with their concerns, but I smile because I trust us and I know you will do what we have always done. Put Adam first in our concerns ahead of other's judgments of how we live. Do only what you know we would have done. Okay?" Ok.

Somehow Jetta knew that people would want to swoop in and help. Help me through my grief. Help me raise Adam once she was gone. They would think they were being helpful. She knew what I did not, that they would be a distraction and might even become a problem for me. Jetta was a very strong woman and had protected me from her friends wanting to rearrange Adam and me. Be nice. Be patient. Remember how we have raised Adam for the past 20 years. She added that she wanted me to date and find a partner and not be alone so Adam would be okay leaving me to be on his own. Jetta's way of saying she wanted me to have another life after she died.

Jetta had cancer for five years. During that time, we lived cherishing every second. Knowing Jetta would die soon changed my perspective. I was more focused and observant of each and every moment. I worked on my thoughtfulness. I lived each day like I would not see Jetta tomorrow. Jetta reacted differently. She dismissed having cancer and focused on relationships. Adam and I became more precious. Her friendships acquired a greater depth and purpose. She did not have time to waste on petty or foolish personal conflicts. She was not distracted by nor interested in what so-and-so was doing; she was too engaged in living her life. She made purposeful connections.

Jetta had cancer, but it did not have her. She refused to be a cancer patient.

Inviting the Mental Health System into Our Lives

We both continued supporting Adam at Hope College but with an addition we made to his formula of supports plan. We added Ottawa County Community Mental Health (OCCMH). When Adam announced that he wanted to move out and become more independent, I started evaluating the availability of supports built into existing community networks. We began considering what Adam's support system would include when he moved out into his own house.

Mental Health had the federal mandate to provide "Community Support services" for people with disabilities starting when individuals reached their 18th birthday. We had chosen to not utilize the family supports services that OCCMH offered to residents of Ottawa County. Jetta and I had waited to invite them into our lives because it was one more system and one more set of entanglements. The school system was difficult enough. When Adam was talking about his independence and Jetta was talking about dying, it seemed a good idea to set up a backup system just in case I died too. We were very cautious and did not invite OCCMH to direct Adam's life; we just wanted to give Adam access to federal dollars provided through Medicaid for him to hire someone to support his independence—his way, a roommate for the time when we were no longer there to support him.

The entire mental health system was another obstacle and could be a chapter in itself. They talked about normalization and inclusion, but they still thought and acted institutionally. I had been the children services supervisor at Ottawa County Community Mental Health for ten years before Adam was born. I was familiar with their Community Support Program funding through Medicaid to pay for some of Adam's roommates' time. Later, I was appointed to their governing board during the State of Michigan's attempt to dismantle their institutional system. It was only partially successful as they still funded Kandu, the sheltered workshop that the *helpful* professional who choked when I had mentioned Adam attending college had wanted us to prepare Adam to work in. OCCMH still had a day treatment program in one of their facilities—a couple of rooms to continue the programming that Adam did not attend at the Ottawa Area Center. Once again, I want to reiterate that separate facilities are not inherently bad or evil. They can be useful for short periods of time, but the danger of the institutional conveyor belt is that separate facilities such as Kandu turns infants into children and eventually young adults who are day treatment workers without ever experiencing community life. They become damaged by the systematic retardation that segregation produces. Their futures are stolen from birth, and their lives are lived under the well-intended supervision of *helpful* professionals teaching them appropriate behaviors to live in institutions.

I was consulting in Allegan County Mental Health in their community supports program designing inclusive supports for Allegan residents. Ottawa County Community Mental Health was not inclusive yet, but both programs were governed by the same federal laws and received the same federal funding. After meeting with Allegan County Mental Health, I was well prepared for meeting with Ottawa County Community Mental Health to assure that Adam received the best services for him to live in the community even if Jetta and I were not there to support him.

Jetta's Graduation

Jetta managed to live with cancer very well. She remained outwardly healthy and always happy. She enjoyed her last five years with Adam and me and her friends. We lived life. We traveled and played, and Jetta scheduled her trips to the University of Michigan Hospital to coincide with art fairs and visits with friends. Some of the trips were to have tumors removed, so involved surgery. Other trips were just check-ups. Jetta chose not to have chemo. Some oncologists recommended chemo, but we knew her "orphan" strain of Hurthle Cell cancer was not amenable to chemo. No one was doing any research to cure this cancer because it was a low incidence cancer. The head surgeon and the cancer advisory panel, a panel of doctors from the University Hospital who consulted on their unique cases like Jetta's, told us there was no viable treatment available. They just had tables of life expectancy and notations that all current treatments were failures. Still, cancer never had her. She even volunteered as a social worker for hospice. I remember her coming home laughing from the interview. She told me they had asked if she had any contagious diseases. She described the looks on their faces when she told them she had cancer and it was terminal, but it was not contagious, and she was fine.

Jetta was an incredible person. Our last five years together were even more amazing than the first 35. Her perspective is sorely lacking in this story, but I cannot speak in her voice. She had a tremendous impact on Adam's life. Although she was at times in great pain after some of her surgeries, she never complained and or spoke with regret, but I always knew, as one knows the heart of their beloved, that her life with Adam and me was not as she had dreamed and was not her initial heart's desire.

I think her chosen path would have been to have a daughter who was just like her, not a son very much like me. She never thought she would die so young before our dreams for our son, whom she now adored, were realized. The one time she complained was one evening. We had just returned from the U of M Hospital, and her latest body scan showed thousands of light spots all over her body. Her lungs looked like the night sky filled with stars. But the stars were cancer cells all glowing. She looked at me, laughed and said, "You smoked. You drank. Your diet is not as good as mine. I was a vegetarian for most of my life. I never smoked or drank, and I'm the one with lung and liver cancer. It really isn't fair." We laughed a lot about life and even about death. I told her I would gladly trade places and she smiled and said, "You'll just

I am seeing angels everywhere

have to wait your turn. I was chosen first, He likes me better."

Her cancer finally reached its tipping point creating catastrophic failures. The last morning in our home in Grand Haven she had gotten up from bed and went into the bathroom. I heard a thud. That morning she fell and could not get up. One of the tumors in her spinal cord was cutting off information from her brain to her body. She could no longer make her body listen to her. We both knew this day would arrive so Jetta and I decided that it was time to go to the hospice house in Holland to let her body die. It was part of her plan to make her death as easy on Adam as she could. She did not want to die at home and disrupt Adam's life. Adam was off with his friends when I called the ambulance. While we waited for it to arrive, I called Adam and told him it was time for Mom to go. She was going to move to the hospice house in Holland, and he could stay or visit as much as he wanted. Adam met us at Jetta's new residence.

Hospice had their own facility with lots of suites and a music room. Every room was private and large enough for a party. Adam and I went to be with her every day. Adam brushed her hair and sang his "I love you" songs to her. As her end became clear to her, I had been tucking Adam in bed at night in our home, then leaving him and returning to hospice to be with Jetta and had friends stay with him while I stayed with Jetta.

Beloved Jetta

When she knew it was her last night she asked me to go home and be with Adam because she was going to die and my love held her here. She wanted me with Adam so she could let go. I wished her a good journey and left her with two of her girlfriends. She was right. I did not know how to let her go. She was my friend, advisor and love for 40 years. She said she wanted me to be the one to tell Adam that God had come to get her and she was fine. That night she left, and I felt it from 20 miles away and knew she was free. She was free while I was still here. Minutes later, I got the phone call. Adam was asleep. The hospice nurse said they would call the funeral home and that Adam and I could come in later. There was no need to rush. When Adam woke up, I told him his mother was now with God. We would have to go into Holland and talk with some people about her body. Adam gave me a hug and a pat on the head and said, "Andy will talk like Grandpa and we will go to the cemetery and bury her body."

Funerals, I'm so Sorry

Adam understood the funeral ritual. He and I had become pretty good at burying our dead. First his grandmother, then his Papa three years earlier, now his mother. He knew what a funeral service meant— sad people but also food and friends and stories about Mom and eventually people laughing.

Adam and I buried Jetta on April 15, 2009. We shoveled the earth over her coffin. Her body died, and she was with God in Heaven waiting for us. Her death was perfect. She was in hospice for two weeks and had no pain. She had taken care of hundreds of her friends and colleagues from work who all wanted to say goodbye. She nurtured even the ones who were all weepy and tearful until I began screening them out as they were taking too much of her energy. Many came to get their last bit of Jetta, not to comfort or celebrate her departure. I remember one person who asked if I was angry at God for taking my wife. I told them I was not angry; I was a little jealous but understood. They were confused. I told them I thought I was a good man, but obviously, God thought Jetta was a little better person, so she went to be with God before me.

Some of Jetta's friends told me that I was not showing my grief (their grief really), maybe I just needed someone, a shoulder to cry on. They felt that I was not giving Adam a good role model because I did not outwardly express my sadness, so he could see what to do. They were wrong. They thought he took his cues from me, and he often did, but Adam was already a seasoned veteran with death. He had his own way already developed; it just did not fit with what they wanted. While I was listening to them, Jetta's words came back to me. Her well-intended friends were here to help me raise my son and help direct his future. But they arrived with their intentions way too soon for me—we had just buried her.

What Jetta and I had taught Adam about life and the body dying was apparently not what most people understood. Jetta was right—her friends all seemed to have the need and felt free enough to tell me how I should raise my son. As Jetta had predicted, each one was sure they were Adam's new mother. Even though everyone marveled at the person Adam was and was becoming, everyone wanted to remake him in their image. Again, on my good days, I would smile and thank them for their thoughts. On my not so good days, I would say Adam is an incredible person and is just fine. Even after her body died, I could feel her soul tap me on my leg and remind me to be nice and whisper just do what we would do. When they pressed too hard and pushed me to live their idea of life, I still managed to thank them and would add, "Adam had one exceptional mother, and he still has me to let him know what life is all about, but thank you for caring." Then, I would try to walk away again. For those few who would not let me go or felt they were entitled to instruct me because they knew best and saw that my gratitude did not stop them from intervening, I would tell them that they were a temporary connection in Adam's life and they had no vote in how to raise my son. That usually concluded the conversation. Jetta had just died, and I had not had time to ground myself. There were no time outs to practice, so when life happened, I did my best at the moment. I could have done better. And so could Jetta's friends.

Adam understood the death process, probably better than they did. I told my son that death is the release from this world. God breathes His spirit into our body in our first breath, and that is our soul. With every breath, we renew our gratitude to God and nourish our bodies. Our bodies are temporary, but our soul is forever. It is a joyful moment when a soul is given to us. It is a joyful moment when our body stops, and we can return to God. Most people cry and get sad about death because they see only their loss and do not understand that birth and death are a natural cycle of God in Heaven and God in the flesh sharing His love. This was my way of letting Adam know that God is eternal. He breathes a soul into us with our first breath. We were created in the image of God, and in every moment we are sustained by Him. It is God's presence within each person that sustains the body. Michael Card, a song writer and a Hebrew scholar, told me that when God first revealed himself to Moses as YAHWEH that the most accurate translation of this word is the sound of a person breathing. So, with each breath we honor Him and bring His life force into our body. God eternal calls Himself "I AM that I AM." He is always present to receive the soul He placed in us when our time comes to return to Him. I told Adam that everyone he knows will have their body die. You will die and I will die. Adam always said to me, "No, I can die, but you can't." I taught Adam that however anyone acted was okay and showed what they understood about life. Knowing that the body will die makes death as natural as breathing. I told him that we are to comfort those who mourn and rejoice with those who celebrate life.

People often asked me what Adam could understand. I just smiled. Many who became Adam's friends when Adam was older never knew he had Autism. Most never knew he had expressive aphasia. Some people just saw the flesh and judged him as a lesser being because he had Down syndrome, but after they experienced his ability to know them and touch the essence of their feelings and their thoughts; he left them confused.

I celebrated my mother, father and wife dying without suffering. With Jetta cancer had spread throughout her body, but it was the tumor on her spinal cord just below her neck that stopped the impulses from her brain to her body and her body first went numb, then stopped completely. It took two weeks to close off the pathways in her spinal cord.

Adam did better than me with the folks who wanted to be sad. The people who wanted me to join them in their moment of shock or sadness no longer had Jetta's protection. My kindness was exhausted, and Jetta's strong influence wasn't quite enough to subdue me. To all who came to me with eyes red or downcast saying they were so sorry, or it was such a shock, or that regrettably, they didn't have the time with her that they wanted, I sometimes said, "A shock? I told you she was dying four years ago." Or worse yet, "Sorry? Do you mean you are in sorrow with me as is the old English custom? But I am not in sorrow. I had her as a gift for 40 years, and now she is free, returned to God." The people coming at me with a Kleenex in their hand was short lived. They quickly learned to go to Adam and Adam comforted them. Even with the loss of his mother he had the capacity to comfort and support them when I faltered and could not.

Just after Jetta died and before her final celebration, Adam and I had read together about Job's three friends who came to visit him: **"Then they sat down on the ground with him for seven days and seven nights with no one speaking a word to him, for they saw that his pain was very great. After this, Job opened his mouth…"** (Job 2:13–3:1). This is what my son understood. Adam learned the three principles to comfort those who grieve: Be there; speak in silence; and hear with your heart. What they could not do for Adam or me, he modeled for them.

Adam understood. He lived every moment in the moment. Maybe the greatest gift I received from being Adam's father was learning to only live in this moment. To live all of life now. Regret, I believe, comes from people living their lives in "as if" time, not really connecting or being intimate. It's the "I will someday" folks who have regrets. Adam did not live there.

What I received from some people was, "I loved her, too." "She was a gift." "I will miss her gentle ways." "What can I do for Adam?" To all of these, I opened my home and invited them to come tell stories and rejoice in the life she lived so well.

When we returned home the day we had buried Jetta's body, our friends had gathered to eat and tell such stories. Adam discovered his gerbil had died. He had been Adam's friend for six years. I never considered how long a gerbil lived until he died. It was a day of passing. Adam knew just what he wanted done. He got a box, dug a grave under a favorite bush and assembled everyone who happened to be present in our home. He asked Pastor Andy DeJong to say a few words for his friend who just joined his mother. God blessed Andy with just the right words and Adam sang and shoveled in the dirt. Amen. After we buried Jetta, Adam and I would visit the cemetery where their bodies were, and he would tell them his stories and sing.

Mourning Light – Life After Jetta

The hospice worker called and asked us to come in about three months after we buried Jetta. She was prepared and had her children's coloring books and storybooks entitled, "When My Mother Died." I could see she was ready to help Adam and me. However, before she got started on her presentation, Adam handed her his book that Jetta had made for him about life and her cancer and what she wanted him to know. It was a talking scrap book format with pictures on each page of Adam and Adam and his mother. There was a button you could push, and Jetta had recorded her story for Adam. The sound of her voice was clear and loving and filled the room as Adam turned each page and listened and talked about his mother. By the last page, the hospice worker was sitting next to Adam, and he was reassuringly telling her that it was okay.

Jetta and I had had five years to get it right. Her departure was not a surprise to Adam. It was part of his real life. When we got up to leave, the hospice worker said we were doing just fine, and what an incredible mother Adam had.

For 29 years, I had joyfully honored my covenant to both of them. Our commitment really, Jetta and mine. Each member of our little family had had some old rituals and some new ones to develop. As we developed our way of being the Winstrom family, we made sure that what we did we did with Adam not just to him. We were taking seriously the admonishment to "teach your children" not command them. Jetta had been successful. Jetta's role was to find and stay in the moment with Adam and allow him to join with her. She had to stay vigilant and available to Adam, matching his attention to the task at hand. She had managed that until Adam changed his rhythm and then she adjusted her way of supporting him, and I had begun to make our special connection. I followed him into and back out of Autism when Jetta could not. It had worked. Adam had been able to discover what it meant to be Adam Winstrom, our son. Here he was a 29-year-old young man, confident in himself and capable of so much more than anyone had been able to imagine except Jetta and me. My obligation to be the father Adam needed me to be was double-edged. First, I was the one responsible to interact with the larger systems creating conditions for Adam to be fully included. Second, I had to always make sure the friction required to reshape the social systems was not experienced by Adam. I did for him what he could not so that he could devote all his attention and energy to becoming the best person he could be. We had all succeeded.

True to his word, Adam stayed with me for

Adam visiting Jetta's grave

another nine months. Adam was still at Hope College, and I would pick him up from his classes, and we would visit Jetta at the cemetery, share his school stories and sing to her. Then we would look at houses, trying to pick a good neighborhood. I started making serious plans for Adam to have his own home.

Just Another Detour

One day Adam started showing signs of getting a cold. His immune system was never great, and Jetta dying had slowed us both down a lot. It was winter and Adam would often get colds and sinus infections this time of year. I called his doctor imagining it was soon time to start an antibiotic. By the time we got an appointment three days later, he was coughing enough to lose sleep and feeling really punk. He started the antibiotics, but by now we were four days into the process, and I was getting nervous. I trusted the doctor, but I saw my son progressively getting worse and slowly leaving me. I called every day, and the doctor reassuringly told me to make sure he was taking the antibiotics and fluids and resting. There was nothing more they could do, and he would be fine. Adam did not want me to leave his side. He did not seem afraid as much as he felt death looming and needed me close to stay in this world. I could tell that he was trying to hold on to staying with me.

I called his doctor one more time and told him that I was going to drive him to the hospital. When we got there, we went from the ER to ICU; he had pneumonia and was not oxygenating enough. His lungs were too compromised with fluids to let oxygen pass into his system. They put him on oxygen and IV antibiotics and said I could go home, but there was no way I was leaving. Even with all that was happening in ICU Adam wanted to reassure all his friends. Because only family were allowed in ICU and he did not want his friends to be worried, he asked for his banana nose and had me take his picture to send them.

When Jim Kruis came up, then I went home. While I was gone, Dr. Ivey, the pulmonary specialist, had been called in because

Adam was not responding to treatment. Pyothorax, as it is also called, is an infection of the chest cavity that resembles spaghetti and grows fast, eventually restricting the heart and lungs. It is serious, and often kills people before it is even diagnosed. Dr. Ivey was in charge when I returned to tell the ICU staff my concerns. Without looking up from

Adam cheering up his friends with a "banana nose" Facebook post

Adam's chart, Dr. Ivey told me, "Yes, Adam has a catastrophic illness that we started treating him for two hours ago. And who are you?" After hearing me say, "I am his father," he walked away, and I returned to Adam. My son was intubated and drugged out with monitors everywhere.

I will not go into detail on this hospital experience except to say that it was another system still influenced by the old eugenics philosophy. They not only underestimated Adam, but true to their eugenics training they viewed him as a mentally deficient person and, therefore, one who could not actively participate in his own treatment. One of the ICU nurses had warned me that the lead ICU doctor did not like working with retarded patients because they could not understand what was happening and often resisted treatment. He typically sedated them so he could just do his job more easily. True to his reputation he did not explain nor prepare Adam for procedures. This added to Adam's anxiety and compromised his ability to work with his doctors to assist in his own recovery. After I had stopped the doctor to talk to Adam and explain the procedures, the doctor placed Adam in a "therapeutic coma" to avoid any further issues. They did not respect him as a human being but saw him as a body to do with as they thought best.

Systems' ineptness and judgments about the "retarded" require parents to guard their children well. Dr. Ivey and the ICU chief were at odds over Adam's treatment and Dr. Ivey's orders to reduce Adam's sedation in order to give his body a chance to respond and heal were being countermanded by the chief who wanted to maintain a coma for his convenience. Their inability to communicate with each other and treat my son in a coherent manor endangered Adam's life. The ICU doctor in charge told me that his plan was to move Adam to his long-term facility in a coma for three months based on Adam's inability to understand his treatment and knew this would be the best for Adam. I told him that was not possible and was not going to happen. He warned me that I was acting AMA (against medical advice) and I agreed and thanked him, then to his amazement, I discharged him. I fired their chief of ICU through the hospital administrator, barring him from entry or involvement in Adam's treatment. I supported Dr. Ivey as he seemed to know what he was doing and had Adam's welfare in mind. When Dr. Ivey discovered what I had done, he asked me once again, "Who are you?" I told him that I was Adam's father, his guardian and a distinguished expert for the State of Michigan in best practice models and that his hospital was a marginally functional system, almost as dangerous as *helpful*. I could hear Jetta say, "Be nice."

When I told Dr. Ivey that I wanted to take Adam home, he told me that I would be killing my son if I didn't send him into the coma treatment facility. Then he walked away to let his words sink in. Dr. Ivey was better than the doctor I discharged but only by a little. He was not free from eugenics and its prejudice about *retarded* patients. I knew he was wrong. I knew putting Adam in a coma for three months would kill him, or at least destroy any semblance of who Adam was. I knew Adam's brain would never recover from the forced coma of that duration.

Then a miracle happened. In the middle of the night Adam's respirator broke, and, thank God, they had no replacement. I insisted that they call the on-call doctor for permission to stop Adam's sedation medications and add some stimulants so his body functions could return to him and he could fight on his own to breathe. The problem with sedation is that it eliminates the body's natural impulse to fight for life. It was repressing the natural desire of Adam's body to breathe and fight for each breath. He needed to be alert enough to fight for his survival. Had he stayed sedated in a semi-coma, I think he would have died. The nurses and I bagged him for a while to help him breathe and encourage Adam

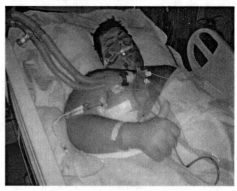
Thumbs up signal -- I'm okay!

to breathe. Finally, the sedation wore off, and I had my son back. He was afraid and confused but able to look into my eyes and listen to me. I told him to fight for every breath. I would help him find his rhythm and squeeze the bag to help, but he had to work now. He began to breathe on his own. They called Dr. Ivey, but with no replacement respirator, there was nothing he or the nurses could do that they were not already doing. The hundreds of prayer groups that had been focusing on Adam were heard, I think.

We made it through the night. The next day Dr. Ivey said he still wanted Adam returned to a respirator with the aim of the three-month coma. I refused. I pointed out the obvious. Adam was strong enough now to breathe on his own even when the respirator tube was blocking part of his airway. I had them remove the tube so Adam could breathe better on his own. Dr. Ivey counseled me on my decision and said he could discharge Adam AMA—a discharge based on noncompliance with *his* medical advice. He could also discharge us to another hospital. I agreed with him and asked if he could continue to treat Adam in a way we could both support. He did not discharge Adam. He let us stay and continued to treat Adam. He acted like he did not listen to me, but he had listened because Adam's chest was clearing. In a few days, the Pyothorax was gone and the pneumonia and was almost gone, and Adam wanted to come home. Dr. Ivey told me his lungs were too weak, his chance of reinfection was too high and I would be making another big mistake. I thanked him, and when Adam's chest tubes were removed and his x-rays were clear, we went home.

Adam was on oxygen continuously, and no one came in or out of my home except the physical therapist who scrubbed in and out and wore a gown. In six weeks, Adam was off all oxygen and was strong again. He had done it. We had done it. Adam had been calling his friends and was hot to go out, but I asked him to take it a little easy and first see what Dr. Ivey said.

When Adam and I returned to Dr. Ivey's office 45 days later, what Dr. Ivey saw was a young man standing in his office breathing naturally with good color and clear speech. He listened to Adam's chest and asked, "How did you do it?" Then Dr. Ivey spoke into his Dictaphone: "Adam Winstrom 8/26/84. From catastrophic illness to miraculous recovery in six weeks." He shook my hand and said he was wrong then asked again, "how did you get him so healthy so quickly?"

"It was the harmonica," I told him. "I got Adam playing the harmonica. Being tone deaf, it was fine with me, and it was a great lung building exercise—it required both resistance and back pressure." Adam had some minor scarring on his lungs, but they were clear, strong and fully functional. As was Adam. Dr. Ivey became a fan of Adam and dropped his detachment when Adam came in for follow up visits. He even joked with me. He had underestimated Adam's potential and how that potential affected Adam's treatment. Adam had fit the medical staff's perception of a retarded young adult. But he broke their stereotype and replaced it with a person capable of being involved in his own treatment even having the will, attention and persistence to overcome major obstacles. That was a new understanding for them. I respected Dr. Ivey not only as an incredible doctor who knew faster than I did what was wrong with Adam, but also risked treating Adam differently than the hospital culture typically did. That was the reason I did not discharge Dr. Ivey; he was bright and willing to follow what he observed even when what he observed contradicted what he had known to be true. As with so many, Adam created a condition to allow Dr. Ivey to grow. At the end, he treated Adam like one of his friends.

With Dr. Ivey's blessing, Adam returned to Hope College part time. By the time another month had passed, Adam was in full bloom, back to his old patterns and going out with friends. Spring had arrived, and Adam was feeling himself again. Adam stayed with me another eight months, going back and forth to Hope for classes and to Compassionate Heart Ministries two nights after school. Then he said that I was doing okay and it was time he moved out.

I was given the gift of life with Jetta and Adam, and I untied the bow on the box in 2014 when he bought his own home.

Compassionate Heart Ministries Camp

Hangin' with the boyz

Chapter 17
Starting Adult Life

We Found a House

Adam and I found a house in the nice, small community of Zeeland. We had looked in Holland close to Hope College, but it did not seem like the right area. Adam had prayed that we would find his new home soon and we did. The house was perfect and had a fenced-in yard with a pool. The for-sale sign was tipped over, and no one else had wanted it. The home was in foreclosure and was just two blocks from Compassionate Heart Ministries, a place that provided a community for Adam to make friends. It was also on the Max bus line that could take him to school. Once again, the direction had been presented. The house was perfect, and we bought it in Adam's name.

The house needed a complete redo. It was a repossession, and the prior owners left trash everywhere, and the house had big holes in the walls. Dogs had lived in the house, and they had not been let outside. The pool had tadpoles and big frogs that were 4" long. Adam and I started washing the brown spots off the wall only to have them return the next day. It was nicotine; they all smoked and the house was an ash tray, so we used ozonators for a week and then applied a coat of KILZ to every room. It would have taken Adam and me months to get everything done just to make it livable.

Once again, the path was illuminated. Our church called me to ask if they could do anything for me, after all, Jetta had just died and Adam had almost died. I think they wanted to send someone to sit with me or make a casserole. I told them that I was well, but Adam needed some help. Could his men's group paint the inside of his house? Silence, then "sure, that sounds like something we can do." Adam was in the men's group and had helped people move, mowed their yard, and even painted the outside of their houses.

I hired haulers to take away the junk, a sheet rock company to patch the holes, carpet removers and floor finishers. Janie, an interior decorator from church who loved Adam, offered to help Adam pick out paint colors. She wanted Adam's home to be cool. Lots of Holland Christian maroons. Janie was especially a gem. She was patient and insistent that Adam pick the colors. When he wanted his bedroom to be black, I balked, but it was his house, and it became his black bedroom. "Nice and dark," he said, "no light, so I can sleep in." The two of them picked the colors. I just bought the paint. And more paint. They came 15 strong and painted every room. Adam also worked, and when they were done a week later, they moved his furniture in. It was God in action. The house was transformed, and Andy came and blessed it.

One day a week he was with Jim, and he still wanted to take care of me three days a week. It was a good (a God) transition. Eventually, Adam expanded to four days in his own home, was with Jim one day and with me only on weekends. He had a swimming pool at his house that we fixed up so he could swim all summer. He really did have his own home.

The Gift of Eli

Eli had been Adam's friend since Adam was eight years old. When Adam and I were developing his next move in life into his own home, we always considered Adam having a roommate. Eli had needed a place to live, and Adam asked him to be his roommate. Adam needed a unique kind of person to live with him—one who could advise him but not be his boss, to have his own life and still be willing to support Adam living his own life.

I had approached Ottawa County Community Mental Health to utilize their community supports program. They were responsible for disbursing Medicaid funds intended to reduce dependence on classical Mental Health Programs and to support more independence for young men and women to be included in their own communities. The idea was to take the money spent on the old institutional model of paying mental health professionals (costing the State taxpayers over $150 an hour) and replacing them with support people in the community (paying them $15 an hour). Instead of spending three hours with a professional learning to cook or shop or engage in learning community safety, the goal was to find more natural community supports. It was the reason Eli could not only be Adam's friend but a mentor for Adam. It was a good trade—replace the three-hour social worker with up to 30 hours of real support in a real community for the same amount of money.

Eli was never comfortable getting paid to do what he loved doing for Adam. He said free rent was enough, but I told him it was the best of all worlds because mental health spent less money and Adam learned more. And, Eli could focus on going to school because he had a good home and a great roommate. And I had done my job to create the best conditions for both of them.

The Police Visit

His roommate, Eli, was working out well. Eli told me a story about a visit one night by the police. They came over because someone had complained that a person living there had shined his flashlight at their house. When Eli (26 years old) answered the door, the police wanted to know who was in charge here and he said, "Adam Winstrom. I will get him." When Adam showed up at the door, the police were ill prepared for the home owner being Adam. Then, when Adam refused their request to come in, they were clearly out of their element. He had learned well that if you do not know the person at your door, they stay *out*. The police were not used to Adam's brand of proper behavior.

Eli said that as the police stood outside the door, they attempted to interrogate Adam, but he answered their questions with yes or no and the truth. Adam told them that a dog had barked as he walked by that house and he flashed his light at it from the sidewalk. The police tried to make it seem that shining his flashlight at the house was wrong. At this point, Eli added that at night, for Adam's safety and anyone else's, if Adam heard a loud noise in the dark, he was instructed to shine his light at the noise until he knew what was there. He had done this from the public sidewalk. The police asked him not to do that again and left. Adam started to get upset, but his roommate laughed and then so did Adam. Eli told the police that if there were no strange noises coming from a dark area, Adam would not shine his light.

Every day the following week I went with Adam to the house that had complained, but no one answered the door. The dog inside barked but Adam suggested we just ignore it. Home owner Adam was in charge of his own life. Eli was a gift to Adam and told me that Adam was a gift to him as well. Eli said that Adam helped him at least as much as he helped Adam.

A Good Citizen

What did that look like? Our 29-year-old son owned his own home. His home. He never lived in the group home the *helpful* professionals had reserved for him. He loved keeping his very own home clean and organized. He could, with the support of his roommate, Eli, decide on the foods he wanted to eat, make a menu, go shopping, put his food away, get the necessary ingredients out of the cupboard, get the pots and pans out that he needed, cook dinner for him and his roommate, set his own table, serve the food, and sit to enjoy what he had done. Eli preferred to cook with Adam because they had fun in Adam's kitchen, laughing and messing around. After enjoying a meal together, they both did dishes. Adam even invited friends over and made the meal.

Adam could take Jack, their dog, for a walk at night *alone*! It was an aim of Adam's to walk Jack by himself. Jack was originally Eli's dog, but

Adam became Jack's best friend, too. Eli had started out taking Jack for a walk, and Adam had just come along. Eli had explained to Adam how important it was for Jack to get out and walk each day and how much Jack enjoyed it. Adam was all about keeping Jack, and incidentally himself, healthy. Eli began having Adam pick the directions until Eli was comfortable that Adam could go different places in Zeeland, maneuver cross streets, take different routes and get home safely. Then Eli let Adam take Jack's leash and walk making sure Adam was kind to Jack and kept Jack safe at street crossings. Eli taught Adam how much pressure to hold on the leash and how to get Jack to walk with Adam and not pull or bolt when another dog, squirrels or cats crossed their path. Then Eli let Adam take Jack on his own with Eli shadowing back about 50 feet until Eli was comfortable that Jack and Adam could take good enough care of each other to really go out alone. Then Eli had Adam plan how long the walk would be and what time they would return. Eli and Adam had the same agreement I had with Adam. If anyone leaves the house, they tell everyone else in the house where they are going and for how long. If the plan was more than an hour, a check-in call was arranged. Supported independence. Freedom of inclusion like Lee DeWitt had done with Adam at CBI and like the ADA representative had done on the Holland city buses. Like I had done. We introduced Adam to the routines then supported him in those routines. Fade, slowly remove support and let Adam continue on his own always checking in to get reinforcement and support to continue to do his best. And, like with each prior experience, Adam added his "Hello, I am Adam" to the people he met as he moved through the world and made each one his new friend. He came to know the names of someone's wife or son or father and enough about them to ask how they were doing each time he saw them. His "Hello, I am Adam" encounters were not too much to stop and bother someone, but just enough to begin a friendship.

Adam Living His Plan

Adam and his roommate went to school together at Hope College. I had to pull some favors to get them into one class in the social work department. Adam's friend, Professor Piers, was the chair of the department, so we had to get his approval. Jim was the guy who had let Adam's neck flop when he was a baby. Adam and his roommate had already been in a similar class and had done fine, so they were admitted. At the end of the first class, the professor invited students to come up to talk with him. Adam reportedly waited for his turn in line and when recognized extended his hand and introduced himself. The professor asked what was on his mind and Adam told him that he talked too fast when he was writing on the board with his back to the class. It was hard to hear and to keep up. Could he please have a lecture outline? Apparently, everyone standing in line to ask a question as well as those still in the classroom applauded.

Jim told me his colleague had come to him after that and told him what happened. He said he expected Adam just to say hi or something and he was both surprised and impressed by Adam. I think surprised was often the response people had to meeting Adam. And after that came a warm glow and often friendship.

Adam continued to explore his community. He would walk to Compassionate Heart Ministries two afternoons a week and stay until early evening. Other nights and weekends he would go out with Brett, Travis, Brittany or Michael and his wife, or...the list went on. When he got home, he would Skype, Facetime and text other friends. Adam took care of his friends. He had an active prayer list of at least 40 different people that he prayed for each night. The Kuipers remained on the top of his goodnight list.

When he stayed with me on weekends, he would make me breakfast and serve it in bed. Two eggs, toast and coffee and always made with love. Like my father who loved to cook and experiment with food when I a child, Adam had to try new and different ways to make eggs for my morning breakfast. Eggs could never be just eggs, that would not do. Adam tried salsa eggs. Onions and sweet pickle scrambled eggs. Peanut butter eggs. Sometimes they were over cooked (maybe deep fried would better describe them), but all were delivered to my bed with his beaming smile and always with a nice cup of coffee. Sometimes he added chocolate syrup or maple syrup to the coffee or enough cream to clog my arteries for days. He would sit next to me as I enjoyed his latest creation. Initially, I had attempted to have him cook for me my way, but that never lasted. I found out that some of his ideas were coming from a local restaurant and burger joint that he loved. They served south of the border burgers, salsa jalapeño pepper burgers, egg burgers and peanut butter burgers. Inclusion and normalization were all against me when it came to my weekend breakfasts. He was exposed to a larger world and was sharing his discoveries with his Dad with love and delight.

When breakfast was over, Adam would invite me to join him in some job. From the time Adam was four years old, he had chores. So, every weekend we would clean the house then mow the yard or shovel the snow, and by noon he was off with his friends. Jetta must have been laughing with delight at our son's joy-filled life and how he shared his discoveries with me.

Blueberry Picking

Adam had a couple of jobs working with Travis on his families' Carini Blueberry Farm. It was a real job, and not a Kandu experience as the *helpful* professional had prophesied. Placing Adam at Kandu would have cost taxpayers $100 an hour or $700 a day, plus bus service. Because Adam had been fully included all his life he could find real work. During high season when the berries had to be picked and processed before they spoiled, they worked hard. Adam knew his job in the cold storage shed well enough to become the boss of that area. He was the boss because he worked hard and steadily and encouraged the other workers to join in at his pace. He led by example and encouraged; he never ordered anyone to work harder than he did.

Before and after high season there was a lot of riding around on the tractor and mowing or taking a semi-full of new bushes to another farm to plant. The off season always included lunch somewhere, usually with one of Travis's girlfriends meeting them. Girlfriends that often became Adam's girlfriends too. During the winter, Travis's family operated West Coast Outfitters, a sporting goods store. Travis did what Eli and I did—he worked with Adam until he became comfortable restocking the merchandise and keeping it orderly. He knew where everything was in the store. Travis said to me that he did not

Adam seeing what the big equipment feels like at the Carini Blueberry Farm

remember where everything was or all the customer's names, but Adam did. Adam would greet people by name and ask with a smile, "How are you doing?" He never pushed a customer for anything. Travis said that customers would usually be looking for something specific and Adam would immediately take them to where it was in the store and come back and stand by Travis until the customer brought it up for Travis to ring out. He was always supporting but never rushing customers. He had learned about the timing of other people and was using that skill as an adult.

Everyone a Peer

Adam had been involved in Compassionate Heart Ministries (CHM) since it began ten years earlier in Zeeland's old hospital building. The city rented the building out to local nonprofits and called it the City on the Hill from Matthew 5:14 because every nonprofit was intended to be a testament to Christian community and support including an at-cost restaurant. CHM was the brain child of Donna Bunce and started out in two rooms in the City on the Hill complex. Donna described CHM as a Christ-centered drop-in program for teens and young adults with mild to moderate disabilities with the goal of building inclusive relationships in Christ through peer mentoring. Part of the decision in purchasing his home was the location of CHM two blocks away. It was close enough for him to be able to walk there easily. CHM developed into an incredible community for Adam. It was a rich environment with lots of people wanting to become friends and enjoy life. He loved it. Adam never got the role distinction between mentors and peers. His inclusive blinders made everyone a peer.

Donna Bunce wanted to have a place of belonging for her son and for all the unique people to have a place to develop a social life. Even after her son had decided it was not for him, she continued to build this oasis, a sanctuary, and an open, inclusive community. So often the kids who are different are not fully included in school, so after school, they are set adrift or pushed into special and artificial programs like the mother's group the *helpful* professional was intending Jetta should go to for support. The error is imagining that if you put ten drowning mothers together they will learn to swim (emotionally). Research shows that grouping people together who are having similar difficulty is efficient but only serves to increase their difficulties. Inclusion in a diverse group is healing. God smiled on Donna and CHM and peers and mentors were homogenized into one compassionate heart. What I mean is that the peers and mentors blended together completely with mentors growing in their faith and awareness just like their peers were. Who taught who the most was questionable. It was and still is a uniquely inclusive community, a place where Adam loved to be and a place where he felt loved. Donna honors Adam every year by awarding the Adam Winstrom Friendship award to someone who embodies the special brand of friendship that Adam practiced.

Shoo, Dad

Adam learned to walk to Compassionate Heart Ministries by himself after Eli went through the procedures to teach him community safety. At first, CHM became a destination on walks with Adam, Eli and their dog, Jack, until Adam was able to walk safely there on his own. I never realized how important "on my own" was to Adam until I had taken him somewhere and I was just hanging around, and my loving son said quietly to me, "Shoo, I do this myself." My being there diminished his independence. For so long I had had to be there for him to feel safe and secure enough to be included. Supported independence means being sensitive to how much support is just right. I was enjoying seeing my son having an expanded social life that I had let my attention slip and forgot to fade out my support so that Adam could exercise his independence. That was the moment when I needed to be around the corner just in case but not be breathing over his shoulder. The next step was not even being there at all except by phone.

Adam continued going to Jim Kruis' house overnight for Adam Winstrom Day. Jim and Adam hiked, swam, played catch, fixed things and painted light posts in Jim's association. They shopped, prepared, cooked and cleaned up dinner and breakfast together. Because Jim was different than me, Adam began gaining independence when he first started Adam Winstrom Day with Jim. Adam polished his work skills and his independence with Jim.

Jim told me one time that he had been reluctant to let Adam cut up vegetables with a sharp knife. That is until Jim cut his own finger and Adam showed how to put sugar on it to stop the bleeding and then how to hold the vegetable so that he would not cut the end of his finger again. When Adam was younger, he had learned to master the skills well enough to teach others.

When we lived in Grand Haven, he began attending the men's prayer group on Friday mornings at our church. Back then, the church only had about 50 members and had no custodians so Adam and I would vacuum the church, wipe down the chairs and clean the bathrooms. As the church grew, they hired Joe who had a heart of compassion the size of Adam's. After getting to know Adam, Joe asked if he and Adam could work together. Adam had begun developing his independent attitude and wanted to do things by himself. As the church grew to 500 members, more men came together to support the church, and the men's group was started. They met for prayer for about an hour before they all started working on projects for the church. Adam loved it, and they loved Adam. They asked me to join, but I declined. It was Adam's men's group, and he wanted to be on his own. I was just his driver. Adam had to create his own identity as a unique person.

Building Community on the Riding Mower

After Jetta had died, I moved out of our old home in Grand Haven, and I bought a house in Holland to be closer to Adam. It was just ten minutes away from his home in Zeeland and a few blocks from Holland Christian. It made football Friday nights easier for me. Our home in Grand Haven was an acre and a half with lots to mow and fix. My house in Holland was on a smaller lot with my neighbor, Randy, owning the open lot next door. I grew up in Holland but had not lived there for many years. When I lived there, Saturday morning started after 9 am, we were not allowed to ride our bikes on Sunday, and most of the stores and restaurants were closed on the Sabbath. Culturally, it was not a day to work.

Adam had been out all day on Saturday with Travis and missed his mowing job at my new house. Every Sunday morning Brett and Darlene picked Adam up for church and went to get donuts afterward. When Adam got home at noon after church, he told me the grass needed to be mowed and he was going out to mow the lawn. It was my second week in the neighborhood, and I had not really paid attention to what the Holland rules were. I figured God would understand that for Adam mowing was not work; it was pure joy because he got to drive the riding lawnmower. It was his way of resting. Sometimes he mowed in circles, sometimes in no connecting lines but eventually he finished it off by making a golf course crisscross pattern.

As Adam finished my back lawn, he headed out into my neighbor's land, the open lot between us, and began his random manicured mowing. I came out and called Adam over to me and was explaining property lines and private property when Randy came over on his John Deere mower and introduced himself. Randy's sons had gone to Holland Christian with Adam and played football. Randy was Adam's newest best friend. I do not think Randy intended to mow the yard at that precise moment; I think he was just being a welcoming neighbor and accepting my son and I as we were. Adam and Randy became mowing buddies.

That fall when the leaves fell, Randy and his sons and daughter raked their open lot all day. The maple trees had filled the lot a foot thick and Adam went to help. The next year Adam mowed Randy's lot with our leaf catcher

Mowing in patterns, Adam-style

every week and deposited the leaves at the curb as the city of Holland required. Randy no longer had to spend two days raking as long as Adam was around. Sometimes Adam would try to overfill the mower bags causing the leaves to get stuck in the shoot. Adam could see that it was difficult to fix it, but I was always happy to do it. But one day, he rode over to Randy's and asked him to help. Bless him, he stopped whatever he was doing and helped get the shoot unjammed. I heard the mower stop and came out prepared to pull wet leaves out of the mower shoot but saw my neighbor figuring out how to fix it for my son. I went over to apologize and remind Adam not to bother Randy, but Randy said it was no trouble. After all, Adam was doing his leaves. From then on, Adam and Randy became work buddies. If Adam was running out of gas he would pull into Randy's backyard, and they would visit, and

Raking leaves for the elderly

Randy would fill Adam's tank. Once Adam had a flat tire, and Randy fixed it and did so with a smile saying, "I sure do enjoy Adam."

Adam also mowed his own yard and occasionally the neighbor's yard for chocolate chip cookies. Adam took care of his own swimming pool. In winter, he shoveled the snow from his own driveway, and if his neighbor was out shoveling, Adam would help him, too, just like he and I had done together when he was younger to teach him cooperation and how people in a community behaved and supported each other. What he learned as a child he did as an adult; he never forgot the ways in which he was instructed.

Normal, Inclusive Life

Adam was free from systemic retardation. His definition socially and personally was Adam Winstrom, everyone's best friend. He was never a Down's child. He was never autistic Adam. He had been allowed to grow and learn and become Adam Winstrom—a spiritual rock able to sustain others in their fears and disappointments. A source of joy and love and excitement and companionship for his friends. As the kids in Canada had promised me, Adam would be safe. Adam would have friends and feel like he belonged. Adam would learn how to be a good citizen. We had managed to achieve this without moving to Canada.

All the things I have described, going to a social club, walking a dog in the city, mowing lawns, making meals, going out with friends and being a charter member of the church men's group is no big deal to most people. They are all just normal things. And that is my point and the reason for my gratitude and my joy. My son as a young adult in 2014 led a normal life doing normal things and feeling independent enough to move freely through his local community. He had an active social life with lots of friends—young, old, men and women.

Temple Grandin said that we should teach our children well and make sure they have the opportunity to be included in all aspects of life not be segregated into special programs. Adam had that opportunity. Twenty-five years earlier in 1989 this was an accurate clinical description of my son: Deficits in social-emotional reciprocity ranging, for example, from abnormal social approach and failure of normal back-and-forth conversation to reduced sharing of interests, emotions or affect to failure to initiate or respond to social interactions. Deficits in nonverbal communicative behaviors used for social interaction, ranging, for example, from poorly integrated verbal and nonverbal communication to abnormalities in eye contact and body language or deficits in understanding and use of gestures to a total lack of facial expressions and nonverbal communication. Deficits in developing, maintaining and understanding relationships ranging, for example, from difficulties adjusting behavior to suit various social contexts to difficulties in sharing imaginative play or in making friends to an absence of interest in peers. Hand flapping, tactile super sensitivity, noise and smell hypersensitivity leading to over stimulation.

Hanging out with Katy Kuiper
1970 Groovy party

Adam outgrew all these characteristics of classical Autism just as Temple said he could. He no longer needed me to guide him through how to relate to people, how to make friends or fit in. What my son needed me to do was continue my covenant to interact with the larger systems to create conditions for Adam to be safe.

Chapter 18
The Best and Worst of Years

What did the Best Look Like?

Everything was going according to plan. Adam was spending most of his week in his own home. He had developed a large and active community. In the three and a half years after we buried Jetta, Adam had blossomed into a wonderful young man and one his mother would have been proud of. He had his own home. He had a very active social calendar. He was part of the Compassionate Heart Ministries community twice a week. He was so proud of his independence because he could walk from his own home up the hill to meet with his friends or go somewhere by himself. He was independent with some support at home—Eli his roommate was always there as his advisor. Zeeland was his community, and he was safe and comfortable taking his dog, Jake, for a walk. He had his many girlfriends to see, have lunch with or just hang out with—Brittney, Katy and too many others to name them all. He had Adam Winstrom Day with Jim every week. The time he also spent with Brett, Travis, Mickle, Kirk and Chris and other friends all intertwined into a life tapestry with a vibrant rhythm.

Adam, Kirk and Chris

Adam was living his life as Jetta and I believed he could. Best of all, Adam was free from systemic retardation. His definition socially and personally was, Adam Winstrom, everyone's best friend.

Full Inclusion Creates a Full Life

I think it is important to take one more look at the life Adam could enjoy because of his full inclusion growing up. Adam was included in all the ways I had hoped for in his church and school. Whatever struggles that had occurred for me raising Adam, he lived his own life and that made it all worth it. Adam had been able to discover what it meant to be Adam Winstrom.

He was a 29-year-old young man, confident in himself and capable of so much more than anyone (except Jetta and I) had been able to imagine. He had been allowed to grow and learn and become Adam Winstrom, a spiritual rock able to sustain others in their fears and disappointments as well as a source of joy and love and excitement and companionship for his friends. As the kids in Canada had promised me, Adam was safe. He had friends and he belonged.

He owned his own home and was proud of that. He didn't live in a group home that the *helpful* professional told Jetta would be where he belonged. He lived with his friend Eli as many of his friends did. He was one of the guys living together as roommates exploring what it meant to be a young single adult.

How to Find an Eli?

Many parents asked me how I found Eli. We had several requirements for someone to become Adam's roomate. First, it was important to us that Adam know the roommate, and Eli had been Adam's friend for almost 20 years.

Then, to make this work, it had to benefit both Adam and Eli financially. Jetta and I had approached Ottawa County Community Mental Health to utilize their "Community Supports Program" back when Jetta had first discovered she had cancer. Ottawa County Community Mental Health was responsible for disbursing Medicaid funds intended to reduce dependence on classical Mental Health Programs and to support more independence for young men and women so that they could be included in their communities. If we accepted Mental Health's recommendations, we would have had a paid "caretaker" who would instinctively try to run Adam's life. Instead, the State paid significantly less for Eli's services and we offered Eli free rent so that he could use the money to go back to college.

Finally, we needed someone who would support Adam, not try and run his life. Choosing Eli worked because he accepted that being a roommate meant he was there to support Adam but understood I that was ultimately responsible for Adam and would support both of them. I told Eli that it would be more like a three-legged race at first, but soon enough they would both gain more freedom.

Adam developed the skills needed to live his supported, independent life when he was young doing his chores with me. It began with helping his mother and I clean the house every Saturday morning and helping do his laundry with Jetta. It began with being included in life and doing all the usual self-care things people must do to survive. It began with not being done *for* but being done *with*, over and over.

Adam was ready to practice all the skills we had learned together and begin living on his own. It would start with Adam living in Zeeland three days a week. For those three days, Eli needed to be available all the time and as time passed could be less and less directly involved. The other four days Adam would be with Jim Kruis for Adam Winstrom day or with me. Over time, this shifted to Adam only spending Friday nights, all day Saturday and Sunday until about 2 pm with me. The rest of his time Adam lived in his home.

My son, who the *kind* doctor had told Jetta and me would never walk, talk, have friends and would always be a burden, contradicted every one of those things. He not only walked, but he skied mountains in Colorado.

Visit to Israel

One day I received a call from Pastor George DeJong inviting Adam to go to Israel, Jordan and Egypt. The invitation was a complete surprise; it was nothing Adam or me had applied for or even knew was possible. George said he was organizing a trip for people who were spiritual influences in their community and he chose Adam. He said that God pushed him to organize a trip to the Holy Land for young adults with different abilities so they could return and share the Word in their community.

After Adam understood what Pastor George was offering and why, he decided he wanted to see where Jesus grew up. George led 20 unique individuals and their buddies through the Holy Land. It was a wonder-filled and rewarding experience for Adam and me as his buddy.

Visit to Israel

It was my honor to listen to Adam deliver his sermon on Sunday on the shores of the Sea of Galilee, the same spot where Christ did. He also received communion from Pastor DeJonge in Jerusalem. I am convinced that God smiled on Adam that day. It was quite a feat for a person who was told would never talk, walk or relate to others to talk and walk where Christ did.

Every place we stayed had WIFI, so my son continued his good night routine to 20 people every night, some he even sang to.

Adam had hundreds of the very best friends. I do not think the world experienced Adam as a burden. It was my observation that he supported others more than he needed support, as his friend Kirk observed. Adam was looking to add his friendship as a gift, not be your friend for what he could get.

All the things Adam learned to do including going to a social club, walking a dog in the city, mowing lawns, making meals, going out with friends and being a charter member of the church's men's group were all just normal activities for a young man. But not for a young man with Down syndrome and Autism. At all times, his nothing special life needed to be defended and protected from being taken from him by a culture that still thinks their special life "best." And that is my point and my gratitude and my joy. My son as a young adult in the year 2014, just led a normal life doing normal things feeling free to move through his community. He had an active social life with lots of friends —young, old, men and women. Like Temple Grandin had said, teach your children well and make sure they have the opportunity to be included in all aspects of life, not segregated into special programs.

For so long I had had to be there for him to feel safe and secure enough to be included. For so many years, I had to be present to stop those who would keep him from his normal life. Now I could let go a bit. Supported independence means being sensitive to how much support is just right. I wanted to be the perfect father in a perfect world always knowing what to do and how to be. When I did not know what to do, I just did what I could and trusted that Adam and I would learn together how best to be in this world. Adam had enough independence that I could let my attention slip a bit and watch my son having an expanded social life. When I was needed I was just around the corner or available by phone but not over his shoulder. My loving son would help me know what he needed. He would say quietly to me, "Shoo, I do this myself." It was the best of years. Adam no longer needed me to be involved in every aspect of his life. He was emancipating and growing into his own independent life.

Reconstruction Starting with the Knees

His life was full enough, and his community support strong enough that I thought it was the perfect time to fix and rebuild my worn-out body.

When I was younger, I thought I would only live until I was about 50 years old. Both of my grandfathers had died of heart attacks around that time in their lives, so I thought my body would probably be wearing out around that time, too. My head-on motorcycle accident, football injuries to my knees and ruptured disks in my back were all converging. I did the best I could physically, getting up and at 'em every day at 6:30 am with Adam until I finally could not force my body to do it any longer. I managed to put off any major reconstructions while Jetta and Adam required my full attention by going to the pain clinic for regular steroid injections in my back and my knees so I could keep walking. Once Adam was doing well I went to the neurosurgeons in Grand Rapids, and we set up a plan. This time the plan was for me. They did an evaluation and concluded that I had no reason to be standing up. My knees were both worn out with most of the socket portion of the joint worn away. My back was equally a mess. I had ruptured disks and bone spurs pinching off my spinal cord. The plan was to start with my knees and work our way up. The first surgeries went very well. Each knee took only three weeks recovery time and no pain pills. I was their poster child for reconstruction and rehab.

Then we started in on my back. The first five surgeries in my back were micro surgeries to clean up arthritis and ruptured disks. The surgeons had wanted to open my back up from my hips to just below my shoulders and fuse my back with titanium rods and screws, but I had asked for a somewhat less invasive reconstruction and one in which I could still be available to Adam. I was two days in the hospital and then three more days in rehab. I fit it all in midweek so Adam and I could still have our weekends. Each surgery reduced the pain and allowed me more movement. I began to plan for my new more active lifestyle with Adam and I taking some trips on our motorcycle.

But the last surgery did not go well. I could feel a difference. It was more involved with a fusion of my lumbar spine. The micro surgeries had cleaned out the bone spurs and ruptured disks, but my back was not stable. The surgeon had warned me that there was a 50/50 chance that my spine would collapse in on itself after he removed the extra bone growth that my body had produced. My body made an additional layer of bone growth that protects itself, but the growth also pinched off the nerves and created pain and lack of mobility. About two months after my surgery, it collapsed, as the surgeon had warned me and I had to have the more involved procedure. This time, I had titanium rods and screws implanted and shark cartilage to grow the bones together for stability. The surgeon was pleased with the results, but I told him that something was not right. He assured me that the surgery went perfectly.

A few weeks into my rehab and I started to lose ground. I could not walk as well even though I was still in my plastic upper body cast and I was losing energy. My hip began to hurt more and more. I walked during rehab but was less able to walk during the week. The doctors told me that I had finally worn out my hips, too, but it did not feel like the joint pain I was familiar with. I had a postoperative infection. I did my best to get the doctors to understand that I had an infection, but they were convinced it was just time to replace my hip. This went on for eight months. The surgeon referred me to a hip specialist and stopped returning my calls.

Adam continued to be with me on weekends and make me his special breakfast. I managed to keep up my smiles and movement with him around, but I really began to fail. I was a touchstone in my son's active life. He wanted to see me and know I was okay. I would pick him up from his house Friday afternoon and bring him to my home to eat and get him ready for "the game"–football or basketball at Holland Christian or Hope College was the order of the evening. Then I would pick Adam up after the game and the after-game party, and he would come to my house, get on my computer, his phone and iPad and say, sing and Skype his goodnights to all. Some he prayed with. Some he sang to. Some he listened to and reassured as only Adam could. He would remind them it was nothing permanent and that they were always loved by him and by God. He took care of his friends, then me and then his day was done.

My hip got so bad that I was no longer able to walk at all. The pain was so intense that I was not very functional. For the last three weeks, I had not had Adam stay with me but only visit because I could hardly tolerate the pain when I tried to stand or use my hip. A friend stayed with me one night and convinced me

Adam enjoying some Facetime with friends

to go to the emergency room in Holland. All my years dealing with the health care system made this feel wrong. My surgeon was supposed to listen to me and refer me for testing, but he would not. My sense of what was right nearly killed me. I was evaluated in the ER within 15 minutes of my arrival. The ER doc said, "You have a serious infection; why did you wait so long?" I was sent to Grand Rapids by ambulance to the infectious disease wing of the hospital in Grand Rapids with a very real infection in my hip.

I don't mean to sound melodramatic, but I was prepared for my life to end. I had thought I had an infection after my last back surgery a couple of months before, but the surgeon said, "No, you do not!" I was not as good at being a self-advocate as I was at advocating for Jetta and Adam. By the time I got my doctors to agree with me, my kidneys had begun to shut down, my heart was going a fib and my liver was failing. I really thought I would die and that was okay with me. I had done everything I could for my son. I had kept my covenant. Adam had his own home and an incredible community of hundreds of good friends. He could work at a real job. He had a very active social life. He was financially secure.

As I laid there in bed with my body was failing, I thought back to all the plans we had put in place. Jetta and I had planned for our son's future as well as ours. Jetta became a school social worker for the lifelong insurance benefits for Adam. When she retired after 15 years, Adam's health insurance was assured for life. I had worked and saved and invested in stocks and in a home in Mexico for all of us. It was a vacation Adam could enjoy for life. My goddaughter had assured me that she would take Adam there whenever he wanted to go. Adam had his own home he owned it free and clear. I had transferred the value of our home into his so he was assured of his home forever. He had an incredible community and a full and active life. Knowing I had a plan in place for Adam, I looked forward to joining my wife. I had fulfilled my covenant, and I was ready to be released from life. I had been the best father I could be, or good enough, I thought. I had supported my son's right to be included in the mainstream of the community, and he was. I had been the best husband I could be, taking care of Jetta as she lived and died. I thought it was finally my turn. I imagined I had done well enough to be allowed to join Jetta.

But Adam was not done with me. When I had told him after we buried his Mom that everyone is born, lives and dies—it is a natural, human process. Every time we talked about this, he always said, "No, you cannot die!" He would not accept the idea that I would die. Grandpa, Mom, even his guinea pig could die, but not me. When he came to visit me in the hospital and saw all the tubes going into me and my not being myself, he recognized that I really was not well. He just said, "I need you home soon." He was not ready to let me go as I had not been ready to let Jetta go.

I spent three weeks on IV antibiotics in the infectious disease wing of the hospital. When that didn't work, the surgeons wanted to open up my hip and physically scrub out the infection, just like the surgeons had wanted to do to get rid of Adam's chest infection. The Infectious Disease Center wanted me to go on IV antibiotics and put tubes into my hip to flush it out. With Adam, the surgeons had wanted to open his chest and remove the infection, but Dr. Ivey had suggested the tube with an enzyme to wash out his chest. Dr. Ivey had reasoned with me that surgery would increase the potential for more infection. I had chosen the tubes for Adam and did the same for me. He survived what they did not think possible. I survived as well.

The tubes were inserted into the pockets of infection in my hip identified by the scans from their machine to drain off most of the infection. I had to be conscious and move for the procedure to work. I remember telling the doctor to put in his ear plugs because I would be making noises to release the pain. I could barely endure the pain of lying flat on my back as the infected hip muscles were stretched into position for them to push in the tubes. They told me to go ahead and scream if it helped me. I was very good at managing pain. I had had both of my knees replaced with no pain pills. But not this time; this time the pain won. They positioned the tubes into the pockets of infected tissue and then drained the infection of the joint. Once that was done, they injected the antibiotics directly into my hip. I screamed until I stopped remembering anything. I was not fully conscious most of that time. I passed out a lot, a gift for me because the pain was exquisite.

I lived, and they put me back together. I had to have the antibiotic in my IV changed every eight hours. I was beginning to recover after three weeks in the hospital, so I was transferred to a nursing home for another month, still living on IV's. It seemed like I had just finished burying my mother, father and Jetta and then I lost myself in delirium for a month in the hospital.

My father called nursing homes *the incarceration* when I had put him in one after he had his appendix removed and needed to recover. It was amazing for me to see first-hand what really went on in a nursing home. There was one doctor and two nurses to one hundred patients. I was there because I needed my IV changed every eight hours and that regiment was to be strictly followed according to the Infectious Disease Center. With two nurses for all of us 100 patients, I could never get my IV's changed every eight hours, and I was not even strong enough to walk. After a week of random IV changes, I learned by watching the nurses how to change my own IV. On schedule, I began to recover. With my medicine administered as prescribed, the hallucinations went away. To be honest, I kind of missed them; they were the best entertainment I had, but they had removed me from the world. Back on the antibiotic schedule, they disappeared, and I started seeing all I had missed. I started rehab again and was walking with a walker again and making my plans to go home. I was anemic because the medication used up all the iron in my system faster than my body could replenish it. They told me that until I was finished with my IV antibiotic that I would just have to get used to the symptoms of anemia: fatigue, shortness of breath when I walked, difficulty concentrating, dizziness, cramps and insomnia. They suggested I not make any major life decisions until I fully recovered.

But it was all okay really because Adam was doing so well.

Chapter 19
Adam Still Needed

When I first went into the hospital, Adam had felt some swelling and pain in his testicles but could not get the message across to anyone. In the hospital, I was unconscious and unavailable; I had not been there for him. He had told a few friends that his pants were too tight and they thought it was just a clothing issue and tried to get bigger pants and new underwear. But it was not a clothing issue. When Adam made it clear to me what the problem was, I immediately made an appointment with our family doctor. The needle biopsy indicated it was cancer. I was still in the nursing home but was getting the doctor reports by phone. I was informed that he could get into a surgeon for an evaluation in Muskegon in three weeks. I called the doctor in Holland and got Adam in the same day, and they scheduled surgery one day later. Adam could not wait. Catching cancer early is the only chance for survival. Jetta had taught me that lesson. It must be removed before the tumors get into the blood supply, metastasize and develop their own highway into the rest of the body. They must be removed before they send their seeds off to grow throughout the body.

Jim picked me up from the nursing home. Adam was relieved that I was there and went into surgery brave and assured. His surgery went very well, and the surgeon reported that to all assembled there: Adam's roommate Eli, Adam's backup guardian and her friend and Jim. He said that they would biopsy the tissue and know what kind of cancer he had. He added that typically testicular cancer was 99%

curable. It sounded just like what the surgeon said about Jetta's thyroid cancer—99% curable. But when Jetta's biopsy report came back, it did not support that description. She had Hurthle Cell cancer that spread and settled in her lungs, heart and spine. There was no cure for Hurthle Cell cancer; it was a rare and untreatable form of thyroid cancer.

But this was Adam and this was now. Adam stayed in the hospital three days, and Eli was there every day. When Adam went to his home to recover, his community supported him with visits and calls. Everyone told him how brave he was. And he was. But I was still in the nursing home waiting for the lab reports about my son. I struggled to get myself healthy enough to fulfill my obligation to Adam. Even as I faltered, I was very encouraged to hear about Adam's community in action while I was still in the nursing home recovering. All of his friends supported him during his surgery. After his surgery, he had so many visitors that the hospital had asked if they were treating a rock star. Inclusion pays off when all is well in the world but even more so in a crisis. The support for Adam was heart-warming for me. It affirmed that all my efforts to include Adam and build an inclusive community were worth it. In spite of all of his friends, Adam still needed me to be in his world to assure him all was okay. He needed his connection to me.

Not Fighting Cancer

Adam having cancer was like reliving my wife's first discovering she had cancer. First the rush to surgically remove the tumor. Then the pause to arrange for the next standard form of care. For Jetta, it was radioactive iodine. For Adam, it was arranging to have one round of chemotherapy. That was the "standard of care" for testicular cancer. It had been four weeks since his surgery, and he had recovered very well. He was back to his typical weekly activities of visiting friends and taking his dog for a walk. He was a little slower, but Adam was back into his community. He had friends coming over to his house and was going out with his friends.

It was different for me with Adam than it was with Jetta. With Jetta, we could share the information and make decisions together. I would read all the reports, not just listen to the doctor. Jetta and I knew from the reports the specific kinds of cancer she had and their prognosis. Jetta knew she would die. She and I could read the research and the reports and know what was real and what was "doctor pretend" to give hope. I could talk with Jetta and together we chose her path of no chemo. She could resist her friend's and the oncologist's need to do something. Together we could decide that literature reported that chemo would only make her sick and weak. Her type of cancer was not curable with chemo and would make her more vulnerable to the cancer. She chose not to suffer chemotherapy and not to get sick, lose her hair, her appetite, her energy and then die. She preferred to live joyfully, poison free and die from cancer, not be killed by the helpful doctor (the doctors who really wanted to be helpful when no medical help was really available). Jetta chose quality of life as doctor-free as possible. She had just one radiation treatment. The doctors told us it was the standard course of treatment to remove any trace of cancer following the total removal of her thyroid. And that one treatment with radiation to remove any remaining thyroid tissue had wiped out her short-term memory and her proprioceptive awareness—her sense of where she was in the world. She could get lost coming home from the grocery store. If she drove for five minutes and did not get home, she would call and tell me what street she was on and I could help her get home. I did not want that for Adam. Jetta could laugh about it when it happened, but I did not think Adam would have Jetta's insight.

My son could not understand the medical professionals need to treat even though they knew the treatment would probably fail. They had to help; they wanted to create hope. They wanted to "buy time" just in case a miracle drug would be discovered. Their view was that if Adam had chemotherapy, he could live happily ever after that extra month.

Everyone wanted Adam to live, especially me. What we did not know was what kind of cancer Adam really had and how virile, fast growing and strong it was. Nor did we know how resistant to treatment this cancer was. They all wanted Adam to fight cancer. They wanted

Adam to want what they wanted—a miracle. I wanted for him to live in grace and not suffer.

Most of Jetta's friends were still recovering from Jetta dying. They had wanted her to want to do chemo and fight cancer, and they wanted the same thing for Adam. Jetta could restrain them but Jetta was not here. It was just me. I knew what Jetta and I would do together, but I was alone and sick and didn't have the strength for relational struggles. I wasn't even supposed to be making significant life decisions because I was not functional

Beginning chemo treatments

enough to even live at home yet and take care of myself let alone take care of my son. Because Adam was over 21 years of age, the court had determined that he needed both a legal guardian and a backup guardian in case the main guardian was incapacitated. I was the main guardian. I was incapacitated. I could not agree and I could not disagree. My own hospitalizations were taking their toll. My ability to think had been affected by the infection, the medications and becoming anemic.

Jim Kruis, Adam's back up guardian, Cindy, and Adam's roommate, Eli, were really in charge. When Jetta first found out cancer was going to be part of our lives, we had created an adult community just in case we were not there for Adam. We put in place protections for our son should we no longer be available to support him. That support system kicked in. They were adamant that Adam receive chemotherapy. They made the most logical loving decision they could at the time. They believed that the chemo would extend his life, if not save it. They believed that time would be on their side and even if this chemo did not cure Adam, modern medicine would find another possibility, and by giving Adam chemo he would be alive to benefit from any possible medical advances. After Adam's surgery Jetta's friends and Eli were adamant that if I did not agree to at least try chemo, I would be killing my son.

Jetta's death was a shock to her friends. For Adam's friends, Jetta dying was an older person who had gotten sick. It was sad, but it fit into Adam's communities' understanding of the order of life. Adam, on the other hand, was the first person in his community to almost die from pneumonia. His recovery reassured his community that the young and strong among them are still vulnerable. Now Adam had cancer, and it was the first real confronting of their own vulnerability and the possibility of death for any them. It was the first introduction to their own mortality. It was the first challenge to their world view that life was fragile and limited, not a timeless possibility. This was especially true for Adam's roommate Eli. He had never before faced anything like what was happening with his friend, Adam.

I had taken care of my mother as she died from cancer. I had taken care of my father as he died from congestive heart failure. For five years, I had taken care of Jetta as she lived and died from cancer. It was only three years earlier that Adam and I buried her. And now my son had cancer. It was difficult for me to separate what I had experienced with Jetta and what was going on with my son. The two processes seemed identical although I hoped they were not. Added to the surreal appearance of Adam's cancer, I began to doubt my own judgment for the first time in my adult life.

The first six months were the most difficult living with cancer as our new companion. The problem with having cancer is becoming a cancer patient. It is that the treatment takes over your life. The ups and downs of hopefulness and disappointment all take time to adjust to and time is so precious. The beginning process isolates the person with cancer and makes them feel alone, and they get physically sick from the "therapy." Adam had to stop all of his activities to do chemo. Adam had to give up his life. Adam had to be very careful not to be around anyone with even a cold because of the risk of infection for him. His lungs still had some scarring from pneumonia but he had recovered completely, but the doctor knew chemo would remove Adam's immune system and leave him vulnerable and at risk for complications. Adam's community rallied around him on Facebook and other social media. This was our process.

A Community Comes Together

Darlene Kuipers put a prayer group up on Facebook to give Adam's community somewhere to meet and share their support for Adam and each other. I posted information about Adam's fight against cancer in this prayer group. I tried to be thoughtful and compassionate in my writing, but some did not approve and told me I was too blunt and uncaring. I tried to accept their responses as part of their grieving process, still, sometimes it hurt.

Facebook | Darlene K. Kuipers | February 3, 2014

Bring everyone up to speed...

Adam began treatment today for non-seminola cancer stage IIb. Lance Armstrong was treated for the same cancer. Today began his journey with chemotherapy. He will receive infusions for 5 hours a day for 5 days followed by rest for three weeks. After that complete cycle, 3 more cycles of 5 days on and 3 weeks rest before the chemo is complete. He is receiving his treatment in Holland and will be home each night.

Chemo will be tiring and he will have to make some adjustments in his activities, but he is Adam Winstrom! He loves all his friends and will thrive off your prayers and Facebook comments and seeing you as he can. Post here or on his timeline - let's shower him with love and prayer. Invite others to this group to keep everyone up to date with how they can support him.

We'll keep you updated here with information and specific prayer requests as they come. Along with prayers for Adam, pray for his care team too! He is blessed to have many people in his life ready to aid him on this journey.

Eli, Jim, Travis, Brett, Darlene, and others came to the oncologist's office to be with Adam as he had his five hour IV of chemo. They watched stupid day time soaps and laughed. They made pictures. And best of all, they loved Adam and were there for him. By the time his day of chemo was over Adam was exhausted. Yet, when he went home, he still made all of his evening phone calls to all of the people on his prayer list, and he sang an "I love you" song to those who needed just a little extra Adam love. Then he said his good nights to the *Waltons*, Brett Kuipers' family before he called me and went off to sleep. Adam stayed at his home and rested every day and night. He walked his dog, Jack, a little but mostly he watched the *Price Is Right* and napped. Eli kept the visitors to a minimum and made sure Adam rested.

Facebook | Darlene K. Kuipers | February 16, 2014

This week marks recovery/rest week #2. With the first week of rest behind him, Adam is in great spirits! The chemo is making him more tired than his usual self at the end of the day, but he still has his spunk. Pray for rest and strength this week, and that the chemo continues to do its job. He has been enjoying the encouragement and prayer posts/messages. Keep them coming!

Facebook | David Winstrom | February 19, 2014

Chemo makes some physical changes for each person. For Adam the time has come when he has just lost most of his hair. He is not sure if his new look is OK. Please let him know that his hair is not what makes him lovable. I have always thought bald was beautiful, but for Adam it is a new experience. Please let him know he is still Adam, the friend you hold dear in your heart.

Adam's oncologist said he was doing well with his treatment, so that became the worldview on Facebook. But that was "doctor talk" and it was relative. The truth was that Adam's physical response to chemo was to immediately lose his hair. He also lost his energy, got a secondary infection because his immune system was compromised by the chemo, broke his foot because his bones became brittle from the chemo and he got blood clots. Like his mother, his attitude never changed. Jetta managed to take care of her friends so they would not worry. I doubt any of her friends ever realized the effects of her one treatments had on her. During chemo, Adam would smile and call his friends to check up on them and pray for them. When he finished the first week of chemo, the blood levels indicated that the cancer cells were shocked, but they continued to slowly grow again while Adam rested.

At Adam's first post-surgery meeting I had signed the permission card so they all could have access to his medical records and his treatment. I had done that because I was in the nursing home and others were taking Adam to his appointments. I thought that was the right thing to do. They still had access to Adam's doctors, and all were invested in Adam's treatment. The problem developed because everyone had their own idea of what to do based on their life experience and the doctor's words that Adam had cancer that was 99% curable. They were all pulled by their own illusions about life and fear of dying. Doctor hope from the oncologist was accepted as truth. For many of them, this was their first experience with the ways of the medical profession. The oncologist wanted everyone to be hopeful so Adam would be in his best frame of mind to endure the treatment. That made assessment and decision making more difficult. Additionally, everyone wanted to come to visit Adam. They were well-intended but not germ-free.

Facebook | David Winstrom | February 24, 2014

Adam starts his second round of chemo Monday. Hopefully, with the shots he has been getting his white cell count will come up so he can do more with his friends. For now it is Adam the masked man, Skype only.

Facebook | David Winstrom | February 28, 2014

A few years ago, Adam was in ICU at North Ottawa Hospital with what Dr. Ivey described as a catastrophic illness. His doctors did not expect him to fully recover. He was so very ill that they wanted to put him in a therapeutic coma for three months.

All who knew Adam formed prayer groups. The last time Dr. Ivey saw Adam he wrote in Adams chart "From catastrophic illness to miraculous recovery." Adam healed completely. I never thanked all who gave their time and energy each day, alone or in small groups, to support Adam's healing. When a community focuses its attention on the well-being of one of its members, it gives strength and hope and protection from the fearfulness that can come from living in the shadow of the unknown.

I cannot know the outcome. Life and death occur as they will, I only observe that today after two rounds of chemotherapy, Adam is an active, loving, hope-filled young man. He feels loved and supported and very much alive. For all who supported Adam in the past and to all who each day focus on Adam's well-being in thoughtful reflection, thank you!

Adam did his best. Like Jetta always did her best. Adam had cancer but initially felt fine. Like Jetta, without any intervention such as chemotherapy, Adam would feel fine and his body would die from the spread of cancer. It was déjà vu. The biopsy report finally came back from the labs. It identified three different kinds of cancer. One that typically responded to chemotherapy, one that typically responded to radiation and one that did not respond to any form of treatment. Adam was once again in the 1% category that treatment would work.

Like his mother, the kind of cancer my son had seemed untreatable. The oncologist said nothing about the biopsy reports. He did say that we should finish this course of treatment and see what was really happening. The biopsy report told me the cancer Adam had was more aggressive than the kind of cancer his mother had. Adam's body would stop in 12 to 18 months if we could not stop the cancer.

Facebook | David Winstrom | March 11, 2014

> *Some things have not changed, his smile and his talking to all of you on his phone.*

I was finally back home and taking care of myself. I was also able to have Adam stay with me. That was fortunate because on Sunday I noticed him favoring his left leg and asked if it hurt. He said a little but it was okay. I knew he was being brave and reminded him that he never had to be brave with me, he just had to be my son and tell me honestly how he felt. I asked him to show me his leg and he slowly peeled his pant leg down. His left leg from knee to hip was red and swollen and hot on the inside right along the femoral artery. I called his doctor to let him know about the problem. He said we should put some ice on it and elevate it a little. So, we iced it and put our feet up to watch a movie. Adam kicked back all Sunday with me. No walking, just movies and, of course, his friends.

Facebook | David Winstrom | March 17, 2014

> *Adam update. He developed an infection in his leg. It is inconvenient and uncomfortable but not contagious and has caused him to postpone chemo this week until the infection is gone. One more example that reminds me that what I expect has nothing to do with what life will bring me.*

Facebook | David Winstrom | April 5, 2014

Cancer is getting better and keep prayers
Cancer is not fun it all
Cancer. Is getting better
Adam's words from last
week.
Still true.
David Winstrom

The cure is more unpleasant
than the disease. So, cancer
is all about surviving chemo
and feeling worse each week
to be "getting better." It is

Award night CHM Courage award

confusing and scary. The only thing that seems to be the
cure to the chemo is all of you. Your thoughts, prayers
and friendship. I am amazed by the amount of love
Adam gives and receives and how your thoughts hold
him when my holding him is not enough. "Cancer...is
(about) getting better" and you all are God's medicine.

His white cell count and cancer markers are "good." He
is going in today for an ultrasound of his groin to see
why it is still swollen.

Facebook | David Winstrom | April 13, 2014

Last week of chemo starts tomorrow. I am tired of
chemo, almost done. ~Adam

Facebook | Darlene K. Kuipers | April 18, 2014

Rocking through his hopefully last day of chemo.
Continue to pray that over the next three weeks the

chemo does its job and his tests post rest cycle show no sign of cancer.

Facebook | David Winstrom | April 19, 2014

Adam is so blessed to have all of you supporting him. Monday he begins treatment for the blood clot that formed in his leg. It came with the infection and now we ask it to leave. Then in three weeks is the PET scan that Darlene wrote about. Please continue your support.

Facebook | David Winstrom | April 25, 2014

I found out today, one of the side effects of Adam's chemo is that the medicine is making his body form blood clots. Two in his left leg so far. Adam missed the 5K walk for CHM tonight because it has become difficult to walk that far. He will begin taking blood thinners, and we pray no more clots form. Who Adam is has not changed, his spirit and passion for living is still just as strong, stronger than his body right now. His compassion and caring about all his friends has not diminished. He accepts his personal circumstance without complaint. He is my son and he teaches me about keeping perspective. He lives in grace. I have never felt sorry for him, just respect. No hero, no saint, just a very good man taking his next step no matter what the obstacle.

Adam's community was confused. The initial word after surgery was that Adam would be fine because the surgery was successful. Next, Adam went in for chemo. Once again, everyone was told that Adam would be fine because this was a standard procedure for testicular cancer. Travis Rieth, a friend of Adam's from Hope College, also had testicular cancer and had been diagnosed before Adam. He published a blog about his experiences. I talked with him often and asked if I cold reprint his observations. He was happy to do whatever he could for his friend.

Facebook | David Winstrom | April 27, 2014

> *Excerpts from a note from Travis, a friend of Adams on a similar journey:*
>
> *I've had my initial surgery. Recovered. Worked a fun job on Donner Lake's Marina. Seen 8 different doctors at 5 different hospitals. Been a sherpa and a quasi-model for a GSI Outdoor photo shoot. Been told I will get chemo, won't get chemo, will have a surgery, won't have a surgery, will have the surgery, and finally won't have the surgery. Life has been good. I still have all my hair and I am very thankful.*
>
> *Most of all I am thankful because I have done nothing recent to deserve it and have had an outpouring of love and support in every way from high school and college friends, old teammates, kids I coached, people I've worked for, relatives, and even complete strangers.*
>
> *This fight against cancer is rough with varying levels of winning the battles. It is impressive to see those battling well and at the same time challenging to see those who are not. Some have little wrong and a lot to complain about while others like my friend Adam are losing everything yet remain the most positive attitude. It is interesting, to say the least.*
>
> *As for me right now I am well. The pros of not being treated are no chemo, keeping my hair, my lungs will continue to be fine (I was told the chemo I would have*

received would have made me less athletic), I do not have to have a foot long cut in my abdomen to remove my lymph nodes nor the 3-6 months recovery. The cons are doing nothing is not easy, I am learning not to waste my energy fighting what I cannot see, gaining some peace learning to live with cancer.

Thanks for writing to me and for letting me share this.
~ Travis

Facebook | David Winstrom | May 6, 2014

Today Adam went to the oncologist to some blood drawn to see if the cancer has left him. He gets a PET scan Friday and we are hopeful. He also got cleared to begin treatment for the clotting condition the chemotherapy created. We are hopeful.

He is happy, still, and I am thankful

Facebook | David Winstrom | June 15, 2014

Today is Father's Day. I am reminded that I am Adam's father but he also has a Father. For some reason, his Father has introduced cancer into our lives, as He did with Jetta. That gift has made clear again the reality that control is an illusion. Not that we are victims but that we are beings of the moment. The future is a hope not a promise, and living in the future is a mistake.

This week, another test, another procedure, another reminder to LIVE EACH MOMENT. As Travis Rieth wrote in his journey with testicular cancer, remission is not cure. And I will add that cancer is not the enemy to fight, the battle is to never surrender a moment's joy or one's love of life to a diagnosis. Cancer can kill the body,

but it does not need to take life. I see Adam live each
day. I see his friends love and be loved by him. That is
my Father's Day present. I am thankful

While I was busily focused on my recovery and on my son's care, Adam kept his focus on living his life. He stayed engaged in each day and with his friends. Imagine with me how far Adam had grown from the child who had meltdowns because a siren went off walking by the hospital and had to be held for half an hour before he could relax. My son who would run the other way with his hands over his ears because a band was coming down the street for Coast Guard Festival as it marched past our house. Imagine the child who could not get to class on time because of the crowded halls of his high school. Now imagine him as a young adult after three rounds of chemo being released back into his world once more and he chooses to go with his friends to Tulip Time, the Dutch festival celebrated every year in Holland. Bands. Dutch Dancers. Floats and parades. Noise. Confusion. 700,000 tourists crowded into a town of 35,000. Adam and his friends had come a long way. My, still hairless son, mingling, no *choosing* to mingle with all of this chaos and he was fine. I did not worry about him getting lost, or confused or having a meltdown. He had his community.

Lee DeWitt from CBI had introduced Adam to down town Holland where the parade was being held. Adam knew the area. Adam knew the businesses and business owners. The parade route was close to Hope College, and again Adam knew the area. He still had friends on campus. His years of inclusion had accumulated into his level of freedom to move through and enjoy this expanded life. Adam was comfortable even in the crowd. Adam was safe. He still would call me and tell me what was happening and send pictures from his iPhone. Adam managed to keep life in focus.

Just after the third round of chemotherapy and the first labs were back, I received a call from Adam's initial surgeon and he said out loud what I already knew. The cancer in Adam was not growing, but it was not going away. This was again just what Jetta and I had just gone through together. He suggested we begin thinking of what to do next after chemo. Again, just what Jetta and I faced with her having cancer. His call confirmed what I knew but had denied. This time a new element was added. His call triggered what is called anticipatory grief. It is the grieving process that occurs for some people when they know they or someone they love is dying. It was not intentional on my part. I did not dwell on the fact my son would die or lament my wife's recent death. It just happened. I did not imagine anything. The doctors had not given up, but he wanted me to be realistic and to make plans to explore all treatment options or, if none were possible, to live with no treatment. Knowing Adam could be dead in two years, knocked the wind out of my sails.

Facebook | Travis Rieth | June 14, 2014

> *"May your choices reflect your hopes, not your fears"*
> *Nelson Mandela*

Facebook | David Winstrom | June 18, 2014

> *I met with Adam's doctor today. He told me that we had "stunned" the cancer but it was still present (remission, not cure). What I am also attempting to say is his life is now. I cannot give him to God today but God has chosen/invited Adam, and my will...will not hold him here. This moment will not last...love now... care now...befriend now...be kind now...not just to Adam but know, learn from Adam's circumstance. If you had no more todays...what one more act do you wish you had done... do it.*

Facebook | David Winstrom | June 19, 2014

> *Adam wanted me to add to his "news" that he broke his left foot now. Another hairline crack. He just got*

the walking cast off from his right foot. I asked the oncologist and he said Adam will be more likely to break bones for a while following chemo. The best news is his joyfulness and smile are unaffected. He stays in grace.

Facebook | Adam Winstrom | June 19, 2014

Hey guys my hair is coming back and I am getting better every day and my left foot is better and I have on my black shoe and cast. My bone hurts and keep prayers my left foot.

Facebook | Michael Scott Pyle | June 19, 2014

Praying for your foot bud! See you tonight!

While Adam's community celebrated his remission like a cure, I tried to tell Adam's roommate Eli and the backup guardian that remission was not a cure. I tried to share what the doctor had told me. I was hoping they would be people with whom I could process this information. But they could not hear me. I was accused of stealing Adam's hope and of having a negative attitude. They told me my attitude would bring the cancer back. They were still in denial and not ready/able to see very clearly what was happening. I had first-hand experience with the insidiousness of cancer's process to rise up and then hide only to blossom more forcefully.

The surgeon told me that the lab reports after Adam's last round of chemo confirmed his preliminary assessment: he did not think chemo was going to work. He wanted one more blood sample after the three weeks of rest to make the final confirmation. He, too, wanted to hope. He wanted to be completely sure that what he and I saw indicated in the earlier labs was true—the cancer was still active. He said it might be possible to still catch the cancer before it was systemic if we operated and removed all of Adam's lymph nodes. It was an option he had initially said would likely not be necessary. I later found out that it was an option not usually successful.

Treating cancer is a very fluid process. It is not a broken bone that is static and once identified can be focused on and fixed. Cancer is a disease process that grows atypically in each individual. I treated Adam like I had Jetta, talking about what was real. I told Adam that the cancer had not gone away but was stunned. It would not go away with chemo alone so I would talk with his doctors about the possibility of another surgery that they said might work.

I told him to trust me to find out everything I could. His job was to live. His job, for now, was to rest and see his friends, and we would be given the best answers soon. Adam shared that with his friends who called. Once the word got out, everyone in Adam's community wanted to know about what was happening with their friend. He was not afraid. He got it that he might be joining his mother and God. He said, "no more talk now. Cancer sucks." Okay. He did better dealing with it than some others. Talking with him I felt no grief in either of us. No sadness in me or him.

When I told Adam's roommate about what the surgeon had told me. That the cancer Adam had was not cured and might not be able to be cured, he said he did not believe me, that I was lying. The backup guardian and the others who had been in the first post-surgical meeting did not accept my words, and they all wanted another meeting. They did not believe me either. They wanted to talk directly with the doctor. I mention this because it is so typical with cancer treatment. Hope gets crushed by fear and then often arises again only to get crushed. What Adam needed was for me to stop this roller coaster. They were all in denial. It was their fear of death and denial that this could be happening that made them think I would lie about my son. It was the power of cancer to make people feel powerless that made them all want to be in charge and in control. Their own personal processes only added to the confusion and difficulty that cancer presented to Adam and me.

The surgeon and I were talking every couple of days as more information came to him. He had sent off more samples to the lab to have more studies done and was waiting to share with me what he was learning. He told me during one of our conversations that he really did not have time to answer all the other people's phone calls. I asked, "What other people?" He told me that all the folks from the first meeting in the hospital still wanted information. I apologized and said I would tell them not to call. I had not talked to the others after they told me they did not believe what I was telling them and it had not occurred to me that they were all calling the doctor for information. I was no longer "incapacitated" so I didn't need their help. I called everyone and thanked them for their concern and informed them I would be the one person talking directly with Adam's doctors. I thanked them again and told them that I removed their names from the doctor's list of people who could call meetings or see his records or call the doctor directly to get information. Some never spoke to me again.

I was responsible for my own son. I removed the backup guardian because they disagreed with my way of taking care of my son. That was unpleasant. I replaced them with someone I could talk with honestly and think through the best course of action for Adam. Jim Kruse was a rock and agreed to be the backup guardian. He had initially been Adam's backup guardian before but had asked to be removed to just be Adam's friend. I explained why I needed him now and he agreed.

An interesting thing about anticipatory grief for me was that when I would talk with Jim about the process the surgeon and I discussed, I would weep. When I talked with Smitty at church, I would weep. When I would talk with Adam's roommate, I would weep. The idea of Adam no longer being around was for me the final loss of all that mattered. My family was no longer with me. Father, mother and wife all gone in ten years. And I knew Adam was next. Yet, when I was with Adam, life was full, rich and engaging. When I was with Adam, I anticipated nothing, and I still had my purpose.

I remembered Adam and I had been in Garden of Gethsemane in Israel together, listing to Reverend George DeJong explain what had unfolded there. I could understand Simon Peter drawing his sword and striking the person who was trying to take away his Rabbi, his friend, Jesus. I could understand all who would turn their sword at me, blaming me for removing their beloved friend. I was the messenger bringing news that Adam might be taken from them. I was the one who finally decided that he would do no more chemotherapy, so they saw me as assuring that Adam would die. They could not see past their grief. They could not see that I was the one who would make sure Adam would not suffer. I was the one who would support Adam living the best quality of life, even if it lasted less time.

Facebook | David Winstrom | June 21, 2014

Adam's doctor told me there is nothing routine about this next step given all the challenges Adam has and has had. It is technically challenging, and he could do the surgery but if possible, he suggested we go to Indianapolis to have the fellow who trained him do this for Adam.

We are working through the insurance restriction working at getting exceptions. His doctor is discussing this possibility with the head surgeon at the National Testicular Cancer Center. It is hopeful Adam will be in the best hands on earth and will have the best chance of a complete cure. Indianapolis is the national center for the treatment of this kind of cancer. I am thankful for all of your support. I am thankful Adam's doctor is more concerned about what is best for Adam. I am thankful that Julie at Priority has made the effort toward getting us approval. It makes making difficult decisions easier to live with. When will this happen? As soon as all the obstacles are removed from going to Indianapolis. Hopefully in the next three weeks...hopefully.

I talked with the surgeon about any other realistic treatment options. He said he had done his training in Indiana at the national center for the treatment and study of testicular cancer. Adam's doctor decided that if Adam were going to have surgery, it would be done by the best surgeon in the country, so we referred Adam's medical charts to the surgeon who trained him in Indiana for a surgical evaluation. This process took at least a month, and every day during that time someone wanted to know what would happen to Adam. I knew, but I was trying to find another path for Adam. The one where he does not suffer *or* die.

Adam left cancer up to me. He went to work with his friend Travis at Carini Blueberries and had fun. He went to CHM again. He went out with his friends. He came to visit me but had to return home Sunday after church with the Kuipers family and went home early because Michael was coming over to play Nintendo—a Sunday ritual. Adam lived. He had a rich, full life that even cancer could not stop.

Adam's doctor called again after reviewing all of Adam's information I was given my options for my son. More chemo treatments then surgery to remove the "sludge" (dead cancer cells that remain after chemo and often regrow into untreatable forms of cancer) and to remove all of Adam's lymph nodes. This would mean two to four months in the hospital and six months of rehabilitation. Then another round of recovery chemo. The surgeon would remove stem cells from Adam and use both chemo and radiation to kill all of the cancer in Adam's body. It would also kill almost all of the good cells in Adam's body. Then Adam's own stem cells would be reintroduced back into his body, and we would all hope and pray that they would regenerate. It would be a six month to a one-year process. Adam's doctor in Holland told me the prognosis was "guarded," medical code for not likely to be successful. We would wait for the final word from the National Cancer Center about what they thought.

Facebook | Darlene K. Kuipers | June 24, 2014

*Please continue prayers for Adam, David and his
support system. Pray specifically for things to logistically*

move forward without barriers, pray for strength for Adam to endure the upcoming procedure and for strength for David, too. Continue to let them know you are lifting them up in prayer via Facebook messages, this group, text messages, FaceTime and Skype calls.

Facebook | Adam Winstrom

thank you so much for prayers guys keep me lot good memories and keep thoughts for me pleas call me on my cel phone tonight

Facebook | David Winstrom | July 3, 2014

I adopted this mantra... I plan...God smiles...I am instructed.

I / we have been waiting for "the scan" to get to the doctor. The plan was to then meet with the doctor and work out the referral. Well, the scan finally arrived at the doctor's office. Eli and I were going to drive to Grand Rapids and get it as we were losing our ability to wait.

Now the doctor is on vacation until next Friday.

The lesson? My energy is best utilized as Adam's is. Live each day as it is. Love my friends. Do each day what I can to better myself and all I encounter.

Talking with a friend after a chemo treatment

Prepare but do not plan or expect.

Facebook | Jim Kruis | July 3, 2014

> *Yes, David. The Psalmist puts it this way, "In their hearts humans plan their course, but the Lord establishes their steps." Actually, I like it better the way you say it, "I plan...God smiles."*

Facebook | David Winstrom | July 5, 2014

> *And then Adam's doctor calls and tells me he (Dr. Ludlow) cannot wait anymore and is driving to get Adam's scan so he can see it and show it to his mentor in Indianapolis this weekend. He cares. He said he will call later today or maybe tomorrow to talk about what they think...adding not to worry he is just impatient*
>
> *Interesting how what he is doing does nothing to change Adam. I see in me hope rising and falling with words like remission, or acts of caring like wanting to see Adam's PET scan now (even though he is "on vacation") instead of in another week. It is not that I wish to be unmoved by all that is occurring, and still... to live as my son does, trust as he trusts that everything is just as it should be ....and today is a good day to go work with his friend Travis on the blueberry farm. He has no apocalyptic concern, nor is he looking forward to Christmas, waiting to be happy...just paddling his little boat letting the day enjoy him.*

Facebook | David Winstrom | July 9, 2014

> *I know nothing more than all is proceeding just as it is intended. Adam is well, loved and loving. The*

doctor has reviewed the data is in communication with Indiana and Adam's HMO. I am adding all the energy to the process i can. I reassure Adam it is fine. Worry if it will help you but mostly just live and enjoy your friends

Facebook | David Winstrom | July 15, 2014

Working with the best doctors in the world from the National Center for Testicular Cancer. Refocusing, time to look at what are the most important things in my son's life. Serve camp (1) and (2) being "the best man" for his friend's wedding. I have been talking with Travis R…helping me recognizing the freedom this process grants the few to live in this reality, it is not how long but how well we live…each day now is a gift. Each moment, a total experience. Adam has an incredible community alive with vibrant friendships and Serve camp…your prayers, your thoughtfulness, your caring friendships…who could ask for anything more?

Facebook | David Winstrom | July 17, 2014

Adam is getting calls and questions about the process he is in, what about your surgery? What about more chemo? I am accepting. "In their hearts humans plan their course, but the Lord establishes their steps." When I talked with Adam's doctors and wrote the post about a surgery, the plan was to go and have the surgery to cure Adam. Those are not the steps that we can take any longer. My son is a seemingly healthy man with cancer who cannot get cured with surgery. When I told Adam that he would not have surgery he was very happy. The idea of surgery worried him and so that worry is gone. My journey with Jetta taught me a lesson I will share.

There is a roller coaster ride living with cancer offers…
hope, despair, hope, despair as we plan our course and
discover what is real. What is real is not despair, it is
also not the hoped-for cure in 10 weeks. What is real is
Adam is a happy, healthy man with cancer.

If there is a way to separate Adam and cancer, working
with the doctors at the national center is the best course.
But today they do not have an answer. Today Adam is
vibrant and Adam is one in a million genetically, a
unique being to behold and that has created a challenge
for the doctors: how to separate cancer from Adam's cells
and keep Adam. So, Thy will be done on earth as it is
in heaven. Give us today grace and acceptance…and
wisdom for his doctors. And of course, Adam, being
Adam, will continue to love you all, it is okay to return
that to him.

Facebook | Adam Winstrom | July 19, 2014

keep on prayers okay. great am i

Facebook | David Winstrom | July 19, 2014

Adam Winstrom, fear not my son for I am with you
always. In your fear and your joy I will be there. Just
close your eyes and feel your father's love holding you
close.

I called the doctor at the National Treatment Center and talked to him directly. We determined that Adam would most likely die going in either medical path. It took me a couple of days to let that news settle in me. I had known Adam's cancer was not treatable, but I, too, held on to some denial, some false hope. That was removed now. There was no more to do only live what is. I called Adam's oncologist to arrange a meeting to go over what I knew. A report would be sent out in a month or so, but the report was not a priority as the doctor had already talked to me.

I met with Adam's oncologist in Holland without Adam. He was reluctant because he could not legitimately charge Adam's insurance for a consultation without the patient being present. I understood his position. His time was valuable, so I paid cash. I told him everything I had discovered. I asked him to refer Adam to hospice. He told me that he had to see Adam one more time to do that and we set the appointment. I asked him to let me explain to my son what was going to happen in the timing I thought best, and he agreed. He would just say that Adam was done with chemotherapy.

Adam's roommate wanted to come to the last appointment. Adam was back at his own home, and he said he could bring Adam and meet me there. He had sat with Adam for all of Adam's chemo, and I thought he just wanted to be there to thank the doctor. I missed his intention. He wanted to talk to the doctor himself about Adam instead of getting second-hand information from me. After my last meeting with the doctor, I thought he was going to tell Adam and Eli that the cancer was not gone, but there could be no more chemo. I imagined that he would then refer Adam to hospice for eventual palliative care. It should have been a fifteen-minute appointment.

I had not considered what happened possible. Adam's roommate asked the doctor if there were any other possibilities. Eli desperately wanted the doctor to tell him he had some new miracle to save Adam, that I was wrong and that his friend whom he loved would live. And the doctor was eager to try a new chemo he had read about using stem cell regeneration. I had already talked with the specialist at the National Center for Testicular Cancer who discovered and utilized this procedure, and we had determined that it would kill Adam after having him suffer for nine months in isolation in a sterile hospital room. But the report had not been sent out, and the doctor in Holland had not been in on our conversation and wanted to *do* something. It was all heading south quickly, as the expression goes. I tried to turn the conversation around, but both Adam's roommate and the doctor were invested. I wanted to remove Adam, but he was already locking up physically. I was not able to pick him up and carry him out of this burning building.

My attempt to correct the discussion and head toward the agreed referral to hospice failed completely. The oncologist said he had tried a new chemo on one person eight months ago. I stopped him and asked, "You have a treatment that has been proven to cure Adam's cancer, correct?" The doctor responded that he might not be able to save Adam, but he could learn something that might help someone else.

I was about to take Adam out of this fiasco, but Eli asked one more question that *he* needed an answer to: "How would Adam die from cancer?" It was too late, I was too late; Adam was beginning to melt into me and weep. The doctor said, "Lung cancer or heart failure. Suffocation. 18 to 24 months without any intervention."

As I held Adam I said, "You two want me to choose between death by doctors or death from cancer. I choose living with cancer. It is much more humane." I thanked them both for all they had just done, stood up and asked Adam to come with me so the doctor could make his referral to hospice.

I wanted to slap them both. I talked to Adam as we left the building and drove home in the car. I believed in telling Adam the whole truth. I also believed in being sensitive to his limits and timing. They did not exhibit sensitivity or good timing. I always respected Adam's wish to hear more or less. They had talked about how Adam would die right in front of him with no concern for how their discussion might affect him. They had talked about him as if he were not there. It took Adam a couple of hugs and about ten minutes of quiet in the car to say, "doing okay. No more talk today, okay? Cancer sucks." And we talked about what he would do tonight, who he would see and what fun he would have.

I left Adam's roommate a message to drop it, regrettably adding that he obviously did not have the sensitivity, experience or temperament to talk to Adam about this. I say "regrettably" because none of my message was really true. Adam's roommate was sensitive. He loved Adam but got lost in his search for hope and a word from the doctor that I was wrong and that Adam could be cured. It took him a week before he came to talk to me and say he was sorry. He had wanted to know what was going to happen and lost sight of the impact it might have on his friend.

I asked if he was ready to return to focusing on what was best for Adam or did he need some time away to process death and dying for himself. Did he need to meet with the hospice people alone before they came to see Adam to get his needs taken care of so hospice could focus on Adam? Adam's roommate never escaped past his own shock and denial; he never accepted that Adam was dying until after Adam had died.

I had been using my posts in Adam's prayer group to create the condition for Adam I wanted. I made it a more conscious effort to communicate to all of Adam's friends how I hoped they could support Adam. I wanted people to get beyond Adam has cancer. Isn't it sad? Adam has to fight cancer, poor Adam. I knew that their grief was not about poor Adam, it was about poor me and dealing with their own loss. It was about covering the pain of letting go of a loved one. I knew my grief was about my life without my son, not about Adam going with God. I wanted Adam to gain support from his community and give them support. Life brings life. Joy begets joy. Sorrow begets sorrow. I wanted to live in grace, insulated from the sentence of cancer. His community wanted to do something for Adam because they loved him. They just needed to know what to do.

All of Adam's life I had engaged the community we lived in to allow him to be included in typical-normal life, just like every other human being. And now, in his final months, I wanted to remove him from the normal cancer patient process. Our Winstrom family had its own way to understand life and death and what happens next. We believed that both birth and the death of the body are cause for celebration.

I have written about how Jetta and I struggled to keep our son included. I have maybe too often shown the difficult side of the work required to create conditions for my son to be allowed to explore his potential just as all children should be encouraged to do. Throughout my struggles and Jetta's struggles we were always working to give Adam one degree of separation from the unpleasant friction that surrounded our efforts that secured his right to be with other children. Children who became his lifelong friends. It was always the children who included Adam until the adults made their including Adam dangerous or harmful for Adam when he was younger. Now I was at the end game. Placed here to finish the work I had been given with my son. I always knew that I had only been loaned Adam and was expected to do the right thing for him. The right thing now was to assure that living was the focus, not cancer until his body died.

Facebook | David Winstrom | July 20, 2014

> *It has become a difficult path for Adam now as what we know and what we do not know begin to merge. What Adam knows is he has cancer. And from his mother he knows what cancer can do to a person. He knows he wants it out of his body. He knows he is afraid of having surgery and afraid of what will happen to him if he does not have surgery. Right now, the doctors do not want to schedule surgery based on the results of Adams latest cancer blood levels, they think a surgery would be more harmful than helpful.*
>
> *What we (Adam and me) do not know is if any treatment is possible. The doctors here and at the National Cancer Center said right now the best medicine is at Serve camp and loving time with his friends. What will be the end result of all of our efforts is unknowable today. For most of us, the unknown has no face, no specific concern. Adam is placing a face on his future he does not like. He sees his mother's path. He sees what will occur but not when. I am encouraging*

him to let go of the unknown future and any thoughts about when. No more what is going to happen, only what is happening right now. Who are you with today? How can you make this moment better, more filled with grace? I am not asking anyone to pretend that everything in this world will always be okay, only to stay focused on the living moment to be in, and let the unknowable (the face of God) shine on my son. We have started working with hospice to keep my son as healthy and happy as we can. He will be at Serve camp next week with all of his friends and not able to call by Skype while he is there. ~David Winstrom

Adam and I talked before he went to Serve camp and Adam knew that his body would die. He told me, "I know…and cancer sucks." I told him hospice would make him feel better. I enrolled Adam in hospice before many in his community were ready for what that indicated. Hospice is an incredible organization. They offered palliative care aimed at comfort and were designed to support Adam staying as active and included as his body would allow. Adam was as comfortable and involved as was possible until his last breath. Adam liked his hospice team. He did start feeling better and getting stronger the further away from chemo we moved. Hospice gave him medications to increase his energy and shrink his tumors. It was the best process.

I talked to Donna Bunce about my son's cancer and told her there was no treatment possible. She told me she would match Adam up with someone who could assess his physical health and endurance and make sure he did not over do or hurt himself.

Adam had a blast at Serve camp. He went to dances and had praise and worship every night. He rode Harley Davidsons. He hung out with his friends. He lived. But every night his body complained and his legs cramped as the chemo worked its way out of his muscles. Rosa, his mentor, practiced her physical therapy skills, prayed with him and was a friend to my son.

Facebook | Rosa De Jonge | July 29, 2014

Hey bud, remember that book we read before bed at camp (Jesus Calling)? I was reading it the other day and stumbled on these words that I thought might encourage you:

"Hope is a golden cord connecting you to heaven. This cord helps you hold your head up high, even when multiple trials are buffeting you. I never leave your side, and I never let go of your hand...."

I can't say I understand what it feels like to have cancer, but I do understand what it feels like to serve a great God who gives us hope no matter how frustrating or annoying our current situation may be. I also know that everything happens for a reason and God is already using you Adam to further his kingdom. You are such a kind, humble and loving person. I'm very blessed to have had the chance to mentor you this past weekend, you are so incredibly loved by great friends and an awesome Dad! Keep on keeping on Adam. Peppers

Facebook | David Winstrom | July 30, 2014

Adam makes each today the totality of his life. He fills his day seeing friends and sharing his life. Kim from hospice works with Adam to manage pain and fatigue every Monday. I raised Adam to be better than I am, to accept what is, be patient with others who mean well but are confused about how to relate or support him, and not to fight. To understand his differences are not what define him...not who he is, but accepted them as a stone to carry in his backpack. Cancer is the same, not who he is, it is just another stone to carry.

He has never wanted to spend time looking through his backpack or taking the stones out for display. I told him everyone carries their own stones in their backpack, too, and it is best to let them be. Thank you all for your thoughts, support and prayers for Adam. Thank you for seeing Adam all of his life and for not focusing on his backpack. He is my son in whom I am so pleased, a 29-year-old man who has touched more lives, lived more fully, loved and been loved by more than I ever hoped for. To all I again thank you and to Adam, my son, you are a good man.

From Serve camp on, Adam lived in grace no longer worrying about what will happen. We already knew. Adam worked with Travis in his capacity of boss of the cold storage shed and giving the welcome to people who came to the farm to pick fresh blueberries. Adam returned to his best life with his friends without the interference of cancer doctors. No more questions about what was next. He walked Jack. He mowed his lawn. He lived knowing it would not last, but that knowing did not take away from the great joy he shared with his friends. It was today and today was a good day.

Facebook | David Winstrom | August 19, 2014

My dear son, remember you are loved by many, and also by me. Loved for your laughter, for your loving nature, for being just who you are and because you love each of us...just for who we are.

Facebook | Adam Winstrom | August 19, 2014

Thanks guys for prayers you are so nice to me always and my birthday is on tuesday I am be 30....... my birthday is on tuesday.

Adam announced his birthday a week in advance. I arranged for a party at his house for many of his adult friends. I talked with Donna and she agreed to a party at CHM with pizza and pop for all. Then he celebrated with Hannah, another time with Brett, still another at our traditional Mexican restaurant where we sang happy birthday and had a whipped cream in the face party with Anna Clawson and her family. Eli also celebrated Adam's birthday. It was a fun filled two weeks.

Facebook | Rosa DeJong | August 26, 2014

Happy Birthday Bud! I had so much fun celebrating with you tonight and on Saturday. David Winstrom is right, life is definitely a party, especially when you're around. I love having you in my life and my prayer for you is for this year to be the best one yet because you absolutely deserve it. You constantly challenge me to live life to the fullest and treat everyone with Compassion. Hope you had a great day. Cya friday!

It was also the beginning of Holland Christian Football season. Games every Friday night and Adam was there on his team's side lines encouraging them. He went to White Sox Baseball games with Rosa on Saturday afternoons when he was not working with Travis at the blueberry farm.

Facebook | Adam Winstrom | October 3, 2014

Adam Winstrom Thanks guys i am coordinator coach for Jim at Holland Christian High School

Email | High School Dad | October 3, 2014

Love seeing Adam on the football sidelines every Friday night--football at HC would not be the same without him there for me. I know the team enjoys having him there--my son is on the team and has said he is appreciated for his enthusiasm.

Facebook | Adam Winstrom | October 12, 2014

hey guys i am getting better everyday hospice in holland every mondays keep healthy see hospice in signal day

Facebook | David Winstrom | October 12, 2014

Adam has a wonderful Hospice team. Kim comes to visit him at his house in Zeeland every Monday. Adam has recovered from his chemo and has his hair and his energy back, better every day. The plan is to keep Adam comfortable and involved with all of you. Thank you all for all your thoughts, prayers, love and continued support. ~David W

Facebook | Adam Winstrom | October 14, 2014

hey guys - keep thoughts about Adam Winstrom

keep healthy every day and energy back and keep on prayers for Adam and david winstrom keep thoughts well. ~Adam Winstrom

As football season wore to its close, Adam asked if we could go visit Grandpa Duke and Grandma in Florida. We made plans. We also made plans to go to Mexico after Christmas.

Facebook | David Winstrom | November 21, 2014

Loving, living, enjoying all of you each day. It is not a "compressed life" it is just a day in the life of my son. I am amazed, thankful and delighted for every moment I witness, each breath I share I am thankful for all of you, each day.

Chapter 20
The Hospice Bag

A Short Floridian Respite

Adam had wanted to go to see his adopted grandparents Duke and Grandma in Florida one more time. Grandpa Duke and Grandma were a friend of Jetta's mother and father and had been adopted by and adopted Adam. Adam and I checked with hospice in Holland and coordinated with hospice in Florida. Adam's energy was good, and the trip was what he most wanted to do. He loved Duke and Grandma and had really enjoyed his time in Florida staying with them two years before when Adam and I had rented a Harley and toured south Florida. He was looking forward to Grandma's big breakfasts that she made for us and getting the mail in the golf cart with Grandpa Duke. That usually turned into a 20-minute affair of touring the park and visiting with folks and Adam loved it. The golf cart had been decorated for Christmas with lights and streamers and one night there had been a golf cart Christmas parade. Adam and Duke were proud participants. Adam and I went airboat riding and swamp buggy touring. Or we went to the hot tub, pool, hot tub, pool and hung out back and forth all day. All the sunshine and fresh air and love were wonderful.

This year when I asked what he most wanted to do before Christmas, Adam said, "Go see Duke and Grandma." They were happy to have us again, and that was that. I told them it would be their last time with Adam and that was why he wanted to see them. I rented a black-on-black 2014 Chevrolet Camaro sports coupe convertible. A "nice ride" as Adam called it. Adam had started a cough just before we left and I had asked to have him start on antibiotics and to take a hospice kit with emergency medications. We packed our swimming suits, sun glasses and suntan lotion and boarded our direct flight. I used valet parking so when we returned our car would be warm and waiting at the airport entrance for us. I also booked wheel chairs for both of us to make the trip as easy as possible. Adam was really excited about it.

We started out with a bang. Our convertible car was waiting for us in Orlando and it was warm and sunny, not like Michigan in December. But it was a little different this year. We did the airboats and swam, but Adam needed a rest midday. That was fine with Grandpa Duke and we all made time for our afternoon naps. Adam rode with Duke in the golf cart to get mail and Grandma made every favorite meal Adam liked. We went for rides with the top down it was so warm outside, and we stopped for fresh squeezed orange juice and fresh orange sherbet.

But after a few days, Adam started losing energy. Every night his lungs would seem to fill, and he would need me to percuss his lungs and help him breathe. I would cup my hands and lightly pound on Adam's back to break up the congestion. He began coughing up stuff, and that seemed to make it easier to breathe. I could sense that Adam's lungs were not right, but each time I asked hospice to come out, they came and said Adam was fine.

The day before we were to return home, Adam had a catastrophic failure. We had just had a lovely day air boating in the Everglades, but on the hour drive back to Grandpa Duke's house, Adam was so tired that he curled up in his seat. As we got close to home, he woke up and asked to get some fresh orange juice from the place we had gone to a couple days earlier. I figured he had some fresh sherbet in mind, but Adam did not want anything else but orange juice. When we got back in the car to head home, Adam said he was having trouble breathing. He could not get enough air into his lungs. His juice was gone, and he started breathing in and out with the cup over his mouth creating some resistance like people do when they are having a panic attack. Putting his mouth inside the cup made it harder but better for him to breathe.

As we drove home, I called hospice to meet us there. The nurse listened to his chest and said it was clear and told me it was a reaction to the humidity and a panic attack. I knew they were wrong. What he had coughed up the night before were brown chunks of lung tissue. But they heard no rattle or wheezing, so the nurse just gave him some fast acting anti-anxiety pills. They also brought oxygen and suggested he sit with the oxygen on for a while. About 11 o'clock that night Adam told me he could not get enough air. I turned his oxygen up full strength and gave him some medication from the hospice kit we that brought with us from Michigan to help relax him and open up his lungs. Adam slept until 10 am and was kind of groggy. His breathing was okay but shallow.

Wheelchairs and a Hospice Bag

It was our day to return home. I had planned to drive my rental car back, and Adam and I would take the bus to the terminal. But I did not think he could endure that much physical exertion, so I asked Duke to take us to the airport and have Duke's daughter, Cindy, return the rental car. Adam and I went directly to the gate. I called hospice in Michigan and told them what I saw—Adam's labored breathing, coughing up what looked like brown lung tissue and loss of energy. They suggested I give Adam more medicine to relax him for the flight. Adam was already relaxed, so I did not give him any.

It was a direct flight, and about half way to Michigan, Adam began to disappear. He put his head on my shoulder, and I felt him leaving me. I held him and he talked about dying. I told him to trust me and just relax. God and his mother would be there to welcome him. The flight attendant asked what was wrong with him and I told her that it was okay, he was dying and I thanked her for her concern, but there was nothing she could do except to please make sure wheelchairs were waiting for us when we landed. She stayed a while and heard me tell Adam what a wonderful a son he was and that I loved him. His breathing slowed too much. The flight attendant and the passengers on the plane were wonderful. I think the hospice bag helped them understand and allowed Adam and I to just be together without outside help.

When we landed in Grand Rapids, the flight attendants and wheelchair service staff helped me get Adam into his wheelchair and out of the airport into my car. No one attempted to help us in any way but the way I instructed. I think being calm and clear and our carrying a hospice bag stopped people from being overly helpful. Before Adam and I left for the airport in Florida, I had talked to Eli, Adam's roommate, about having hospice meet me at the airport in Grand Rapids, but we decided instead that it would be better if hospice met us at Adam's house.

Adam was nonresponsive as I drove him to his home. He was resting on my arm as I drove to his house. His breathing was too slow and had too many spaces between breaths for him to live very much longer. As he melted into my side, I told him again how wonderful heaven would be and how he would see his mother.

Adam's roommate met me in the driveway, and we carried him into his bed. Hospice got there shortly after we arrived. She listened to his chest and said she thought it could be pneumonia and asked if I wanted Adam to go to the ER. I knew in my heart it was not pneumonia. I also could see that Adam's roommate, Eli, was not ready to let Adam go. I also knew that Adam hated the hospital after his stay in the Grand Haven Emergency Room and Intensive Care Unit. And, I knew he would want me to do what I could to make it easier for his friends and roommate. I knew the right things to do, but they did not fit together.

To assure that Adam did not suffer and to let Adam's body die peacefully now would be to not go to the ER. The right thing to do would be to give Adam some Roxinal under his tongue, and my son would relax further so we could keep him comfortable until his spirit left his body. He would almost assuredly slip further into a coma and his body would die. I had held my father in my arms when his body relaxed and released and stopped. Adam was lying peacefully in his bed. The only pain was coming from his roommate. The only anxiety was from the hospice worker. The other right thing to do would be to call an ambulance and let Eli and the nurse take my son to the ER. I said okay to taking Adam into the ER and the nurse called for an ambulance.

When the ambulance arrived, I signed the consent form to admit Adam to the hospital. They gave him adrenaline and more oxygen then whisked him off to the hospital. Adam's roommate wanted to ride in the ambulance, and I gave him that moment with his friend, my son. Eli loved Adam completely and was like his brother. But he had never seen death. I had just been on the brink of my son dying in my arms and felt him slipping away, and I needed a moment to let that settle in. I thought Adam would be pronounced dead in the ER. As I was driving to the hospital, slower than the ambulance, the ER doctor called and asked me to hurry—he needed me to sign another consent to treat. I had registered Adam as a DNR (Do Not Resuscitate) patient. That designation only allowed them to make him comfortable, not use any extreme measures.

The Right Thing for Adam and His Friends

When I arrived, the doctor asked me what I wanted them to do. He told me Eli had wanted him to try to save Adam but the DNR designation had prevented him from opening Adam's chest to take the fluids out of his lungs. I told him that it felt like my son had already died and I just wanted him comfortable. He told me they were prepared to crack his chest open and drain the fluid from his lungs and put in chest tubes to try to manage the fluid build-up. When the doctor could see that I wasn't moving in that direction with him and did not want Adam's chest cracked open, he asked me if I wanted them to do everything they could to keep him alive. I said no, I wanted my son comfortable.

He then took me into another room and showed me x-rays of Adam's lungs. Cancer had filled 90 percent of my son's lungs. Fluid from the cancer had filled the rest. That was why Adam was not conscious. That was why he had had a difficult time breathing in Florida. Not the humidity. Not anxiety. He had no lung capacity. He asked again if I wanted them to crack open Adam's chest and put in tubes to suction off the fluid. I looked at the x-rays of my son's lungs and imagined the difficulty he was silently enduring for each and every breath.

When I asked, "Can you cure cancer?" he said, "No."

"Then anything you do will never save him, will it?" The doctor seemed to relax out of his emergency "stat mode" pace. He added that Adam would most likely not survive any procedure.

I told him I never wanted Adam to feel like he was drowning and this looked like the same congestive heart failure that my father had. Adam's lungs could not provide enough oxygen to keep his body alive ever again. I did not want my son fighting for every breath or to feel like he was drowning in his own fluids. I told the doctor my father had chosen to go into a deep induced coma until he died. The doctor promised me that he would not let Adam feel like he was downing. What he could do was increase the oxygen to 40 liters and medicate Adam, and it might let Adam return for a day or two to give Adam and his friends some last moments. The doctor could not save Adam's life, but he could keep him comfortable for a few days for Adam's friends. I agreed. It was the right thing to do for Eli and all of Adam's friends who dearly loved him. It was also the right thing to do for Adam. He was given two more days to spread his joy.

Adam was miraculously returned, pulled back from what I thought was his scheduled meeting with God. The doctor had put Adam on 40 liters of oxygen and would make him as comfortable as possible with medicine. Adam would wake up for short periods of time, but he would not have to fight to breathe. True to his word, the doctor's formula allowed Adam to be alert and comfortable. He was not drugged, and he was not drowning. He was alert and hungry. I was relieved and so was Eli.

I called all of Adam's closest friends and told them that Adam was alert and himself and to come to the hospital *now* to see Adam if they had any last moments they wanted to share with him. Some came and received Adam's love. Some waited. He had no fear or anxiety but was smiling and taking care of his friends.

At the end of the long day, Adam wanted to go to sleep and Eli wanted to stay with him. Adam was okay with me going home as long as I returned in the morning. It was after midnight when I left.

The next day, the doctor told me that Adam could be comfortable and survive on oxygen for maybe a few days but not for weeks. He could be maintained in the hospital, at his home or at mine. I told Eli this and said that if he was ready to let Adam go, Adam could go to his own home. If he wanted Adam to fight to try to stay alive, Adam would come home with me. The aim had to be keeping Adam comfortable and letting him go. Eli agreed to help his friend die comfortably in his own home.

Hospice returned to help us get Adam home and keep him comfortable. They consulted with the hospital doctors, and we ordered a bed to be put in Adam's living room and ordered an oxygen generator. Adam and Eli rode in the ambulance with Adam on 40 liters of oxygen. Consuming that much oxygen with every breath is like being hit in the chest with a sledge hammer, but Adam smiled. Eli told me that Adam almost died on the way home and needed to be revived.

We got Adam settled at home and that evening the 20+ friends and family who came to visit that last night in Adam's living room were treated to Adam at his finest. He was laughing and smiling. He was loving and comforting each one, taking care of them one last time. When they left and the night progressed, his body began to fail as the doctor had predicted. Eli worked with Hospice managing medications to keep Adam comfortable, which allowed me just to sit next to my son and stroke his head and talk about going with God and about how his mother would come for him when it was time to leave me and go. I sat with him all night.

Life's Natural Cycle

Eli was a gift. He worked with hospice over the phone and balanced Adam's medication so that Adam was alert but never felt like he was drowning or coughing out his lungs. When the coughing increased at all, they increased his medications so Adam was as comfortable as we could make him. Between the pressure of the oxygen slamming into his chest and the instinct to cough out the cancer that filled his lungs, that last night was long and difficult for Adam. I wanted the night to be over, and I wanted it to last. I knew my son would not be with me much longer.

When morning light came, the hospice nurse, myself, and Eli were present. Adam sat up in bed and intently took off his oxygen mask. Eli put it back on his face and told him he had to have it on to live. I thought, *just relax, Eli.* Adam took one more breath then took his oxygen mask off again. Again, Eli said, "Adam you need this to live." Adam looked at me and took off his mask. I told him it was okay. He took one more breath and looked up, then laid back down in his bed. After another breath, he looked into my eyes and through my soul, and when he exhaled, it felt like he returned back to me everything I had given him—a lifetime worth of caring and doing and loving. Then he looked up past me, raised his hand up one last time as he had done in church, and with his last breath I felt him leave. I felt his heart stop and his eyes went empty, dilated and dark. Silent and still his body lost all its tone. He had gone off with his mother, I thought.

The nurse asked if I wanted to try to revive him. I told her he had decided to leave and was already gone. His body was dead. I could feel his peace and for that moment it joined with my own. The nurse instinctively wanted to put his mask back on, but I stopped her. With my hand on his cheek, on the same comforting spot that I used to stroke him from the time he was a baby until just now when he released this last breath, I could feel the artery in his neck, and there was no more pulse. There was no more light in his eyes. There was no more living in Adam's body. My son had decided it was time to leave. All the life of Adam that had filled the room and shone through his eyes was gone and was given back to me. His eyes were dark, black and empty and I closed them for the last time.

Once Adam and I released our physical connection I remember turning to Eli to thank him and ask what I could do for him. Eli was in shock. I remember him standing up from his chair at the foot of

Adam's bed that still held Adam's lifeless body and saying he had to take care of himself this time. He told me, "When Jetta died, you took care of me. You have to take care of yourself this time. Don't take care of me." Another gift from Eli. He had stayed with his friend and with me all night, calling hospice for instruction when Adam seemed distressed. And now he released me from my instinctive caregiver role. I asked him if he wanted some time with Adam's body because it would be his last opportunity. He said, "No" and then asked what was next. I told him the plan I had made. Nothing was required of him anymore for Adam or me.

Eli left the living room where Adam's body rested and went to his own bedroom in the home he had so loved sharing with Adam. My friend Jim had just arrived, and he joined me as we bathed Adam's body, washed his hair and shaved him. The hospice worker had brought everything to clean Adam up for the day and we used it to prepare Adam's body for its departure. We recited a last prayer of transition and prepared to let his body go. I helped put Adam's body onto the cart and remember thinking how like Jello a body is without a being in it. The body was no longer my son; Adam was gone. Off with his mother and his heavenly Father.

When the hospice social worker showed up about an hour later, I talked with her briefly then I asked her to talk with Eli as I was going home to sleep. I knew Eli would need someone, but it was not me.

That was the end of Adam's life with me. There was no more gauntlet to run.

Facebook | David Winstrom | December 27, 2014

Adam is with his Father and his mother. He left today at 11 am. Yizkor...remember in love.

Facebook | David Winstrom | December 29, 2014

This is from Adam's father. There are two memorial services. The service in Holland is more participatory and expressive. The service in Grand Haven is more traditional and reflective. You may come to either or both.

The Memorial Service at Maplewood is intended for Adam's Compassionate Heart community (if you are not part of that Community you are still welcome).

On Sunday, January 4, at 2:00 pm at Covenant Life Church in Grand Haven another memorial service will be held for Adam's community in Grand Haven and all others who would enjoy a traditional service.

Adam always managed to have two or three birthday parties. Two celebrations of his life, one early one later, one in Holland one in Grand Haven seemed proper. I did not intend to confuse anyone. But like my son, I just wanted to have a couple of chances to celebrate him and to make it easy for everyone who loved him to find a place to come and share that memory.

As I write, I still have mixed feelings about my **decision to send** Adam to ER instead of letting him remain at home. Adam was a DNR (Do Not Resuscitate), so I imagined they would make him comfortable and see if his collapse was from pneumonia or as I thought, from cancer. I am convinced that it was a gift and a sacrifice that Adam was willing to give to his roommate and to those who gathered around him those final two days. They had not seen nor considered his end and that his death was imminent. They had not prepared themselves. For Adam, those last two days were physically very unpleasant, yet he endured them continuing to pour out his love, kindness and joy to others until he decided he had done enough and let go to join his mother and God. He had no fear or sense of confusion or panic. Just a peace-filled release.

He was my son whom I loved and felt loved by from the first moment I looked into his eyes and heard his first breath to the moment he looked back into my eyes and released his last breath.

Going out to talk to God

Chapter 21
Celebrating Adam

How to Celebrate a Life?

After my last phone conversation with the doctors at the testicular cancer center, I knew my son's body would die. I had just buried my mother, father and my wife, and knew that soon I would bury my son. I wanted to focus on Adam as he lived and I had time when he was in his community living his life to consider and make plans for what was to be next. I did not look forward to Adam's funeral. The reason for a funeral is for the community to come together to mourn our loss, celebrate the life of the person who died and offer support to the surviving family. I was reluctantly preparing to do this again and to complete my social obligation by having a funeral, knowing it was the right thing to do and not right for me.

Jetta had orchestrated her departure knowing from our experience with my parents how draining the funeral process is and how much more so her body dying would be for me. She had made her plan to go to hospice in Holland to have her body die. Her plan was to have her friends stop by and say good-bye to her. Hundreds did, but most were gloomy, sad faced, uncomfortable folks. I understand sadness quite well, and I understand the need to express one's sadness over the loss of a friend or loved one. I just did not have the personal energy to create the conditions for everyone else to express their sadness. I did not want to put aside my own grief to take care of all those I knew would come looking for support and relief, but I did it anyway.

My father and Jetta had both attempted to make the death gauntlet easier for me to run. My father prearranged what he could and told me what he wanted so I would not have to suffer his loss and still organize the event. Even as I was happy for my father and Jetta to be released back to God, their support and comfort offered to me in life was gone leaving a hole in my life.

The gauntlet starts the day after the person you were caring for and most cared about dies. It is often not a surprise, but it is still a shock. Running the gauntlet means going to the funeral home to pick out a casket, pick the dates for visitation and the public viewing of the body, arrange the obituary, order the grave stone and talk with the minister about the actual ceremony. Then you get to decide to do or not do an additional grave side ceremony and decide where everyone goes to meet, eat and greet afterwards. Then they all leave and you clean up. Each meeting and executive decision took energy and removed me from my own processing of my now different life. It put me into my care giver role, a role that takes energy. Next comes living through the three-nights of visitation with hundreds of people who do not know what to say or do so they say with great sincerity, "I am sorry." It is the proper thing to say, often followed by, "they will be missed."

By the time I was running the gauntlet when Jetta's body had died, I had run thin on my ability to fulfill my part of the ritual. My part was to say, "Thank you" and "yes she will be missed." Adam did it very well often adding an arm on their shoulder or a hug for those in tears. I started out strong, but by the time the last night of visitation came around, I was not able to comfort her friends. What I had wanted was uninterrupted time with my son and time to be alone for the first time in 40 years, to process the feeling of being alone, not just separated for a few hours or a day, but alone. After living with and loving Jetta for 40 years, I needed time to adjust. My instinctive need to take care of others compelled my to do what I really did not want to do—support Jetta's friends who were involved in organizing me and the proceedings. They were helping me as best they could, knowing that was the right thing to do.

Knowing I would need to make final arrangements for Adam's body, I did not want to suffer through this unfulfilling ritual one more time, and still, I wanted to do the right thing for Adam's friends. But this time I wanted to do what seemed right for me.

I began talking with Smitty, my friend from church. He was also the support minister. We had many lunches together, and he listened to what I thought I should do. Let me weep and feel sorry for myself—the real sorry as in I am in sorrow, not looking for sympathy and he just let me be. And we prayed together. Then he asked, "What do you *need* for you in this process and what do you *want?*" He had listened to me talk about making arrangements for visitations in Holland in the evening for Adam's friends from CHM, Hope College, Zeeland and Holland Christian and having the funeral in Grand Haven in the afternoon at our church. All that was what I knew was the correct thing to do. He reminded me that funerals were not only for the living but were specifically for the family. The funerals were not for Adam and me; we always said our last prayers of parting and good-byes at the cemetery, alone. Then we shoveled the dirt in to bury the dead body of our loved one. My father's funeral was for his friends and Adam. Jetta's funeral was for her friends and Adam. I ran the funeral gauntlet both times. Smitty asked me what I wanted at Adam's funeral *just for me.* At first, I said nothing public. What I wanted was care for my son until his body died, have his remains cremated, get on my Harley and head south until I hit Key West, then head west until I found San Diego, then south again until I hit Cabo, Mexico. All I had dedicated my life energy to would be gone. My purpose concluded. My covenant completed. I just wanted to let the wind and the sun wash over me for as many months as it took to find my own rhythm again. I just needed to find my own way through such an enormous transition. I had spent 40 years being a husband to the love of my life and 30 of those years being Adam's father. I could not find a perspective for what was becoming "my life, but not yet." I was still letting go of who I had become for most of my life with Jetta and now it was time to give my son, Adam, back to God. What I wanted was not really a possibility.

Smitty both gently and firmly asked what could I handle. What I knew I did not want was having to support hundreds of distraught people telling me they were surprised and sorry and wanting to know what happened. I had not handled that very well when Jetta died even with Adam still there to help me.

As Smitty and I discussed the memorial service, I thought of Adam's community from Holland and all of his friends at Compassionate Heart Ministries and his roommate. For many of them, it was their first significant death. I realized that Adam's memorial service was the last gift Adam could give to them. It had to be a celebration, just as Adam's life was a celebration. I wanted it to teach people that death is part of a natural cycle. I wanted it to celebrate a friend's return to God; it did not have to be a funeral ritual about death and grief. Death had come and gone. Grief would come when mourning light shines and not sooner or later. Like breathing, death is not planned yet impossible to avoid.

I went to the funeral home four months before Adam's body died. I made my decisions at the pace I could without letting them interfere with my time with Adam or my own processing pace. I asked Barb Newman, Adam's friend and mine, to host the celebration and teach Adam's friends about going with God. I approached her four months before Adam died and she said she would but never imagined it was really going to happen. I asked Donna Bunce, the Director of Compassionate Heart Ministries if it could be held at there in Zeeland, not at a funeral home with a viewing of Adam's lifeless body. I would not have Adam's body present with Adam no longer connected to it. Adam had lived an intense life and in 30 years exhausted his earthly shell. He was free, and I did not want this to be anything like a funeral; I wanted this to be a celebration of his life. Donna agreed and liked the idea of a celebration led by Barb Newman.

Smitty reminded me about Adam's community in Grand Haven and said they would like to honor him and his life as well. He asked if it would be okay to do the same thing in Grand Haven on an afternoon. Many of Adam's friends through his church and in his men's group no longer drove at night, and it would be difficult to come to Zeeland. I was clear about what would be offered as his farewell—a celebration of life. I had asked Andy DeJong to host the Grand Haven event, and he also agreed but said it would not be for a long time. Everyone was in denial.

When Adam left his body, all the preparations were already made for Adam to be celebrated twice—once in Zeeland with his friends from Compassionate Heart Ministries, Zeeland Christian School, Holland Christian School and the Hope College community; and once more in Grand Haven with his Covenant Life Church community, grade school friends and old neighbors. On some cosmic level, it fit. He had died twice.

Like the celebration in the football stadium when a thousand voices sang Happy Birthday Adam, his memorial service made it clear how wrong the kind doctor was. Adam had a huge community of friends. I knew that Adam would be with God and with Jetta and that they would be smiling as we celebrated his well-lived life.

After Adam went with God, I called Barb and Donna and Jim together. It was time to finish the plans for the celebration of Adam's life. Our meeting was nothing like going to the funeral home to make arrangements—we laughed and told stories, cried and told more stories. We talked about Adam in his community and released Barb from her concern that she was not a minister. The celebration was not about having a minister guiding Adam's soul into heaven; Adam was there, I had no doubt. It was about creating a condition for an inclusive community to make meaning out of life's natural process. To paint a last picture of their friend Adam living with God. Jim wanted to make sure both celebrations were open to everyone. He did not want people to feel excluded or unwelcome if they went to the Zeeland celebration or the Grand Haven celebration

Barb created the condition I had hoped for at the first celebration of Adam's life in Zeeland. People told stories and laughed and sang and ate. Adam's friends learned about death being a natural part of being human rather than something to fear. Several people came up to me and said, "It's too bad Adam is missing his party, he would have loved it!" The atmosphere was not at all funeral-like. I was asked to greet everyone as they entered the church and I did. I did not hear, "I am so sorry" or feel any funeral heaviness. I heard lots of "I miss him, but he is okay and I will be okay, too." Not one person mentioned Adam having Autism or Down syndrome. There was no dwelling on what did not define his life; it was all about love and the incredible human being he had become. It was about life and about how Adam had lived it. The band who played at Serve camp rocked Adam's fave tunes. People laughed and told funny stories about how wonder-filled their lives had been because they knew Adam. Folks came up to the front of the church to tell stories about Adam. Rosa Donna and her daughter, Adam's football coach and his daughter, Chris Doornbos and his friend Kirk Cousins spoke and told some great stories. It was just the perfect celebration of a life lived by a unique man fully included in his community.

The second celebration at Grand Haven was more traditional but was equally a joy-filled send-off. Adam's home church packed with all who wanted one last chance to celebrate who Adam was. The praise group played his favorite songs. Andy DeJong, Adam's minister who had welcomed Adam into the church on Adam and Jetta's first day at church 25 years earlier, was leading the church community in their goodbye to Adam. Brett and his wife, Dale, along with Kirk Cousins talked about the kind man Adam was. Other people talked about what a gift he was in their lives. Smitty had his wife Janie read what Smitty had written for the occasion. Smitty was once again having to have his body repaired and could not be present. All spoke about the joy Adam brought to everyone he touched. Smitty wanted everyone to know that many people pray, some with eloquence and some with emotion, but all pray to God. But not Adam. For Adam, prayer was different; it was personal because he talked with Father God just like he would with his father. Adam grew up understanding that I was his temporary father here on this earth and that God was his Father for eternity. Adam and I often talked honestly, personally and sometimes with humor to our Father but always from our hearts to the heart of God.

Smitty's Eulogy

Smitty couldn't do it, so he had his wife, Janie, read to Adam's Grand Haven Community what he wrote:

Adam Winstrom

A Child of God

Loving Son

Loyal Friend

Teacher

Mentor

Coach

Encourager

Joyful

Sargent at Arms

Chick Magnet

Hopeful

Helpful

Generous

Full of Grace

Adam was bigger than life with his smile, his hugs and his vitality. The world is a better place because Adam Winstrom walked among us. While we may miss Adam, he is now in heaven being taken on the grand tour with his Mom, Jetta.

For many years, Adam, Jetta and David sat in the row in front of Janie and me at Covenant Life Church. First, Jetta would come in and a few minutes later David would amble in and then Adam would come in after greeting half the congregation and have David and Jetta move over so he could sit with either of them...one never knew which side he would choose, left or right or move them both so he could sit between them...and then he'd look at David and say, "You need some coffee?" and off he'd go to get Dad his coffee.

And how can we ever forget Adam's closing benediction – HAVE A GOOD DAY! at the end of Sunday morning services. After our Pastor would give his benediction, Adam would give us the real benediction. One of my favorite memories is Adam raising his hands in blessing at the end of our month-long celebration of the 25th Anniversary of Covenant Life's founding. But more than his Sunday blessing, he blessed us in his everyday presence just by being here and by being Adam.

For many years he was the Sargent at Arms of the Friday morning men's group as he took his "protected" place alongside Bob Parker, our leader, and we would all hear Adam's voice boom out, "ALL RIGHT GUYS...SIT DOWN, SHUT UP! BOB IS READY TO START." Right now, Adam is probably telling St. Peter where to sit and to be quiet because Jesus has something to say.

Each week, Adam would close the Bible study time with prayer, praying not only for the prayer list but for Holland Christian High School Football, Hope College Football, his friend Kirk Cousins, and of course, for his Dad and others especially those who had lost loved ones or their pets had died. He even prayed for David's different cars and gave thanks for his new phone(s). Throughout his prayer was this phrase: THANK YOU FOR THIS DAY. I hope my prayer life can be so practical. We know that God understood Adam's each and every word even tho' we sometimes couldn't.

But more than just being a blessing, Adam was a teacher. I don't know if he realized how much he taught me, and I'm not trying to speak for others, but I have a feeling that most of you also can relate. Here are just of the few things he taught me.

LIVE ENTHUSIATICALLY AND GENEROUSLY. Who could ever match his laughter and his smile. He loved to buy the pizza or dinner whenever we went out...with his own credit card.

LOVE PASSIONATELY AND UNCONDITIONALLY. He never met a person he didn't like.

LAUGH OFTEN AND MEAN IT. LIFE IS GREAT NO MATTER WHAT IS GOING ON AROUND US.

ACCEPT WHAT IS.

ACCEPT LIFE GRACIOUSLY NO MATTER WHAT OBSTACLES YOU ENCOUNTER

NEVER COMPLAIN.

LIVE IN THE PRESENT, YOU CAN'T CHANGE THE PAST NOR WORRY ABOUT THE FUTURE. Some time ago, Janie and I attended a funeral and Adam made this comment about the deceased, "He died, he was a good man and he died. He's dead!"

Well friends! Adam was a good man. He was like the rest of us—a sinner saved by grace. And because of his confession of Jesus Christ as his personal savior, Adam didn't die...his life continues on in heaven with greater enthusiasm, passion and love than when he lived on earth, but now he is in the presence of our Lord and Savior.

As I finish I'd like to say this to David. You and Jetta raised not only a good man but a great man full of compassion and caring and I believe a man after God's own heart. A job well done! I'm looking forward to seeing our friend again.

As we said goodbye to Adam, we can say the same thing that I'm sure was said in heaven upon Adam's arrival, "Well done! Well done! Thou good and faithful servant."

Friends Sharing

Dale Kwekel wrote a letter to Adam and shared it at the memorial service. In it he apologized to Adam for the times he thought he was too busy to say hello and how he longed for one more hello from Adam. He reflected on Adam always being available to cheer him up and pray for him. Nothing was more important to Adam at the moment than the person he was with or the person he was talking to on the phone and he told how great that felt. He talked about how much he missed basking in Adam's love.

Kirk Cousins talked about how Adam lived his life from a unique perspective. He said most of us live our lives looking in our own mirror. We are focused on ourselves and how we are being impacted in each of life's situations. Adam, on the other hand, lived life looking through a window. His concern was how others were being impacted by life. He wanted to be there when support was needed. And he was.

Memorial Service from Barb Newman's Perspective

God gave me a gift. Yes, Adam was a gift. His parents were gifts to me. But Adam's memorial service was a precious gift and a picture of something I had been implementing, teaching, suggesting and creating since 1989. It was a picture of the profound beauty of inclusive community.

While I do quite a bit of speaking, I am not a pastor. And of all the jobs a pastor does, the last thing I would want to do is some sort of memorial service, especially for someone I know and love. So, when David called and asked me if I would do this when Adam died, I was stuck. I would do anything for Adam and David, and I would never want to lead that type of service. In the end, I agreed and prayed that God would give me wisdom.

When Adam died, I ran over to my brother-in-law's house (he is a pastor) and asked him, "How do you lead a memorial service?" He gave me some valuable advice and I set up a time to meet with David and a few close friends. We told stories about Adam and I was listening carefully to some major themes that were part of those stories. Also, I asked David what he wanted, and it was clear he wanted a place for Adam's friends—of all abilities—to celebrate Adam's life and understand death as part of life. We needed a differentiated memorial service with visuals.

Donna and I started thinking about the details and decided we might be best to hold the service in a church. After all, we thought perhaps a hundred people might show up for this first of two services. It was a Friday night and some people were still gone on Christmas vacation. We wanted people to have a chance to participate, so we asked several to speak to one of the five qualities we saw in Adam's life—his contagious joy, servant's heart, compassion, strength, and friendship. We constructed prayers to say thank you to God for Adam's life. We had time to ask why to God and ask Him to help us as we looked now to life here without Adam and not having him to ask us what we had for supper, to pray for us, to join us on outings, to chop our wood, to phone us at night, and to lead us in singing to God with great abandon.

We watched as people started to come. Our guess of maybe 100 people turned into 500 people. 500 people were all gathered because Adam had touched their lives in some way. From a doctor who once predicted that this little baby boy would have no friends and would be a burden his entire life to a service celebrating his life that pulled in 500 people who had Adam's fingerprints all over them, we gathered. And given Adam's ability to be welcoming, the people attending displayed varied ages, cultures, IQ scores and socio-economic status.

I had prayed that God would hold back my own tears during the service and God answered that prayer. I handed many people the microphone during the evening and listened to the testimonies they gave to the power of "Adam" in their life. So many commented that when in the presence of Adam, it was so easy to feel God's presence. Those who spoke included friends and teachers and one NFL quarterback who texted and talked back and forth with Adam before and after each game. After all, that football team from school is still there for one another.

I made it to my car and then the tears started to flow. I was crying because I, too, would miss Adam and the way he loved and cared for me. I was also crying because I realized that God had just given me a picture of the power and beauty of inclusive community. I recalled that from the many words given about Adam, not one person happened to mention that he had Down syndrome or Autism. I saw clearly what inclusion created. If the Winstroms had followed the kind doctor's advice, there would be an entire community of people who would have missed gifts God had intended to give us through His servant, Adam Winstrom. I saw in the eyes and hearts of the 500 who were there to celebrate Adam that night a living picture of 1 Corinthians 12, God's picture of inclusive community.

We had closed the memorial service with a time of worship. After all, gathering and singing before God's throne was something we could do together with Adam. That ride home I kept singing the chorus from Matt Redman's song "10,000 Reasons." For Adam, for his life, for the picture of an inclusive community, for our God who clearly weaves together His people, "Bless the Lord, O my soul. Worship His Holy name. Sing like never before, O my soul. I'll worship Your Holy name."

It was all I hoped for, just as my son Adam had been all I hoped for in a son. I felt supported by Adam's community, not exhausted. My anticipatory grief had vanished the moment Adam breathed his last breath with me.

Chapter 22
Adam's Community Speaks

Adam didn't just meet people, he engaged people and he offered and maintained friendship for eternity. Some people he even adopted. All of them he loved and supported and gave them his friendship. Adam's friend, Kirk Cousins, said that some people want friends for what they can receive from that friendship, but Adam made friends so he could give something to them. Here are a few stories from a few of Adam's 960 closest friends. The *kind* doctor was so wrong when he said that Adam would never have any friends.

The Walton's: Friends for Eternity

Walton's–that was the name I gave them. They are a family who were the last ones on Adam's list to call every night. He would go through a good night routine with the entire family of three brothers, one sister and Mr. and Mrs. Kuipers (their real name). At the end of the daily evening call, they all said, "Good night, Adam" and in my head, I heard, "Good night, John Boy." He loved them. He had connected with Brett when Brett was playing football at Holland Christian School. They never let go of each other all through High School, even during summers. When Brett went to college and on to graduate school, he would come home on weekends and would pick Adam up to go to church to sit with his family. They did not talk about being Christians, they just lived a life of faith. Some days, Adam became Adam Frank Winstrom Kuipers.

He also knew Grandpa and Grandma Kuipers. When Grandpa got sick, Adam told me that Grandpa was dying before the rest of the family were ready to see it. This was after Adam's Grandfather, and Grandmother and Mother had all died. Adam could see death as could I, and he had no fear of it, unlike many of the people we knew. Adam told me he prayed with Grandpa and that Grandpa was okay. Adam meant he was okay with dying and okay with God. During Grandpa's last days, he asked Adam and me to come into his room and spend some time alone with him. He wanted me there, but he had Adam come close next to his bed and held Adam's hand. He looked Adam in the eye and told him to listen carefully to what he had to say. Adam looked back into Grandpas eyes, something Adam rarely would do to anyone else. He told Adam, "I will die very soon, and I want to bless you." I heard Adam's soft "okay." Grandpa said, "Your name is Adam, Adam Frank Winstrom, and you are a good man, upright and honorable. I am so proud of you. Continue to honor His name and to honor your own name always and thank you, Adam, for your friendship. Thank you for praying with me." Then he wanted to pray with Adam one last time, and they did, each in their softened voices. I could hear them each thanking God for the other, Grandpa Kuipers affirming Adam as a man of God and Adam telling Grandpa to have no fear because God was with him, then their words just fell together. I had no words to add to that moment except "Amen" when they were done praying together. Grandpa was not afraid of dying. He, like Adam, knew what was coming was not to be feared or resisted. Grandpa Kuipers told me that I was a good father who had raised up a good son. We left and Grandpa called in his family to bless them and assure them each that he was okay with his death. He died a short while later that day.

Each one of the Kuiper family was so very precious to Adam. At one point, Katy caught Adam's eye and he asked her out on a date. She was working so much it didn't work out, but Adam did not give up. He saw her every Sunday. He even invited himself or got invited to family dinners. Finally, I talked to Katy to see for myself if Adam was pushing too much. She had the perfect response. She told me that she just didn't have time to date right now and that she thought of Adam as one of her brothers. When she had time, she would go out with Adam. I suggested that she and a girlfriend let Adam take them both to dinner at a very nice restaurant. I asked Katy to teach Adam how to go on a respectful date. The night came and Katy and Darlene (Dar, who was dating Brett) went out with Adam. Adam insisted that Brett come along and they all had a very good night. After that, Adam hung out with the girls from time to time. Adam had a lot of girlfriends but considered Dar his special girlfriend. Brett eventually married Darlene.

As each of Adam's girlfriends married someone else, Adam learned to share them with their husbands. What was clear was that all potential husbands had to be willing to share the girls with Adam, too. When Adam was in the hospital, one of the nurses noticed that all the women who came to see Adam brought their boyfriends. The nurse told me that Adam had some wise friends. She said she watched as the couples would go into Adam's room. The young women, who Adam called his girlfriends, would each sit next to Adam on his bed and visit with him, then invite their boyfriends to join in. She said every one of those girls watched like hawks how their new boyfriend treated Adam. Some of those boys were not keepers, and Adam was their test. Those who related easily and respectfully got a subtle approval, and the nurse could see a cold shoulder developing for those who could not relate.

One night out of the blue, Mr. and Mrs. Kuipers told me not to worry—if something ever happened to me, Adam would have a family and a home if he needed one. My body had begun to fail, and that assurance that Adam would be fine was very meaningful. When Brett married Darlene, Adam was Brett's Best Man in the wedding. I warned the minister that he might be marrying the three of them. He and I laughed, but midway through the ceremony when Adam gave Brett the ring, all three of them hugged each other and laughed and cried. The minister had to separate them to pronounce Brett and Darlene husband and wife. Brett and Darlene bought their first home with an extra bedroom for Adam just in case he needed it.

Katy Kuiper's note to Adam

To the best man I have ever known. You have changed my life and my family completely. I will never forget you. I hope one day I can be as great of a person as you were. You have touched the lives of many. You were my brother and a wonderful friend. No one will ever take your place in my heart. You will be greatly missed. I love you Adam. 12/27/14

Brett Kuiper's Tribute

The last time there was a speech given between the two of us, it was at Dar and I's wedding and Adam was giving a speech for me as my best man. Adam spent months preparing Bible verses and he even found an extensive PowerPoint presentation on married life in his research. I was honored to have him speak as my best man; I considered him like my own brother. He would jokingly call me "his son." The least I can do today is to give a speech honoring his memory.

Adam had many names. The number of names he had grew by the day. At one point, he went by Adam Frank Peppers Stylish Winstrom with the addition of Kuipers following my wedding.

Adam, the Best Man

Adam was always joyful and a selfless servant. He loved to work and was always wanting to help people. He couldn't always help, but he would always try. He showed the joy of Jesus in every moment of his life.

Adam dressed up as Elton John at Brett and Darlene's wedding

The first time I met Adam was in the Holland Christian football locker room. We would spend much time in there together during high school. While I would be weight lifting, Adam would be stationed at the exercise bike. Typically, we would crank up Queen's greatest hits on repeat nearly every session. Adam's favorite song was "Another One Bites the Dust," which he referred to as "The Dust." When the song would come on, he would yell, "THE DUST!" and do an air guitar with his hands. Everyone knew when Adam was leaving the weight room because he would announce in a loud voice, "I'm taking off!" It seems like he left this earth in the same way he would leave the locker room.

Adam and I have been there for each other over the past ten years through good and bad times. On average, he would call me ten times a day and always had to close the day with his good night ritual. It would go like this: We would talk and then he would remind me to take a shower, brush my teeth, get to sleep, eat breakfast, put my pants on and get moving, get moving, get moving. While I was at my parents' house, he would have to say goodnight via speaker phone to every member of my family in order to go to bed. It was like being at the Walton's house from the popular TV show. Many times, previous to his good night ritual, he would play his guitar for us, sing a song or dance via Skype to "Shake Your Booty" by KC and the Sunshine Band.

Together we worked through the passing of his Mom, Jetta, and his guinea pig, Cole, coincidentally on the same day. I would stay up late at night on the phone with him as he cried about missing his Mom. He helped me through the passing of my Grandpa, Fred. Through my Grandpa's fight with cancer, Adam would visit him often. I did my best to encourage Adam during a tough bout of Pneumonia when he almost died. Because of his joy and love of life, he struggled through this tough time and beat his illness despite the doctor's doubting that he could pull through.

When Dar and I got engaged, it was as if all three of us got engaged. I got on one knee, asked Dar to marry me, and Adam got so excited he was jumping up and down. Later we found out that he broke his foot as a result of all the jumping. Our engagement took place at Holland State Park where Dar and I rode in as the two of us, but we rode away from the engagement three across in my truck with Dar in the middle. We went back to Starbucks to celebrate with friends. Adam was the first one inside and announced to everyone that we had gotten married.

Adam was the best man at our wedding and also showed up as Elton John to the reception. David called him Elton John after he put on all the props from the photo booth including a masquerade mask, feather boa, cowboy hat, peacock feathers and a bandana to name a few items. I am also pretty sure he thought all three of us were married into the Kuipers' family that night.

Through his chemotherapy, Adam showed everyone his joy and strength. If you didn't know Adam was going through chemo, you probably wouldn't have known other than the indication of his newly bald head. He didn't let on that he was in a lot of pain; he didn't let cancer take the joy of life from him.

Anyone who knew Adam received many phone calls. So much so, that his Dad said that he would be the first person to get a phone implanted into his brain. He would call me so many times that his Dad would call me to make sure that Adam wasn't wearing me out. Whenever a thunderstorm was coming through the area, Adam called to alert everyone and instruct them to go inside and be careful.

Every Sunday I would pick Adam up for church. When Darlene and I were dating, I would pick them both up for church and we would ride three across in my truck with Adam's arm around my girlfriend. Sometimes I would be late and Adam would definitely let me know. He left video messages telling me that he was waiting forever. When we would finally get to church and sat down, it was like we were still sitting in the truck with Adam's arm around Dar and sometimes both of us.

For Dar and me, our dates were very similar to our church outings with Adam. At times, I felt like I was the chaperone for his date. On one date in particular, I was the chaperone when Dar and my sister, Katy, took him to CityVu on a special outing. I was not supposed to go along, but Adam insisted on me coming. That night he practiced being a gentleman with one lady on each arm. He proceeded to open the door for both of them, pull out their chairs and pour their water at the table.

My wife, Darlene, and Adam had a special relationship. He considered himself her protector and at all times her boyfriend. When we got engaged he told me after deep deliberation and inner conflict, "you may keep her." It was a struggle for him to say that because deep down I think he was in competition to marry her. He seemed to be okay with the idea of us married when we brought him back a family ring from our honeymoon. It was then official, he was a Kuipers. Not by blood, but by ring and heart.

Adam was very upset that he could not come on our honeymoon. We cheered him up by taking him on a family trip to a cabin near Traverse City. At first, he was upset since he had it in his mind that he would be sleeping three across in the same bed as us. He settled for sleeping upstairs after we snuggled him to sleep. The following morning, he lumbered down stairs waking everyone up and literally jumped into bed with us. Later that weekend, we received a swimming clinic from Adam as he towed us by rope in the canoe across the lake.

One of my earliest memories with Adam was cutting down a cherry tree in his backyard at his home in Grand Haven. All the wood that I cut was put into a pile in his backyard. Over the next year, he shaved every inch of bark off the entire tree. Adam knew that I was a forester, and he wanted to do the same type of work as me. In his woodshed with his guinea pig, he would chisel off the bark of the wood while calling me on the phone to tell me "he was working wood." When I would visit him, he would ask me to come see the work he had been doing in his workshop. The workshop floor was covered with at least a foot deep of wood shavings from all his wood peeling.

Adam loved cleaning, and he wanted badly to come help me clean as I moved my belongings back home from Michigan State. Adam's dad dropped Adam off and then the fun began. While finishing a few things on campus, I left Adam at my apartment. I came back to him lying in the middle of my apartment vacuuming wherever his arms could reach. When I opened the door he said, "I do good work." Adam did great work, and he loved to work. I never saw someone who loved working as much as him.

I miss my friend very much, as we all do. To miss Adam is to miss Jesus; if you did not see the love of Jesus in Adam, you missed who Adam was. Adam was constantly pouring himself into others. Adam wanted to be part of people's lives through good and bad times. Evident in Adam was his tender heart. Life was precious to him, this was seen when he would cry about obituaries that he would read. Most of the time he did not know the individual, but it would break his heart. He would call me and be sobbing about someone he did not even know. Adam always wanted to make sure that Dar and I were okay. He would always ask, "Do you need anything?"

Let's not miss out on the opportunity to learn from Adam's example. Many of us have experienced the outpouring of Adam's spirit into our lives. We should learn from his example and pour ourselves into the lives of people that we meet.

Hanna's Tribute

One of my absolute favorite memories is when Adam's family moved to the green house in Grand Haven. I remember playing cowboys there. We were just little kids and Adam "shot" me with a toy gun and I fell down and played dead in the hallway outside his bedroom door. I did my best not to move or breath because I was "dead." He ran to Jetta slightly panicked to tell her that I was dead and I can still hear her voice in my head saying, "Oh no!" Adam took a blanket and covered me up and laid in the hallway beside me stroking my hair and waiting for me to be "undead." Then, when I couldn't fake it anymore, I burst out laughing and Adam erupted in laughter, too, and we just sat there and laughed until our bellies hurt. Then he told me to get up and the game started all over. If I didn't fall down, he would order me to fall down. We played that game for multiple years until we both got older and outgrew it.

I remember there was a kid's TV show we would watch full of silly games that would make us laugh. I remember the winner on the show would have the honor of riding the pie train. It was a little train that the winner sat on and rode it through a maze where at every turn they would get a pie in the face. It was so silly that it was funny. For Adam's birthday one year, I came over and we put on our swimming suits and took turns putting pies in each other's faces and laughing. We did so many fun silly things.

I remember when I got accepted to Liberty University that Adam was just as excited as I was (and he reminded me for quite a while after getting accepted that he had a dog named Liberty who I remember fondly). He told everyone that I was going to Virginia he was genuinely proud and excited for me, the big "college girl." Then I got to share in his joy as he graduated high school and moved on to college, too. Our life milestones were never too far off if I wasn't living life with Adam, we were living it parallel.

My whole life is flooded with the most joyous memories of Adam. Thank you for sharing him with me for nearly all of my life.

Travis' Tribute

I met Adam Winstrom at Holland Christian High School in 2003. We remained friends for life. Me, Gus and TJ all hung out together and were known the "Bad Boys." We were a little rowdy, but we all had great hearts. Adam found us and held on.

Adam and I were in our first class together. I recall it being an art class in the morning or end of the day. At our school, we prayed in the morning and the end of the day for things like who was sick or someone died or for thankful nice fun things. Adam had asked to pray for a dog that had died. I asked him after we said a prayer for his dog when did this happen? Adam replied a few years ago. Now to be honest, I thought to myself inside a little laugh why is this guy praying for his dog that died a couple years ago. I did not understand why but he sure liked that dog and I think I could relate. I learned to pay attention to how caring of a guy he was from that day on. I thought I would like to get to know this guy better. As high school went on we shared a lot of time together as we had math and English together for a couple of hours a day.

On weekends, I worked in my Dad's store and Adam went along. I liked hanging out with Adam because it kept me real. A lot of Adam's friends said he kept life real because with Adam life was real. Adam loved to work and knew where everything was in the store better than I did. People came in to talk with Adam and he would get them the stuff they wanted.

After high school, everyone went separate ways, but a close group of friends made a vow that would make sure no matter what we that we stayed in touch with Adam as it was hard for him to get around to see friends. We would go to lunch often on Saturdays or whenever we could get together. It became not only Adam time, but it kept people in touch. The camaraderie went on for a lot of years.

I learned some things along the way from Adam. One was his amazing ability to genuinely care about everyone and another to be himself no matter what. I know I learned to change myself along the way and we became quite the pair after I realized it was okay to make funny faces and be loud sometimes in public. We had some funny names we had for each other he would call me Mustard sniffer. One time we were at a sushi place

Adam Winstrom and Travis Carini

and I told Adam that they came out with this new green catsup he should try it out. I know he did not particularly like spicy things and it would be harmless. So, I encouraged him to put a little bit about the size of a tic tac on his sushi. Ha ha, he, of course, was surprised!! He looked at me, knew it was game time to trick me back. I went to the bathroom and when I came back he patiently waited for me to eat about a quarter sized glob of wasabi that was under my sushi that I did not see! I ate it and, of course, it lasted longer and I made some very hilarious faces. I don't think we ever laughed so hard!!!

Another phase we went through was we spent Saturdays with a group of guys on my farm. This included golf carts, brush fires, grilling out and sometimes beers. A group of us would meet up and just hang out we would give each other a hard time and push each other's limits. I assume this is what all guys do. I have a passion for shooting guns, and Adam really enjoyed this hobby as well. One thing about Adam, and why I trust him so much as a friend, was how disciplined he was and rule oriented he was. When I trained him on firearm safety, I knew he would be the safest one out of the group. He also had a steady hand and loved the loud bang!

I know for me those are some of the best times ever of my life.

I farm blueberries with my Dad, and I was fortunate enough to have my friend come and work with me by my side during harvest season. Some of that "work" entailed riding the tractor or the quad around the blueberry fields. After some play time, we would get to business and work in the production room where we packaged the blueberries for retail. I taught him how our number one priority is quality.

One thing I loved seeing was Adam's care and kindness for his fellow workers who spoke Spanish. Adam got along with everyone. He was the El Jefe (the boss). I think we also got along so well because we are both bossy. One time I gave him a supervisor position and made him some business cards and then it really set in and worked out well he was a good leader! When the migrant workers from Mexico were around, Adam would help show them what to do. One day, an older Mexican lady was upset about something, and I didn't know what to do. Adam went right to her and put his arm on her shoulder and spoke Spanish to her. She cried and talked and said, "Gracias" several times, then went back to work. Adam had just made another friend.

We were on the way to get some blueberry plants for a couple of new acres we were planting, and we had one of our best friends and co-workers Shari Jo with us. Adam was riding up front in this big semi-truck, and Shari Jo was in the back. We saw this State Trooper following us and I said, "Oh, crap, we are getting pulled over again, buddy!!"

So, the cop comes up and is kind of tough to me and asks for my ID. I handed it to him then he asks Adam, "Can I see your identification?" When Adam told him no, I thought we might be heading to jail together. He asked Adam again, "Sir, can I see your ID?"

Again, Adam said, "No!"

The Trooper was still standing at the window. I looked at Adam and asked, "Where's your wallet?"

"In my pocket!"

I said, "Can I see it?"

"No!!"

I turned to the policeman and asked, "What's the problem?"

He said, "Nothing, but I have never been told 'No' that sternly before." I think he was trumped by Adam's authority.

He listened to Adam explain that we were going to get blueberry bushes to plant on some new acreage and he let us go with no ticket. After we were back on the road, I asked Adam why he didn't want to show the Trooper his license. He told me that he just didn't want to and that he was mad that I broke the rules and got us pulled over. I found out later that his father had taught him to never give up his wallet. He could give his passport to travel but never his wallet.

On that same trip, we stopped at a local apple stand with a little petting zoo. We wanted to get a snack and see what kind of critters they had. They had this pen that had a small building, and they had these Alpacas or Llamas in there. One of these creatures had kind of a fuzzy haircut and a bad attitude, and it even looked mean. I said, "Hey, why don't you give that thing an apple we found on the ground?"

Adam said, "No way!!"

I assured him that this thing was as nice as a kitten and tried to feed it the apple. Then the next thing I knew, it grabbed my arm and shook it so violently I thought I'd been bitten by a shark! I swear this thing had two front teeth that were 2" long. I thought that was it for my arm. Adam grabbed that ugly alpaca and got it off of me. Once my arm was out of its mouth, we laughed so hard we almost fell over. We never stopped at one of those small petting zoos again.

When Adam was looking for a "real job," he applied at Carini Farms and was hired as cold room supervisor. He had a time card, ID badge, and business cards. The business cards were a treat from Mr. Carini. Adam got the job because he was different. The difference that Mr. Carini noticed in Adam was that he loved to work. Production was always up 30 percent when Adam ran the show. Adam was invited to fiestas and parties and became part of the Carini family also.

I have 100 more great stories, and I think we could tell them for days! I learned a lot from Adam about how to be a consistent person in life. He was the most consistent friend I have ever had. I knew that if I wasn't consistent or kept plans, it was not just rude, but it hurt his feelings. Adam would never do that to me, so I better not do that to him or any other friends.

I saw how he was so disciplined and that helped me realize that I needed to be aware of that.

Adam was my buddy. When we left hanging out or chatting on the phone, I would say, "I love you, bud!" and he would say the same thing back to me. I am at peace knowing he knew that every time. I did not know Adam's parents early on, but as we grew our friendship we became closer. I am thankful to carry on a friendship with his Dad, and I can say that Adam is a product of caring and compassionate parents.

Brittany Van Byssum's Tribute

Adam Winstrom was such an important person in my life. He was my best friend. He was my go-to person when I needed to talk. He was my go-to person when I needed to be cheered up. I felt like I needed Adam more than he ever needed me. Because of Adam, I look at life the way I do. I celebrate differences. I look at the gifts and abilities that individuals have. I can see how each person is valued and needed in the body of Christ. Without one member, the body of Christ is weak and cannot function to its fullest. Without one member, the body of Christ suffers. Adam proved that to me.

I met Adam when he was in my brother's class in middle school. I was in elementary school at the time, but I remember seeing Adam interact with his peers and thinking that he was such a fun kid. He really intrigued me. When I got to high school, I mentored at Summer Serve Camp. Adam and I were paired up together and what a week we had! One of the best of my life. He looked out for me, taught me how to love and care more for others, and to not worry about what others think of me. He was the true example of what Christ wants us to be. After Summer Serve Camp, we would call and text each other and would meet up every once in a while. We would go out for lunch almost every Saturday and have great conversations about his latest technology. He knew so much about the latest cell phone and he had everyone's phone number. His phone was almost always occupied with him checking in on his friends and asking them what they had for dinner! He was such a nice and thoughtful guy.

Brittany remembering Adam on her wedding day. They had planned the day with Adam, but he was already with God, so she wore his leather vest to celebrate their friendship.

Because of Adam, I decided to go into special education. Once college started, some of the hardest years of my life, Adam stayed by my side. He would always answer my phone calls when I needed him most. He was the friend I could depend on. During my time at Calvin College, I met a special guy. Of course, I had to introduce him to Adam. Once Adam definitely approved, our lunch dates for two were turned into three. A few years down the road, that special guy proposed to me! The first person that I had to tell was, of course, Adam. Adam played such an important role in my life. He inspired me, he encouraged me, and he made me a better person. He was the reason that I ended up teaching special education at Zeeland Christian School. I have a picture of Adam on my desk at work. I am reminded by that picture to be a good dependable friend, to encourage others, to see gifts that others have, and to live for Christ.

Kirk Cousins - Adam's High School Quarterback

Adam stayed connected to his friend Kirk Cousins all through High School. When Kirk went to college and played ball, Adam would call him before every game and after the game. Kirk always took the calls. Adam and Kirk went to lunch whenever they were both in town. Adam was there the night Kirk got his job offer to be an NFL quarterback for the Redskins. They each took their time to find and remain friends. Adam stayed in touch with Kirk until in December Kirk flew into Holland to say his last goodbye.

Here are some of Kirk's memories of Adam:

Adam Winstrom, you've always reminded us that no matter what you're going through in life, you can still keep a smile. God works in mysterious ways, my friend, He put you in our lives for a reason. You were always there encouraging me on the football field and kept in touch throughout the years.

Adam, Trainer for Holland Christian Football Team

Your parents are in our prayers; you were an incredible soul that will always be remembered, buddy. Thanks for the life lessons you've taught me... H5H

- *Post-game prayers at HC football games. Win or lose, Adam often prayed, and it was special.*

- *He would consistently ask people, "Are you tired?" It was precious. He usually was also a little tired himself.*

- *I would receive post-game voice mails from him in college and early in the pros. It was always so special to hear his thoughts on the game, win or lose.*

- *Whenever I would go to lunch with him, he would choose to wear all Spartan and Redskin gear. He was 100% supportive at all times.*

- *After tough high school basketball game losses, he would sit next to me in the locker room patting my knee and just letting me know that he was willing to sit with me as long as necessary to help me feel better.*

- *At football practice on hot August days, he would spray us with water from the hose and ask if we wanted a "cold shower" ... ha!*

- *I love the memory of him wearing the motorcycle gear: leather chaps, helmet and jacket, specifically in the weight room. It was so cool.*

- *I remember the day I was drafted to the Redskins, he came over to celebrate and just could not get enough of the homemade cheese dip my mom had made. We all marveled at the way he inhaled the cheese dip so casually. Just a funny memory.*

- *The picture is from our 5-year high school reunion party. Adam didn't technically graduate with our class, but he was such a friend to all of us, that he needed to be there.*

- *At my graduation open house, my Mom had placed a large poster on the wall where visitors could write a supportive, encouraging message as I left for college. Adam wrote a message saying: "good crats - Adam." He meant "congrats," and we all knew what "good crats" meant. It was just Adam being Adam, which is what made him so special. To this day, when our group of friends wants to congratulate another friend, we say "Good Crats."*

Donna Bunce, Compassionate Heart Ministries

Donna Bunce was witness to the infectiousness of Adam's friendship. She knew the depth and genuineness and unrelenting love he was capable and willing to share. Adam is remembered through the annual Adam Winstrom Friendship Award. These are her words:

Love you, Adam Frank Winstrom. Where does one even begin to describe this one-of-a-kind, extraordinarily unique young man? His gift and ability to live, love and have joy were unexplainable. He taught all of us more about living life large, laughing big belly laughs, and loving everyone, unconditionally.

Donna Bunce and Adam

Adam was the kind of guy who everyone wanted to be with. You wanted to be his friend. He treated ladies with respect and kindness. He was a gentleman. When he entered the room, you knew that he was there because he would always say, "Hey guys!" He made you feel like you were the most special person in the world and gave everyone the individual attention that we all crave. If you were sad or lonely, you can be sure that Adam would be by your side; praying for others and carrying your burdens was his specialty. Adam laughed and celebrated life like no one else... He was truly the best and will forever live in our hearts and put smiles on our faces!

Dale's Tribute

There was Adam, the first man, then there was Jesus who was called the second Adam, and then came Adam Winstrom, the personification of unconditional love, generosity, and loving kindness! I weep at your passing! Tend the garden until we all can join together once again my friend!

My heart is breaking with the loss of a sweet friend today. Adam was such a blessing to all he came in contact with. He taught me how to live and love life to the fullest. I'm so thankful I was able to get to know him. Rest in peace, Adam. You will be missed by many.

Gus' Tribute

There is a select number of people in your life who you will truly call friends. We meet many pleasant people including those who are friendly and those we become acquaintances with throughout life, but very few who grow with you, change with you and stick with you for life. If you move away, they still call you. When you come home, they act like you never left. There is even a smaller number of people you will meet in your life (and if you do, you're lucky) who teach you what it truly means to be a friend. Someone who loves unconditionally, sees the good in you and in everyone they meet and can brighten up your day and everyone else's that they come in contact with. I have to say a premature goodbye to one of those people today. Someone who taught me so much about what being a true friend (and great human being) was all about without even knowing he was teaching me anything at all. His demeanor and love for life and everyone around him is something I truly look up to and strive for, and he did it effortlessly. Always able to make you laugh, smile and give back-breaking hugs (even lifting you off the ground), he never lost sight of you, always kept in touch with you and most certainly would never forget you. It's been truly a blessing and a privilege to call you my friend and you have given us so much, we will miss you dearly Adam Winstrom, and we love you forever. Let us be the friend to each other that you were to us.

"Bookie - boojie" my friend.

Rabbi David J.B. Krishef

Mr. Winstrom, I want to tell you how much I enjoyed seeing Adam at Torah study. He just put a smile on my face every time he would come into Schuler's, get about half way back to the music area where we met and shout, "Hi, Rabbi!" He was a delightful person, happy, fun to be around, always reading something on his iPad. Periodically, when I wanted to compare translations, I'd ask him to read his, and he always had it on his screen. Even though he was often doing something in addition to what we were studying, he always was following along right where we were.

I'd tease him about his hair, or lack of it, at times and tell him he was trying to look like me, and I'd tell him how good he looked bald. But when he finished a round of treatment and his hair grew back, I told him how great that looked at well. He didn't talk about his health, and neither did Jim, except mentioning cancer treatments one time. Adam was one of the most positive people I have ever met, simply a joy to be around and a privilege to know.

Michael Scott Pyle's Tribute

I'm laying here thinking about just last week on Sunday when we had FaceTime with Adam and he was showing us the sweet ride him and his Dad had for the week in Florida....I'm going to miss that weekly sound of FaceTime going off with Adam just wanting to check in, share his positive joy and see what we are up to.... I'm going to miss seeing him show up to my Thursday night volleyball games...I'm going to miss him coming over for dinner, usually followed by Forrest Gump......
he was always so happy and no matter how stressed out I was about the work I still had for school, he would always make me smile and laugh. He is a friend who will be missed by so many. He knew

Michael Scott Pyle and Adam

what it meant to be a true friend and showed that to so many people! No matter how much he had going on in his own life, you felt like you were his number one priority. He called almost every day that my Dad was in the hospital to see how he was doing, to tell us he was praying for him and to tell us he was going to be okay. Adam Winstrom, you truly were one-of-a-kind, heaven sure gained one heck of an angel on Saturday!! Love ya, Buddy!!

The world lost a great man today in you, Adam Winstrom. I have yet to meet another person who can light up a room as quickly as you did. You had such a positive impact on more people than you will ever know. Thank you for being a true friend. We love and miss you. H5H.

Coach's Tribute

"SharaLee Attema, this is coach Adam calling."

Brave • Passionate • Radiant • Giggly • Loyal

My heart is hurting so badly right now. Adam always knew exactly how to make my day. And usually, that just consisted of him coming up to me, wrapping his arms around me, and saying "SharaLee!!" in a way that made me feel like the most important person in the world during that single moment in time no matter how I looked, smelled, or felt.

I am going to miss my Skype going off, telling me that Adam is calling. They were always at the most random times, completely filled with laughter and often ended in him serenading me with his guitar or harmonica while I studied. I will miss his phone calls, updating me on the Redskins, keeping tabs on Kirk Cousins for me, and his voice mails that always began with "SharaLee Attema, this is coach Adam calling."

Adam taught me more about what it means to worship with your whole heart (I'd assume he's doing a lot of that right now), how to be a good friend (let's just admit it, he was literally everyone's best friend), and how to love Jesus with a type of passion that is contagious. He definitely wasn't perfect, but I'm quite positive that he was the closest thing to that here on earth. Adam is not only the man I hope my little brother grows up to be but also the kind of person I want myself to be.

Through all these tears, there is hope. If Adam were sitting beside me right now, he would put his arm around me and tell me, "It will be okay honey." Thank You, Jesus, for blessing my life so richly by Adam Winstrom.

*Thank you, **Adam Winstrom** for always making me laugh, for remembering my # in football, and for some of the most heartfelt prayers I have ever heard. Love you and miss you and glad you get to call Jesus on your new phone.*

Rosa De Jonge

I was and continue to consider myself blessed, privileged and honored to have shared a friendship with Adam. I have and continue to say that Adam was not just my friend but the greatest friend I have ever known who became a part of my family. I met Adam in 2010 when I started mentoring at Compassionate Heart Ministry while I was in high school. I had very little experience with special needs people and felt very out of place. Despite the discomfort, I was drawn to this ministry and kept coming back week after week. Adam was one of the participants who came alongside me and made me feel welcomed, accepted and important, and for that, I knew Compassionate Heart would become more than just a place to get volunteer hours but rather a second home. It wasn't until the summer of 2014 when I was Adam's mentor at Summer Serve camp that I got to know what makes Adam uniquely himself. I've come to learn many life lessons from my short but ever meaningful relationship with Adam. Among those are the importance of relationships, a sense of humor and the power of prayer.

I will forever remember Adam as the friend who changed my life by his overflowing kindness. The way he put his friend's needs ahead of his own is something I will never forget. I remember toward the end of the summer; Adam had asked if we could hang out that week. I told him I was busy every day but on Tuesday I was going to run a 5k, I asked him if he wanted to come to the race and cheer me on with my parents and go out for ice cream or we could pick him after the race and go out then. Right away he said, "I am coach Adam, I will cheer you on."

Rosa De Jonge and Adam
Whipped Cream Pie Challenge

That night Adam was in the most pain that I had ever seen him in, it was the first time I had ever heard him complain of any pain through his battle with cancer. Even though he struggled to even sit on the curb, he cheered loud and proud, not just for me but every runner at the race. As I turned to cross the finish line, Adam used every bit of strength to stand up and cheer me on to the very end. In every way, Adam understood the true meaning of friendship. He took the little bit of love you showed toward him and returned it back times ten. I truly believe God puts certain people in our lives at exactly the right time to teach us how to be better people. Although I did not know it at the time, God placed Adam in my life to teach me the real value of relationships, acceptance and belongingness. Love knows no boundaries and Adam understood the very extent of that in ways most people search their entire lives to understand. He truly cared for everyone he came in contact without condition and chose to see the good in every person he encountered. I love what the Bible says in the 2nd part of 1 Samuel 16:7 "For the Lord sees not as man sees: man looks at the outward appearance, but the Lord looks at the heart." I've come to learn from Adam and that his disability never disabled him but instead gave him the ability to look into our hearts and love each and every one of us for exactly who we are.

If anyone knew how to have a good time it was Adam. I think part of the reason we got along so well was our mutual love for dancing. The first night at Summer Serve we had a party bus that would give rides around the neighborhood, and within this party bus was a pole. I was looking the other way taking to someone and all the sudden I heard laughing and it was directed toward Adam showing off these dance moves that I didn't even know existed. I don't think I have ever laughed so hard, part of me wanted to stop him because, after all, Serve is a Christian camp but the other half was too busy enjoying his laugh and hearing him say, "Hey guys look at me shaking my booty!" To anyone who says white people can't dance, you clearly never saw Adam when any kind of music was playing because based off that, he was probably more black on the inside than I will ever be my whole life and I'm from Kenya. I especially loved how he never took himself too seriously. One night after dinner we were sitting on the couch, he had taken his shoes and socks off and was relaxing after a full day of vacuuming the church. I was painting my nails with my friend and Adam kept looking my way, so I asked him if he wanted his toenails painted too. And he looked at me, rolled his eyes and said, "De Jonge please, no way!" In the meantime, his friend Chris came to sit by us and had overheard our conversation and said he wanted his nails painted. As soon as Adam saw that, he wanted his nails painted, too. Afterward, he went over and showed Donna who said, "Wow, Adam those are some hot nails!" and for the rest of the night he was walking around showing off his polished nails and shouting, "Look guys, I'm a hot man." There are a lot of things I miss about my friend, but his contagious smile and belly laugh is top of the list. Oh, what I would give to hear that laugh one more time.

Above all, Adam was truly a man after God's own heart. He lived out the mission and vision of Jesus Christ in a way that never left you questioning who had his heart. During Summer Serve camp, I started reading my Jesus Calling devotional with Adam every night before bed. It was in those moments that Adam began to open up with his struggles with cancer and how much it sucked. He gave all of his worries to God every night in prayer. Listening to Adam pray was one of the most inspiring moments. He always started with, "Thank You, God." To come to the Lord every day in thanksgiving even though your situation is hard is one of the greatest forms of worship in my book. Adam was the best prayer warrior I knew. If anyone conveyed a prayer request to Adam, he wrote it down and covered you in every day. He had a notebook with hundreds of prayers for others about struggling relationships, health issues, job search, success in school and anywhere in between. I was lucky to have my name on this list. I had a full class load at school the fall of 2014 and Adam was always there asking what I was studying for or what research paper I was working on and many times he offered to help. The week before exams I was feeling extremely overwhelmed and just when I was ready to call it a night, Adam called me and asked the typical questions: "What did you have for dinner?" "How was it?" and "How was your day?" and I told him about my upcoming week and right away he said, "You will be okay. I'll pray for you." Those two simple sentences are just what I needed to make it through because when Adam said he was going to pray for you, it came from the heart and he would follow up. Almost every day that week he would text me asking how my exams went and to remind me just as I was praying for him he was praying for me.

The weeks and months following Adam's death left me feeling cold, empty and alone. Although my family and friends meant well with their words, it never seemed to provide comfort. I pleaded with God over and over again to why he would take my friend who was so God-fearing, compassionate and joyful and how can a God who is so good take such a son from his earthly father whom I have come to love, cherish and respect. The Lord has taught me many lessons in the early stages of grief. Grief is the ultimate price for loving someone so deeply. God's thoughts are not our thoughts nor are His ways our ways. He allows us to ask why, to be angry and sad but He never leaves us or forsakes us in our darkest day. I know without a doubt Adam lived out his purpose on earth and that brings me the most peace.

There's not a day that goes by that Adam doesn't cross my mind. I see him in the new facility at Compassionate Heart. I see him when I watch sports, especially football, even though we never agreed on teams (Go Blue!). I see him as the backseat driver when I drive. I see him in my residents whom I care for as a constant reminder of joy and grace. I see him celebrating with me, and I also see him comforting me on the hard moments of life because Adam was so good at both. I see him in the early morning sunrises and summer sunsets. I see him in and all around me. One thing is for certain, I cannot wait to see my friend in heaven. I have no doubt it will be a joyful reunion and for that, I still consider myself blessed, privileged and honored to have shared a friendship with Adam

Maya Clawson–His Footprint in My Life

Hero: a person, who is "idealized for courage, outstanding achievements, or noble qualities" (Google). For many, Superman or Avengers come to mind. My hero is far more than that. My hero is compassionate, uplifting, and selfless. Adam Winstrom is my breath of fresh air.

Adam is the "big brother" I looked up to. He has touched so many people in this world in such a special way. He is our angel sent from heaven to care for us. Adam is very different from most people: he has a special gift from God called Down syndrome. Most think of Down syndrome as a disability, but anyone who knows Adam sees it differently. We see a unique characteristic that makes him the wonderful person God meant for him to be. Adam is a graduate of Holland Christian High School, Hope College through the Ready for Life Program, and a member of the Compassionate Heart Ministry—all of which are places where he left his footprint upon everyone's hearts.

To me, Adam defines "hero" perfectly. He tackled obstacles with a contagious smile every step of the way. When I looked into his eyes, I saw pure kindness and love with his actions for everyone. He showed me not only to always have a bright smile

Adam and Maya

on my face but also to look through a window, not through a mirror. He remained positive through the rough times and brought God into everybody's life. He was a very big impact on Kirk Cousins' life as well. He would call him before every Michigan State game and pray for him. Whether it was college football or NFL, he did that before every game. He inspires me to do great things in life: to help people by bringing them up with kindness. He showed me how to bring out and see the happiness and love of God in everyone.

Adam was diagnosed a couple of years ago with a rare type of cancer. Although in great pain, he remained positive and strong. On December 27, 2015, my mom received a shattering call from David Winstrom. Adam had taken a turn for the worst. David had requested that we try to visit him, for it could be the last visit we might have with him. I was in such disbelief. I wanted to leave my house right then and there to see him. Having house guests prevented us from visiting Adam that morning. Later that night, Adam lost his battle to cancer. He ran his race with courage, strength, and love for everybody. Plus, he left this world with much faith in Jesus Christ.

We could only dream of being just like Adam. He exemplifies courage and selflessness. He was protective, funny, and much more. I couldn't imagine my life without him. Adam has touched many people's lives in such a way that no one else could. He most certainly lived his life to the fullest. I could not have asked for a better "big brother." I will forever be "his girl" and he my hero.

Adam Winstrom Day by Jim Kruis

One day, I bumped into Adam's father, Dr. Winstrom as I knew him before Adam came into my life. We were both waiting to get our cars fixed. He was just talking about his son and how Adam wanted a job. Adam was interested in working part time. I was winding down a building maintenance company and owned a few rental properties. The way he talked about his son made me curious. I told him, sure, I knew of a part time job cleaning offices. When he asked where I said with me, I thought a part time job was possible working for me.

He made the arrangements, and I met Adam at Zeeland Christian Junior High. I liked Adam right away. He had big eyes, direct eye contact, a broad smile, and a firm handshake. He topped it off with a robust, "Hi, I'm Adam." (I found out later that Adam was looking between my eyes, not into my eyes. David and Jetta trained him to make nose contact not eye contact. Apparently, direct eye contact is often difficult for people with Autism.) Still, he fooled me.

I offered Adam a job, and we cleaned offices one afternoon/evening a week. Initially David joined us, but eventually, it was just Adam and I. Usually I picked Adam up at school about 3 PM, then we would go to work.

I often became friends with my employees, but Adam was different. Adam and I became close friends. After cleaning offices for few hours, we decided we would also play a little ball, take a hike, have dinner, and what not. I would take Adam home about 9 PM, every Wednesday evening.

Adam Winstrom Day
with Jim Kruis

We had a lot of fun. But it was not always easy for me to be with Adam. I often made things too complicated. Adam has Autism and Down syndrome. And those were my problems. In my conscious mind, I had it straight. I knew Adam was first and foremost a human being, a brother in the Christ. A god-son? But I often failed to see that Autism and Down syndrome were things he had, not who he was. When I made Autism and Down syndrome primary, I would fail to connect well with Adam. I would mistakenly explain things to Adam that needed no explanation. I would help Adam where he needed no help. I would do things for Adam that he could do for himself. And I would fail to help him when he would truly benefit from my support. It was all because I confused Adam with his Autism/Down syndrome. This was not good for me or him, and I could feel it. My blunders did not bother Adam much. He would look at me and smile. I think maybe he was saying to himself, "Jim needs help."

I asked David for help. I told him Adam's Autism and Down syndrome often threw me off balance. They blinded me. David said, if I stopped thinking of Autism and Down syndrome as belonging to Adam and understood Autism and Down syndrome better, it would be easier to keep them in their proper place. So, we talked. And I read a couple of books that David recommended.

Eventually, I found the right balance. I guess it took about a year. I learned to keep Adam as a friend and brother in the foreground, and Autism and Down syndrome in the background, where they belonged. For me, the trick was doing this without denying that, yes, Adam, my friend and brother, does have Autism and Down syndrome, but Autism and Down syndrome are not who he is. David said to think of them as adjectives, like Adam has brown eyes, brown hair, Autism, Down syndrome. They modify who Adam is; they do not define him.

Adam and I continued to meet to work and play for a few years. It was great fun, and I learned a lot about myself, and I made a great friend. It was my curiosity that first got me interested in meeting Adam. Learning is important to me. I intend to be a lifelong learner, discovering something new every day until the day I die.

Then, Jetta got cancer. That was unexpected, of course. I thought Jetta and David might like one night alone, so I asked Adam if he would like to stay at my house overnight. I remember Adam saying, "A sleep-over, cool!" He liked the idea so rather than only having him until 9 PM on Wednesday evenings, I took Adam back to school on Thursday mornings. We soon called this, "Adam Winstrom Day." I did this because I enjoyed my time with Adam. It worked out for them to take care of Jetta's doctor's appointments on those days without involving Adam.

In the fall of 2012, "Adam Winstrom Day," became "Adam Winstrom Week." A local minister invited Adam to experience the Holy Land with a group of "special needs" young adults. I said yes, I am happy to do that. Subsequently, I was Adam's roommate and companion for a full week in Israel. This trip involved a lot of hiking. No problem, since Adam and I were already hiking buddies due to the walks we took on "Adam Winstrom Day." David was in Israel too, but his back and hips were failing, so the long hikes were often without David.

The trip to Israel was like so many things Adam had done, such as downhill skiing in Colorado, flying airplanes, and traveling to Mexico. They gave him experiences to talk about with his friends. This trip would give him stories to share at church. Naturally, I reaped similar benefits from the trip. Now I also have stories to tell about Israel.

Adam and I had connected before we took the trip to Israel. The trip had an unintended benefit for one of my fellow "leaders." During the trip to Israel, she came to know Adam. On the return journey, she told me she had gone to school with Adam, but never really got to know him because she was scared. After traveling with him for over a week, she got over her fears. She said he was kind, thoughtful, patient, polite and had a strong faith. She regretted not knowing him sooner. She realized she was never afraid of Adam; she was afraid of difference. It was her judgments about Adam being outwardly different that kept her from being his friend for all those years. I understood everything she said. She had only seen Autism and Down syndrome, and that had blinded her to who Adam really was.

After coming back from Israel, we returned to our "Adam Winstrom Day" routine. This was a chance for me to have "a family meal" one night a week. As much as I treasure the great time I spend with my own son, he, as a teenager, was not interested in having "a family meal" with the old man and understandably so. But Adam was all for it.

Adam Winstrom was like a godson to me. I looked forward to "Adam Winstrom Day," because he made it "Jim Kruis Day" for me. He returned all my love tenfold or more. I felt a sense of belonging and friendship. I slept better on the nights he stayed with me because he made my house feel like a home.

I have read many books, but Adam taught me lessons about life that I do not find in any books. One of the lessons I learned from Adam and David was to stop overthinking and to let myself just be with Adam. I didn't have to outsmart him, stay ahead of him, or control him. I was simply with him. We enjoyed life because we were friends and brothers doing life together.

No doubt I was the responsible adult but only when it was necessary. And I came to realize that was not nearly as often as I had thought. I also learned to be with Adam as his resource rather than being in charge of Adam as his overseer. That made my time with Adam fun for both of us and a lot less work for both of us.

Then Adam died. When grief overwhelms me, I think of Adam Winstrom day. I let my gratitude for the good times replace the grief in the loss. That seems to work for me.

So, I miss you, Adam. And thanks for Adam Winstrom Day.

Chapter 23
Honoring Adam's Right to
Belong and Change the World

Full Circle

Bobby, one of my friends at Jefferson Elementary School when I was eight years old, called me tusuperman mafred. He would say this to me when someone or some group was picking on him or another one of the "special" kids. With Bobby, it usually started with "Hey, retard," and ended with pushing his face in the snow just because they could... until they couldn't because I was standing between them and Bobby. I stopped hitting the bullies and putting their face in the snow as my grandfather required, but I did not yield. I just physically interjected myself between them, then planted myself like a shield. I could never understand what Bobby said to me until I had Adam. Translated for those less familiar with the diction and timing a Down Syndrome enlarged tongue can create, Bobby was saying, "Tough Superman. My friend." He would step away with self-assurance from all the others and walk with me. I became a rock for Bobby to stand on in a sea of oppression. All these years later, I returned to again be a tusuperman mafred, whom my son called "Father." We stepped away from all who would oppress or segregate my son and found our path to walk through life.

How Did Adam Change Our Lives?

For Jetta and me, having our son, Adam, become part of our family changed our lives much like landing in Oz changed Dorothy's life. When Adam was born, everything we thought we knew was going to happen didn't happen. We were going to the hospital to have a child, celebrate and rest, then return to our familiar home and community in Grand Haven. We never imagined the wicked witch from the West would try to take our child away from us. We never knew Munchkins, Winkies, Quadlings and Gillikins were real. The day Adam was born, Jetta and I experienced culture shock. For Jetta especially, it was as if she had gone to sleep one night as a princess and awoken as Cinderella. Overnight she became an outcast, unacceptable in her own community, or at least what was her old community. That better describes her transformation. I cannot put in these few words how Jetta adjusted to losing her friends, her community, her dream for our future and adjusted to being a first-time mother at 30+ years old. She was rocked and shocked and tumbled all ways in the extreme. Like Dorothy's ride to OZ in a tornado, Jetta rode the whirlwind into motherhood. And like Dorothy gathered herself up and started her journey, she managed to find her footing and walk on, loving her son and enduring with grace and beneficence a culture that did not love her son.

My reaction was just the opposite. The duality of my existence concluded on August 26, 1984. I discovered my purpose. Thomas Jefferson penned these words in 1776 to make sense out of events that were transforming his nation. My revolt was forged and fueled by the same forces—a refusal to no longer stand by idle and suffer evils' rule.

Jefferson wrote,

> *Prudence, indeed, will dictate that Governments long established should not be changed for light and transient causes; and accordingly all experience hath shewn that mankind are more disposed to suffer, while evils are sufferable than to right themselves by abolishing the forms to which they are accustomed. But when a long*

train of abuses and usurpations, pursuing invariably the same Object evinces a design to reduce them under absolute Despotism, it is their right, it is their duty, to throw off such Government, and to provide new Guards for their future security.

I understood both the passion and the desperation in his words. I did not throw off an oppressive government; I threw off an oppressive culture. My father instructed me to consciously suffer normal privilege to avoid the inevitable response of all who challenge the status quo, the unearned right of the privileged to their presumed privilege or experience. I did this as my way of honoring my father's will. He knew I would be marginalized more if I resisted the culture's way of doing things than if I just silently endured. He told me that all the folks I saw shaming me were just acting out of their presumed birthright to act privileged. Just as I, by my birthright of difference, held my obligation to suffer their station in life. I was to forgive them because they did not know the harm they did. My Grandfather told me that their privilege blinded them so they could not recognize their actions as evil. I thought I was doing the right thing. I thought I was doing what the men of my family had asked. Turn the other cheek. Walk away. Recite "sticks and stones." Forgive and forget.

But some spirit deep within me knew there was more to be done. Dietrich Bonhoeffer wrote, "Silence in the face of evil is itself evil. God will not hold us guiltless. Not to speak is to speak, not to act is to act." Like Plato, Thomas Jefferson and Leonardo Da Vinci all wrote that all it takes for evil to prevail is for good men to be silent. Dr. King said the same thing. Until the day Adam was born, these words were just a philosophical idea. The kind of rhetoric many of the folks who grew up in the 60's would utter with some sense of false pride having always closed their eyes, hiding from evil, complacently tolerating evil, like the colonists initially did before they came to America.

Then Adam came into my life, and I could not be silent and allow the evil I had prudently and patiently suffered take another victim. I could bear this evil in my life but not in my son's life. The focus of evil shifted from my shoulders and landed on my son's. It was a weight he could not bear and survive, nor could I suffer one more second to endure evil's consequences for my son. All the years of feigned deference and pseudo accommodations, my façade of being one of the guys evaporated. I had silenced myself trying to be nice in the face of the "Dick jokes." I tried to turn a blind eye to the subtle shunning that I observed every day being called stupid or weird. I had even learned to be silent to all the shunning the Bobby's in my life had to endure. And I could no longer be silent.

Jetta had wanted me to believe along with her that the evil witch was dead. It was 1984, and the world was different than the one I grew up in. The law had magically changed discrimination into accommodation, only no one told the Munchkins, Winkies, Quadlings and Gillikins that. They all still knew that witches ruled Oz. And we discovered discrimination and segregation still ruled Ottawa County. The new laws had landed on discrimination like Dorothy's house landed on one witch. But her sister, Prejudice, still lived and was not in an accommodating mood. She knew that Munchkins and Winkies did not mix and that Quadlings and Gillikins each belonged separated and grouped with their own kind. That was the best way to keep Oz in proper order.

It was not Adam who initially transformed our lives any more than any new born child does. That change we delighted in. In the beginning, it was the continual stream of surprises the culture interjected that moved and reshaped Jetta and me. Having Adam as our son was not hard. Having Adam as our son and living in this culture was.

The Gift of Adam in Our Family

All through my life I have had experiences that have been transformative. I learned to call them gifts but not because each one came in a bow-wrapped box containing my new favorite toy. Gifts in my life have been the situations that necessitated my going beyond what I believed I was capable of doing, beyond my self-imposed limitations. Adam was a gift. The challenge to become a good enough father for Adam made me become a better person. That same covenant to become the mother Adam needed her to become pushed Jetta into becoming a better woman.

I do not remember Jetta telling me that having her understanding of the world becoming so radically changed was a gift. She had been, after all, a princess. Until Jetta became a mother, she was given a blank invitation to enter every aspect of life and was welcomed. She was unaccustomed to my warrior's ways (that was the reason for her knee-tapping-be-nice reflex), just as I was unaccustomed to being welcomed. Jetta had grace and style and an ease about her. She had been raised in a more affluent and cultured life. I had learned to be quiet and more invisible while she had developed the social skills to meet and greet anyone. That is until she had Adam and was transformed into Cinderella.

David aged 21 and Jetta aged 20 pretending to be adults for for their wedding picture

When we first met, she was 18 years old and was rebelling against what she had grown up with as phony and was seeking something she could call real life. I was war weary and seeking inner peace and a truce with the world. It was the 60's, and the United States were not so very united. Vietnam divided our one nation politically, and the resistance to that war divided our one nation culturally. In the midst of all the friction, Martin Luther King, Jr., Gloria Richardson and others were working to establish equal treatment between the races, and the

David, 18 years old

Civil Rights movement emerged. It was a tumultuous time to be 18. I had found Jetta in the confusion and chaos of the 60's and convinced her to marry me. My friends all told me that I had married above my station and that I was probably just part of Jetta's rebellion. I thought they might be right, but I knew I would be just the right husband for her…at least eventually.

We married and for 12 years grew together and matured as individuals. We had left the 60's behind and settled into what we thought were professions that supported the values we had integrated into our present lives from the 60's. We were both social workers by profession, working to improve the culture and support those who were oppressed by their circumstances.

Then she invited Adam into our lives, and being Adam, his uniqueness invited the world into our lives in unexpected ways. Surviving our experiences in the hospital and asked to abandon her newborn son, Jetta was slowed to a half step like a sprinter who has been injured. The experience accelerated my transformation, freeing me from my earlier obligation to suffer evil in silence. Jetta's grace and patience never left her but added was a space. It did not come between Jetta and her son or between Jetta and me, but in public, she learned to safeguard her emotional self. I had seen that same insulation develop in the children I worked with who had been abused. It was nothing most people would notice, but it was there as she greeted each new situation involving *helpful* people. She became more thoughtful, more reserved, less vulnerable and no longer open to their influence. She used her social skills like a shield. The behaviors she despised in her parents as phony she adapted and honed into impeccable graciousness without any personal exposure or investment. This was the persona she eventually served up when faced with *helpful* professionals.

But never with Adam. To Adam, she remained open and available. She adored her son. With Adam, her guard was always down; she remained completely vulnerable so he could always find her when he was able. She wanted to be a mother and she was a very good one. She salvaged as much of her dream as the world allowed. If only the world would have embraced her son in the beginning. If only her friends would have rallied around her as she would have rallied and supported any one of them. But it did not. They did not. I watched helplessly as her optimism turned to resolve and acceptance, now knowing the world would not support her son. My love for her, like my father's love for me when I was being shunned in grade school was never quite enough to offset her pain. Maybe there is no offsetting that kind of personal injury. It is a crucible not all can survive. It is just experienced and let go of arming one with a depth of wisdom or hung on to as it eats at your heart. Jetta, for the most part, let it go. The kindness in Jetta never let her blame them for their judgments nor me for my inability to change quickly enough in this world to a kinder more accepting place.

I loved Jetta all the more as we moved together to hold our son safe from others' prejudice. Our bond grew, and I was able to open some parts of me that had been too well protected to share with anyone until she arrived in my life. I became more focused and more vigilant than ever before. I had been trained by life to support and defend the vulnerable and that accelerated. I learned from Jetta some kinder ways of deflecting what she identified as their "unintended unkindness." It was through understanding their intention through Jetta's eyes that she taught me a better sense of who needed correction, who could benefit from education and who were intentionally unkind and needed to be rebuked. Together we supported and loved and nurtured our son and each other. Together we challenged the systems in Ottawa County. She did it politely keeping her kindness in the forefront. My kindness carried a more forceful friction.

The Cost of Silence

"In the end, we will remember not the words of our enemies, but the silence of our friends," Martin Luther King, Jr. said. Until the day Adam was born I had silently endured. I could never stand in silence again. Had the *kind* doctor's words shocked me into silence as it had Jetta or had I failed to speak out against his invitation to send our son away, I would have relived my moment of silence for eternity. If you look into the eyes of the families in the documentary "Willowbrook: 25 Years Later" (available on YouTube) and take the time to listen to their stories, you will know as I do the price of choosing to listen to the *kind* doctor. Their torment would have been mine had I let evil prevail.

The *kind* doctor's words were the perfect shock to stop my old world and force me to see what would happen when evil goes unchallenged. I had barely survived my wounding as a child, but it was clear that Adam would not survive my silence the day he was born. Prejudice would take my son from me if I were silent. What blossomed within me was that clarity Richard had told me would be available to me. I was forced by Adam's birth to see that graciously accepting others prejudice (evil) destroyed lives and would have taken our son from us and from his community.

Segregation is harmful; it is an evil to be identified and resisted. I felt no respect for the doctor, but I did not act disrespectfully or in an unkindly manner. I told him a simple truth not from any titled authority, just the truth and that stunned the *kind* doctor. The truth is that we should not dispose of our children to try again for a better model. The truth is that we must not abandon children. Not our own children. Not any children. A person, a community, a country is judged by how they deal with their most vulnerable members. Abandoning the lesser among us is to let evil grow and tyrants flourish; it marks our very soul and culture as putrid and tainted by evil.

The *kind* doctor's response was surprise and retreat. His response to my sense of clarity was repeated throughout Adam's life. His *intended celebration* of my son's birth—to give Adam a special life—was the catalyst to understanding why I was born. It was clear to me that I was born to be Adam's father. To keep this one child from being put in the special place for children who are different. To assure that he would always be proud of being Adam and free to discover his potential and make his own place in the world.

Jetta's kindness would not have worked to keep Adam free from the offered (directed) institutional specialness. My warrior ways also would not have worked to reshape the culture of Ottawa County. It was through our blending and because of our mutual respect that we were successful in keeping Adam in the mainstream of life. Nether Jetta nor I had all the required skills, but together within our family Adam was safe. The school system thought I enjoyed the fight; I did not. They never knew it was often Jetta saying, "Okay, David, it's time for Dr. Winstrom to go get 'em." They never knew sweet Jetta had them in her mother's sights. Her velvet hand calling on the thunder.

Jetta forever forgave all who without intention (or as I saw it through their lack of attention) acted foolishly and hurt her. But she changed. She was more deliberate, more able to stay focused on what was presented in the moment even when they attacked her motherhood. She was no longer naïve. She was no longer surprised by people's prejudice. I think that was her biggest change. Just as Jetta's perceptions altered mine to see the nice people doing what their prejudice pushed them into (evil acting on them), she was newly able to see the folks who were simply unkind and wanted discrimination to return so they could live within their normal privilege and keep those retards in their place. Even as Jetta would unleash me, she cared about and wanted to be there to pick up their pieces and make their reorganization as easy as possible. To borrow a phrase from Dan Fogleberg, she learned to "play life with a thundering velvet hand." She was the balance to my knight's steal glove.

I have written about evil as I now understand it. Jetta helped me see evil for what it is. She read this excerpt from Aleksandr Solzhenitsyn to me one time:

> *If only it were all so simple! If only there were evil people somewhere insidiously committing evil deeds, and it were necessary only to separate them from the rest of us and destroy them. But the line dividing good and evil cuts through the heart of every human being. And who is willing to destroy a piece of his own heart?*

> *Aleksandr Solzhenitsyn, Gulag Archipelago 1918-1956*

Growing up I thought evil was just as simple as Solzhenitsyn first identified—bad people doing bad things. I was sure that was the truth about evil. As I have run into what I experience as evil I had to change my understanding. I take evil to be an action that has the consequence of distorting good and causes harm beyond complete recovery. Evil leaves scars on one's sense of self, one's soul. It is difficult to admit that with in each of us lies evil and therefore the potential to wound a soul.

The *kind* doctor dedicated his life to doing good but was corrupted by his training in eugenics. His training taught him the right thing to do was to sentence a two-hour old child to life in an institution where he knew the conditions were not anything he would allow his own child to endure for a second. Acts of evil spread as the *kind* doctor's influence infected the nurses and they became corrupted.

Teachers, ministers and friends most truly wanted to do the right thing. If I asked any of them, "Do you want my son to have the best life he can possibly have?" all would say, "Yes!" "Do you want my son to learn and interact with others?" Again, "Yes!" "Do you think Adam should have friends?" All would say as one, "Yes!"

Then we cross their dividing line into evil. Do you think Adam should be in a "special" place and not with his parents? Doctors and nurses said, "Yes, in a special school designed just for him so he can be safe and learn." Even teachers and some preachers susceptible to their evil within would say, "Yes!" It is at that point the line of evil that Solzhenitsyn identified is clear. These are basically good people. Evil's distortion of good intention is manifest in the eugenics rebranding of "special" from meaning *better, greater, uniquely designed for safety* to really mean neglected, treated expediently in a *segregated facility, often dirty, with too few staff, no programing, brutal treatment by staff and peers and probable sickness and death.* There is no longer anything special in "special." Evil has distorted and drained any good out of it.

Sadly, even when all this was pointed out by Geraldo Rivera in his documentary Willowbrook, the next level that evil twists is that people with retardation are bad people who should not be supported at our expense. If they or their parents had lived better lives, they would not have problems. We have special places for those kinds of people if only parents would do the right thing and place their kind in the facilities we made for them. Or, if their faith were stronger, they would be cured. This rhetoric is straight out of the original eugenics philosophy. Poverty and physical ailments are the results of moral turpitude, their own moral failing. I have listened to people who speak with impunity (privilege) that the Adams of this world should not be allowed in their classrooms, Sunday schools or communities and refer to those Adams as stumps, drunken yottas, time wasters, distractions, black holes and retards. As children, people like John Forbes Nash, Stephen Hawking, Temple Grandin, Howard Hughes, John Cougar Mellencamp and Steve Jobs would be removed and placed in special facilities if Eugenicists had their way. This is a short list of *thems and those* from our society whose absence would be noticed.

Eugenics was not one of my intended points of this book, but I fear it is returning into our governmental policies in 2017. It is evil's seductive voice that whispers *self-responsibility* and then twists good into, "I am not responsible for them." *Evil* is blaming victims for their plight. The evil within us is once again focusing on the mentally and physically impaired, the poor and the new "Jews"—the Mexicans. Like Hitler, moved by evil, who wanted to make Germany great again by eliminating uniqueness, so the USA seems headed down that path. I fear evil has the ear and the heart of my government. Education, healthcare and social supports for the disabled, the elderly and the infirmed are all to be removed. Evil is whispering once again it is too expensive to include "those" people. They have a choice to be the way they are, we are not responsible.

The Difference Between Having a Cause and Being a Cause

Marsha Forest was my friend. She was also a leader in the inclusive movement in Canada. She told me there is a difference between having a cause and being a cause. I found out how true her words were. Before Adam arrived, I had causes. I wanted to become a healer for the children wounded by their circumstance. Once Adam came into my life I was compelled to address the systems and people who wound our children. I became a cause to protect children from prejudice and segregation and the injury these practices inflict on them.

John Forbes Nash developed a negotiation protocol that worked, and he was awarded the Nobel prize for his work. Martin Luther King, Jr. won a Nobel Prize for his nonviolent style modeled after Gandhi's way of opposing discrimination in social systems. King proved power and force fail when met by nonviolent active resistance. I renamed it compassionate noncompliance.

What I am trying to say is that I could always see what to do and how to do what is correct, that was not the mystery. For Adam, inclusion was the right thing. For Adam, being treated as a valued human being was the right thing. Making sure he had that opportunity was the right thing. That was irrefutable. A poignant line from the movie, "The Scent of a Woman" that always stuck with me is, "It wasn't that I did not know what was the right thing to do. We all know what the right thing to do is. It is just that it is too damn hard, so we retreat. We surrender our integrity for a moment's reprieve."

Being Adam's father forced the confrontations I had tried to avoid all my life. The *kind* doctor made it clear the side I had to choose. From that day on, the only fear I lived with came from my Grandfather's words. He told me that if I knew the right thing to do and did not do it, he would still love me, but my soul would be in jeopardy. All his love and all his prayers could not protect me from the consequence of abandoning what I knew was right.

I always tried to do what I knew was right for Adam and all others (thanks to Jetta). What I did for Adam was to remove the barriers to full inclusion that prejudice and fear erected. What Adam did for me was to change my fundamental understanding of the world from a dangerous place to maneuver through, to a place of wonder and possibility. Set free, Adam did the same for everyone he came into contact with. His entire community felt his freedom and joy-filled wonder. He never stopped exploring what was possible in his life to find ways to befriend everyone.

Removing Barriers

When Adam was in school and the school went too far in their attempt to segregate my son, my objection resulted in a Due Process Hearing. Both the Montessori school and Ottawa County Community Mental Health were corrected by the court. That was my way of rebuking their system.

When Adam was in ICU and his doctors were contradicting each other's orders and harmed my son, I tried to talk with them. When that failed I went to the hospital administrator to talk with her. When she began to back paddle, I offered to file a medical malpractice suit if they did not correct their system to best serve Adam. They corrected their confusion and served Adam. One doctor gave all orders, and Adam began to recover.

When I applied for supported independent services for my son Adam, then 26 years old, from Ottawa County Community Mental Health (OCCMH), services that the law really required them to provide from birth, they said, "No." I asked to meet with the Director of OCCMH to avoid the friction I could see was coming, but he would not meet with me. He sent me to deal with his assistant, and it culminated in a Due Process Hearing. The judge agreed with my request for proper services for Adam and wrote in her decision how OCCMH would be required to fund Adam for more support hours than I had asked for. The county appealed, and the three appeal judges supported the initial decision and added that the instrument OCCMH utilized to determine the number of hours of support needed was not an acceptable method. That precedent still stands.

The absurdity in the OCCMH system was that they would "allow" Adam into their day treatment program or their sheltered workshop for 40 hours a week at more than $120 an hour but not support Adam in the community costing them $15 an hour for 20 hours. For that disagreement, they paid for eight staff at $50 to $85 an hour and their attorney at $250 an hour to waste 10 hours or over $6500 to attempt to maintain the legitimacy of their separate-but-equal institutional model. That doesn't include the expense of their filing an appeal. They wasted 50% of the cost to fund my son for a year in that one day because they were willing to defend their institutional model instead of letting us save them $80,000 by keeping Adam out of their day treatment and sheltered workshop. Separate but equal is expensive financially and kills the souls of those served. OCCMH said I was expecting them to do too much and was abandoning my obligation as Adam's father. This is the typical Eugenicists response. The hearing officer said she did not think that was true. She wrote in her opinion that from birth Mr. Winstrom was providing a home for Adam to live in, his health insurance, his food and clothes and had waited 26 years to ask for the assistance that they should have provided since Adam's birth. Mr. Winstrom does not ask too much; he asks too little. The judge awarded Adam more support than I had asked for. The system does try to shame parents. Adam lived in his own home with a house mate. Adam at age 26 had his own health insurance. He bought his own groceries. He paid for his own transportation. Adam just needed some additional support to live semi-independently.

When I finally got to meet with the Director of Ottawa County Community Mental Health, I started our conversation with, "Why did you make me do this? You have wasted my time and your agency time and thousands of dollars." He came out from behind his desk and said, "I needed someone to challenge the system so I could fix it. We have operated this way since before I arrived, and I could not fix it any other way." He thanked me and said that whatever Adam needed, as long as it was within the law, he would receive without a fight from then on.

The Director of Mental Health had utilized my obligation to my son and my skills to fix his system. I think the hospital administrator found me useful to adjust their system and improve their services when Adam was in ICU with pneumonia. Bill, the Principal of Zeeland Christian, used my reputation to smooth the way with the public school when it benefited students from Zeeland Christian. And, Jetta, whom everyone would prefer to deal with, would say "Time to go get 'em, Dr. Winstrom." I accepted being the problem.

I mention these areas of friction for all parents who do not find a Zeeland Christian Sanctuary or a Compassionate Heart Community for their son or daughter. The unwilling systems will yield to what is right if you apply enough friction. Many systems want to do the correct thing but are stuck in their traditions. Eugenics has deep roots. They need someone to set them free, but remember, freedom has a price—it never comes free; every messenger will get shot or crucified.

Dear Dads, (Mom's, Too)

Don't be surprised by how the kind and helpful systems respond to you. When I tried to help them add to the plans for my son, I was initially surprised by how I was received—I was labeled angry and told I just could not accept "my" sons condition. It was a perfect paradox. When I spoke, I was dismissed as angry, and when I was quiet, they talked about Jetta and me as depressed or overwhelmed by our son's disability.

Shaming is eugenics' most-often used tool. Their arrogance would be felt when they would attempt to add guilt to shaming. Their verbal assault usually flowed from "let us protect your child in our special institution." Next, if you refuse, their institutional plan they would say, "you can't expect us to do everything so your child can live in our community."

They seemed to want Jetta and me to feel guilty because we had created something bad. Because we chose not to have an abortion, now they had to waste their time and resources assisting us with our substandard child. We were a drain and we owed them gratitude and respect for having to spend time fixing our mess.

Wolfensberger writes about the deep wounding inflicted upon individuals and their families by the entitled system. If they had succeeded in making us feel devalued, their solution of clustering all of us retarded folks together and isolating us would have moved us easily toward our fate of segregation. It was their way to wear us down. First, the *kind* doctor took his best shot, then the rest of the system followed up with the same message: "he will be better off with his own kind."

Systems operate like people. Change comes from the top down. Down from the person in charge of the system as instruction and up from the bottom as success ignites the system to reorganize and improve. Children are your allies; they get inclusion naturally. Boards and committees are obstacles because they are intended to keep the status quo to make "adjustments," and beware of the "special."

Who I became as a father to Adam I am okay with. Who Adam became as a man whom I admired and loved makes me burst with pride. He and the journey were worth everything. I never picked a fight, I just planted myself and deflected all their made-up laws and protections that would have isolated Adam and used active nonviolence or compassionate noncompliance and redirection.

In writing this story, I have been able to reflect on my life and remembered Mark Twain's observation: There are two important days in your life. The day you are born and the day you discover why you were born. I was born on August 4, 1949, and discovered my purpose on August 26, 1984. I see clearly that I was born to be Adam's father.

A Lesser Man

My last experience with a system was for myself. It was in a hospital for an evaluation in 2015 that resulted in my being paralyzed from my chest down. My brain, heart and lungs continued, but that was all. I couldn't walk.

I had tried to avoid this. I had explained to everyone I contacted that I needed to see the neurosurgeon before I had an MRI because I could not lay flat on my back. The stenosis, an excessive calcium sprue in my thoracic vertebra was pinching my spinal cord and it was too painful to lay on my back. I needed to see the surgeon *before* I had the MRI to talk to him about adjusting my positioning to protect me from hurting myself by lying flat. I told them that I could not lay flat on my back because it would compress my spinal cord and I could not stand the pain. They refused and said I could be sedated for the MRI or not be treated at all. The doctor needed the MRI to see what was wrong. I tried to explain I already knew what was wrong and only wanted a fifteen-minute appointment with the surgeon to explain why an adjusted position for the MRI was essential. I was not refusing to be treated, I understood no treatment would eventually mean I would become paralyzed from the chest down and eventually die. I was already falling down and losing my bowel and bladder control. My choice was to submit to their procedure their way or slowly have the stenosis cut my spinal cord and stop my existence. I chose to accept their way.

I was just as successful talking with them about adjusting my position for an MRI as I had been convincing them I had a hip infection. No one listened. I walked into the hospital to have my MRI, they sedated me, and I was laid flat on my back. That positioning compressed my spinal cord, and I could not walk out of the hospital when it was over. When the anesthetic wore off I was paralyzed from the chest down. They acted surprised. They decided I really needed to see the neurosurgeon right away. All I could do was laugh. I think they thought I was becoming hysterical, but it was just the irony.

A week before Jetta had her catastrophic failure we had been in the neurosurgeon's office because I could tell by her symptoms that she had a tumor growing on her cervical spine at the base of her neck. We had had an MRI, but it was not conclusive because it was a poor image. I wanted another one done that day but both the surgeon and Jetta had decided to wait. Jetta had just endured a surgery two months before. I think she had decided it was time to let it be. Two weeks later the tumor pushed into her spinal cord and two weeks after that Jetta was with God. She said she was ready. Adam was doing very well, and she knew I would be there to assure he was always okay. I think I understood her surrender and willingness to allow whatever natural process was moving her to come to its conclusion. Even if I could have convinced the surgeon to remove this tumor, another one would follow.

There was something about having five back surgeries in the last four years with the last one very nearly killing me, along with my belief that Adam and Jetta were fine now that made what ever happened next be okay. It is fortunate for the hospital and doctors that I am retired now. Like Chief Joseph, I have chosen to fight no more. Now that

Adam and Jetta are safe, I have no more need to protect them. Growing up I had always thought that I was not very smart but believed my body would never fail me and here I was a paralyzed Mensa member. I laughed. My plan was to hike through all the pyramids in Mexico when they fixed my stenosis. It would only have required a laminectomy. Tricky, but it was minimal back surgery, and I could continue to hike. Again, God laughed and gave me the time to write this story about living with Adam, our son.

After my "emergency" surgery and three months of rehab, God and Jim Kruis said it was time to go home, even though I was still mostly moving around in my wheelchair. Jim told me he was moving in until I was really able to care for myself. He took care of me for another three months. This was a gift for me, just as being given time to write this story was a gift for me and maybe a source of hope for you. We are one people in the body, none lesser and none expendable. It seems telling my story about living with Adam and Jetta was what was intended. Hiking and motorcycle riding were not.

When Pastor Andy came to visit me after I got home from the hospital, he said it was official, he was going to put my name in his book replacing Job, or at least alongside Job. Andy said I had officially qualified as someone who had lost it all. I smiled and told him that I think I understood what he was telling me about submission. I had learned many lessons, mostly from Adam.

What Adam taught me I have attempted to pass on through telling our story. If I had just said okay to the *kind* doctor instead of choosing Adam, my life would have been easy, and the social systems would have been undisrupted. But, without Adam, the world would have been a lesser place and I a lesser man.

I am always near

About David Winstrom

David Winstrom is a warrior, pacifist, husband, doctor, father, mourner, and storyteller. After learning that school psychologists dictated whether Adam was educatable or trainable and what academic classes he would be able to take, David decided he would be the one to make those decisions and went back to school to get a dual Ph.D. in Educational Psychology and Clinical Psychology. After learning from the physical and occupational therapists that riding a motorcycle would help Adam's balance, David purchased a Harley Davidson took Adam on many glorious trips together through Michigan, Colorado and California. On one visit to San Francisco Bay Area, Adam had the stereo on the motorcycle cranked up with ZZ Top at full blast. Everyone was looking and laughing at the two guys in leathers coming into town. When they got into the little bakery and Adam took his helmet off, they all started laughing and very much enjoyed meeting father and son.

CPSIA information can be obtained
at www.ICGtesting.com
Printed in the USA
FSOW02n1510070817
37215FS